THE HISTORY OF JAPAN

URA AND OMOTE

Edited by Eric Messersmith

Florida International University

cognella™
San Diego, CA

Bassim Hamadeh, Publisher
Christopher Foster, Vice President
Michael Simpson, Vice President of Acquisitions
Jessica Knott, Managing Editor
Stephen Milano, Creative Director
Kevin Fahey, Cognella Marketing Program Manager
Zina Craft, Acquisitions Editor
Jamie Giganti, Project Editor
Erin Escobar and Brian Fahey, Licensing Associates

 cognella™

www.cognella.com 800.200.3908

CONTENTS

INTRODUCTION

Without dwelling on the distant past, one could argue that there were four major events that shaped the Islands of Japan to this day: the introduction of green tea by the monk Eichu in the Heian period (9th century); the ascendancy of the warrior class beginning in the 10th century; the introduction of Zen Buddhism by the monks Eisai and Dōgen in the Kamakura period (12th century); and the introduction of firearms by the Portuguese in the Warring States period (mid-16th century). This is not to say that there wasn't another very important indigenous feature of Japan—that being the animistic religion of Shinto.

Like any introduction from a foreign land, these events did not have an immediate effect on the lives of the people. Tea, for example, made its way from Emperor Saga's palace to the Zen monasteries, then to the warrior class, and finally after some 500 years, trickled down to the masses of merchants and farmers.

The warrior class, later known as the Samurai (lit. "One who serves"), got its start by protecting the vast landholdings of the nobility and the transport of rice from the fields to the various palaces in Kyoto, the Imperial capital. As rice was the most valuable commodity, payment for the Samurais' services was in this product. It was not too long before their terms came to not only include rice but also the land it was grown on. By taking payment in land, the power of the Samurai increased substantially over time and led to vast landholdings and wealth, some encompassing entire islands, as in the case of the Shimazu Daimyō in Kyushu. The term "Daimyō," or "Great Name," was reserved for the controlling family patriarch of the district. In order to qualify for this title, one had to have a minimum of 10,000 koku of rice (1 koku = approx. 5 bushels) under cultivation in his province. This allowed the Daimyō to employ hundreds if not thousands of armed Samurai to protect his status. It also led eventually to neighboring Daimyō to attack each other in hopes of increasing their power and wealth.

It was not until the mid-16th century with the ascendancy of the "Three Great Unifiers"—Oda Nobunaga, Toyotomi Hideyoshi, and finally Tokugawa Ieyasu—culminating in the Battle of

Sekigahara in 1600 and the victory of Tokugawa over the opposing forces, that in 1868 the beginning of the end of the Samurais as a class was ushered in with the return of power to the Emperor Meiji. Of course this is a highly compressed account and one would need an entire volume just to cover this one period. It is, however, one of the most intriguing periods for those who are students of Japanese history.

"Why the end of the Samurai class?" one might ask. The Tokugawa era lasted close to 250 years and gradually the need for armed warriors was diminished due to the hegemonic control of the Tokugawa bakufu (tent government) over all aspects of the people's lives. Soon the Samurai class became the bureaucrats of the Shogun and less and less his army of warriors.

One of those warriors, Miyamoto Musashi, didn't fall under the patronage of a Daimyō. He chose a much less certain life, that of "mushashugyō," or more popularly known in the West as a rōnin—masterless samurai.

Another samurai, some say the last samurai, Saigo Takamori from the Shimazu domain, led the Battle of Shiroyama against the newly formed Imperial army. It was a lopsided victory for the new Meiji government and signaled the death of the samurais as a class.

One of Saigo's followers was a young man from a nearby domain who survived the battles. His name was Toyama Mitsuru. Up until his death in 1944, Toyama would continuously agitate for Japan's intervention in China, Korea, and Manchuria. His group, the Genyōsha or Dark Ocean Society, was made up of the remnants of the samurai class in Northern Kyushu plus some very unsavory characters picked up along the way.

One of the most unsavory was Kodama Yoshio, who plundered East Asia on behalf of the Japanese military in an attempt to secure vital natural resources to continue the war effort. As a consequence of his activities, he was classified a Class A war criminal and sent to Sugamo Prison to await his possible death sentence. Instead of hanging him, the CIA hired him as a consultant in anticipation of the Korean Conflict.

One of Kodama's prison mates was Sasakawa Ryoichi, the self-proclaimed "World's Richest Fascist." He, along with prison mate Kishi Nobusuke, a future Prime Minister of Japan, became fabulously wealthy from the war. Kishi was the Governor General of Manchuria and thus controlled everything and everybody who could put money in his coffers. Rumor has it that Kodama offered Emperor Hirohito a large box of diamonds in gratitude for being allowed to serve his country. After buying their way out of prison, Kodama went on to be the godfather of organized crime in Japan. Sasakawa continued his proclivity for making a fortune off pari-mutuel motorboat racing throughout Japan. Later in life he would use these enormous profits in hopes of being awarded the Nobel Peace Prize.

Where was the Imperial family during all of this? What was their responsibility for the war and the accompanying atrocities? These are difficult questions with many conflicting opinions as to whether or not Emperor Hirohito had direct responsibility and should have been tried as a war criminal with the others. I think that it was wise to spare him the embarrassment of facing the War Crimes Tribunal or having to sign the surrender agreement on board the USS Missouri. As a consolation, he had only to renounce his divinity to the public via a radio broadcast.

His younger brothers had been put in charge of repatriating the plundered gold and precious stones looted from all Japanese-controlled territory. Among the billions was a one-ton solid-gold Buddha statue stolen from a Thai temple. It was melted down along with all the other gold and hidden in caves in the Philippines to await recovery after the war. Some of this gold actually made it back to Japan in cargo ships disguised as hospital ships. Once safely back in Japanese waters, the ships were scuttled, along with their crews, for later salvage.

Another "crafty" character was Tanaka Kakuei. Before becoming the Prime Minister of Japan during the Nixon years, Tanaka ran his own construction business. Once bombing of the homeland began under the raids by General Doolittle, Tanaka was contracted to move a vital bearing factory from Japan to Korea. He was paid an enormous sum upfront in full, but the war ended before the factory could be moved in its entirety. Since the ministry that hired him was no longer in existence, Tanaka pocketed the money and went on to an illustrious—and dishonest, I might add—career in politics.

It is my hope that by adding all these disparate but somewhat related entries to the text, students of Japanese history will see not only the "omote" or out-front side, but the "ura" or back side of what makes up this fascinating country.

THE WAY OF THE SWORD: BANSHU TO GANRYU ISLAND

William Scott Wilson

One morning in 1596, just outside the village of Hirafuku in the province of Banshu, Arima Kihei, a swordsman of the Shinto-ryu, sat waiting for a formal apology. This was to be delivered by a thirteen-year-old boy, Miyamoto Bennosuke, the local *gaki daisho*, or "commander-in-chief of every ruffian in the area, and the chief instigator of every outrage in Hirafuku.

Kihei had arrived in the area a few days earlier, put up a simple bamboo fence and erected a placard announcing in large gold letters that he would accept a match with anyone willing to enter a contest of skill with him. Why he chose to come to such an out-of-the-way place as Hirafuku is uncertain. He may have heard that a master of the sword and the *jitte*, a certain Hirata Munisai, lived not too far away, and hoped to attract his attention.

He was, however, to be disappointed. It was a young Bennosuke, rather than the seasoned Munisai or any other wandering swordsman, who noticed the placard. On his way home at the time from a calligraphy lesson, Bennosuke took out his brush and ink, smeared over the gold letters of Kihei's sign and, in a fit of bravado, wrote, "Miyamoto Bennosuke, residing at the Shoren-in, will give you a match tomorrow."

When Kihei returned to the spot and saw this bit of vandalism, he responded by sending a disciple to the Shoren-in, where the youngster Bennosuke lived with his uncle, the priest Dorinbo. As Kihei's disciple informed the priest that his master wished to accept the challenge from this Bennosuke, the priest turned ashen and explained that Bennosuke was only thirteen and that his challenge was just an adolescent prank. When informed of this, Kihei magnanimously sent a message to Dorinbo that he understood, but would need a formal apology from the boy in order to clear his honor. The priest readily accepted these terms.

So the following morning Kihei sat waiting for the priest and the boy to set the matter right. A number of villagers who had heard of the incident also gathered, probably to witness and enjoy the humiliation of this wayward child who was always causing so much trouble.

But as Dorinbo and Bennosuke approached, people noticed that the latter was carrying a six-foot staff. Then, to everyone's surprise, just at the moment the apology was to be made, instead of bowing in humility, Bennosuke charged. Kihei was not expecting this and may have been caught off guard, but he was a practiced swordsman. Dodging the blow, he unsheathed his sword and took a stance. Surely the onlookers must have thought that the brash young challenger had no chance at all. But after a few exchanges, Bennosuke suddenly threw down his staff and grappled with Kihei. He then picked the swordsman up bodily and threw him down headfirst. Recovering his staff, he beat Kihei to death and returned home.

Long before writing *The Book of Five Rings*, Bennosuke would become known as Miyamoto Musashi.

In that book he refers to this match quite simply: "From long ago in my youth, I set my mind on the martial arts, and had my first match when I was thirteen. My opponent was a martial artist of the Shinto-ryu, Arima Kihei, whom I defeated."

But another record, the *Tanji hokin hikki*, provides insight into Bennosuke's mental attitude at the time of the match: "At this point [Bennosuke] thought, 'I was unbeaten by the enemy because I gave no thought to my life. I simply walked in and struck.'"

This attitude would inform his psychology for the rest of his life and become one of the main undercurrents of *The Book of Five Rings*.

His "enemy," Arima Kihei, was most likely one of the many *shugyosha* of that period; a sword practitioner who perfected his skills and enhanced his reputation by wandering through the provinces of Japan engaging in combat—often mortal—with other swordsmen. A *shugyosha* took disciples or established his own style or school, but also always hoped to be noticed by the local lord, who might offer him an official position as sword instructor to his clan. The life of the *shugyosha* was by no means an easy one. It involved a long list of rigorous ascetic practices: in his travels, the *shugyosha* was exposed to cold and hot weather, often sleeping in the mountains and fields with little shelter from the wind and rain; he bore hunger without carrying money or rations for his travels; he walked through the most inaccessible places and was always in danger of losing either his reputation or his life in a chance match along the way.

Of the unfortunate Kihei himself, almost nothing is known, but he may not have been the most exemplary of *shugyosha*. One account, the *Sayo gunshi*, published in Hyogo Prefecture in 1926, relates: "There was a certain Arima Kihei who gambled and acted outrageously. Although an accomplished swordsman of the Shinto-ryu, in town he was despised as though he were a snake or scorpion."

His style, the Shinto-ryu, was that of the legendary Tsukahara Bokuden, a master swordsman of a generation earlier; but the word "Shinto-ryu" may indicate any number of styles or substyles. There were, and still are, the Katori Shinto-ryu, the Kashima Shinto-ryu and Bokuden's style as well. All of these came from the eastern provinces at that time and were offshoots of one basic tradition. (Interestingly, there was also an Arima Shinto-ryu created by a certain Arima Yamato no kami, and it may be that Kihei was either a member of that family or a disciple of the school.)

Nothing else is clear: only that Kihei was killed by the thirteen-year-old Bennosuke (it should be noted in Kihei's defense that, according to some accounts, Bennosuke had the stature of a young man three or four years older).

For his part, Bennosuke coolly returned to the Shoren-in to continue his studies in calligraphy, Confucianism and Buddhism under the loose—and perhaps, after this turn of events, timid—direction of his uncle Dorinbo. He also studied some painting, probably on his own; when he departed the temple for good, he left a painting of the Zen patriarch, Daruma, presaging his emergence some thirty-five years later as one of Japan's finest india ink painters. But for the three years following the match, he lived now at the Shoren-in near Hirafuku, and now with his sister, Ogin, in the village of Miyamoto, close to the provincial border in Sakushu. Finally, in the early spring of 1599, he deeded all of his family's possessions—weapons, furniture and family tree—to his sister's husband, Yoemon, and walked out of Miyamoto and up into the hills with one of his friends. At Kama Slope, having been presented with Bennosuke's staff as a keepsake, his friend turned back to Miyamoto and obscurity. Bennosuke—who from this point became known as Miyamoto Musashi—walked out of obscurity and on to become Japan's most famous and singular swordsman.

Origins

There is nothing particularly remarkable about the low mountains and hills between the villages of Hirafuku and Miyamoto. In the late 1500s, the area contained scattered farming villages dotted with houses and fields and, in Miyamoto, a river of no very great size. Yet while the landscape was generally one of peace and tranquility, if a traveler climbed the Kama Slope, as Musashi did on his departure, he would come out onto a pass in the middle of the mountains. This was the highway between Harima (Banshu) and Mimasaka (Sakushu), which during the ensuing Edo period (1603–1868) was part of the road used for the *sankin kotai*, the journey to Edo (Tokyo) taken by the *daimyo* every two years. The road itself was an ancient one, probably used as a trail first by the bear and deer that had inhabited the forests, later by hunters and finally by merchants transporting wares from the western seaboard to the capital. No doubt it would have been a thing of wonder to a small boy of great curiosity and imagination, growing up in one of these otherwise remote country villages. It was the road out.

Harima, however, did have a colorful history. The Akamatsu clan had settled there early in the twelfth century, eventually building Shirahata Castle and establishing itself as the local *daimyo* family. The Akamatsu were descended from a Minamoto Morofusa, who in turn came from the Genji line of the Emperor Murakami, and thus the clan could consider themselves distant relatives of the imperial family. The Akamatsu did well in the area for three hundred years, but came to their end in 1441 when the head of the clan, Mitsusuke, made the great tactical error of assassinating the Ashikaga shogun, Yoshinori. Although the shogunate itself was not very strong at the time, other *daimyo* led by Hosokawa Mochiyuki took this opportunity to destroy Mitsusuke and his clan's castle.

The Bessho, a junior line of the Akamatsu, survived this disaster and prospered enough to built several castles in Harima. One of these castles, commanded by a Bessho Shigeharu, was attacked and fell in 1578; Shigeharu escaped by the skin of his teeth to the village of Hirafuku, where he changed his name to Tasumi, literally "one living in the fields." It was Shigeharu's daughter, Yoshiko, who gave birth to Musashi in 1584, thus linking him to the Akamatsu, to the Minamoto or Genji and, anciently, to the imperial line.

Musashi's father was Hirata Munisai, a landed samurai with the status of senior vassal to the Shinmen clan, whose last name he was eventually given permission to use as his own. The Shinmen family was a pillar of the warrior community in Mimasaka and its progenitor was Tokudaiji Sanetaka, the twenty-eighth-generation descendant of the famous Fujiwara Kamatari. Involved in the attempted restoration of Emperor Godaigo between 1334 and 1338, Sanetaka was exiled to Awai-no-cho in Mimasaka. His son, Tokuchiyo, went to Kyoto and asked for absolution (shamen; 赦免) of the family's crimes. This was granted, and the clan was given the status of warrior and changed its name to Shinmen (新免), or "newly absolved." Tokuchiyo, now called Shinmen Norishige, married the daughter of Akamatsu Sadanori, the governor of Mimasaka; his son Naganori also married into the Akamatsu clan.

Finally, Munisai's father married into the Shinmen clan and Muni-sai's first wife, Omasa, was the daughter of Shinmen Munesada, the fourth-generation Shinmen. It is in light of this genealogy that Musashi sometimes stated his full name to be Shinmen Musashi Fujiwara Genshin.

Munisai thus became a minor power in the area and was invested with a small fief; his house in Miyamoto was an old-style mansion, surrounded by a good bit of land enclosed by walls of stone and no doubt including a fine *dojo*. It was here that Musashi played as a young child, climbing the trees and roaming the low mountains. His older sister, Ogin, married into the nearby Hirao family, and in the garden of that house today stands a zelkova tree that is said to be the second generation of one from which the young Musashi took a branch to make into the first of his many wooden swords.

An instructor to the Shinmen clan, Munisai was a master of several of the martial arts including the Two-Sword Style, the use of the *jitte*, *jujitsu*, and the proper use of armor. He was known in particular as a skilled practitioner of the Tori-ryu of swordsmanship, a style he would use to good effect against Yoshioka Kenpo in Kyoto. Munisai also taught *jujitsu* to Takenouchi Hisamori, who stayed as a guest at the Hirata house when Musashi was about four years old and who would later establish the Takenouchi-ryu of that art. Thus, Musashi was raised in a household that placed a great emphasis on the martial arts and he most likely began receiving some instruction from his father at an early age. Certainly weapons of all kinds were constantly around him and he must have often sat enthralled at the conversations of the talented men who came and went, gathering around the stern Munisai for instruction and edification.

But Musashi's childhood was not a happy one. Not long after he was born, Munisai divorced his second wife, Yoshiko, who was Musashi's mother, and she moved back to her home in Harima. Munisai then married yet again, and Musashi seems not to have gotten along well with his new stepmother. In addition, there were hurtful rumors that his real mother was not Yoshiko at all, but in fact was Omasa, Muni-sai's first wife—a claim that the village of Miyamoto (now Miyamoto, Ohara-machi, Aida-gun, Okayama Prefecture) officially makes to this day. When he was about eight years old, Musashi's relationship with his father began to deteriorate to the point where the young boy began making the difficult trip over the mountains to visit Yoshiko and her family, eventually dividing his time between Harima and Mimasaka. It was at about this time that his formal education was placed in the hands of his uncle, the priest Dorinbo.

One day, the situation with his father came to a head. The following story is found in the *Tanji hokin hikki:*

> Bennosuke watched his father's martial arts from the time he was quite young. As he got older, he gradually started to voice critical remarks. Munisai began to think that this child was not very likeable, despite the fact that he was his own son. One day, while Munisai was carving a toothpick, his son approached and began criticizing his *jitte* technique. Angered, Munisai took the dagger he was using to carve the toothpick, and threw it at his son as though it were a *shuriken*. Bennosuke dodged the weapon and it lodged in the pillar behind him. Munisai became all the angrier, took out his short sword and used it too as a *shuriken*. Bennosuke dodged this as well and fled outside. After this, he never

returned to the house but, rather, lived with a priest related to his mother in Banshu. Thus he abandoned his hometown.

Musashi now considered Hirafuku to be his real home, and it may be for this reason that he declares in *The Book of Five Rings*, "I am a warrior born in Harima." But local records in Miyamoto copied as far back as 1689 clearly state that Musashi—officially, at least—lived in that village until 1596, and so would have retained a strong sense of its rhythms and environment. One of his favorite haunts would have been, just as it is to village children in Japan today, the local shrine, with its wide spaces and old trees. In ancient times, the Aramaki, or Sanomo shrine, had once stood at the top of the mountain to the rear of the village—hence the village's name: Miyamoto, "at the foot of the shrine." The shrine was later moved to the base of the mountain, close to the northern side of the Miyamoto River. Here the young Musashi would have watched the Shinto priests as they beat a huge drum throughout the day; at night he would have drifted off to sleep to the same sound: that of two drumsticks, constantly in motion, swirling like swords in expert hands.

Finding His Strength

When Musashi climbed the Kama Slope at age sixteen, he embarked on the homeless, ascetic life of a *shugyosha*, a life that he would continue in one form or another until his final years. His belongings were few: the clothes on his back, perhaps a small sewing kit, a bamboo canteen, at the most a very small amount of pocket money, an ink stick and writing brush, and, of course, his sword. As he walked over the stony mountain paths, he wore a pair of straw sandals that would quite often need repairing or replacing. If he was lucky, he might find a straw hat for his head. There was unlikely to be anywhere to stop for food when he was hungry, or a pleasant place to lie down when he was tired. For those who believed in folktales, the dark mountains were filled with foxes and *tanuki* (a sort of badger), both experts at bewitching the unsuspecting. For those who did not believe such tales, there was still the very real danger of bandits.

In the spring of 1599, Musashi walked through the mountains and into the neighboring province of Tajima. Here he had a match with a swordsman by the name of Akiyama, whom he defeated. Nothing is known of where the match took place or of Akiyama's lineage, and in *The Book of Five Rings* this opponent is simply described as "strong." But the memory of this fight must have been an intense one for the sixteen-year-old Musashi. Of all of his more than sixty matches to come, he seems to have remembered this one perhaps most clearly as he reviewed his life some forty years later, alone in the Reigan Cave.

As Musashi walked on alone, large groups of warriors were beginning to gather slowly around Sekigahara, a large plain to the north and east of Tajima. In October of the following year, a battle would be fought there that would settle both Japan's course for the next three-and-a-half centuries and the direction of Musashi's life.

For several decades, two men had been directing the reunification of a Japan badly splintered by the ineffectual Ashikaga shogunate. Oda Nobunaga (1534–82) had emerged from a small fief in the middle of nowhere to nearly succeed in unifying the country with his ruthless and creative military genius, and had been stopped only when he was assassinated by one of his own generals, Akechi Mitsuhide. Toyotomi Hideyoshi (1536–98), another of Nobunaga's generals, quickly squelched the rebellion and had brought the country to the verge of total unification and control when he too passed away, possibly from a brain tumor. Before he died, Hideyoshi appointed a board of five *tairo*, or chief ministers, to govern the country until his son Hideyori reached majority, hoping that in this way the Toyotomi clan would continue to rule the country. Now, one of those *tairo*, Tokugawa Ieyasu (1542–1616), was bringing those hopes to naught.

Due to a complicated balance of ever-shifting loyalties, Japan in the year 1600 was essentially divided into two camps: those generals and *daimyo* who favored the more-or-less incumbent Toyotomi clan (largely from Kansai and western Japan), considered the Western forces; and those who were betting on the increasing strength of the forces of Ieyasu (mainly from Kanto and the eastern part of the country), the Eastern forces. There were several battles in different locations, but the main battle took place at Sekigahara on the misty morning of 21 October 1600. It is uncertain how many troops eventually engaged in the fighting, but the initial balance was approximately even, at about eighty thousand men on each side. By the time the battle was over, sometime during the Hour of the Sheep (from one to three p.m.), the Tokugawa armies had routed the Toyotomi, helped in part by the perfidy of some of the generals on the losing side. The casualties were in the tens of thousands. Many of the defeated who had not been killed in the battle itself were hunted down in the rain and mud and slaughtered in the days and weeks to follow. Some, however, were able to escape to fight another day. Musashi, although still only in his teens, was one of these.

The Battle of Sekigahara was a *shugyosha's* dream. Along with the life of ascetic self-discipline he put himself through, he would welcome the chance to join in a battle—this was referred to as "borrowing the battlefield"—to prove his mettle. For an unemployed warrior, fighting in battle gave him a chance to be noticed for his skills and, if he excelled, to be taken on as a martial arts instructor under the patronage of the lord whose forces he had joined. Thus he might become a samurai in the true meaning of the word, "one who serves."

So Musashi now traveled on toward Sekigahara, eventually joining up with the forces of the Shinmen clan. This clan was under the command of Ukita Hideie, who had been one of Toyotomi Hideyoshi's favorites; he had been chosen to be one of the five *tairo* by the dying Hideyoshi and was a mainstay of the Western forces. Hideie's father, Naoie, had conquered Bizen, Mimasaka and Bitchu and established Okayama Castle a generation earlier, and the Ukita was considered one of the most powerful clans in the area. With his mother's connection to the Shinmen, it is not surprising that Musashi would have cast his lot with that clan, but it may also be that Hideyoshi's dreamlike rise to power from peasant status inspired Musashi to join that great man's side. Musashi had been six years old when Hideyoshi had destroyed the powerful Hojo clan, and seven when Hideyoshi conquered the great city of Odawara. Two years later, Hideyoshi had begun his invasion of Korea. These stories were the talk of the nation, and the young Musashi would have listened to them as any child would, dreaming of what he would do when he grew up.

All sources indicate that Musashi fought with extraordinary valor at Sekigahara, despite his youth. One typical account, from the *Musashi yuko gamei*, states: "Musashi's achievements stood out from the crowd, and were known by the soldiers in all camps."

According to the Kokura Hibun monument erected in 1654: "Musashi's valor and great fame could not be overstated, even if the oceans had mouths or the valleys had tongues."

If we look to Musashi's own comments about the battle, however, we will be disappointed, for he alludes to it only once, in a note to Hosokawa Tadatoshi written decades later, and then only in the broadest terms: "I have participated in over six battles since my youth."

In the end, the Western forces lost the battle. Ukita Hideie was condemned to death by Ieyasu, but his sentence was commuted to permanent exile on an island off the Izu Peninsula. He eventually shaved his head and became a monk, living to the great old age of ninety. Other commanders were not so lucky: many lost their fiefs and their families and of course many lost their lives. The battle had been one of the most definitive in Japan's history, marking its course for the next two hundred and fifty years. And much as it defined the Yagyu clan, who had fought for the Tokugawa, as permanent members of the establishment, it would also define Musashi—who had fought on the losing side—as an outsider for the rest of his life. The Tokugawa hegemony was now evident everywhere and marked the future of the battle's participants well beyond the grave. Even the composers of the Kokura Hibun, erected in faraway Kyushu nine years after Musashi's death, needed to be circumspect in their language. They did not, for example, mention on which side he had fought, and they even felt compelled to describe the actions of the Western forces as an "insurrection of the Taiko Toyotomi's favorite retainer, Ishida Jibunosuke."

After the battle, seventeen-year-old Musashi was once again on his own. He had lost his gamble at war and had nearly lost his life. But he had gained the pride of having served the Shinmen, the Ukita and even the late hero Hideyoshi. He had also gained experience in a protracted battle. He would think about this experience for the rest of his life and record many of these thoughts in his final statements *in The Book of Five Rings.*

It is interesting to note that Musashi's father, Munisai, also participated in these conflicts, but in Kyushu and for the Eastern forces. For unknown reasons, he had previously resigned from the Shinmen clan and gone to Nakatsu in Buzen to serve Kuroda Yoshitaka (Josui), receiving an annual stipend of two hundred *koku.* As part of Ieyasu's forces in the southwest, the Kuroda attacked Tomiki Castle in Bungo, and Munisai would have seen action there. It was in Kyushu that Munisai met the important Hosokawa vassal, Nagaoka Sado no kami Okinaga, and became his instructor in the martial arts. This relationship would play a critical role in Musashi's career.

Like most of the survivors on the losing side of the Battle of Sekigahara, Musashi spent a number of years after the war keeping a low profile, doing his best to keep body and soul together. He spent some time secluded in the mountains, but also did a lot of traveling, no doubt meeting other *shugyosha* on the road and testing his skills. What would soon become apparent, however, was that his self-discipline and training during this time must have been rigorous and intense. In 1604, at age twenty-one, he would walk into Kyoto and bring to ruin one of the most respected schools of swordsmanship of that time.

Kyoto and Matches with the Masters

The Yoshioka clan had been well-known residents of Kyoto for generations. The earliest Yoshioka Kenpo, whose personal name was Naomoto, was a master of black and tea-colored dyed goods in the Shijo area of the capital. It was in the constant rolling back and forth of the dyeing implements that he was enlightened one day to the special style of sword handling for which his school would become famous. The name "Kenpo," which became the hereditary title of the head of the family, connotes a man who adheres to righteousness, and his dyeing methods and prices were said to be just and proper.

It was this Naomoto who attracted the attention of the twelfth Ashikaga shogun, Yoshiharu, with his great feats in battle, and who thus became the first Yoshioka instructor to that house. The second generation was his younger brother, Naomitsu, who also took the name Kenpo and became a martial arts instructor to the Ashikaga clan. It was Naomitsu who was instructor to the "Swordsman Shogun" Yoshiteru, who also employed Tsukahara Bokuden and Kamiizumi Ise no kami Nobutsuna, founder of the Shinkage-ryu. And it was Naomitsu who opened the Heihosho, or Place of the Martial Arts, in the Imadegawa section of Kyoto. Naomitsu's son, Naokata, became the third generation and instructor to the fifteenth and final Ashikaga shogun, Yoshiaki.

Finally, there were Naokata's sons, Seijuro and Denshichiro. The family annals, the *Yoshioka-den*, remarks of them:

> Here, then, the Yoshioka brothers. They gained fame in the style of the martial arts, and were unprecedented in past or present in the mysteries of the arts. The elder brother, Seijuro, and his younger brother, Denshichiro, were the so-called Kenpo Brothers. It was from the time of the Kenpo Brothers that the art was daily renewed, becoming more prosperous day by day and transcending the art of former generations.

Seijuro, in particular, was considered to be an excellent swordsman. He had become the fourth-generation head of the Yoshioka clan, but the Ashikaga shogunate was now defunct and the clan enjoyed no special standing. One of his methods of training was to go out late at night to a forest on the outskirts of Kyoto and, as a spiritual discipline, exercise the practice of "fixing the vision" (*shikan*; 止観). This was originally a practice of Esoteric Buddhism in which, in contrast to the Zen practice of filling the mind with Emptiness, the practitioner was to concentrate on a single object of worship and, so, sweep away any other extemporaneous thoughts. Seijuro was said to have reached such a level of concentration that, when he focused his thought on a single bird on a treetop in the forest, hundreds of birds would fly up to the treetops at once. It was this Seijuro, the almost transcendentally skilled scion of the respected Yoshioka clan of Kyoto, that the twenty-one-year-old self-taught Musashi challenged to a duel.

Musashi's decision to challenge Seijuro was not random. By defeating Seijuro, he would not only show the whole world what he could do but also demonstrate a thing or two to his father, Munisai, who was still teaching martial arts in Kyushu.

A generation earlier, Munisai's talent had come to the attention of the Ashikaga shogun, who had called him to Kyoto for a "comparison of techniques" with the shogun's own instructor, Yoshioka Naokata. The Kokura Hibun gives this brief description: "With a limit of three matches, Yoshioka had the advantage once and Shinmen won twice. At this point Shinmen Munisai was awarded the designation of a martial artist 'with no equal under the sun.'"

One can imagine that Seijuro would have been quick to accept this challenge, regardless of the fact that Musashi seemed to have no experience, no status, and probably little skill. With this fight, Seijuro planned to ensure that the residual spot on his family's name would be eradicated forever.

The place for the match was to be outside the capital, at the moor adjacent to the Rendaiji temple. Seijuro was armed with a real sword, while Musashi carried the weapon that would become one of his trademarks—the *bokuto*, or wooden sword. The Kokura Hibun describes the fight:

> Musashi and Seijuro fought with the power of dragon and tiger at the Rendaiji Moor outside of Kyoto, but with one blow from Musashi's wooden sword, Seijuro collapsed and fell unconscious. This match had been promised beforehand to conclude with a single blow, so Seijuro barely escaped with his life. His disciples carried him away on a plank and nursed him back to health. He eventually abandoned the martial arts and became a Buddhist priest.

The unproven youth from the countryside had beaten the head of the Yoshioka family so thoroughly that the humiliated man withdrew from his famous clan's profession and took the tonsure.

No doubt Musashi beat Seijuro with unexpected skill, but he had also used psychology in arriving late enough that the proud man, anxious to clear away this small embarrassment from his family's name, became agitated with anger and expectation. Musashi had broken Seijuro's famed concentration before the fight ever began, and so secured his victory beforehand. No birds flew up to the treetops at this match.

The Yoshioka, however, were duty-bound to regain the family honor. Hadn't Seijuro's defeat been a simple fluke? Could the respected Yoshioka school, for generations instructors to the shogunate in the capital, lose its reputation—and thus its future—to a nameless, uncouth *ronin* from a farming village? To let the debacle end at this juncture would be unimaginable. And so a second match was arranged, this time pitting Musashi against Seijuro's younger brother, Denshichiro.

Denshichiro had a reputation as a very strong man and was, after all, one of the Kenpo Brothers. He carried a wooden sword over five feet long and sharpened at the end, a weapon that would have required considerable strength to handle at all, let alone with any skill. The bout was to be held at a location outside the capital, and a time was set. It would be astonishingly short. Musashi, having studied the Yoshioka character and gauged Denshichiro's temperament, showed up late once more, with the desired effect. When Denshichiro made an aggressive and angry attack, Musashi dodged the blow, wrested the sword from his opponent and stabbed him through. According to a number of records, "Denshichiro fell where he had stood, and died."

The match was over in a matter of seconds, and the astonished disciples who had come to watch their teacher make quick work of the upstart Musashi could do nothing but carry Denshichiro's lifeless body back to Kyoto. The fourth generation of the Yoshioka Kenpo had come to a devastating end.

It is not difficult to guess what happened next. Stories of revenge, or *adauchi*, have always occupied an important place in Japanese history, which is not surprising given the crucial role that honor plays in traditional Japanese culture. Whether the damage to one's honor was egregious or subtle, the wounded party was expected to take revenge. And in a society where news spread like ripples from a stone thrown into a still pond, there was no escape: the dishonored party was absolutely bound to action. Not to act would mean perpetual disgrace.

This was the situation in which the remnants of the Yoshioka clan, their disciples and students, found themselves: they had an inescapable obligation to act, regardless of how tragic the consequences might be.

And so yet another match was arranged with Musashi, this time against Seijuro's son, Matashichiro, now considered the fifth-generation Kenpo. But the match was only a ruse—a fact that seems to have been known to everyone, including Musashi. Matashichiro was just a symbol of the clan's honor. The real plan was for battle.

The place was again to be on the outskirts of Kyoto, at the famous spreading pine at the Ichijoji temple. To make sure that there was no chance of suffering another defeat, the Yoshioka brought more than a hundred men, armed with everything from swords and spears to bows and arrows.

Meanwhile, Musashi's reputation had skyrocketed, and he had taken on some very eager students himself. Just before the match, a number of these students learned of the Yoshioka family's plans, warned their teacher, and offered to accompany him to the bout. Musashi, however, knew that involving students in an *adauchi* would be considered the same as enrolling them in a battle, something strictly prohibited by the authorities. The Yoshioka clan was essentially finished and so perhaps had no other recourse. But Musashi had his life ahead of him, and had somehow gained a confidence and an inner strength far beyond that of ordinary men. His students were forbidden to walk with him into the trap set by the Yoshioka.

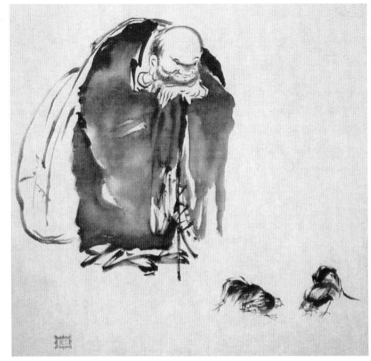

Above: Hotei watching a cock fight by Miyamoto Musashi

Left: Miyamoto Musashi self-portrait

Earlier in the year, when he fought Seijuro and Denshichiro, Musashi had put his opponents at a psychological disadvantage by causing the men to wait and thus lose their mental equilibrium. This time he reversed his strategy and started off early. On his way, he passed by a shrine to Hachiman, the god of war, and stopped for a moment to pray for victory. But as he walked up to the altar and was about to shake the gong's cord to get the god's attention, he suddenly realized that in ordinary times he had never put faith in the gods and buddhas. To do so now would be wrong. Chagrined, he released the cord and backed away. Why would the gods listen to him now, when he had never relied on them before? In truth, was he to rely on the gods or on himself? Dripping with sweat from embarrassment, he bowed to the shrine in thanks for the revelation and hurried on.

This incident made a deep impression on Musashi and when writing *The Book of Five Rings* nearly forty years later he made it clear that the principles of swordsmanship must be understood as though the student himself had discovered them. This was a major departure from other sword styles of Musashi's time. Of the great number of styles that arose in about the mid-sixteenth century, many of their progenitors let it be known that they had learned those styles not on their own, but through divine revelation. Tsukahara Bokuden of the Shinto-ryu, for example, received a "divine decree" at Kashima Shrine; and Ito Ittosai, the founder of the Itto-ryu, had his style revealed to him after seven days and seven nights of seclusion at the Grand Shrine at Mishima. The list goes on: the eyes of Okuyama Kyugasai of the Shinkage-ryu were opened by the gracious deity of Mikawa Okuyama; Jion of the Nen-ryu was enlightened to the secrets of his styles at Kurama Temple in Kyoto; Hayashizaki Jinsuke, founder of *iai-do*, discovered his new Way at Dewa Tateoka Hayashizaki Shrine; and Fukui Hei'emon had the principles of the Shindo Munen-ryu revealed to him by the Izuna Gongen in Shinshu.

Musashi bowed in veneration to the gods and even worshipped the Buddhist bodhisattvas, but the ever-practical swordsman had little patience with revelations or secrecy. These, he felt, were nothing more than impediments to self-reliance. As he lay dying years later, he wrote in "The Way of Walking Alone," his last testament for his disciples, that one should "Respect the gods and buddhas, but do not rely on them."

Musashi walked on and studied the topography on the way: the fork in the road that passed by the northern stretch of the Shirakawa River, the rice fields with narrow paths running between them, and even Mount Ichijoji and Mount Uryu at the back of the road. By dawn he was waiting to face the Yoshioka at the Spreading Pine.

Presently, Matashichiro and his accompanying "troops" arrived at the pine, carrying lamps and muttering that their opponent would probably be late again. Suddenly, Musashi jumped out from behind the pine and yelled, "Did I keep you waiting?"

Once again, his psychological tactic worked flawlessly. The Yoshioka were thrown into confusion, and, not yet able to see well in the half-light of dawn, each no doubt had the grim fear that Musashi might be just behind him. For his part, Musashi dashed straight into the crowd of men as they fumbled for their swords, found the cowering Matashichiro and cut him through the middle. The shocked students slashed about, thrust their spears and shot off arrows in total disarray. Taking advantage of the general panic, Musashi herded the frightened men together like so many cattle, cutting them down one after another before he finally withdrew along the route he had planned earlier.

It was a complete rout. The Yoshioka men who had somehow escaped with their lives now fled back to the capital, their disgrace so complete that no chance of recovery was possible. The last of the Yoshioka line had been cut down in the first moments of battle and a single swordsman had put to naught a sword style that had been celebrated for generations. Although an arrow had pierced his sleeve, Musashi himself had received not a single wound.

Nothing remains of the Yoshioka style today, so it is difficult to know what it actually entailed. The *Musashi koden* states: "As for their martial art, either they had studied from Gion Toji, a man who had understood the mysteries of swordsmanship, and were continuing his line; or they were the descendants of the Eight Schools of Kyoto in the line of Kiichi Hogen."

Both Gion Toji and Kiichi Hogen are legendary figures without clear historical origins, but the "Eight Schools of Kyoto" represent the Western style of swordsmanship and are often compared to the "Seven Schools of Kashima," representing the Eastern tradition. In traditional accounts, at least, Hogen lived in the twelfth century at the Ichijo Canal in Kyoto and was a master of the esoteric study of the yin/yang. He is said to have taught the martial arts to the famous twelfth-century general and strategist Minamoto no Yoshitsune, but he imparted the truly secret skills of the sword only to the "Eight Priests of Kurama," and it was with these that the Eight Schools began. Hogen was famous for his strategy, part of which is contained in his enigmatic saying:

> If the opponent comes, then greet him; if he goes, then send him off. To five add five and make ten; to two add eight and make ten. By this, you create harmony. Judge the situation, know the heart; the great is beyond ten feet square, the small enters the tiniest atom. The action may be fierce, but when facing what is in front of you, do not move the mind.

According to a book circulated among the adherents of Hogen's style during the Edo period, their swordsmanship was for the most part that of the Chujo-ryu. The *tachi* they used was short, and the distinctive feature of their martial technique was to press in close on the opponent's chest.

We will encounter this style again in connection with Musashi's famous bout on a small island far to the southwest.

The famous school of the Yoshioka was closed, never to reopen. The remaining members of the clan went back to, or perhaps had never really left, their craft of dyed goods; and for some generations after these events, their store remained open in Kyoto's Nishinotoin district, where they had once proudly traded upon their skill at a much different art.

The dream of the first Yoshioka, Naomoto, had floated like a bubble along the Kamo River through the city of Kyoto, only to disappear with the flash of a new morning's light.

At this point people were no doubt beginning to wonder and talk about the quality of that light.

But one who we can be sure was not interested in talking about that subject was Musashi himself. Musashi's laconic style is well known: even about his famous fights with the Yoshioka he wrote nothing specific, but noted in *The Book of Five Rings* that "I went to the capital and met with many famous martial artists; and although I fought a number of matches, I was never unable to take the victory."

Sharpening His Tools

In the Earth chapter of *The Book of Five Rings*, Musashi compares the warrior to a carpenter, noting that "the carpenter skillfully prepares all the different kinds of tools, learns the best way of using each one, takes out his carpenter's square, works correctly according to the plans, does his work unfailingly, and makes his way through the world."

As we have seen, his father, Munisai, was an expert at the sword, the *jitte*, the proper use of armor and even *jujitsu*. Thus, as was mentioned, Musashi must have been exposed at an early age to a great variety of weapons. Not long after his defeat of the Yoshioka clan, he turned his attention to other forms of the martial arts, and his steps toward the ancient capital of Nara.

The Buddhist monks at Nara had long been known for their prowess with military weapons and their willingness to use them in times of conflict. One of their favorite weapons was the spear, and the temple most closely associated with the spear was the Hozoin, a subtemple of the famous Kofukuji.

The first generation of the Hozoin style of spear technique was Kakuzenbo Hoin In'ei. Born in 1512 during the violent years of the Ashikaga shogunate, he first studied the spear under the martial artist Daizen Taibu Shigetada. Once In'ei was visited by the famous swordsman Kamiizumi Ise no kami, who soundly defeated him. Kamiizumi had already defeated In'ei's friend, Yagyu Muneyoshi (Sekishusai), and so the two friends now became Kamiizumi's disciples. In'ei became an expert with both the sword and the spear under Kamiizumi, but his specialty was the forked spear, which he would develop to great deadliness.

In'ei was from the famous Nakamikado clan, and was of the same generation as the famous generals Takeda Shingen and Uesugi Kenshin. This was a period of intense interest in the martial arts and In'ei, although a priest, was at the vanguard of his times. Eventually banished from the Hozoin temple for his love of weaponry, he took the opportunity to wander the provinces and visit more than forty martial artists before he was allowed to return to the temple. One of those martial artists was the above-mentioned Daizen, from whose lessons In'ei developed his own *kamayari*, or sickle-spear, technique.

Priest-soldiers had traditionally used the halberd, which they considered a holy weapon for the protection of Buddhism, as opposed to the straight spear, the weapon of common soldiers. The innovative In'ei, however, found that fixing a sicklelike blade to the spear increased its efficiency. This was the *kamayari*. The secret poem that expressed the virtue of the weapon goes:

Thrust, and it's a spear;

Hurl, and it's a halberd;

Pull, and it's a sickle.

In any and all events,

You should not miss.

This weapon was far more efficient than the regular spear or halberd. It was used not only for thrusting, but for sweeping, cutting, dragging and striking. Because of this innovation, In'ei's fame spread to the surrounding areas and he attracted many disciples.

By the time In'ei turned eighty-three in 1603, he had come to the realization that Buddhist priests should have nothing to do with instruments of violence and death. He closed the *dojo* that had once employed over forty teachers and forbade his successor, Kakuzenbo Inshun, to teach the martial arts. He died four years later, at age eighty-seven.

But the Hozoin spear tradition did not die with In'ei, for a few years after his death it was re-established by Inshun, who had become abbot of that temple. Born in 1589, Inshun was five years Musashi's junior and was rumored to have been In'ei's son. He continued studying spear technique from a Nichiren priest at the neighboring Ozoin temple who had also studied under In'ei.

It was this priest from the Ozoin—known to us only by the name of his temple—that Musashi met in a match not long after the fight at Ichijoji temple. The priest was armed with a *kamayari*, while Musashi stood his ground with a short wooden sword. Despite his apparent disadvantage, Musashi beat the man in both of two matches, showing no concern about being in a compound surrounded by warrior priests who very much wanted their man to win. For his part, the monk felt no rancor but, on the contrary, was so impressed that he had Musashi stay for a sumptuous meal. The two became so engaged in talk about the martial arts that the sun had risen before they became aware of the time. Then Musashi thanked his opponent-host and went on his way.

After Musashi left Nara and the Hozoin, he disappeared from the written records for about three years. But there is little doubt that during that time he continued to live the life of a *shugyosha*, meeting other such men and wandering the country. Musashi, like other *shugyosha*, learned firsthand on his travels about nature, topography, local customs and the character of men—especially of other swordsmen. He also no doubt learned about the characteristics and features of local castles, the production of local goods and the cultures of the various provinces. This was exactly the sort of information that was valued by the feudal lords, who were happy to hire *shugyosha* with expertise in such matters. In turn, this was the outcome that most wandering swordsmen sought: a position as trusted servant of a prosperous master and a stipend worthy of his talents. Musashi, however, turned neither his knowledge nor his talent into practical security. His sights were set much higher.

In 1607, Musashi was passing through the province of Iga when he met a man known only by his family name, Shishido, who was a master of the sickle and chain, the *kusarigama*. This Shishido lived in a relatively isolated part of the mountains in Iga, where he farmed and ran an informal local smithy, making his own weapons. The sickle was originally a farming instrument, but according to the chronicles of the Genpei wars, it was used as a weapon called the *naikama*, or *nagikama*, as early as the twelfth century. The *naikama* was a sickle attached to a long handle and was used to cut the opponent's feet and ankles with a sort of mowing motion. According to tradition, when used as a weapon in China it was attached to a nine- or ten-foot chain. The chain was attached to either the upper or lower section of the sickle's handle, which was a little over one-and-a-half feet long. The chain was then used to immobilize the opponent's body or weapon, while the counterweight at the end was used to wound or kill him. The sickle was employed to finish him off.

The match between Musashi and Shishido took place in an open field, and once again Musashi had to fight while being watched closely by a number of his opponent's disciples. After successfully arresting Musashi's sword with the chain, Shishido moved slowly in to finish him off with the sickle, when Musashi suddenly unsheathed his *waki-zashi* and, throwing it like a *shuriken*, fatally pierced the man's chest. At this point, Shishido's shocked disciples all drew their swords and slashed out at their leader's assailant. Musashi, however, chased after them and they scattered, running "off in the four directions."

Musashi was an expert at throwing blades. The Kokura Hibun states:

> He either let fly with a real sword or threw a wooden one. But there was no way for either a fleeing or running person to avoid it. Its force was exactly like unleashing the strength of a bow made of stone: one hundred releases, one hundred hits. It cannot be thought that even Yang Yu-chi [a famous archer of the Spring and Autumn Period in China] had mysterious skill like this.

He also taught this skill to his disciples. According to the *Watanabe koan taiwa*, published about twenty-five years after Musashi's death, Takemura Yoemon, who was either Musashi's adopted child or his disciple, was no less expert with the *shuriken* than was Musashi himself. Yoemon, it notes, "could float a peach in the river and then pierce it to its core with a sixteen-inch knife."

Tokugawa Ieyasu had politically unified Japan by December 1602. The following year the imperial court awarded him the ancient title, Sei-I Tai-Shogun, or Great General Who Conquers the Western Barbarians, which gave tacit court approval to his assertion of ultimate authority. By February of the following year he began rebuilding the castle at Edo (Tokyo), which was to be the new capital. By June he had declared that every *daimyo*, from fiefs around the country, would be required to leave members of his immediate family in Edo year-round, to ensure his "good intentions" toward the Tokugawa government; in other words, family members of all *daimyo* were effectively to be held hostage in the capital to prevent rebellions from starting in the countryside. To make sure that these hostages could live in dignity commensurate with the status of their clans, mansions were built, quarters for samurai were established and roads were constructed. With the labor, materials and supporting businesses involved in the reconstruction, Edo was quite suddenly transformed from a backwater town to the new center of politics, business and, if not high culture, at least cultural activity. Money and power had come to town.

Swordsmen had also arrived in great numbers. Yagyu Munenori had become sword instructor to Ieyasu's son Hidetada as early as 1601, and had now established his line of the Yagyu-ryu in the new capital. The Toda-ryu was there as well, and the Itto-ryu under Ono Tadaaki, who was also an instructor to the shogunate family. Edo had become a magnet for those *shugyosha* who hoped either to be noticed by a visiting *daimyo* or to meet other martial artists and sharpen their skills.

Musashi was in Edo by 1608 and, preceded by the reputation he had gained at Kyoto, met a number of talented men. To survive, he started his own small school and took on such students as Hatano Jirozaemon, who later had a number of disciples of his own. Another disciple was Ishikawa Sakyo, a retainer of Honda Masakatsu. Sakyo is said to have been skillful enough to combine the Unmoving Sword and the Diamond Sword techniques, and this synthesis was eventually added to the Musashi style. It is easy to imagine that Musashi's *dojo* was a busy place, despite the fact that he was only twenty-five years old.

One day early on, a man by the name of Muso Gonnosuke walked into Musashi's *dojo* accompanied by eight disciples and requested a match. Gonnosuke was a big man—well over six feet tall—who had learned the deepest secrets of the Shindo-ryu and was invested with the secrets of the Kashima-ryu's One Sword technique. After further study in Hitachi under a Sakurai Yoshikatsu, he had toured the northern provinces wearing a *haori* that bore a large crest of a crimson sun on a white background. On his shoulders was embroidered in gold characters: "Greatest Martial Artist in the Realm, Founder of the Hino-moto-ryu, Muso Gonnosuke."

It should be noted here that, while Gonnosuke may have had a flair for style, his dress and braggadocio were no more unusual for *shugyosha* than Arima Kihei's self-promoting, gold-lettered placard. Flamboyantly dressed swordsmen were not rare during this time. Their clothes were a means of gaining attention, and carried two messages: "I'm a skillful swordsman ready to be hired by an appreciative lord," and "Anyone, at any time, is welcome to test his skills against mine." Clothes on occasion either made or unmade the man, depending on the relative skill of the swordsman who happened to notice him.

Musashi, on the other hand, did not conform to this style, and in fact did not comply with many of the sartorial rules of his day. He was an independent, and in large part a nonconformist. He dressed and bathed as he pleased. At any rate, Gonnosuke walked into Musashi's *dojo* and requested a match, and one of his disciples produced a four-foot wooden sword from a brocade bag. Musashi, who at the time was carving a small willow bow, quickly accepted the challenge and took up a piece of firewood as his only weapon. Gonnosuke attacked without further ado, and Musashi sent him tumbling with a single blow.

Gonnosuke was humiliated and left without a word, but he was a man of great determination and skill, and this would not be the end of the matter. Dismissing his disciples and retreating to Mount Homan in Chikuzen to pray and meditate over this defeat, he was answered one night in a dream with the words: "Know the reflection of the moon in the water with a log."

Gonnosuke understood this "log" to be the five-foot staff, or jo, and the moon in the water to mean the center of his opponent's chest. Soon thereafter he was employed by the Kuroda clan in the Fukuoka fief of Chikuzen for the *jo* technique he then originated. Much later, he returned to challenge his nemesis again, with the match this time resulting in the only draw of Musashi's career. The technique that Gonnosuke created is called the Shindo Muso-ryu, and it is practiced to this day.

Musashi stayed on in Edo for another two years or so, continuing to teach students and take on opponents. His matches in 1610 with two of these opponents, Osedo Hayashi, a Yagyu stylist, and Tsuji-kaze Tenma, known more for his strength than his swordsmanship, are described in the *Nitenki*:

> When Musashi was residing in Edo, Osedo Hayashi, a samurai in the Yagyu clan, went with a certain Tsujikaze, a strong martial artist, to ask for bouts with the swordsman. Musashi gave his consent, and immediately stood and faced them. Osedo advanced and

was about to strike, but Musashi took the initiative and struck first. Osedo collapsed where he stood.

Next, Tsujikaze attacked, but for some reason fell backwards, hit his back on a water-jar at the edge of the veranda and died. Generally speaking, this Tsujikaze was a man of great strength. He was able, for example, to run alongside a galloping horse, and to bring it to a halt by wrapping his arms around its neck.

By 1612 the situation in Edo had become tedious for Musashi. He was essentially barred from comparing skills with the best swordsmen of the day, such as Yagyu Munenori, because of Munenori's connection with the Tokugawa and because of the precarious political status Musashi had after having fought for the Toyotomi. To make matters worse, the tension between these two clans was escalating day by day. The Toyotomi were ensconced in their castle at Osaka and still had the backing of a number of *daimyo* and *ronin*. So early in the year, Musashi traveled on foot to the Fujiwara area of Shimousa Province, ostensibly for the opening of new land. This was probably a ruse, because he did not stay there long, nor had he likely decided, at age twenty-nine, to give up the sword and begin a career in agriculture.

Musashi clearly had something else in mind, and by February or March he had already started on the long trip to the southwestern island of Kyushu.

Demon of the Western Provinces

Musashi's mark for an appropriate match was Sasaki Kojiro, a swordsman popularly known as the Demon of the Western Provinces. Kojiro had arrived in the port city of Kokura in Buzen some two years earlier and, as his nickname implies, had attained great fame. Certainly he had caught everyone's eye with his striking appearance—he wore a crimson *haori* with his long sword, known as the Drying Pole, slung across his back—but his skill too was astonishing and he had thus far defeated every opponent he had faced.

Hosokawa Tadatoshi, who six years later would become the lord of Kokura, had been enamored of the martial arts from his youth and was himself a skilled practitioner of the sword. Thus, when news of Kojiro's presence in Kokura reached him, he happily interviewed the man and soon hired him as an instructor to the Hosokawa clan. Although Kojiro was not actually taken on as a retainer to the clan, he received a substantial fee and was able to open his own *dojo* in the castle town, eventually gaining a great number of disciples.

Ganryu Sasaki Kojiro was born in Jokyoji Village at Ichijogatani in Echizen. Ichijogatani was the home of the prosperous and cultured Asakura clan, who had been the lords of Echizen over the course of five generations spanning more than a hundred years. Their instructor of the martial arts was one Toda Seigen, the main heir to the Chujo-ryu. It, like the Shinto-ryu and the Kage-ryu, was a fundamental style of the Japanese martial arts and had been established as far back as the Kamakura period (1185–1333) by Chujo Hyogonosuke. Seigen himself was an extraordinarily accomplished practitioner who continued to perfect his martial art after he retired from teaching in his old age due to an eye disease. Secluding himself at his home in Jokyoji Village, he was commonly known as "the blind swordsman." His ideal had been a technique called the "No-Sword" (*muto*), exemplified by the phrase, "If shortness [of the sword] is taken to an extreme, it becomes nothingness" (*Tan kiwamareba mu*); as his art advanced, his short sword became shorter and shorter still.

Seigen had met Kojiro when the latter was quite young, and had recognized in him the makings of a great swordsman. For the purposes of his own research, he hired the teenaged Kojiro as a sparring partner. In their daily matches, Seigen wielded a short *tachi* about one-and-a-half feet long, while requiring Kojiro to oppose him with a much longer blade. With this intense training, Seigen developed a style he hoped would eventually lead to the abandonment of the sword as a weapon altogether; but for his part, Kojiro eventually gained great ability with the long sword and became one of Seigen's top disciples. The moment of truth came when Kojiro was able to defeat Seigen's younger brother, Jibuzaemon, in a match; at which point Kojiro went out on his own. He wandered the provinces of Japan as a *shugyosha*, eventually arriving in Kokura and establishing himself under Tadatoshi's patronage.

Musashi came to Kokura from Kyoto in April 1612, visiting the mansion of Nagaoka Sado no kami Okinaga, a chief retainer of the Kokura fief and, it will be recalled, a former student of Musashi's father, Munisai. Musashi was now twenty-nine years old. After a short while, he made his wishes known to his host in a formal request, which records note as follows: "It would seem as though a Ganryu Sasaki Kojiro is now residing in this area, and I have heard that his technique is excellent. My request is for permission for us to have a 'comparison of techniques.' I make this in reference to your relationship with my father, Munisai."

Okinaga, whether out of deference to his old teacher or his impression of the intense Musashi, was quick to comply. Putting Musashi up at his own mansion, he contacted his lord, Tadaoki, and made the petition his own. Martial arts enthusiast that he was, Tadaoki had no doubt heard of Musashi's bouts with the Yoshioka in Kyoto, and must have been quite curious about this man. But he was also acting out of respect for Sado, a trusted and respected retainer, when he gave his permission for a match to be held the following day, April 13.

The place was to be a small, lonely island between Kokura and Nagato Shimonoseki, a little less than two-and-a-half miles from either shore. Known in ancient times as Anato no Shima, it was in Musashi's time called Mukaijima ("the island over there") by people in Buzen on the Kyushu side, and Funa Island ("boat island") by those in Shimonoseki on the Honshu side, because of its boatlike appearance from that shore. The match was set to begin during the first half of the Hour of the Dragon (seven to nine a.m.). A decree was posted throughout the castle town and the surrounding area stating that absolutely no favoritism was to be shown either man and that spectators were strictly forbidden to travel to the island.

Okinaga quickly informed Musashi of the decision and offered to escort him to the island the next day in his own boat. Overjoyed, Musashi thanked Okinaga for his efforts in arranging the match that he had so greatly anticipated.

That night, however, Musashi disappeared. A search was made through the castle town, but he was nowhere to be found. Word spread quickly, as did rumors that Musashi, when confronted with the prospect of a bout with the Demon of the Western Provinces, had turned tail and run.

Okinaga, as might be imagined, was chagrined. He had his own prestige on the line in this matter, having taken up Musashi's petition and encouraged Lord Tadaoki to agree to the match. If Musashi had now truly fled, it would be a source of embarrassment not only for him, but worse, for Tadaoki as well. Upon some reflection, however, Okinaga realized that if Musashi really were a coward, he would not have waited until the night before the match to escape. He also reasoned that, as Musashi had come to Kokura from Shimonoseki, he may well have gone back to that city to spend the night away from the inevitable distractions in Kokura, and would probably go to the island from there.

A courier was sent and, sure enough, Musashi was found staying in Shimonoseki at the residence of a wholesaler, Kobayashi Tarozae-mon. The courier explained the situation in Kokura, and Musashi responded with a letter that demonstrated both his respect for Okinaga and his circumspection.

> I have heard that, concerning tomorrow's match, you would send me in Your Excellency's boat, and I am heavily honored by your solicitude. However, at this time, Kojiro and I are hostile opponents; and if Kojiro is sent by Lord Tadaoki's boat and I am sent by Your Excellency's boat, I wonder if this would not place you in opposition with your lord.
>
> Please let me be of no concern to you in this affair. I considered speaking to you about this right away, but thinking that you would not agree, purposefully did not make any mention of it. I must strongly refuse Your Excellency's boat. Tomorrow morning I will cross over to Mukaijima from this place. Please do not be the least bit concerned, and be convinced that I will come in good time.
>
> April 12
>
> Miyamoto Musashi
>
> —To Lord Sado—

Musashi was clearly concerned that any sign of favoritism toward him on Okinaga's part might result in some friction between lord and retainer, and he was determined to prevent this. His actions had predictably resulted in doubt about his courage and sincerity, but Musashi seems to have been concerned only for Okinaga's relationship with the Hosokawa. It was important to him that this relationship would continue smoothly for his sponsor long after the following day's bout had ended.

Nevertheless, when the sun came up the next morning, Musashi was still sound asleep. The master of the house, Tarozaemon, woke him up and informed him that the Hour of the Dragon had already arrived. At this point, a courier came from Kokura, informing Musashi that Kojiro's boat had already left and made the crossing. Musashi responded that he would be there soon, but then got up, washed his hands and face, and ate a leisurely breakfast. Requesting an oar from Tarozaemon, he sat and carved a large wooden sword until another courier arrived urging him to make the crossing immediately.

Musashi then dressed himself in a silk-lined garment, folded a towel over his sash, put a wadded cotton garment over the silk one, boarded the boat and left. At the helm was Tarozaemon's servant. Musashi sat in the middle of the boat twisting a paper string, with which he then tied back his sleeves. Finally, putting the wadded cotton garment over his head and shoulders, he lay down.

On the island, Kojiro and the verifying officers waited with impatience and consternation. In the boat, Musashi was apparently asleep.

In the end, Musashi arrived at Mukaijima after the Hour of the Serpent (nine to eleven a.m.). He had Tarozaemon's servant stop the boat on a small, narrow sandspit projecting from the island, and removed the wadded cotton garment. Placing his sword in the boat and his short sword in his sash, he pulled his sleeves up high and got out of the boat, barefooted, into the shallow water. Holding his wooden sword in a lowered position, he took several steps in the little waves and walked up the beach. As he walked, he took the hand towel from his sash, folded it into the length of a *hachimaki*, and tied it around his head with the knot in the middle of his forehead.

In contrast to Musashi, Kojiro was dressed colorfully in a sleeveless scarlet *haori* and dyed leather knickers. On his feet were new straw sandals, and in his hand was a sword over three feet long, reputedly fashioned by one of the great swordsmiths of Bizen.

Kojiro felt insulted at having been made to wait. Seeing Musashi approaching in the distance, he rushed to the water's edge. He angrily informed his opponent that he himself had been on the island at the appointed time and demanded to know whether Musashi had come late out of fear. Musashi silently ignored him and simply advanced. In a rage, Kojiro unsheathed his sword and dramatically threw the scabbard into the water. Musashi stood in the shallows, smiled and uttered his now-famous words, "You've lost, Kojiro. Would the winner throw away his scabbard?"

Inflamed, Kojiro moved quickly toward Musashi and swung his sword straight forward, aiming for the middle of the forehead. At the same instant, Musashi struck with his wooden sword in the same way, hitting Kojiro directly on the head. Kojiro fell where he stood. The tip of his sword had cut through the knot of Musashi's *hachimaki*, and the hand towel had fluttered to the ground, but Musashi's wooden sword had made a direct hit. Musashi lowered his sword and stood motionless for a moment, then quickly raised it to strike again. Kojiro was lying flat on the ground, but at that moment he wielded his sword to the side in a mowing motion, aiming for Musashi's thigh. Musashi leapt back, and received a three-inch cut in the lining of his *hakama*, probably less than an inch away from his femoral artery.

Musashi's wooden sword now came down, splitting Kojiro's ribs, and Kojiro, blood flowing from his mouth and nose, lost consciousness. Musashi crouched down and put his hand above Kojiro's mouth and nose, checking for signs of life. There were none. He turned to the verifying officials, bowed briefly, then stood up and walked briskly to the beach. Jumping deftly into the boat, he helped the helmsman pole away from the island, and could soon be seen only dimly in the offing.

It was noontime, and in the spring sea between Kokura and Shimonoseki, the bright sun reflected off the wavelets and a breeze began to rise. Musashi had fought the greatest fight of his life, one that is still discussed with great animation nearly four hundred years later.

Musashi's approach to the fight with Kojiro seems to have involved a two-tiered strategy. The first tier involved psychology, the same weapon he had used against the Kenpo Brothers. By making the opponent wait, he disturbed his equilibrium: anger and consternation thwarted the necessary concentration. Kojiro had had to wait in the bright morning sun, eventually, no doubt, clenching his fists in frustration. By the time Musashi arrived, refreshed and fully focused, his opponent was completely distracted by his hurt pride and impatience. The second tier was Musashi's knowledge that Kojiro had a preference for long swords and would likely rely on the advantage of that length. It was a long sword that he had used to defeat Toda Seigen's brother Jibuzaemon and every opponent since. Musashi therefore fashioned his oar into a wooden sword just a bit longer than Kojiro's weapon, to take that advantage from Kojiro and make it his own. According to the Kokura Hibun:

> Ganryu said, "I would like to settle the match with real swords." Musashi replied, "You handle a naked blade and show me every mystery it has. I will raise my wooden sword and manifest its secrets." Thus the promise was made as hard as lacquer.

Musashi's "secret" may have been as little as one inch. At any rate, many years later, in the Wind chapter of *The Book of Five Rings*, he would warn his students against depending on the length of a weapon:

There are other styles that prefer a long sword. From the standpoint of my own martial art, this can be seen as a weak style. The reason is this: not knowing how to defeat others in any situation, they put virtue in the length of their sword and think they can win by the distance from their opponent.

Those who prefer long swords will have their explanation, but it is only their own individual quibbling. It is unreasonable when seen from the True Way in this world.

But Kojiro was just as famous for his lethal *tsubame-gaeshi* ("swallow return") style. Seigen himself seems to have initiated this style, but it was Kojiro who developed it further, or at least made it famous. The technique itself is not well understood today but it seems to have been based on an instantaneous return of the blade after the first strike, and it was probably modeled after or compared to the swallow showing its white underside when suddenly reversing its course in midflight. The *Ganryu hidensho* describes it this way:

The sword is held straight ahead, as though to strike the opponent on the forehead. Advancing straight ahead, you keep your eye on the tip of your opponent's nose. Then, striking all the way to the ground, you immediately bend down to a crouch, bring your sword up over your shoulder, and thereby defeat your opponent.

In other words, the first strike is a feint, and it is the return strike that is the actual attack. Essentially, this is a *kaeshiwaza*, or "returning technique."

Kojiro, nevertheless, did not use his famous technique against Musashi, unless the final strike at Musashi's thigh might be considered the "return." Instead, he went straight for his opponent in a *jodan* position, his long sword held high over his head. What happened? Was Kojiro too rattled to use the technique that had always brought him success? Was there a fear factor? Certainly he, too, was aware that Musashi had single-handedly dismantled the Yoshioka, but that was a decade earlier. Did he simply not have time for a return blow when Musashi's wooden sword cracked down on his skull? We will never know. But the old swordsmen's saying, "To catch a tiger, you must enter the tiger's den," may apply here. In this one strike, Musashi must have been within an inch of Kojiro's very real and very sharp blade as it made its downward swing. His timing and sense of distance had to be perfect. As it was, his *hachimaki* was neatly severed by Kojiro's sword, and it was the knot of that towel that received the tip of the blade of the Drying Pole.

To say that Musashi had perfectly calculated the strikes of the two swords misses the point, however, for what brought him the victory was nothing so cerebral. Musashi himself addressed the matter in the Emptiness chapter of *The Book of Five Rings*, noting that all techniques and actions of either mind or body must have their foundations in Zen Buddhist Emptiness: "The heart of Emptiness is in the absence of anything with form and the inability to have knowledge thereof. This I see as Emptiness. Emptiness, of course, is nothingness. Knowing the existent, you know the nonexistent. This, exactly, is Emptiness."

The reader senses that in the absence of Musashi's intuition and discipline, language itself fails here. Thus we go back to Mukai Island (Mukaijima), now called Ganryu Island (Ganryujima; *jima* means "island"), time and again, looking for the key to the most famous one-on-one fight in Japanese history. Until we are able to enter Musashi's spirit that day, however, we will be left with only the sand and the sound of waves on this little island.

It is interesting to note that Musashi was asked years later why he did not deliver a *todome*, or coup de grâce, to Kojiro. His response was that such an action was for true enemies, and there had been no enmity between himself and his opponent. Their match was one of a "comparison of techniques."

There are two meanings to the word *todome* that might apply to this case. The first and more common meaning is a simple stab to the throat that quickly and reliably ends a fallen man's life, but this would make little sense in the context of this match: Kojiro had died immediately from the combination of Musashi's two blows. The more esoteric meaning, however, is to finish off the opponent in a manner that prevents his angry spirit from returning to take revenge. In this case, the *todome* would have been delivered by stabbing him "just below the left nipple and twisting the blade from edge up to edge downward as it was withdrawn." Musashi's response indicated that he understood the question in terms of this second meaning, and that there was no need for such a *todome*. Kojiro himself had been eager for the match and while his spirit might lament the result it would honor Musashi for his victory.

But if Kojiro's spirit honored Musashi, there were those still living who did not. The surviving Yoshioka had slandered him, some declaring that Musashi had actually been beaten by Seijuro and then run away from a fight with Denshichiro. Others circulated a story that the fight with Seijuro had been a draw, or that both had cut each other's *hachimaki* but that the blood simply did not show on Musashi's persimmon-colored *hachimaki* and did on Seijuro's white one. How they accounted for the complete disappearance of the Yoshioka brothers and their school from the swordsmanship scene is unknown.

In the case of the fight at Ganryu Island, there were partisans in favor of Kojiro, or disciples of his, who claimed that Kojiro had only been knocked temporarily unconscious by Musashi's blow, and that Musashi's disciples, who had hidden themselves on the island, had rushed forward and finished Kojiro off when he started to regain consciousness. How Musashi's disciples might have managed to get onto the tiny island, evade detection by the Hosokawa verifying officials, and escape is not explained.

Some people may have stopped and listened to these stories, but Musashi was not one of them. After returning directly to Shimonoseki, he wrote a letter to Nagaoka Sado Okinaga, thanking him for his graciousness and help, then left again for ports unknown.

ODA NOBUNAGA: THE WARLORD AND POETRY

Hiroaki Sato

The life of Oda Nobunaga (1534–82), who started the process of unifying war-torn Japan but was assassinated before achieving his goal, is linked to verse in a fascinating way: No versifier himself, he made his debut as a warlord singing a song about the transience of life; and his assassin, who in effect helped fulfill that prophecy, took that step after participating in a verse-composing session.

One of the most inspiring battles in Japan's "age of warring states" is the one at Okehazama. In it, Nobunaga, leading less than 2,000 men, attacked Imagawa Yoshimoto (1519–60), leading 25,000, and won. In the fifth month of 1560, Yoshimoto, the most powerful warlord along the Pacific Coast ("The Number One Bowman of the Eastern Sea"), headed west for Kyoto with an army combining the forces of the three provinces of Suruga, Tōtōmi, and Mikawa. Nobunaga, situated in Owari, was in his way but was not regarded as capable of putting up a credible fight. Indeed, by the morning of the nineteenth of the fifth month, only a day after arriving in Owari, Yoshimoto brought down two of the five forts built against him: Marune Fort, commanded by Sakuma Daigaku Morishige, and Washizu Fort, commanded by Oda Genba, with both commanders killed.

How Nobunaga faced an invader with overwhelming forces and mounted a successful counter-attack is memorably told by Ōta Gyūichi (1527–1610?) in his *Shinchō-kō Ki* (Biography of Lord Nobunaga), which he is said to have written on the basis of notes he took while still "running about on active duty" as a bowman under Nobunaga.

On the eighteenth, when he received news of Yoshimoto's arrival in his territory, Nobunaga was in his main fort, Kiyosu Castle.

His conversations that night contained nothing remotely related to military matters, as they consisted of social gossip. When he found it was very late, he gave his men leave to go home. His house administrators derided him among themselves as they left, saying, "Well, the adage, 'When luck runs out, the mirror of one's wisdom clouds up, too,' is meant for this kind of behavior."

As expected, toward daybreak, messages from Sakuma Daigaku and Oda Genba arrived, one following the other, reporting that the enemy had already begun attacking Mt. Washizu and Mt. Marune.

On hearing this, Nobunaga danced the Atsumori dance, singing;

A man lives for fifty years.
When compared with the Lowest Heaven,[1]
it's like a dream, an illusion.
Is there anyone who, given life once,
never fades away?

This done, he commanded, "Blow the conch shell! Give me my equipment!" He then put on his armor, ate his breakfast standing, put on his helmet, and sallied forth. Accompanying him at that moment were his pages, Nagato Governor Iwamuro, Hasegawa Hashisuke, Sawaki Tōhachi, Hida Governor Yamaguchi, and Gatō Yasaburō.

The six of them, master and retainers together, galloped straight over the seven miles to Atsuta, where, in front of Gendayū Shrine, he looked east and saw smoke rising from Washizu and Marune, both forts evidently fallen. At the time there were six men on horseback and about 200 foot soldiers. If he pushed forward from the beach side, that would have been the shortest way, but the tides were up and would not have allowed horses to pass. So he and his men galloped through the hillside road from Atsuta, first arriving at the fort at Tange, then at the fort at Zenshō Temple where Sakuma [Uemon] had set up camp. There he counted his men and reviewed the situation. The reports said:

His enemy Imagawa Yoshimoto, leading an army of 45,000 men,[2] was resting his men and horses on Mt. Okehazama. At noon on the nineteenth, he lined up his men to face northwest and said, "I couldn't be more pleased that you men attacked and brought down Washizu and Marune." He then had three rounds of nō chanting performed. This time Ieyasu[3] was the first to attack; leading men in red coats, he carried provisions into Ōtaka Castle, struggled at Washizu and Marune, and, because of all the difficulties he had had, was now resting his men and horses at Ōtaka, where he set up camp.

Seeing Nobunaga going to Zenshō Temple, the two commanders Sasa Hayato no Shō and Chiaki Shirō headed toward Yoshimoto with a light brigade of 300 men, but they were swamped in a sudden onslaught, both men, along with fifty riders, killed in battle. Yoshimoto saw this as a sign that even Heaven's demon or devils or gods would not be able to bear the brunt of his might. Feeling delighted about this, he had nō chanting performed in leisurely fashion as he laid out his camp.

These reports heard, Nobunaga decided to move to Nakajima. His house administrators loudly protested, holding on to the bit of his horse, saying, "Sir, the road there is flanked by deep paddies. Once you step into them, you won't be able to move. Besides, you'll be forced to march in a single file. That will make the puny size of our forces perfectly visible to the enemy. This is out of the question, sir!" But Nobunaga wrung himself free and moved to Nakajima. At the time his men are said to have numbered less than 2,000.

---

1 *Geten.* It refers to *Shio-ten,* one of the Six Realms of Desire, and *Shio-ten* is called *Geten* because it is located at the lowest stratum. In this "heaven" one day and night is the equivalent of fifty years of a human life.

2 Yoshimoto spread the rumor that he was leading an army of 40,000 men. The biographer further inflated the figure.

3 Tokugawa Ieyasu (1543–1616), who unified Japan and established his own shogunate. At the time he was going by the name of Matsudaira Motoyasu and, though he had his own castle, was Yoshimoto's virtual hostage. Sometime after Yoshimoto's death, he became Nobunaga's important ally. Hence this special reference to the enemy commander.

JAPAN
IN THE
AZUCHI-MOMOYAMA PERIOD
安土桃山時代の日本

Land of the Oda clan, 1560

Area conquered by Oda Nobunaga and
Toyotomi Hideyoshi by 1582

Main Daimyō opposed to Hideyoshi in 1582

Other areas

• Castle town

○ Town

× Battle

Ukita Daimyō house

Hokkaidō

• Hirosaki • Hachinohe

• Akita • Morioka

Sea of Japan

• Ichinoseki

• Tsuruoka

Sado

• Sendai
○ Shibata Yamagata
Niigata
Nagaoka • Aizu • Shirakawa • Iwaki

○ Takata Shirakawa
Uesugi

Kanazawa • • Toyama Takeda *Honshū*
Sasa • Utsunomiya

• Fukui Maeda Takasaki

Shibata Hojo
Edo • ○ Choshi

• Ilda
Obama × *Sekigahara (1600)* Odawara
Akechi Azuchi • Nagoya Ōdawara (1590)
Kyoto ○ Momoyama Tokugawa
Ukita Himeji Kobe Osaka • Yoshida
Okayama ○ Sakai • Toba
Mori
Hiroshima Takamatsu
Izu Islands

Matsue • • Yonago • Tottori

Hamada

Tsushima • Hagi

Inland Sea

○ Kitakyushu • Matsuyama • Tokushima
○ Hakataka • Tanabe
Hirado Chosokabe • Kochi
Kobayakawa Funai • • Uwajima *Shikoku*
Hara Otomo
Fukue Nagasaki ○ • Higo

Kyūshū

PACIFIC OCEAN

Shimazu • Miyazaki
Kagoshima •

Korea

Oki

*East China
Sea*

Tanegashima

Yakushima

0   100   200
km

At Nakajima he again tried to move his men forward. This time, his administrators held on to him and succeeded in stopping him. Thereupon, he harangued his men:

"All of you, listen to me carefully. The enemy soldier came here, eating food in the evening and marching throughout the night. He had to carry his provisions into Ōtaka, worked hard at Washizu and Marune, and is exhausted with all the difficulties he's had. We, on the other hand, are a fresh army. Besides, you all know the saying, don't you, 'Don't be afraid of a large enemy because your forces are small. Luck resides in Heaven.'

"If the enemy attacks, retreat. If he retreats, give chase. The idea is to wrestle him down and destroy him in the chase. Don't capture anybody. Just leave him alone. If we win in this battle, those of you taking part will bring honor to your houses, your reputation assured in generations to come. So do your best!"

While he was making this harangue, the following men—
Maeda Matazaemon, Mōri Kawachi, Mōri Jūrō, Kinoshita
Utanosuke, Nakagawa Kin'emon, Sakuma Yatarō, Mori Kosuke,
Ajiki Yatarō, and Uozumi Hayato
returned, each carrying the head or heads of the enemies he killed. After repeating his words to these men, Nobunaga took his forces to the hillside. Suddenly a downpour as fierce as catapulted ice stones struck the enemy in the face, Nobunaga's troops from the rear. The rain was so powerful

that the camphor tree growing near the pines on Kutsukake Pass that would have required two or three men with arms spread to surround it tipped east and fell. The fierceness of it was such that people wondered if the Great Deity of Atsuta had started his own war.

The moment the sky cleared, Nobunaga lifted his spear and shouted loudly, "Attack now! Attack!" The enemy, seeing an assault coming forward like black smoke, suddenly fell back like a wave rolling back. Bows, spears, guns, banners, and battle-markers were thrown into confusion, as the enemy fell back and retreated, abandoning even Yoshimoto's lacquered palanquin.

Nobunaga barked a command, "That's his camp. Attack!"

It was around two in the afternoon that he directed his attack east. At first about 300 riders made a complete circle around Yoshimoto as they retreated, but as they fought the assaulting forces two, three times, four, five times, their number gradually decreased, and in the end only about fifty riders were left.

Nobunaga himself dismounted and rushed forward with young warriors, felling enemies forward and backward, as young men in their fury attacked chaotically, blade clashing against blade, swordguard splitting swordguard, sparks flying, fire spewing. In all this, enemy and friendly warriors never confused themselves with each other, distinguishing themselves by color. Many of Nobunaga's horse-tenders [cavalrymen] and pages were wounded or killed.

Hashimoto Koheita attacked Yoshimoto, but, his knee slashed, fell down. Mōri Shinsuke cut Yoshimoto down and took his head. …

The place known as Okehazama is a valley, an extremely difficult terrain where deep paddies prevent mobility and high and low places are combined intricately. Those who fled into deep paddies could only crawl about, unable to get away. With these Nobunaga's young soldiers caught up, each taking two or three heads, bringing them to him. Nobunaga announced that he would conduct formal inspection of the heads at Kiyosu but he was more than satisfied to see Yoshimoto's head. He returned to his camp along the road he had taken earlier.

The "conversations" mentioned at the outset are *o-hanashi*, sometimes called *o-togi*. The conversations a master or a lord had with his ranking aides, though often idle or merely entertaining, formed a vital source of information or provided an occasion for assessment or analysis. This particular night Nobunaga's aides who gathered around him must have expected him to discuss how to respond to Yoshimoto's invasion, asking each one for his opinion. Instead, he whiled away most of the evening or most of the night, *not* talking about the pressing issues. That is why his house administrators were put off.

The verse Nobunaga sang as he danced is from a Kōwaka dance called *Atsumori*. This dance-narrative is an extended version of a brief, affecting episode in the *Heike Monogatari* where Kumagae no Jirō Naozane (1141–1208) is forced to kill Taira no Atsumori (1169–84), a teenage enemy commander his own son's age.[4] The verse is part of Naozane's thoughts as he realizes the transience of this world and decides to take Buddhist vows.

Such explanations aside, imagine a modern-day general dancing a dance expressing the transience of life, accompanied by his own singing, before leading his men into battle!

Nobunaga is known to have often sung this particular verse from *Atsumori*. But his love of songs was obvious. For example, he is said to have encouraged his soldiers to follow him and sing a song three times before springing out of their positions for assault on a battlefield. Still, as noted,

---

4   See note 10, p. 117.

he himself evidently did not compose much verse. There is, however, one episode where he appears as a versifier.

The episode, which forms a part of *Shinchō Ki* (Biography of Nobunaga) by Oze Hoan (1564–1640),[5] describes the time when Nobunaga entered Kyoto as the first official military backer of the fifteenth and last Ashikaga shogun, Yoshiaki (1537–97). Some decades before then the Ashikaga shogunate had come to exist in name only. Yoshiaki's own brother, the thirteenth shogun Yoshiteru (1536–65), was attacked and killed by his aides, and he himself became a refugee. (How Yoshiteru refused to flee from an on-coming army and, by implanting a number of drawn swords in the floor of the middle of his room, fought, wielding one sword after another, until he was overwhelmed and killed, is part of samurai lore.)

The shogunate had come to exist in name only, but it had one vital reason for existence. Ever since Japan became the so-called warrior's domain in the mid-twelfth century, anyone willing to engage in struggles for hegemony, provincial or national, faced a dilemma: if you say you can do anything you please to grab the position you want, you're also allowing that anyone can usurp your position. To deal with this dilemma, most warlords issued stern injunctions against violating the master-subject relationships, while strongly affirming the ultimate one—that between emperor and his top aide in charge of military affairs, the shogun.

So Yoshiaki, even while leading a precarious life as refugee, could still make shogunate claims as he sought from warlords military support to enable him to become shogun. In the second month of 1568 some of those who had assassinated Yoshiteru installed Yoshihide (1540–68), Yoshiaki's nephew as fourteenth shogun. But Yoshihide was obviously a puppet and lineally not legitimate. In the end, in the seventh month of the same year, one of Yoshiaki's chief vassals, Hosokawa Fujitaka (better known by his later name, Yūsai: 1534–1610), persuaded Nobunaga, the rising star then, to back Yoshiaki.

Here's the episode in question from *Shinchō Ki.*

When Lord Nobunaga reached Kōjō-in, of Mii Temple, whispers spread here and there and people throughout Kyoto, both noble and base, high and low, who had often heard that he had defeated all his enemies, no matter how strong, and pacified a number of provinces, wondered how much more terrifying than a demon or a god he must be; and, now that he was about to enter Kyoto, they became fearful of all sorts of calamities that might befall them.

Indeed, their fears seemed to far exceed those of children who scare themselves by talking about demons who cross the oceans from a foreign country, strike and kill them with pebbles,[6] and devour them as their only food. Some people fled to such neighboring provinces as Tanba and Wakasa, whether they had relatives or not there while others boarded riverboats on Yodo to go to distant islands. Still others, especially those with names to protect, sent away their wives and children as well as furniture and other valuables to acquaintances they thought trustworthy, while themselves staying home so they might congratulate Lord Nobunaga on his entry into Kyoto. However, even

---

5 A revised version of Ōta Gyūichi's *Shinchō-kō Ki.* In defense of his rewriting Hoan said that Gyūichi's account was "simplistic" and "choppy," and that it had "oversights" and "omissions," which made him "worried that those achievements have been overlooked might be aggrieved." Arai Hakuseki, whose account appears on pp. 273–286, reports his mother's remark that her forbears are mentioned in *Shinchō Ki.*

6 Pebbles were vital weapons for boys when they fought among themselves. In addition, pebble-throwing was often an integral and of course dangerous part of a rambunctious festival. So the image of a demon killing children with pebbles was, at the time, far less incongruous than it may appear today.

Samurai in full armour, circa 1888

these people continued to worry, as those who knew one another got together and wondered what might befall them, some trying to convince themselves by thinking aloud, "Well, who knows, something good may happen to us because we're staying here." Finally on the twenty-eighth of the ninth month, Lord Nobunaga arrived at Tōfuku Temple, and all the assessments made earlier proved useless.

At once the renga masters, Shōha and Shōshitsu Shinzen, and among doctors, Nakarai Roan and Suichiku-in Dōzō, and those who'd established their reputations, each in his own field, plus the so-called elders, of Upper and Lower Kyoto, who would take part in any council at a moment's notice, all came to thank Lord Nobunaga with various presents. Among them Shōha went straight to him, with two tip-spreading fans on a tray. Everyone held his breath, thinking, What in the world is he doing? when Shōha, kneeling in front of the lord and even before adjusting his formal attire, said:

Nihon te ni iru kyō no yorokobi

two held in your hands, the joy today

Lord Nobunaga followed it with:

mai asobu chiyo yorozuyo no ōgi nite

these are the fans with which to dance and play for thousands of generations!

When they heard this story, the old and the young throughout Kyoto were so impressed they couldn't say anything more. "This gentleman is such a ferocious warrior that we had expected him to behave the way Kiso did when he entered Kyoto in the ancient Juei era,[7] but he's turned out to be such an elegant person, hasn't he? Now we can expect nice things from him perhaps," people said, encouraged in their hearts, and breathed a collective sigh of relief.

Here, what I have translated as "tip-spreading fan" is *sue-hirogari no ōgi*. This translation, no less than the original expression, is redundant in a way: When you open a fan, its outer end spreads out. But *sue* of *suehiro* also means "the future," and *suehiro* or *suehirogari* is a celebratory name of the fan. By presenting Nobunaga with *suehirogari no ōgi* the renga master Shōha (also known as

---

7   Kiso Yoshinaka (1154–84), the first Minamoto commander to enter Kyoto after the Minamoto rebelled against the Taira in 1180. See pp. 113–114 and note 6.

Jōha; the family name, Satomura: 1524–1602) was congratulating the warlord for entering Kyoto as shogunate military supporter. Evidently everyone saw that by making this move, Nobunaga, in effect, placed himself in the position of "issuing orders to the world under heaven," as the expression of the day went.

However, Shōha's real trick lay in bringing *two* fans or *ōgi nihon*, for *nihon* also means "Japan." In other words, by saying "two of these propitious things held in your hands, today you must be overjoyed," Shōha also meant "Japan held in your hands, today you truly deserve our congratulations!" In response to this invitation to take part in the composition of a renga, Nobunaga tactfully ignored the blatantly flattering pun and said that the fans—in a traditional Japanese dance an indispensable prop—were only proper for a celebratory dance. The phrase, *mai asobu*, "dance and play," conjures the images of the crane and the tortoise, two creatures inherited from China as symbols of longevity, and the phrase, *chiyo yorozuyo*, "a thousand, ten thousand generations," is a congratulatory set phrase.

Shōha may have been a remote relative of one of Nobunaga's commanders, Akechi Mitsuhide (1524?–82), who killed his lord fourteen years later, in 1582. By that year Nobunaga had gained control of one third of the country, by one estimate. Even though not all the warlords may have had the ambition to "issue orders to the world under heaven," he still had a number of powerful contenders to subdue.

In the third month of the year, Nobunaga destroyed Takeda Katsuyori (1546–82), a menace to the northeast, and turned his attention to the west. He ordered his ablest commander, Toyotomi Hideyoshi (1536–98), to start a massive campaign to subjugate the western warlords who had not yet pledged allegiance. Hideyoshi brought down one fort after another, until he reached Takamatsu Castle, in Bitchū Province. It was a difficult castle to scale, so he surrounded it with water to starve them out. But then Mōri Terumoto (1153–1625) came to the rescue with an army estimated to be six times as large as Hideyoshi's. Hideyoshi sent a request to Nobunaga for reinforcements. Nobunaga, apparently deciding to use this opportunity to subjugate not only the warlords of Chūgoku, but also those of Shikoku and Kyūshū, first ordered Mitsuhide and five other commanders to repair to their home provinces and raise armies. He himself planned to lead an army.

For Mitsuhide's subsequent action, we turn to *Shinchō Ki*. In both Sakamoto and Kameyama he had a fort, and the one in Kameyama was his residential castle.

On the twenty-sixth of the fifth month of the tenth year of Tenshō [1582], Koretō, Governor of Hyūga [Akechi Mitsuhide], before leading an army to Chūgoku, went from Sakamoto to Kameyama Castle, in Tamba. The next day he climbed Mt. Atago and while staying at the shrine that night he is said to have drawn a sacred lot[8] two or three times. On the twenty-eighth of the same month he held a renga session at the Nishi no Bō. It began:

> *Toki wa ima ame ga shita shim Satsuki kana*   Mitsuhide

> Now is the time to rule the world: It's the fifth month!

> *mimkami masaru niwa no natsuyama*   Nishi no Bō

---

8   *Mikuji*, a small, folded piece of paper in which your fortune is predicted.

the water upstream increases at the summer hill in the garden

hana otsuru ike no nagare wo seki-tomete   Shōha

the brook from the flower-scattering pond having been dammed

This hundred-unit sequence finished, he returned to Kameyama. He must have drawn the sacred lot with something in mind as well; for from the make-up of the opening verse it was later guessed that this renga was planned as a prayer for [the successful execution of] a secret scheme. ...

On the first of the sixth month, Koretō, Governor of Hyūga Mitsuhide, in Kameyama Castle, summoned Akechi Samanosuke Akechi Jiemon no Jō, Fujita Dengo, Saitō Kuranosuke, and Mizo'o Katsubē no Jō, and said to them secretly: "Gentlemen, I'd like you to give me your lives. If you agree, we may continue our discussion. If not, behead me this instant."

He said this so bluntly the five men were startled and their good spirits vanished. With their breathing quickening, they merely looked at one another. At last Samanosuke spoke up: "Sir, we have held you up as our master until today. Why, then, shouldn't we see you through this grave crisis? No matter what you may have in mind, I, Sama-no-suke, will follow you." At these encouraging words, the remaining four also gave consent.

When he heard this, Mitsuhide said, "Gentlemen, I'm pleased that you've agreed to work with me. To put the matter simply I have several reasons to kill Lord Nobunaga. And I think the time is pressing. I've been driven into a corner from which there is no escape. This is why I've decided to revolt. ..."

That day, around seven in the evening, he left Kameyama, with those five men as spearheading generals. After passing Mt. Ōe, they pressed forward at utmost speed, so that by the daybreak of the second the forerunning groups arrived outside Kyoto. As soon as they did, they surrounded Honnō Temple, where Lord Nobunaga was staying and, after raising a great battle cry, shot arrows and guns into the temple. ...

A number of reasons have been advanced to explain why Mitsuhide, who had served Nobunaga since as early as 1567, decided to revolt at that particular juncture. The most persuasive reason, according to the historian Kuwata Tadachika, is Mitsuhide's accumulated resentment against his lord who often treated him, a commander of distinction, like a mere foot soldier, publicly insulting him on some important occasions. Considering Nobunaga's tyrannical nature, recorded by his contemporary foreign observers such as the Jesuit priest Luis Frois (1532–97), some of the insults Nobunaga is said to have accorded Mitsuhide ring true.

At any rate, Nobunaga had left his main fort, Azuchi Castle-the most extravagant military structure ever built in Japan till then-on the twenty-ninth of the fifth month, and arrived in Kyoto the following day. The purpose of his stay in Honnō Temple was to hold a tea ceremony to display the great Chinese tea utensils he had collected since his first official arrival in Kyoto, in 1568. This partly explains why he took only about thirty pages along with him, but not a sizable group of armed soldiers. In contrast, his son Nobutada, who had preceded him to Kyoto, had taken 2,000 cavalrymen.

On the first of the sixth month he had the tea meeting as planned, with Torii Sōshitsu, a wealthy merchant from Hakata, Chikuzen, as guest of honor. Along with a group of aristocrats as "companion guests," Nobutada also took part. Following the tea ceremony, Nobunaga played go with the master Hon'inbō Sansa until late into the night. After Nobutada took his leave, he went to bed. For the rest of what happened the following morning, we go back to *Shinchō-kō Ki.*

…. both Nobunaga and his pages at first thought that some lowly people were making the racket, but in time that proved not to be the case. There were battle cries, and gunshots flew into Nobunaga's quarters. He asked, "Is this a revolt? Whose plot is this?" When Mori Ran[maru] said, "These appear to be Akechi's men, sir," he said, "There's nothing we can do," and, without a moment's hesitation, withdrew into his quarters, with the men on duty there joining him.

Yashiro Katsusuke, Ban Tarōzaemon, Ban Shōrin, and Murata Kichigo ran out of the stables brandishing swords and were killed. Other than these, a total of twenty-four *chūgen*[9] were killed in fighting at the stables, among them Tōkurō, Tōhachi, Iwa, Shinroku, Hikoichi, Yaroku, Kuma, Kogomawaka, Torawaka, and his son Ko-Torawaka.

Those who were killed in the inner quarters were—
The three brothers of Mori Ran[maru], Mori Riki[maru], Mori
Bō[maru], Ogawa Aihei, Takahashi Toramatsu, Kanamori
Ginyū, Sugaya Kakuzō, Ueozumi Katsushichi, Takeda Kitarō
Ōtsuka Mataichirō, Karino Matakurō, Susukida Yogorō,
Imagawa Magojirō, Ochiai Kohachirō, Itō Hikosaku, Kukuri
Kame, Oida Kame, Yamada Yotarō, Iikawa Miyamatsu, Sofue
Mago[maru], Kashiwabaranabe Brothers, Hariami, Hirao
Kyūsuke, Ōtsuka Magozō, Yuasa Jinsuke, Ogura Shōju [maru].
These pages were killed while attacking repeatedly. Yuasa Jinsuke and Ogura Shōju[maru]—these two heard the news at an inn in the town, mingled among the enemy, ran into Honnō Temple, and were killed. At the entrance of the kitchen, Takahashi Torazō put up a good defense for a while, doing incomparable work.

Nobunaga at first took up a bow and shot two or three times but his time must have come: his bowstring snapped. Afterward he fought with a spear but was wounded at the elbow and withdrew. Then to the women who had been around him until then, he said, "There's no need for you women to stay with me. Hurry out!" and chased them out. By then the fire set to the temple was coming close to him. He must have decided he shouldn't show his body; he went into the innermost part, closed the door from inside, and pitilessly disemboweled himself.

It happens that Luis Frois, whose church, as he explained in his letter, was "situated only a street away from the place where Nobunaga was staying," has left us a somewhat different account of Nobunaga's last moments:

> … some Christians came just as I was vesting to say an early Mass, and told me to wait because there was a commotion in front of the palace and that it seemed to be something serious as fighting had broken out there. We at once began to hear musket shots and see flames. After this another report came, and we learned that it had not been a brawl but that Akechi had turned traitor and enemy of Nobunaga and had him surrounded. When Akechi's men reached the palace gates, they at once entered as nobody was there to resist them because there had been no suspicion of their treachery. Nobunaga had just

---

9 Men whose status is between servant and samurai.

washed his hands and face and was drying himself with a towel when they found him and forthwith shot him in the side with an arrow. Pulling the arrow out, he came out carrying a *naginata*, a weapon with a long blade made after the fashion of a scythe. He fought for some time, but after receiving a shot in the arm he retreated into his chamber and shut the doors.

Some say that he cut his belly, while others believe he set fire to the palace and perished in flames. ....[10]

Not long after Nobunaga's assassination, some people began linking Mitsuhide's opening verse to his action several days later, as Hoan did in his account. *Toki*, which means "time," also was the name of the clan from which Akechi branched out, so one can be more explicit in interpretation and read a straightforward announcement in the verse: "Now's the time for a Toki to rule the world: It's the fifth month!"

Legend has it that the renga master Shōha was taken to task by Hideyoshi, who hurried back from the west and attacked and defeated Mitsuhide. Shōha wriggled out of the predicament, it is said, by saying that someone had changed a single character in the transcript of the renga session, from *ame ga shita naru* to *ame ga shita shiru*, thereby changing the meaning of the verse from "we're in the rain" to "to rule the world." It is also said that because he immediately sensed what Mitsuhide meant in his opening verse, he tried to counsel against this with his link, by using the word *seki-tomu*, which means "dam," "block."

Some have discounted the linkage, so to speak, arguing that a commander as cautious as Mitsuhide would not have revealed his rebellious intent in such a public forum. Still, to us of later generations, it is fascinating that Nobunaga, who made his debut as a warlord with a snatch of verse on his lips, should be linked to another verse in his death.

On the fifteenth of the following month Hosokawa Fujitaka, who had refused to respond to Mitsuhide's invitation to join him, held a renga session with Shōha and others to commemorate Nobunaga's death. The three opening verses of the hundred-unit sequence are recorded in *Sōken-in Dono Tsuizen Ki* (Record in Memorial to Lord Sōken-in), which Hideyoshi's scribe and ranking aide, Ōmura Yūko, wrote, following the grand funeral Hideyoshi gave Nobunaga. Sōken-in was a temple Nobunaga built next to Azuchi Castle;[11] it was also his posthumous Buddhist name.

Kurozome no yūbe ya nagori sode no tsuyu   Fujitaka

Black-dyed, evening lingers with dew on my sleeve

Tama-matsuru no no tsuki no akikaze   Ryōgo-in

over the field for the requiem, the moon, the autumn wind

wake-kaeru kage no matsumushi ne ni nakite   Shōha

as I return, bell-crickets in the shadow cry out

---

10   Michael Cooper, *They Came to Japan: An Anthology of European Reports on Japan, 1543–1640*, p. 103.

11   To have himself worshipped, according to Frois. See *They Came to Japan*, pp. 101–102.

THE DESTRUCTION OF THE TOKUGAWA REGIME, 1865-8

Charles Yates

During the first half of 1865, as the remarks quoted above indicate, it became clear to Saigō and others in Satsuma that there was no longer any point in trying to envision a future for the bakufu. Its determination to conduct a second punitive campaign against Chōshū, combined with its unconscionable treatment of the Mito insurgents, had angered so many people that the only support it still enjoyed came from those who had a personal stake in its survival. Aside from its own members, that included only the French ambassador Leon Roches, who had begun searching for a way to rescue both the bakufu and the Tokugawa family from disaster so as to piece together a client government that would give preferential treatment to French interests in Japan.

Britain, France's chief competitor for advantage in Japan, had realized the futility of supporting Edo, and had begun searching for ways to establish a beneficial relationship with those who seemed most likely to become the new rulers in whatever arrangement emerged from the collapse of the old order. The British ambassador, Sir Harry Parkes, had begun courting Satsuma's leaders, who had accepted his offers of help only with great caution. With no desire to become British proxies, they were willing to let Parkes help them establish contacts through which to purchase Western armaments, but they rebuffed his offers of direct material and financial assistance.

In any case, Saigō and his comrades tended to view the diplomatic contest between Britain and France as a peripheral matter. They realized that unless they could find a way to guide Japan toward stable government, and lay new foundations for Japanese security and sovereignty, it would not matter very much which European power ended up with the greatest advantage. A number of interesting proposals for a new government emerged during the last years of Tokugawa rule, but those in a position to choose among them had little sense as to what alternatives made the most sense. They could only speculate about what might work best, and until the bakufu's remaining political influence in Kyoto was neutralized and they had acquired the power to put their choices into action, even speculation was no more than a secondary concern. The time had now come for them to decide what to do about the bakufu, and to take whatever measures might be required to get it done.

Saigō's trip to Kyoto in 1865/5 marked the beginning of a new pattern in Satsuma's leadership. He had spent most of 1864 in Kyoto, while Ōkubo had stayed in Kagoshima, and though they were directly responsible for carrying out han policies, their authority and their guidance came consistently from Hisamitsu in Kagoshima and from the han elder (karō) Komatsu Tatewaki in Kyoto. From early 1865 on, however, they both travelled between Kagoshima and Kyoto more frequently, but they were rarely in the same place at the same time. For the most part, when Saigō was in Kyoto, Ōkubo was in Kagoshima, and vice versa. In the months leading up to 1868, their control of Satsuma's political agenda became progressively more complete, and by the time the court announced the abolition of the bakufu in 1868/1, Hisamitsu and his advisors had receded into the background. Still in full possession of their titular authority, they had nevertheless lost most of their real power.

How this happened is not clear. A large part of it no doubt resulted from Ōkubo's impressive ability to spot opportunities when they arose and to capitalize on them without delay, and from Saigō's equally remarkable ability to mediate between disputing parties and bridge their differences with his considerable powers of persuasion. It is also likely that as these two continued to demonstrate the accuracy of their instincts and to deliver gratifying results, Hisamitsu and his subordinates came to trust them more, and to leave more of the details of the making and implementation of policy in their hands. In the end, what matters is that in Satsuma, as in Chōshū, by the time the final confrontation with Edo came to pass, it was the samurai, mostly of middle and lower rank, who were in charge. Their traditional masters, though still in their traditional positions, had become little more than rubber stamps, with few meaningful prerogatives left other than to validate policies in the making of which they were sometimes not even consulted.

Saigō played a central role at several points in the drama that led to the birth of Meiji Japan, but one can argue that he had already done his most important work in facilitating the negotiated conclusion of the first bakufu campaign against Chōshū at the end of 1864. In saving Chōshū from destruction, he had given its leaders the extra time they needed to consolidate their strength and establish a new agenda for the han. Perhaps more importantly, he had won the trust of a number of men who would soon be in positions of power in that han. The next step was for Satsuma and Chōshū to act on their growing recognition that the dangers they faced together were of more import than the long-standing animosities that divided them, and to work from the interests they had in common to establish a shared program of action that could guarantee their own survival and also could provide the basis for Japan's future survival.

The Satsuma-Chōshū Alliance:

1865–6

Once Saigō realized that the bakufu was determined to carry out a second attack on Chōshū, he went back to Kagoshima with Komatsu Tatewaki and Sakamoto Ryōma, intending to unify opinion in the han against the bakufu's plans. His resolve was hardened by his sense of outrage at the harsh treatment the bakufu had enacted against the Mito insurgents. Nakaoka Shuntarō had then arrived in Kagoshima with another Satsuma samurai, Iwashita Masahira, whom he had met at Shimonoseki. These two urged Saigō to consider going up to Shimonoseki for a meeting with Kido Takayoshi, to which Kido already had agreed. Saigō concurred completely, and set out at once with that aim in mind. As noted above, however, before the meeting could take place, he received word of new developments in Kyoto, and went directly there instead of keeping his appointment with Kido, leaving no explanation for his failure to appear as promised.

Responding to imperial summons, the shogun had made another trip to Kyoto, eliciting the comments from Saigō and Ōkubo quoted at the end of the last chapter. He arrived on i5/22, and immediately asked the court to issue orders for a second Chōshū campaign. The court refused, telling him to avoid any further violence, and to try instead to find a way to settle the dispute with Chōshū through consultation. The shogun accepted the order, having little alternative, but no one believed Edo could be made to give up its hostile intentions toward Chōshū as easily as that. Ōkubo had proposed that he should go to Kagoshima and try to persuade the han government to intervene formally on behalf of Chōshū, but Saigō disagreed.

The Last Samurai, Saigo Takamori, circa 1878

For now, he argued, it was better simply to do nothing, and to let matters unfold. No one in Kagoshima had any hope of persuading bakufu leaders to rethink their plans at this point. Officials in Edo had lost touch with reality, and Saigō saw no point in trying to negotiate with what he called 'a pack of fools.' Trying to talk sense to the bakufu would only cause frustration and anger, and so for now it was better to let them go ahead and try to have their way with Chōshū. It was to be expected that they would try to sow distrust between Satsuma and Chōshū, to forestall the possibility of concerted action. Saigō believed these circumstances presented the two han with a great opportunity, and he warned that failure to take advantage of it might lead to untold difficulties later on.

Ōkubo did return to Kagoshima on 7/8, but as Saigō wrote to him there from Kyoto, if the bakufu did try to go ahead with its second Chōshū campaign it would harm only itself. Officials in Edo had ordered Chōshū to send the hanshu of one of its collateral han to Osaka for cross-examination, but there had been no response. Anti-bakufu feeling was widespread and potent in Chōshū, Saigō reported, while in the Kansai people criticized Edo routinely and openly. A strike against Chōshū could succeed only if it were to be delivered swiftly and precisely, but alas, few of the bakufu's recent moves had been either swift or precise. Once again, Saigō called the bakufu leadership a pack of fools.

Several days later Saigō reported that there appeared to be serious dissension growing within the bakufu, and wondered whether this might lead to even more serious trouble if the shogun were to remain in Osaka, where he had taken up residence after completing his formal business in Kyoto. Saigō concluded that the bakufu was falling apart, and eventually would collapse on its own. There was no way to justify another campaign against Chōshū, Saigō asserted, and in any case, the bakufu would not be able to finish what it began. Saigō's main concern was the welfare of the five nobles, who were still under guard in Dazaifu. He feared that bakufu agents would manage to intimidate Fukuoka han officials and gain custody of the nobles, and he insisted that Satsuma must be ready to intervene if that happened. Those five men must be protected at any cost; Saigō had promised in Satsuma's name that they would be safe, so the good faith (*shingi*) of the han was at stake.

As Saigō was making these observations, during the summer of 1865, Sakamoto and Nakaoka had continued in their efforts to get Kido together with Saigō for discussions. On 6/24 the two Tosa samurai arrived in Kyoto from Chōshū and told Saigō that Chōshū leaders were still willing to talk, provided that Satsuma could do something to demonstrate its own sincerity. As a symbolic gesture, Saigō proposed that Satsuma might employ its connections with Thomas Glover, the English merchant in Nagasaki, to help Chōshū acquire the ships and firearms it needed but had been unable to acquire on its own. In return, Chōshū might supply rice and other provisions for the maintenance of Satsuma's troops in Kyoto, since that would save Satsuma the trouble and expense of shipping those supplies all the way from Kagoshima. By the end of 1865, with the way smoothed through these gestures of good faith, both sides were ready to talk, and Sakamoto began urging Saigō to make the first move.

In the meanwhile, however, Saigō and Sakamoto had gone back to Kagoshima on 9/24 to bring Hisamitsu up to date, and to urge him to lead troops to Kyoto. Instead, Hisamitsu sent Saigō and Komatsu back with the troops. They arrived in Kyoto on 10/25 and immediately sent Kuroda Kiyotaka, another Satsuma samurai, to Chōshū to begin conversations with Kido. Because other leaders in Chōshū were in favor of an agreement with Satsuma, the habitually cautious Kido had to put his own reservations aside and agree, but as with Saigō, it was Sakamoto who finally managed to persuade him. He arrived in Osaka on 1866/1/4. Saigō met him at Fushimi on 1/8, and escorted him to the Satsuma residence in Kyoto, where Ōkubo, Komatsu, and Saigō's old friend Katsura Hisatake entertained him lavishly. The atmosphere was cordial, and there was a great deal of talk and agreement about the crises facing Japan, but neither Kido nor anyone from Satsuma wanted to be the first to broach the subject of a formal alliance between the two han. After nearly two weeks, Kido was out of patience, and was about to leave when Sakamoto arrived, on 1/21.

Astonished that nothing had happened yet, Sakamoto got Kido and Saigō talking substance the next day, and with his help they quickly worked out the terms of an agreement. The resulting alliance between Satsuma and Chōshū was of decisive importance for the fate of the bakufu, though it is important to note that the two han had by no means joined forces to create a new government, but only to forget past hostilities and join forces for mutual survival. As Inoue Kiyoshi puts it, they had agreed to recognize a common foe in the bakufu. As we have seen, Saigō had discovered this truth for himself during 1864; the new alliance now gave it formal expression. The main significance of this alliance was that it formally acknowledged the bankruptcy of the bakufu, and thus also, at least implicitly, the need to replace it with some other form of government. By the end of 1864, in other words, a few influential individuals had given up on the bakufu; by the beginning of 1866, the two most powerful outside domains in Japan had done so.

Saigō had already made his feelings about the bakufu abundantly clear, however, before 1866 began. On 12/6 he wrote to Minoda Denbei, one of Tadayoshi's advisors in Kagoshima, arguing that Satsuma should remove all of its personnel from Edo and close down its establishments there. With the relaxation of the alternate attendance (*sankin kōtai*) system under the reforms resulting from Hisamitsu's visit to Edo in 1862, there was no further need to maintain residences in Edo, and even some of the Tokugawa family's own relatives (*shinpan*) already had withdrawn from the city. As Saigō saw it, the only Satsuma personnel still arguing in favor of remaining in Edo were either afraid of the bakufu, which was patently silly, or reluctant to move away from the sordid pleasures of Edo's brothel district, which was despicable. Already, in Saigō's view, the national unity once predicated on the bakufu had been lost, and Japan had fragmented into self-sufficient local units (*kakkyō*). Civil cohesion no longer existed, and civil war was bound to erupt eventually. When the crisis came, moreover, the outcome would be settled in Kyoto, not in Edo.

In another letter on the same day, Saigō spoke of the bakufu's ongoing failure to elicit any responsiveness from Chōshū. Most people were simply disgusted with Yoshinobu's efforts to gain control of national politics, and his only remaining supporters were the Tokugawa vassal domains of Aizu and Kuwana. Only a hero could save the day now, Saigō argued, and only an assembly of daimyo like that earlier proposed by Katsu could now hope to govern the realm (*tenka*) effectively. On 12/12 Saigō reported with disgust that Shibata Tōgorō, a direct bakufu vassal (*hatamoto*) originally from the Satsuma collateral han of Miyakonojō, had tried to talk Satsuma officials in Kyoto into helping the bakufu.

Meanwhile, the dissension Saigō had noticed earlier in the bakufu was resolving itself into a clear rift between officials in the bureaucracy in Edo (*bakkaku*) and those around Yoshinobu in Kyoto. Representatives from the Edo bakkaku already had tried to bribe Satsuma into siding with them against Yoshinobu's faction, offering the sum of 5,000 ryō as a reward for Satsuma's services during the Chōshū attack on Kyoto on 1864/7/19. Saigō responded to this overture with open disgust, and approved of the han's decision to reject the money. After all, Satsuma had not defended the imperial palace in the hope of material reward, but rather out of a sense of loyalty and duty. To accept the bribe would be to cheapen the han's integrity, to insult the hanshu Tadayoshi, and to invite ridicule from all other han.

In short, as far as Saigō was concerned, the Tokugawa world of bakufu and han (*bakuhan seidō*) was already in effect a thing of the past, its eventual destruction no more than a matter of time after the beginning of 1866. What would replace it was still a matter for open speculation, and there was still a great deal of hard struggle ahead, but in Saigō's mind it was now clear which options for the future no longer remained viable. Of course, there were a good many others who did not see things this way. Some still believed the bakufu could be saved. Some had given up on the bakufu but still hoped to keep the Tokugawa family in power. Some hoped for the creation of a genuine deliberative assembly of major daimyo, including the Tokugawa, to be sure, but ranking them as equals with all the others. And some feared that Satsuma and Chōshū would combine forces to destroy the Tokugawa bakufu and replace it with a new bakufu of their own.

The Second Chōshū Campaign:

1865–6

When the squadron of Western ships left Yokohama to conduct a second attack on Shimonoseki in 1864, it had been widely assumed that they would not stop with the punishment of Chōshū, but would eventually turn up at Osaka to press their demands for the opening of Hyōgo. On 1865/9/16, nine steamships dropped anchor at Hyōgo, and those assumptions became a reality. Saigō and Sakamoto went down to Osaka to look at this flotilla, and then left there on 9/24 hoping to persuade Hisamitsu to lead troops back to Kyoto. This was an opportunity for which Saigō had been waiting ever since his meeting with Katsu.

This new move by the Western powers presented a challenge to the court itself, and the only way to meet that challenge safely and effectively was to assemble the daimyo council, proposed by Katsu and advocated by Saigō at every opportunity since their meeting, to hold 'deliberations on the affairs of the realm' (*tenka no kōron*). Unfortunately, the court was still paralyzed by the same lack of vision and conviction Saigō had lamented in the spring of 1864. If the bakufu were to prevail on the demoralized court and get its approval for the opening of Hyōgo, 'nothing would be more shameful for the imperial realm' (*kōkoku*). However, thanks to the skillful maneuvers of Yoshinobu, that is almost exactly what did happen.

On 9/20 there was a meeting at the court to discuss the opening of Hyōgo, and most bakufu representatives argued for approval, but Yoshinobu had an agenda of his own, and used his influence in the court to prevent the formation of a consensus. Using the threat of resignation, as he had done before, he persuaded the court to issue orders on 9/21, not for the opening of Hyōgo, but for a second punitive campaign against Chōshū. The court insisted on calling a daimyo council to discuss the Hyōgo question, but on 10/1, before this deadlock could be broken, the shogun Iemochi packed up and left Osaka for Edo without warning. Yoshinobu, together with Matsudaira Katamori, the hanshu of Aizu, persuaded him to come back, and in the wake of this unexpected move, the court on 10/5 announced its approval for the bakufu's treaties with the West, but not for the opening of Hyōgo. A daimyo council would convene to decide that issue. The foreign powers hoisted anchor and left Hyōgo for Yokohama on 10/8, evidently satisfied by these developments.

No one emerged from these events in a better position than Yoshinobu, and for Saigō this meant that a collision between Satsuma and the bakufu was now the only way to preserve the interests of both the han and the country. As we have seen, he returned to Kyoto on 10/25, soon after Yoshinobu's success, and at once began making the preparations that led eventually to the Satsuma-Chōshū alliance. While this was happening, Yoshinobu was instructing the court concerning the need to humble Chōshū, and on 1866/1/23 the court accepted Yoshinobu's recommendations. Within Satsuma, these events caused the balance of feeling to shift decisively toward a confrontation with Edo. On 3/4, Saigō left Osaka, accompanied by Sakamoto and his wife, and reached Kagoshima seven days later.

Saigō's first concern after returning to Kagoshima was to check on the well-being of the five nobles at Dazaifu. As he had feared, the bakufu had sent agents to Fukuoka to arrest the five men and bring them to Edo. To prevent this, Saigō sent Kuroda Kiyotsuna to Dazaifu with a contingent of troops and orders to defend the nobles at any cost. As it turned out, the bakufu agents did not give up until Kuroda's troops confronted them with drawn swords.

During 1866/2, Saigō had expressed regret that Yoshinobu, supported staunchly by Aizu and Kuwana, had gained control of the court, and was flirting with the French ambassador Leon Roches, whose own efforts to ingratiate himself with Edo continued unabated. Edo was caught in a bind, with no idea how best to reconcile the conflicting demands of court, han, and foreigners, and Saigō took some relish in observing that for the bakufu, choosing a policy likely to satisfy everyone was 'about as risky as trying to stack eggs.' In particular, Edo officials were at a loss as to how to get any response from Chōshū, and had been sending officials to Hiroshima, still the bakufu military headquarters as it had been during the first punitive expedition, with one set of demands after another. Saigō believed the outcome of this process might well determine the future shape of the country (*tenka no keisei*). Moreover, if Chōshū and Edo were to go to war, the resulting disruption might well provoke widespread peasant uprisings, and that in turn would only hasten the collapse of the bakufu. When Saigō left Osaka on 3/4 with Sakamoto and his wife, it was with the recognition that the situation was nearing a point of crisis, and it was urgent for Satsuma to prepare itself for whatever might come next.

In the meantime, Saigō had heard from Iwashita Masahira about meetings the latter had had in Edo with Leon Roches and Sir Harry Parkes. Iwashita had told both men that if the Western powers expected to realize the ambitions that lay behind their treaties with Japan, they had best forget about the bakufu, and begin relying on the court and the great daimyo. These latter had a reasonable chance of keeping their promises; Edo no longer had any such hope. Roches was not interested in anything Iwashita had to say, committed as he was to forging some sort of unilateral link with Edo. Parkes, on the other hand, was so impressed with Iwashita's arguments that he requested a meeting with Saigō and Satsuma's other leaders in Kagoshima, to which we will return presently.

On 1866/5/1, Saigō was appointed along with Komatsu Tatewaki, Katsura Hisatake, and a number of others to carry out reforms in Kagoshima. Some of these men, including Godai Tomoatsu, had just returned from Europe, where they had been negotiating with various commercial firms both to arrange for help in setting up new industrial facilities in Kagoshima and to initiate regular trading relationships. On 5/10, Saigō wrote to Ōkubo that the reforms were proceeding well, adding that he felt confident that the affairs of the han and of the country were in capable hands with Ōkubo. He himself had meanwhile taken some time off to recuperate at a hot spring, he said. The waters evidently did not have the desired effect, because Saigō had further problems with his health in the autumn. When he was promoted to chief inspector (*ometsuke*) he declined on account of illness. However, he was not so ill as to reject his appointment at about this same time to the han's council of elders (*karōza*), which was the highest and most powerful political body in the han after the daimyo himself.

Saigō's confidence in Ōkubo was well-placed, as the latter demonstrated between 3/11 and 10/15, while evading bakufu efforts to order Satsuma to mobilize troops for the second Chōshū campaign. Saigō was ecstatic when he learned of Ōkubo's refusal to involve Satsuma in this new campaign. On 5/29 he wrote Ōkubo to tell him how his courage had galvanized popular feeling in Satsuma. Both Hisamitsu and Tadayoshi were pleased with Ōkubo's actions, while he himself could only dance with delight. Ōkubo's exemplary action, he asserted, would help to clarify what was at stake in the national political struggle; moreover, it was a 'beautiful thing for the domain.' However, regardless of Satsuma's refusal to participate, bakufu forces began fighting along Chōshū's borders on 1866/6/7, in what was to evolve into an unmitigated disaster for Edo.

Not long after this, as noted above, the relationship between Satsuma and England, which had begun unfortunately enough at Namamugi in 1862, and had then evolved even more regrettably in the bombardment of Kagoshima the following summer, took a more constructive turn. After meticulously careful preparations on both sides, Sir Harry Parkes visited Kagoshima from 6/17 through 6/22. On 6/18, Saigō and Parkes exchanged views aboard HMS *Princess Royal*, with Terajima Munenori, recently back from studies in England, acting as interpreter. In England, Terajima had become friends with prominent government and business leaders, including Laurence Oliphant. He had told Oliphant that most of Japan's trade goods were produced by individual han, not by the bakufu, and that it therefore made more sense for Western countries to deal directly with the han. As a result of these conversations, the British government had told Parkes to seek closer ties with Satsuma.

Asked about Terajima's claims by Parkes, Saigō agreed that they made sense, but only up to a point. In theory, practically any of the han, backed by the authority of the court, had the power to guarantee the observance of agreements between Japan and the West, whereas the bakufu had lost the ability to guarantee much of anything, because it no longer represented the popular will. However, the han, like the bakufu, were fundamentally incapable of representing any interests but their own, so it was not a good idea to negotiate directly with them. International agreements binding on the whole country could only be made with the country's sovereign government, which was in Kyoto. The best way to protect the interests of both Japan and the Western powers was to convene a daimyo council. For one thing, such a body would speak for the leaders in the court, standing between them and the foreigners with whom they had no desire for direct contact, and thereby winning their support away form Yoshinobu, who had more than once been able to influence them by threatening to resign and leave them to face the West alone. For another, it would eliminate the dangers of particularism inherent in direct negotiations with any single han. Parkes made no comment on Saigō's statements, but by the time he left Kagoshima he seemed pleased with all he had seen and heard.

If things appeared to be getting better for Satsuma, they were getting drastically worse for the bakufu, whose forces had met with one defeat after another in Chōshū, and whose fortunes seemed to have hit bottom on 7/20 when the shogun died in Osaka castle. On the same day, the court received a memorial from Hisamitsu condemning the Chōshū campaign. Hisamitsu called on the court to recognize the evidence accumulating everywhere, and to give serious thought to a change in government structure (*seitai henkaku*) so as to facilitate more effective handling of public affairs (*tenka no kōgi*). Commenting on this memorial, Saigō wrote to Ōkubo that, since it was daily more obvious that neither France nor any han would be able to rescue the bakufu, perhaps the time had come to return the emperor to power. Meanwhile, unable to prevail militarily, the bakufu had sent Katsu Kaishū to Hiroshima to try to negotiate a cease-fire with Chōshū. On 10/15, Saigō set out for Kyoto to meet with Ōkubo and discuss the new possibilities created by the death of Iemochi. Then, on 12/5, the bakufu named Yoshinobu the new shogun. Twenty days later, on the 25th, the emperor Kōmei died, and was succeeded on 1867/1/9 by the young Mutsuhito, whose reign was designated Meiji. These events altered the political situation dramatically.

Since 1853, Kōmei had been unflinching in his refusal to contemplate a foreign presence of any kind in Japan, and it had been in response to his firm position that Iemochi had been obliged to make his promise of expulsion in 1863. However, Kōmei had also been a stauch supporter of the institutional status quo, with the bakufu exercising delegated authority to govern the country. With Kōmei removed from the picture, there was no longer any significant force within the court to keep people from thinking about some alternative to the bakufu and its rule. With the convenient breaks in continuity provided by the deaths of Iemochi and Kōmei, and the appointment of Yoshinobu as shogun, then, it appeared that there might be no better time to call a daimyo council so as to try working out some new arrangement.

Yoshinobu's appointment as head of the bakufu had already given Edo an important jump on this process, but bakufu opponents had an equal advantage in the malleability of the new emperor, whose youth and lack of experience meant that he would pose no obstruction to their plans, and to whose authority they could appeal as a check on bakufu initiative. Ōkubo was particularly intrigued by the new possibilities opening up. He had been in contact with Iwakura Tomomi, a young noble who had been purged from the court for his extremist views before Chōshū was driven out of Kyoto by Satsuma and Aizu on 1863/8/18, and had been confined to his lodgings north of the city ever since. Ōkubo and Iwakura had begun talking in detail about the possibility of an imperial restoration. Saigō was also beginning to see new possibilities. On 12/9 he went to Osaka and met for the first time with Parkes' capable interpreter, Ernest Satow.

Saigō had learned from Godai Tomoatsu that Satow was at Hyōgo and wanted to talk to someone in authority from Satsuma. As Saigō reported the conversation to Komatsu on 12/9, Satow was having trouble understanding why, if the bakufu was actually the government of Japan, it could not control the behavior of the domains under its authority, such as Satsuma and Chōshū. How could it hope to govern the entire country if, as it had shown, it could not even defeat a single domain? England could hardly make treaties with a powerless government, Satow stated, but it was impossible to tell where to turn, if not to Edo. In fact, it was not clear that Japan had any government at all. Saigō replied that Satsuma and Chōshū intended to combine their resources in support of the court, and that within two or three years the confusion would be resolved. Astonished, Satow pointed out that Japan did not have two or three years to play with, and that the issues of Chōshū and Hyōgo must be resolved without delay. Moreover, England was worried about France's efforts to join forces with Edo, and unless Satsuma took the lead and moved quickly, Yoshinobu, backed by France, might well finesse the entire game. If Satsuma moved promptly, on the other hand, it probably could take advantage of the unresolved Chōshū and Hyōgo issues to corner Yoshinobu and force substantial concessions from him.

Satow's view of the situation, no doubt rendered more plausible by his impressive command of Japanese, erased whatever doubts may have remained in Saigō's mind about the advisability of convening a daimyo council. On 1867/1/22 he left Kyoto for Kagoshima, determined to persuade Hisamitsu to take part in a meeting of great han leaders in Kyoto.

The Failure of Deliberation:

1867/4–9

Saigō reached Kagoshima on 2/1, but before he could do anything, he was immobilized by illness, as he reported to Ōkubo at the end of the month. While he recuperated, he lobbied influential members of the han government, so that when they met to consider Hisamitsu's involvement in the daimyo council, they were already in agreement. Hisamitsu agreed to participate in a meeting of daimyo, so Saigō hurried to Shikoku, where he met with Yamauchi Yōdō in Kōchi and with Date Munenari in Uwajima. Both men agreed to join the council, and Saigō hurried back to Kagoshima, arriving on 2/27. A month later he left Kagoshima with Hisamitsu, accompanied by some 700 troops, and they reached Kyoto on 4/12. Munenari and Shungaku arrived soon after them, and Yōdō, the final member of this core group, got to the city on 5/1.

This was the second time these four men—Hisamitsu, Shungaku, Munenari, and Yōdō—had gathered in Kyoto for deliberations, but their chances of achieving anything were not much better than they had been the first time. Yoshinobu still enjoyed considerable influence in the court, and these four were not united in their views. Hisamitsu was clear about one thing, at any rate. On 4/20 he was summoned to pay his respects to Yoshinobu at Nijō castle, but he politely refused, stating that he must make his bows at the court first.

Discussions began on 4/21, before Yōdō's arrival, and continued for over a month. As before, the stumbling block proved to be the question of whether Hyōgo or Chōshū should be dealt with first. Hisamitsu and Shungaku argued that an appropriate settlement of the Chōshū question would enhance bakufu credibility within Japan, while Yoshinobu, supported chiefly by Yōdō, held that the international issue raised by the Hyōgo problem should take precedence over the purely domestic question of Chōshū. When they moved their discussions to the court, this deadlock persisted. On 5/24 the court finally decreed that Chōshū should be treated leniently and that Hyōgo should be opened for foreign trade.

This amounted to complete victory for Yoshinobu. Hisamitsu, Shungaku, and Munenari petitioned the court to stipulate that the bakufu must pardon and reinstate both the hanshu of Chōshū, Mōri Yoshichika, and his son, but before this matter could be discussed, Yōdō left Kyoto for home on 5/27, effectively dissolving the council. Thus the meetings accomplished little, though Hisamitsu, with Shungaku's help, had managed to gain some concessions for Chōshū. With Yoshinobu the clear winner, the other members of the group had little reason to remain.

Shungaku, Munenari, and Hisamitsu all left Kyoto by the middle of 1867/8. Hisamitsu had moved from Kyoto to Osaka, and after getting court approval for a proxy to represent him, he left for Kagoshima on 9/10.

The great han council which Katsu had proposed and in which he and many others had placed such great hope thus had proved a mere straw in the wind. If the four core members had been more united in their thinking, or if they had had a less determined and resourceful adversary than Yoshinobu, they might have accomplished more. As it was, the times had changed too much, and it was far too late for any combination of constituents drawn from the traditional bakuhan order to address the problems now facing Japan.

While the daimyo council met, Satsuma's lower ranking leaders met also, and on four occasions Saigō conveyed their views to Hisamitsu in memorials. In all four documents, Saigō insists that loyalty to the court and concern for the will of the people must be uppermost in Hisamitsu's considerations, but the first memorial is of particular interest because in it Saigō argues for the first time that 'a restoration (isshin) is of first priority.' The most trenchant statement of his views comes in the third document.

There, he argues that the way to put the minds of the people at ease is to restore power to the court, reduce the bakufu to the same status as other han, and decide the fate of the country on the basis of 'public affairs' (tenka no kōgi). The court must then negotiate new treaties with the foreign powers, within the framework of international law. Saigō urges Hisamitsu to do his utmost for the imperial realm, restore power to the emperor, and carry out a restoration. In the fourth document, Saigō argues that it is vital to gain popular support by recognizing the will of the people and displaying sincerity which, as the manifestation of administrative integrity, is the essence of good government. In other words, Saigō is here asking Hisamitsu to behave in the manner and by the criteria that took form in Saigō's mind during his years in exile. Thus, after working his way toward the idea by a number of different routes over the course of the preceding five years and more, Saigō had finally arrived at the belief that imperial restoration was the solution to Japan's problems. And in arguing for it, he had appealed for support to the beliefs he had put together while on Okinoerabu.

While the great daimyo group attempted to settle disputed matters through deliberation, other developments continued apace. On 6/16, Hisamitsu had an audience with two Chōshū samurai, Yamagata Aritomo and Shinagawa Yajirō, in which he explained Satsuma's position on the state of national affairs. They then met with Saigō, Ōkubo, Komatsu, and Ijichi Masaharu, to discuss details. On 6/17 they headed back to Hagi to brief Mōri Yoshichika, and to tell him that Satsuma, like Chōshū, was now ready to start preparing for what they all had begun to call buryoku tōbaku, the overthrow of the bakufu by armed force.

In the meantime, two different agendas emerged from Tosa. On 5/21 there was a meeting at Komatsu's residence where Itagaki Taisuke explained that while Yōdō was clearly pro-bakufu, most of Tosa's lower-ranking samurai were not, and wanted to join forces with Satsuma and Chōshū in planning the destruction of the bakufu. Then, on 6/14, three other Tosa samurai—Sakamoto, Nakaoka, and Gotō Shōjirō—arrived in Kyoto with a proposal for a Satsuma-Tosa alliance. During their sea voyage from Kyushu, Sakamoto had spoken to Gotō about an eight-point outline he had devised for government reform and Gotō, who was close to Yōdō, was much impressed. After talking with these men, on 6/22 Saigō agreed to an alliance between Satsuma and Tosa in which the two han would cooperate. This pact was based on the assumption that something like Sakamoto's eight-point outline would serve as a starting point for the creation of a new government, but it made no mention of armed force. Gotō left Kyoto on 7/3 to meet with Yōdō and discuss with him the posibility of trying to persuade Yoshinobu to avert a military confrontation by surrendering his authority to the court voluntarily (*taisei hōkan*).

With the forging of the Satsuma-Tosa alliance, Saigō had once again gotten himself caught between mutually exclusive commitments. Strictly speaking, the Satsuma-Chōshū alliance was not an agreement to destroy either the bakufu or the Tokugawa, and the two han did not formally agree on those aims until 10/ 8, but by the middle of 1867/6 those were their aims, in fact, and they had already begun making preparations to carry them out. Now Saigō had committed Satsuma to a new pact with Tosa, whose effect would have been to sacrifice the bakufu deliberately in order to save the Tokugawa family and its power. On the face of things, Saigō was now deceiving either Chōshū or Tosa. According to the editors of the *Saigō Takamori zenshū*, Saigō did not think Gotō and Yōdō would be able to persuade Yoshinobu to surrender his authority to the court, and so their plans posed no real threat, but since neither Saigō nor anyone else yet had any good ideas about the shape of the new government, he had decided that Sakamoto's eight-point outline would serve as a place to start, and so had agreed to the Tosa alliance as a way to give that outline some formal status. It is also possible that Saigō saw his show of support for Tosa's taisei hōkan strategy as a way to distract Yōdō and other bakufu supporters, and thereby to gain some time for Satsuma and Chōshū to complete their preparations for the coming confrontation.

I have argued that Saigō was attracted temperamentally to a formulaic or aphoristic style of thinking, and that therefore he sometimes found it difficult to grasp the subtleties of complex propositions. I think that difficulty was real enough that it should be part of any interpretation of Saigō, but it is hard to believe he was so profoundly obtuse as to be unaware of the apparent duplicity of his agreement with Gotō. Writing to Shinagawa and Yamagata in Chōshū on 7/7, Saigō described the alliance with Tosa as an 'expedient' (*watari ni fune*), which suggests that he did understand what he had done. If that is the case, then this stands as the most conspicuous instance of willful deceit in a life that was otherwise remarkably free of double dealing. One wonders how Saigō may have felt about this flagrant inconsistency as time went on, but he has left us no clues about that.

About a month after Saigō signed the Satsuma-Tosa alliance, he had a second meeting with Ernest Satow in Osaka, which he reported in letters to Ōkubo on 7/27 and to Katsura Hisatake on 8/4. Satow, he said, was still angry about Leon Roches' continuing machinations in Edo, and Saigō played on Satow's sense of righteous indignation in the hope that anger might prompt him to reveal more about Britain's intentions than discretion would allow. Satow warned Saigō that even if Satsuma and Chōshū did combine their forces, they would not be able to resist a bakufu army trained and supplied by France. Such an eventuality would cancel any hope the two han had of replacing the bakufu with a more effective government for Japan. Such a change of government was what Britain hoped for also, but its official position of neutrality would keep it from intervening in Japanese affairs unless asked to do so. If Satsuma and Chōshū so desired, Britain would provide all the help it could, but it was up to them to make the request.

As Saigō explained in his letters, this was exactly what he had hoped to achieve by provoking Satow's anger. He had had no intention of asking for British aid, but he had feared that if he simply said that, Satow might misunderstand his disclaimer as a covert request. By getting Satow to make an explicit offer of help, Saigō also could make his explicit refusal that much more unequivocal. In any case, he made his position quite clear. Japan, he said, would take care of its own domestic problems, and would transform its government to the best of its ability without foreign help. Satsuma and Chōshū meant to go it alone against Edo, and accept whatever consequences might follow, relying only on what support they could get from Tosa, Higo, Aki, Fukui, and a few other han. Satow pointed out that there might be some reason for optimism: France was likely to be at war with Prussia soon, and certainly would not give the bakufu resources it needed to fight its own battles closer to home. Saigō agreed that a war between France and Prussia undoubtedly would be a boon for Japan. But he also admitted that he felt profoundly ashamed at finding advantage for Japan in the tribulations of other peoples.

Out of the failure of the daimyo council experiment, then, three strategies had taken shape by mid-summer, 1867. In the first (buryoku tōbaku) Satsuma and Chōshū, aided by Tosa, Higo, and Aki, envisioned the destruction of the bakufu and the removal of the Tokugawa from power. Success in this approach would clear the ground completely for the creation of a new Japanese government. In the second (taisei hōkan) a small group from Tosa envisioned a less drastic scenario, predicated likewise on the destruction of the bakufu, but assuming also that some way could be found to retain the Tokugawa family in power under a different institutional arrangement. The feasibility of this outcome was to be guaranteed by Yoshinobu, who would take the initiative and return to the court all powers and entitlements he enjoyed as shogun. This would cut the ground from under the bakufu, leading to its demise, but it would not endanger the prerogatives of the Tokugawa family. The third approach (kōgi seitai) likewise saw the removal of the bakufu as the first priority, and the preservation of the Tokugawa family as the second, but it was willing to go further in disempowering the Tokugawa, so as to make possible the creation of a more egalitarian deliberative form of government with its center of gravity no longer located in the Tokugawa family.

Leaders in Satsuma and Chōshū understood clearly that neither taisei hōkan nor kōgi seitai would go far enough to solve the problems of the Japanese polity they had joined forces to address. Thus, in the final months of 1867, there evolved a contest whose purpose was to decide which of these three agendas would prevail. The outcome may have been a foregone conclusion, as it certainly appears to be in hindsight, but Saigō and his colleagues faced a number of extremely resourceful opponents, and there were still many among the elite in their own han who disapproved of their plans, and resisted their implementation however they could.

The Destruction of the Early Modern Order

One of the first things to happen as autumn began was the failure of the Satsuma-Tosa alliance. On 9/7, Gotō attended a meeting of Satsuma's leaders, and learned for the first time of the tobaku plans taking shape. He pleaded with Saigō to delay acting so that Yōdō would have time to try his taisei hōkan approach, but Saigō refused, saying that the time for talk was past. He promised that no one would interefere with taisei hōkan, but he formally repudiated the alliance with Tosa. In no case, he warned, would Satsuma and Chōshū alter their plans for the sake of Tosa's.

This attitude created some problems with the tobaku alliance as well. Aki han had expressed interest in joining forces with Satsuma and Chōshū, but was reluctant to commit itself fully to the tōbaku agenda until Yōdō had had a chance to see whether taisei hōkan might work. Even after joining the tōbaku alliance formally inaugurated on 10/8, Aki continued to harbor doubts. Except for Satsuma and Chōshū, most of those involved in the events of late 1867 continued to vacillate until the ambiguities were summarily erased by the outbreak of fighting between imperial and Tokugawa armies at Toba and Fushimi. In the meantime, forces that had been in motion since as early as 1862 continued to focus and converge, and the pace of events accelerated steadily toward the denouement.

Early in 1867/10, Ōkubo met with Shinagawa and Iwakura to plan the logistical details of the coup d'etat they were calling the 'return to rule by the emperor as in the days of old' (ōsei fukko). Naturally their primary concern was with such practical matters as where to position troop units, and what to do in case things went contrary to expectations. Writing to Kuroda Kiyotaka on 11/27, Saigō reviewed the essentials of their strategy. Troops from Satsuma, Chōshū, and Aki would use Osaka as their base. Satsuma would occupy and secure Kyoto, while Chōshū and Aki would deploy around the city to serve as relief if needed. If things went badly, Satsuma troops would disguise the emperor and slip him out of the palace to a place of safety in Aki. No doubt Saigō's prior experiences of combat in the streets of Kyoto qualified him to evaluate strategic problems and address them effectively.

Ōkubo, who had looked forward to the second Chōshū campaign as an 'interesting drama' in 1865, was careful to see to it that the coup he now plotted would have ample dramatic elements of its own. Like most of his colleagues, he understood that their actions must include good theater, as well as good strategy and tactics; the history of previous transfers of power in Japanese politics made it clear that whether a turnover *was right* or not, it could not be guaranteed success unless it also *looked right*. Thus, he agreed with Shinagawa and Iwakura that they should have an ample supply of silk battle flags made up in advance, bearing the devices of the imperial army, to help make it clear to bystanders both who they were and what were the sources of their legitimacy. These plans were worth the effort, evidently. When the imperial armies advanced through Toba and Fushimi to confront bakufu loyalists in battle, people along the way greeted them as liberators, cheering and dancing, running into their midst, and offering them food, liquor, and other gifts. According to Saigō, these same crowds greeted Satsuma's banners with cries of 'Satsuma, Great Radiant Deity' (Satsuma daimyōjin sama).

Saigō was only slightly less conscious of appearances than Ōkubo, and often referred to the emperor as 'the jewel' (tama), expressing an attitude that was widespread among the bakufu's enemies. As they put it repeatedly in their diaries and letters, they must 'seize the jewel' (tama o obau). It would not be enough, in other words, merely to control the imperial palace or the members of the court; they must control the physical person of the emperor himself. It would be risky, if not actually impossible, for them to issue decrees in the emperor's name, or to speak in his behalf, if he were himself at liberty to come forth and issue conflicting decrees, or to speak in his own behalf. As they understood keenly, one cannot manipulate the contents of symbols unless one has uncontested control of the physical objects in which they are embodied. Thus these men were all mindful of the need to secure the emperor, whom they understood to be the most important symbol of all.

With all preparations completed, on 10/8 Saigō, Okubo, and Komatsu submitted a petition to the court asking for a decree to topple the bakufu. It justified the destruction of the bakufu as a step necessary to clarify the obligations (taigi) incumbent on the emperor's supporters, and to bring into play the true will of the emperor himself (magokoro). The crimes of the bakufu included violating court decrees, forgetting the duty of an imperial servant, failing to expel the foreigners, losing the confidence of the people, and generally bringing chaos upon the realm. That is, the bakufu was to blame both for domestic unrest (naiyū) and for external peril (gaikan). Yoshinobu had committed violations of his own, employing threats and guile to manipulate the court for his own selfish ends, and obstructing the sincere efforts of others to find solutions to Japan's problems. Tōbaku orders were issued as requested, to Satsuma on 10/13 and to Chōshū on 10/14, thus giving the two han imperial authority to make war on the bakufu and its supporters, specifically Aizu and Kuwana. By the time these orders came out, however, Yoshinobu already had taken the initiative, changing the political stakes once again, and cutting the ground from under his opponents.

On 10/3 Gotō had delivered Yōdo's proposal for taisei hōkan, and on 10/13—the same day Satsuma's tōbaku order was issued—Yoshinobu assembled all of the daimyo then in Kyoto at Nijō castle and informed them of his decision to return his authority to the emperor. His own petition to the court arrived there on 10/14—the same day Chōshū's tōbaku order came down—and was accepted the next day. Thus, before Satsuma and Chōshū could act on their authority to destroy the bakufu, Yoshinobu effectively dissolved it by giving its prerogatives back to the court. Ten days later, on 10/25, Yoshinobu resigned his appointment as shogun. The court deferred acceptance of this resignation pending deliberations by a council of all major daimyo in the country, including Yoshinobu. He had surrendered his political authority to the court, but he had retained his court rank and the other perquisites of his status as head of the Tokugawa family, including all hereditary lands and vassals belonging to them. Thus he was no longer shogun, but he was still far and away the most powerful daimyo in the country, and still well placed to take control of whatever new political arrangement might take shape.

The struggle was far from over, then, in spite of the careful manipulation of all the right symbols by the leaders of Satsuma and Chōshū. These men had left Kyoto in a body on 10/19, before Yoshinobu had completed his preemptive maneuvers. After presenting Chōshū's tōbaku order to Mōri Yoshichika and his son, they went on to present Satsuma's to Tadayoshi and Hisamitsu, arriving at Kagoshima on 10/26, the day after Yoshinobu had unilaterally ended over two and a half centuries of Tokugawa rule.

It took some time for Saigō and Ōkubo to persuade everyone in Kagoshima that it was time to terminate Tokugawa rule. In particular, a number of monbatsu opposed the dismantling of the system under whose institutions they enjoyed their personal status as the han's elite. Both Hisamitsu and Tadayoshi, however, were in support of tōbaku, so it was only a matter of time before they simply ordered opponents of the agenda to be quiet and get out of the way. Tadayoshi left Kagoshima on 11/13 at the head of 3,000 troops, joined up with Chōshū forces at the Inland Sea port of Mitajiri, and arrived at Osaka on 11/20. Three days later the combined army took up positions in and around Kyoto.

On 12/5 Saigō wrote to Minoda Denbei in Kagoshima that all was ready. Shungaku of Fukui and Yoshikatsu of Owari had arrived in response to the court summons for a daimyo gathering, and only Yōdo, late as usual, had not yet made his appearance. Loyalist samurai from Tosa were gathering in Kyoto, and both Shungaku and Yoshikatsu had declared themselves in support of ōsei fukko as a first step toward the realization of the kōgi seitai agenda. The only serious opposition appeared likely to come from Aizu and Kuwana, long Yoshinobu's staunchest supporters. With all in readiness, coup leaders had set 12/8 as the date for action. The only thing detracting from Saigō's sense of satisfaction was the murder on 11/15 of Sakamoto and Nakaoka at the same Teradaya inn where Satsuma's young samurai had killed each other on orders from Hisamitsu back in 1862. Saigō was outraged, and lamented the loss of these two exceptional men.

As the deadline drew near, Iwakura apparently lost his nerve, and Saigō had to write him a strong note of encouragement, enjoining him to stand firm lest all their hopes be lost. Nothing was more important now, Saigō insisted, than to keep Yoshinobu from taking advantage of the confusion to escape the fate planned for him. He must be made to surrender everything—not just his office, but also his lands, titles, and other perquisites. Otherwise he might well come out of the transition in control of whatever emerged. Iwakura vowed to do everything he could.

On 12/8 the court convened to address the question of what to do about the Mōri and the five nobles, all of whom had been under official censure ever since they had fled the city after the 8/18 changeover in 1863. After considerable wrangling, all were pardoned and allowed to enter

Kyoto again. While this was going on, troops from Satsuma, Chōshū, Owari, and other han quietly moved into positions around the palace, causing Aizu and Kuwana forces to pull back in angry confusion. With Yōdō's arrival on the same day, there was no further need for delay. On 12/9 the court announced that all the offices of the Tokugawa institutional order, from shogun on down, were forthwith abolished. In their place would be a new office of state, the *dajōkan*, staffed by three tiers of officials to be known as *sōsai*, *gijō*, and *sanyō*, and staffed by appointees from among the nobility, the daimyo, and the samurai, respectively. Following these announcements, a meeting convened in the Kogosho, a ceremonial building within the palace compound, with all the major players and the young emperor present.

The central question was the fate of Yoshinobu. Ōkubo and Iwakura insisted he must be stripped of his rank and his lands; Yōdō held that no decision concerning Yoshinobu could be made unless he were present himself. A deadlock resulted, and late that night Iwakura called for a recess to give everyone a chance to cool off. He then notified Yōdō that he would bring a short sword with him when they reconvened, and would use it without hesitation against Yōdō unless he ceased obstructing the meeting. According to the biographical tradition, it was Saigō who gave Iwakura this idea. Outside supervising the guards, Saigō did not learn of the deadlock until the recess. He told Ōkubo to advise Iwakura not to waste time with words, but to adopt the last resort, or, as some biographers would have it, he said, 'All you need to resolve this problem is one short sword.' Whatever the case, the rest of the meeting went smoothly, with no further resistance from Yōdō.

The group then promptly decided to notify Yoshinobu that his resignation as shogun had been accepted, and that he must also surrender his lands and titles. Shungaku and Yoshikatsu were delegated to report these decisions to Yoshinobu, but on 12/10 he asked for permission to delay his reply so that he could quiet the growing anger of his supporters. Two days later he left Kyoto and withdrew to Osaka, taking the men of Aizu and Kuwana with him.

This withdrawal brought on another stalemate, during which Gotō, Shungaku, and Yoshikatsu attempted to modify the decision reached in the Kogosho meeting so that Yoshinobu could be permitted to join the new government if he capitulated. According to Saigō, if things unfolded that way, Yoshinobu probably would be appointed to the post of *gijō*, and if that were to happen, he still had enough influential supporters in the court to be in a good position to gain control of the government. Even the five nobles, who had finally returned to Kyoto from Dazaifu on 12/28, would not be able to offset Yoshinobu's influence, and Saigō was very worried. He did not know it yet, but Yoshinobu had already resolved these uncertainties with his own decisions.

On 12/26 Shungaku and Yoshikatsu met with Yoshinobu in Osaka, and he told them he had decided to go back to Kyoto with his troops to discuss the new government's demands on him. Two days later he rejected the Kogosho decision, refusing to surrender his hereditary landholdings. Shungaku and Yoshikatsu reported these developments to Kyoto on 12/30, but by then a series of events in Edo had altered the political atmosphere, offering Yoshinobu a provocation he could not ignore, and turning the course of events irrevocably toward a military solution.

The same day Yoshinobu's reply was reported in Kyoto, Saigō had a visit from two Akita han samurai who had just arrived from Edo. The next day, 1868/1/1, Saigō wrote to Kagoshima that on 12/25 troops from Shōnai han on guard duty in Edo had surrounded Satsuma's residence in Mita and burned it to the ground. There had been an unexplained fire in Edo castle, and Shōnai had blamed Satsuma for it. In fact, it was not Satsuma, but Saigō himself, who lay behind these events. In the autumn of 1867, he had sent two Satsuma samurai—Imuta Naohira and Masumitsu Kyūnosuke—to Edo, evidently on his own initiative. Their mission was to recruit vagrants, masterless samurai (*rōnin*), and others in Edo and roam the city doing whatever they could think of to provoke bakufu supporters and create a volatile atmosphere. For Shōnai samurai, already pushed to the limit, the fire in the castle was too much, and so they had struck at Satsuma. By the time news of these events found its way back to Osaka and Kyoto, Yoshinobu was already in a belligerent mood, having decided he would condemn Satsuma in a memorial to the court. When the troops of Aizu and Kuwana, gathered around Yoshinobu at Osaka, learned of the recent excitement in Edo, it was all the provocation they needed.

They set out from Osaka toward Kyoto, but in the vicinity of Toba and Fushimi they ran into troops from Satsuma, Chōshū, and Aki, who refused to let them pass. On 1/3 Saigō wrote to the Satsuma forces at Fushimi that Yoshinobu's army must not he allowed to proceed without written permission from the court. He suggested to Ōkubo that the plans they had made to move the emperor might need to be altered, so that it did not look like he was being taken against his will. Then he went down to Fushimi, where fighting had already begun. From there he reported that the imperial troops were performing magnificently, and he urged that the silk battle flags be brought out to improve morale. The court, he urged, should name a commander to lead a punitive army against Edo.

By 1/5 Yoshinobu's army was in full retreat and the imperial forces had entered Osaka. The next day Yoshinobu escaped from the city and headed back for Edo by sea. Saigō reported to Katsura Hisatake in Kagoshima that, while they had taken Osaka, they had not captured Yoshinobu. Though outnumbered five to one, he told another correspondent, the imperial army had scored one victory after another. The western half of Japan had become the emperor's territory, but Saigō expected stronger resistance in the northeast, where Aizu han might provide the nucleus for a more concerted defense of Tokugawa rights. He suggested that a reduction of taxes by half ought to bring the support of the people over to the imperial cause. In fact, Aizu did exactly as Saigō had expected, and the hardest fighting of the Meiji civil war (*boshin sensō*) was in the heart of the Tōhoku region, in and around Aizu, which occupied roughly the same territory as present-day Yamagata Prefecture.

At this point, with things going so well, Saigō wrote to his old friend Kawaguchi Seppō, who had passed the hours with him on Okinoerabu, and had coached him in both his calligraphy and his Chinese poetry. After summarizing recent events, he then added that Tadayoshi had reproached him severely for risking his life at the front during the Toba-Fushimi fighting. In response to that, he had the following to say:

> So, I've joined the company of the elderly, and I'm no good for fighting any more, only for looking after. What a disappointment. I've decided that once the fighting has quieted down, I'll ask for leave and go into retirement. I'm no longer fit for public service. I'm just too timid, and there's no help for it.

Saigō wrote this letter on 1/16, and it was discovered only recently. Certainly it is not difficult to understand Tadayoshi's concern for Saigō's welfare; Saigō himself had expressed the same concern for Ōkubo, writing him on 1/7 to cut short a tour of the battlefields around Osaka and return to Kyoto. Saigō's response to Tadayoshi's concern, on the other hand, is intriguing. Perhaps it is nothing but another example of the hyperbole in which he occasionally indulged himself. Or perhaps it offers a vital clue to his behavior in the years that lay ahead.

He had passed his fortieth birthday during 1867/12, and perhaps he was becoming more conscious of his own mortality. He had already been seriously ill several times, and his bouts of illness were becoming more frequent. Moreover, with the emperor restored to power and his enemies nearly all put down, Saigō may have begun thinking that he had outlived his usefulness to the realm, and that it would be inappropriate for him to remain in public office when there was no longer any reason for him to do so. There is little doubt that after 1868 Saigō gradually became more and more troubled about the policies of the new government and the behavior of his former friends, though one can find no single obvious reason for his unease. Inoue Kiyoshi argues that Saigō's doubts about the Meiji government began to grow only after the heavy-handed destruction of the Tokugawa partisans known as the Shōgitai in their stronghold at Ueno. This letter to Kawaguchi suggests that he has already feeling ambivalent about the future within days after the imperial army's first victories outside of Kyoto.

At any rate, there was still work to be done. On 1/23 Saigō wrote to Ōkubo proposing that since Aizu was bound to become a focal point for organized resistance on behalf of Yoshinobu, a quick move against that han would help to shorten what otherwise might be a long war. Sendai han, Aizu's neighbor, was ready to join a combined force, and Saigō thought the bulk of the imperial army should be transferred to Sendai by ship to help pacify Aizu. Ōkubo and others did not agree with Saigō about this, but they all agreed on the need for haste in cornering Yoshinobu before he could rally new support for the Tokugawa. By the time he reached Edo on 1/13, Yoshinobu probably had already decided that his only remaining option was surrender, but no one on the imperial side yet knew that. On 2/2 Saigō argued adamantly that there must be no quarter given, and that nothing less than Yoshinobu's suicide would be acceptable. For his own part, Yoshinobu had withdrawn to Kan'eiji, the Tokugawa family temple in Ueno, and was beginning to indicate his desire to capitulate.

Orders for an armed pursuit were issued in Kyoto on 2/3, and the army set out toward Edo at once, encountering only token resistance along the way. By 1868/3 it had reached Shizuoka, and preparations were underway for the final assault on Edo. However, influential voices had begun calling for leniency, and if Saigō could have disregarded most of them, he could not ignore that of Katsu Kaishū, who wanted to get the matter settled quickly. Katsu sent a messenger to Saigō, proposing that Edo might be surrendered peacefully in exchange for Yoshinobu's life. Saigō had been eager to attack the city, but now he decided to try Katsu's proposal first. He hurried to Kyoto, where he persuaded his colleagues to accept Katsu's overture, and then returned to Edo, where he met with Katsu on 3/13–14. The army entered Edo on 4/4, and the next day Saigō wrote to Ōkubo that all resistance appeared to have collapsed. Yoshinobu left Edo on 4/11, and while he would occasionally advise the government in years to come, his hour in the spotlight was over.

Saigō reported to Ōkubo on i4/27 that the pacification of Edo was going smoothly, but that hospital facilities for the army's wounded were inadequate, and too many were dying. He asked formal permission for Parkes' staff physician, William Willis, to begin treating the injured, first in Kyoto, and then later in Edo also. Saigō's concern here was not only with proper medical care for wounded soldiers, but also with appropriate treatment for the samurai who had been injured while fighting the emperor's battles.

Once again what was at stake for him was the question of virtue implied by the reciprocal nature of relations between people of high and low status. However lowly the imperial army's troopers might be, they had risked their lives in the noblest of causes, and that made them noble in their own right. To treat them with less than the utmost care and solicitude would have brought dishonor on their superiors. This view is fully consistent with the arguments we have seen Saigō making about the proper treatment of the peasants, which suggests, among other things, that his main concern now was not so much with the samurai as such, but rather with the danger that higher-ranking people responsible for their welfare might dishonor themselves through inappropriate behavior.

If Saigō's concern for the fate of the samurai class is sufficient to explain his behavior after 1868, then it would seem that the first evidence of that concern appears in these arrangements he made for the care of those injured in the Meiji civil war. However, his views about the samurai are not sufficient to explain his behavior, however necessary they may be as a part of any interpretation of what he did between 1868 and 1877. On balance, his often repeated wish to retire from public life seems no less important than whatever sense of obligation he may have felt toward the samurai, and his feelings about the behavior of his former colleagues are probably just as important as the other two factors. The tendency has been to explain Saigō's choices after 1868 entirely by reference to one single factor or another, but the available evidence simply does not lend itself to single-factor explanations.

MINZOKU

Kevin Doak

Nationalists, who write so much of the material on nationalism, unfortunately are not the most reliable source of information on the history of nationalism. Leftwing ethnic nationalists, like Inoue Kiyoshi, have tried to pin the origins of ethnic nationalism in Japan on the *sonnō jōi* activists who overthrew the *bakufu*.[1] Rightwing ethnic nationalists in contemporary Japan also trace the history of their nationalism to those opponents of the *bakufu's* policies of Westernization (*Oka*) who led the movement for direct monarchy and expelling Westerners. But, as they tell the story, their nativist forefathers were betrayed by the likes of Iwakura Tomomi and Ōkubo Toshimichi when they turned back to the same policy of Westernization after their 1871–73 journey to the West. They see the rejection of Saigō Takamori's proposed invasion of Korea as a bonding moment among early *minzoku* nationalists, and they lay claim to early rebellions such as the 1874 Saga Uprising, the Jimpūren Incident and Hagi Uprising of 1876, and even Saigō's Satsuma Rebellion of 1877. But the most important of their predecessors is Tōyama Mitsuru. What they see in Tōyama is his anti-government nationalism revealed in the legendary tale of how he approached Itagaki Taisuke, after the 1878 assassination of Ōkubo, seeking Itagaki's help in raising an army to overthrow the "Westernizing new Government."[2] That request, needless to say, went unheeded, but Tōyama went on to form key organizations of rightwing nationalists, especially the *Gen'yōsha* (est., 1881). The *Gen'yōsha* spawned a good many other rightwing nationalist groups until it was finally disbanded in 1946, the most important of which was undoubtedly the *Kokuryūkai*, founded in 1901 by Uchida Ryōhei with Tōyama as its chief advisor.

This history, so replete with facts, seems quite compelling. But this self-narration by postwar ethnic nationalists of their own historical origins is flawed, and it ought to be a cautionary tale to

---

1   Hashikawa Bunzō, *Nihon nashonarisumu genryū*, reprinted in *Hashikawa Bunzō Chosakushū* vol. 2 (Tokyo: Chikuma Shobō, 1985), 3–4.

2   Ino Kenji, "Uyoku minzoku-ha undō o tenbō suru," in Ino Kenji, ed., *Uyoku minzoku-ha sōran*, 71–72.

anyone who blithely projects certain concepts back onto the past. The problem, simply put, is that it loads a heavy argument on flimsy historical evidence. Inoue could not convince even his fellow leftwing ethnic nationalist Tōyama Shigeki, who called the *anti-bakufu* activism nothing more than a reactionary feudal movement against foreigners. Like Inoue, Ino Kenji, albeit from the other end of the political spectrum, tried to establish the origins of what he called the "right-wing ethnic nation school movement" (*uyoku minzoku-ha undō*) at a time when the evidence for the existence of the key concept of "ethnic nation" is questionable at best.

It may be useful to begin with a review of the early origins of the concept of *minzoku*. The earliest known instance of the concept in modern Japanese discourse was in 1875, when Murota Mitsuyoshi's translation of Guizot's *A History of Civilization in Europe* appeared. But Murota used different *kanji* than the usual ones for "nation" to render the homonym word *minzoku* and indeed his reference is not to the nation *per se*, but quite clearly refers to Guizot's concept of society.[3] The earliest use of the concept of *minzoku* as "nation" (with the same kanji used today in the word for nationalism, *minzokushugi*) was Miyazaki Muryū's 1882 translation of Dumas's concept of "assemblée nationale" as *minzoku kaigi*.[4] Yet, as we saw above in Chapter Two, this concept was conceived as a means of juxtaposing the people to the aristocracy in revolutionary France. Whether it carried the same relationship to ethnic nationalism that Ino associates with his postwar nationalist group is quite dubious. And while Miyazaki was affiliated with the Freedom and People's Rights Movement, the concept of *minzoku* was incidental to his text, just as it was marginal in two other texts of the Freedom and People's Rights Movement during the 1880s. These nearly simultaneous appearances of the concept include the 1882 translation of Mirabeau's "On the Abuses of Despotic Government" (the translator is unnamed, but was probably Nakae Chōmin) which introduced the homologous term *minzoku* in Nakae's *Seiri sōdan* (the *Seiri sōdan* instances used different *kanji* than Miyazaki, returning to the *kanji* used in Murota's translation of Guizot). The exact concept referred to by this term is not self-evident, but it was not "society," as the text used *shakai* for that concept.[5] It seems to refer to something like national mores or customs, but it could even refer to the people as "the nation," as we find it used in that context in the same issue of the journal in the translation by a pseudonymous "Kōya Sei" of an article by "Oujean Ballot" that criticized the centralized government's destruction of national culture. In what was clearly a case of political criticism of the Meiji government by metaphor, "Oujean" argued that centralized governments like Imperial Rome harm the "national people" (*kokufū minzoku*).[6] States do not always enhance national identity.

In any event, in these early years, there is little, if any, record of the extension of this concept of *minzoku* (which at the time could mean anything from "people," "folk," "society," "nation" and even "race") to the term *minzokushugi*, or nationalism. The term *minzokushugi* (nationalism, in the ethnic sense) arises much later in Japanese discourse and appears to have emerged around the First World War. One sourcebook on Japanese social thought concludes that *minzokushugi* did not enter

---

3   Haga Noboru. *Meiji kokka no keisei*, 236.

4   Yasuda Hiroshi. "Kindai nihon ni okeru 'minzoku' kannnen no keisei: kokumin, shimmin, minzoku," 61–72 *Shisō to gendai* 31 (September 1992): 62.

5   Mirabeau, [Nakae Chōmin, trans.?], "Sensei seiji no shukuhei o ron su (zoku)" *Seiri sōdan* no. 6 (May 10, 1882): 233–9, at 233.

6   Oujean Ballot, (Kōya Sei, pseud., trans.), "Chūō shuken no sei wa kokka no fūzoku o jōhai su" *Seiri sōdan*, no. 7 (May 25, 1882): 5–13, at 5.

public discourse until after that war.[7] This view gains additional weight from the reminiscences of an active participant in the *minzoku* discourse, Kamei Kan'ichirō, who wrote in 1941 that "the word *minzoku* first appeared in print in actual world politics after the Versailles Treaty."[8] Since it is quite clear that the word *minzoku* was used in printed debates about world affairs quite a bit earlier than the Versailles Treaty (1919), it appears that Kamei must have meant the word *minzokushugi*.[9] Saitō Tsuyoshi's linguistic study of how the suffix *shugi* got applied to words in modern Japanese in general also raises some intriguing questions about the relationship of *minzoku* discourse to *minzokushugi*. Saitō notes that Inoue Tetsujirō pointed out that the practice of adding *shugi* (C: *zhugi*) as a suffix to words was a common linguistic pattern in Chinese long before it was adopted in Japanese. But this suffix did not necesssarily render the composite word an "ism" as in modern concepts like individualism (*kojinshugi*) or socialism (*shakaishugi*). Rather, in this practice, the meaning is that the concept so inflected "is the main principle." Saitō concludes that the Japanese may have coined the use of *shugi* for modern "isms" and reimported it back to China.[10] This may be a more useful way to understand the earliest expressions of *minzokushugi*, i.e., to assert that it is *minzoku* that is the main principle of the nation (not the *kokka*, *kokutai*, *tennō*, etc). But it also raises the question of whether Japanese discourse derived the word *minzokushugi* from Chinese, since Sun Yatsen had been propagating the concept of *minzokushugi* in Chinese between 1904 and 1924. But which way the linguistic influence flowed remains shrouded in mist, as Sun himself was also closely advised by Japanese who were deeply involved in the *minzoku* movement back home. What does seem clear is that *minzoku* emerged as a concept before *minzokushugi*, and the meaning of both must be understood historically, through close attention to both intra-discursive developments and to international and domestic events that shaped the rise of nationalism at that time.

Minzoku and Empire

As with the emergence of the concept of *minzokushugi*, exactly when the concept of *minzoku* became an important factor in modern Japanese nationalism is a contested issue. Hashimoto Mitsuru argues that it was not until the Shōwa era, 1928 to be exact, that "Japan started seriously asserting an image of itself as a particular *minzoku*."[11] But most scholarship on the question concludes that *minzoku* discourse originates much earlier, even as far back as the late nineteeth century. Yasuda Hiroshi has concluded that there are few instances of the word *minzoku* in Meiji discourse prior to 1890, but thereafter it exploded across the pages of the journal *Nihonjin* and the newspaper *Nihon*, as journalists like Shiga Shigetaka and Kuga Katsunan tried to clarify the meaning of the national essence (*kokusui*).[12] Yamamuro Shin'ichi agrees that the beginnings of ethnic nationalism are to be found in the 1880s, and he points to Shiga Shigetaka's use of the concept of *minzoku* to mean

---

7   Habu Nagaho and Kawai Tsuneo, "Minzokushugi shisō," 326–346 in Tamura Hideo and Tanaka Hiroshi, eds., *Shakai shisō jiten* (Tokyo: Chūō Daigaku Shuppanbu, 1982), 330–3.

8   Kamei Kan'ichiro, *Dai tōa minzoku no michi*. (Tokyo: Seiki Shobō, 1941), 301.

9   One instance of *minzokushugi* in political discourse that well-predates the Versailles Treaty is Tanaka Suiichirō's article on "Minzokushugi no kenkyō," in *Mita gakkai zasshi* (1916) 10: 1–22.

10   Saitō Tsuyoshi, *Meiji no kotoba*, 370.

11   Hashimoto Mitsuru, "Minzoku: nihon kindaika wo tōgō suru chikara," Senjika nihon shakai kenkyūkai, ed., *Senjika no nihon*, 6.

12   Yasuda Hiroshi, 66.

that which constitutes the essence of our nation is accepting the influence of all sorts of foreign things in our country and mixing appropriately with them like a chemical reaction, thereby planting, giving birth, and developing them, while at the same time continuing to preserve for the current era what has been transmitted and purified among the Yamato *minzoku* since ancient time.[13]

Nonetheless, Yoon Keun-Cha argues that "in the first half of the Meiji period [i.e., until 1890], there was an absence of collective or group consciousness as a single ethnic nation, which is to say that 'the ethnic nation' did not exist or at least was still not fully formed, and in reality, one can hardly find any actual instances of the word *minzoku* then, and certainly not in the late *bakufu* or Restoration years."[14]

Clearly the word (and with it, the concept) of *minzoku* grew increasingly prominent in nationalist discourse in post-constitutional Meiji Japan. But even then, one has to be cautious about assigning a single, fixed meaning to the concept at this early date. Yonehara Ken has demonstrated that in Tokutomi Sohō's writings around that time, the concept of *minzoku* was used interchangeably with class, but to refer to Tokutomi's ideal of the "country gentleman."[15] What is clear is that the concept was neither introduced nor promoted by Katō Hiroyuki, as is sometimes thought to be the case. As late as 1887, Katō was still employing a now obsolete term, *zokumin*, to render this sense of nationality, the nation as a popular body, and his point was to deny its legitimacy as a real form of the nation.[16] Given the historical point of erupture of this discourse, and the arguments it spawned, it does seem plausible that *minzoku* emerged as a challenge to the Imperial Constitution's denial of legal nationhood and its substitution of the status of imperial subject (*shimmin*). It was trying to assert that this principle (*minzoku*) was the heart and soul of what the nation truly is, or at least should be.

Yet, other historians who accept the general time frame of late nineteenth century as the point of departure nonetheless look to other sources of the discourse. Oguma Eiji, for example, traces the beginnings of *minzoku* discourse to a debate among anthropologists over the origins of the Japanese people. Western anthropologists who, like Edward S. Morse, Erwin von Bälz and Heinrich Philipp von Siebold (Philipp Franz's son), came to Japan during the 1870s brought with them their Orientalist and imperialist assumptions about peoples and cultures, and they applied these assumptions to the quest for the origins of the Japanese people. In looking for enduring patterns of ethnological identity among the Japanese, these Western academics promoted a "composite nation" theory that held that the Japanese people were the result of mixtures among several distinct lineages. Oguma notes that while most mainstream Japanese anthropologists adopted the "composite nation" theory of their Western teachers, a few such as Kurokawa Mayori and Naitō Chisō were offended by the notion that not all the Japanese were members of the same group who

---

13   Shiga Shigetaka, cited in Yamamuro Shin'ichi, *Shisō kadai to shite no Ajia: kijiku rensa tōki* (Tokyo: Iwanami Shoten, 2001), at 110.

14   Yoon Keun-Cha, "Minzoku gensō no satetsu," 9.

15   Yonehara Ken, *Tokutomi Sohō: Nihon nashonarizumu no kiseki*, Chūkō Shinsho 1711 (Tokyo: Chūō Kōronsha, 2003), 74–75.

16   Katō's term *zokumin* was his translation of Bluntschli's *Nationalität*, presented in his 1887 translation of *Allgemeine Staatslehre*. Cf. Katō Hiroyuki, "Zokuminteki no kenkoku narabi ni zokuminshugi," *Doitsugaku kyōkai zasshi* vol. 40, no.41 (January 1887); reprinted in Tanaka Akira and Miyachi Masato, eds., *Nihon kindai shisō taikei: rekishi ninshiki* (Tokyo: Iwanami Shoten, 1991): 432–441.

Toyama Mitsuru center, at the founding meeting of the Genyosha. Kodama Yoshio second from right

had descended from the gods. Characteristic of their work is their reliance on the concepts and methods of ninetheenth century physical anthropology, and thus the resulting confusion of the concepts of race and ethnicity. The result of this anthropological inquiry was not so much distinctive theories about race and ethnology, but competing conceptions of the Japanese people that were informed by "two forms of nationalism."[17] In short, while the anthropological search for physical traces of the Japanese people's early origins left a racial ring to some forms of *minzoku* discourse, it was not free from the same divisions that marked the broader political discourse over whether the nation was the people or the Imperial State.

The question of Japan's ethnic origins, particularly whether the Japanese were originally the same or different from other peoples in East Asia, became an increasingly urgent matter as the century closed. The 1870s saw the incorporation of Okinawa within Japan, and in the 1880s Hokkaidō became part of the territorial realm, even before Japan itself had established its own legal contours of identity as a state through a constitution. But it was the acquisition of Taiwan in 1895 that most acutely brought forth the question of who the Japanese people were, are, and should be. Prior to the 1890s, even "integral" units of Japan proper found their administrative incorporation into the new imperial state far from a natural transition. But with a constitution in place, a constitution that by design refused to answer the question of who was a Japanese national and instead referred to all residents of the empire as "imperial subjects," further incorporation of other peoples raised the question of how far the boundaries of "Japan" could be extended. This was particularly true when the new members of the realm had a distinctive culture, were located far from the center, and spoke an entirely different language. Moreover, just as Taiwan was added to the empire (as the

---

17   Oguma Eiji, *Tan'itsu minzoku shinwa no kigen*, 27–32.

result of a war fought with China over Korea), another war was heating up with Russia, once again over Korea. So, as the century ended, ethnicity and race intermingled over the issue of whether the Japanese nation was a nation for the Japanese ethnic people, and how far the definition of "the Japanese ethnic people" could be pushed.

The interwar period of 1895–1905 proved to be a formative moment in the emerging *minzoku* discourse. Having defeated China, Japan was experiencing a surge of nationalism that at first seemed to legitimize the direction that the Westernizers and architects of the imperial state had set. The sacrifices of the last two decades had yielded real results, it seemed, in demonstrating that Japan was superior to China. In 1897 Kimura Takatarō captured this feeling in an article he called "The Japanese Are a Superior *Minzoku*."[18] Here, the concept of *minzoku* performed two roles. First, it separated the Japanese from the Chinese in ways that appeals to a common Asian race could not have done, while at the same time not excluding the theoretical possibility of assimilating the Taiwanese through this concept of national identity that relied on a culturalist and assimilationist notion of who was Japanese. Second, it located the motive force for military victory in the cultural essence of the Japanese people themselves, rather than in the machinations of military and civil bureaucrats who guided the state. *Minzoku* was being wedded to a cultural ideology that would disappoint state officials who had hoped victory in the Sino-Japanese war would unite the nation behind His Majesty's government.

In May 1897, Kimura had joined with Inoue Tetsujirō and Takayama Chogyū in forming the Great Japan Society and espousing a brand of cultural nationalism they called Japanism (*Nipponshugi*). This nationalism looked to the core of Japanese culture and argued that unless that core identity was purified and strengthened, Japan could not continue to achieve victories like that of the Sino-Japanese war. And with the humiliation of the Triple Intervention by Russia, Germany and France still stinging, and a general recognition that war with Russia was around the corner, the Japanists began to regard Western culture in Japan, not as the reasons for Japan's victory over China, but as a fifth columnist influence that had to be rooted out. Inoue, as we have seen in Chapter Three, was already embroiled in the "clash between religion and education" and this "clash" indicated where the influence of Western culture was most dangerous: Christianity. From the very first article of its founding charter, the Great Japan Society declared that "we worship the founder of our country" and their journal *Nipponshugi* took the lead in publishing attacks on Christianity. It was a popular position to take: as Oguma notes, "the intellectuals of that age joined the Great Japan Society one after another."[19]

Christian intellectuals quickly responded to this attack on their loyalty to the nation, just as they had five years earlier during the attack on their loyalty to the emperor in the aftermath of the Uchimura *lèse majesté* affair. Many Japanese Christians in the late nineteenth century had an affinity with the *minzoku* movement and shared social and political roots with activists in the Freedom and People's Rights Movement. To them, especially after the elevation of the monarch and the rise of State Shintoism, conceiving of the true nation as the *minzoku* rather that the now-Shintoist State was an essential means of asserting the compatibility between their national identity and their faith. Watase Tsunekichi's rebuttal of the Japanist attack on Christians is illustrative of this effort. Watase did not reject the concept of *minzoku* or its importance to national identity. But he countered that it was too narrow a concept for the kind of civic consciousness required by a cosmopolitan, modern government with the dynamic and democratic aspirations he attributed to

---

18   Kimura Takatarō, "Nipponjin wa yūshōteki minzoku nari," *Nipponshugi*, no. 3 (1897); cited in Oguma, 63.

19   Constitution of the Great Japan Society (1897); cited in Oguma, 57.

Japan. He rejected the narrow ethnic nationalism of Kimura and Inoue, arguing that the founding spirit of modern Japan was one that was open to peoples of various races or ethnicities.[20] Watase and other Christians quickly sensed that the victims of such an exclusivist ethnic nationalism were not only Taiwanese and Koreans, but also themselves and anyone else who professed a faith that did not permit the worshipping of the monarch as a Shinto god. They did not reject the claim *minzoku* made on individual identity; rather, they merely sought to subordinate it to the universal transcendence of their Christian faith.

That was not enough for the Japanists; or perhaps it would be more accurate to say that it was too much. They found their best spokesman in Takayama Chogyū who developed a wide-ranging theory of cultural nationalism between 1897 and 1902 that mixed *minzoku* and race, nationality and Asianism, all the while drawing heavily on Western theorists in order to denounce the deleterious effects of Western culture on Japan. Takayama understood Japan's growing tensions with Russia as part of a broader idea of global "racial war" that Ludwig Gumplowics had sketched in *Der Rassenkampf* (1883). From this racial lens, Takayama was certain that the Triple Intervention, Russian designs on Korea, and even the 1875–78 war between Russia and Turkey and the 1897 war between Greece and Turkey (Takayama believed Turkey was part of the East, or "the Turanian race") were indicative of a "600 year old racial war between the Aryan race and the Turanian race."[21] Against Watase's argument that a modern state was able to withstand the challenges of a multiethnic populace, Takayama drew from Max Müller and Henry George to argue that a state cannot simply be a territorial administrative unit, but must be built on, with, and through, a single people with a shared cultural identity. Thus, even through the Japanese, Koreans, Taiwanese and others were all part of the Turanian race, their distinctiveness resulted from the fact that this race, like all races, was divided into *Naturvölker* (*shizen minzoku*) and *Kulturvölker* (*jinbun minzoku*). The *Naturvölker* were those peoples who had yet to develop an integral, shared culture that provided the dynamism for their own independent states; the *Kulturvölker* were those ethnic groups who had emerged out of the state of nature to built an independent state on the basis of their unique culture.[22] Of course, among the Turanian race, only Japan met the requirements of a *Kulturvölker*. In one broad sweep of the pen, Takayama had sketched the conceptual foundations for modern Japanese imperialism as well as the grounds for culturalist attacks on Christianity as a foreign creed incompatible with the culture of the emperor-nation. Not surprisingly, his last work published in 1902, the year he died, was an exploration of the thinking of the medieval xenophobic Buddhist monk, Nichiren.

The annexation of Korea in 1910 renewed and sharpened the debate on whether Japan should be a homogeneous ethnic nation-state and whether the concept of *minzoku* was flexible enough to incorporate Koreans in the Japan *minzoku*. Again, Christian intellectuals played a leading role in asserting an optimistic, open reading of the potential limits of ethnic assimilation, while the Japanist and statist intellectuals like Takayama and Inoue Tetsujirō were slow to accept a sense of *minzoku* that was not thoroughly and exclusively racist. Yamaji Aizan had laid the foundations for his fellow Christians, arguing several years prior to annexation that the Japanese were a "composite" nation, historically formed through a combination of Ainu, Malay, and the Yamato (a branch of the Turanian race). On the eve of annexation, he refuted the argument presented in Takekoshi

20   Oguma, 57–8.

21   Takayama Chogyū, *Chogyū zenshū*, volume 5. 313.

22   Takayama, volume 5, 20–22.

Yosaburō's 1910 *Nankokuki* that the *Tenson* (descendants of the gods) group was entirely Malay.[23] Yamaji's arguments were controversial, but the helped spawn a sense that Japan's national identity, even when conceived in ethnic or racial terms, was more open, more pliable, to the forces of history than some anthropologists and racial determinists were willing to acknowledge.

Christians in particular had reason to argue in favor of this multiethnic notion of Japanese nationality. Their interests were complex, involving both domestic and regional concerns, but it is not accurate to say that they simply were promoting imperialist intervention against a mono-ethnic interpretation of the nation that might have prevented imperialism. The crux of the matter was not imperialism (both sides supported the annexation of Korea), but over how Japan's new imperial subjects should be treated: compassionately, as members of the same family; or as a conquered people to be exploited. Influential Christian intellectuals like Ebina Danjō and Ukita Kazutami argued the former line, with Ukita stressing that the annexation of Korea was not the result of a self-interested policy on the part of Japan and that intermarriage between Japanese and Koreans, and thus Korean assimilation, should be encouraged.[24] Japanese Christians generally welcomed the incorporation of Koreans into the empire since they hoped the relatively larger number of Korean Christians would strengthen the voice of Christianity within the empire and counter the rising Shintoist nationalism at home. (It is also not unreasonable to assume that they had a personal interest in intermarriage, so that their own sons and daughters would have a wider pool of Christian marriage partners.) This position was in sharp contrast to the views of the national polity (*kokutai*) and Shinto nationalists for whom Japan's annexation of Korea was proof of Japan's superior ethnic identity and the necessity of keeping Koreans in a separate and inferior social position. Even for those like Inoue Tetsujirō who grudgingly came to accept the "composite nation" theory of the origins of the Japanese, the true underlying moral fiber that held together the empire was to be found in the monarch as a moral figurehead for his subjects. These tensions over how the concept of *minzoku* was to be deployed continued to play a role in nationalist discourse throughout the imperial period.

Minzoku and Liberal Political Theory

The outbreak of world war in Europe, sparked by a nationalist Serbian revolt against the multi-ethnic Austro-Hungarian empire, had a significant impact on Japanese concepts on nationhood. While Japan played an extremely limited role in the fighting of the war, no one in Japan could ignore the resurgent ethnic nationalism (*minzokushugi*) that the war had unleashed in the world, particularly as a tool against multi-ethnic empires like their own. As Benedict Anderson has noted, "by 1922, Habsburgs, Hohenzollerns, Romanovs and Ottomans were gone. … From this time on, the legitimate international norm was the nation-state, so that in the League [of Nations] even the surviving imperial powers came dressed in national costume rather than imperial uniform."[25] Legitimacy now meant a government had to make a persuasive case that it represented the nation, which is to say, the people. This national principle was a new and revolutionary idea. In 1914, Matsumoto Hikojirō recorded one of the earliest recognitions of the new challenge posed by this

---

23   Oguma, 99–100.

24   Oguma, 109–113. Ebina also went so far as to praise the patriotism of An Chung Ken who had assassinated Itō Hirobumi in 1909.

25   Benedict Anderson, *Imagined Communities: Reflections on the Origin and Spread of Nationalism* (London: Verso, 1983): 104.

rising ethnic nationalism, as it struck close to home in the form of attacks by Chinese nationalists on Japanese in China during September 1913. Clearly, Takayama and the Japanist belief in Asian racial solidarity against the West was revealed as limited in its appeal and, as a consequence, the racial flavor of their understanding of the nation was also losing any attraction it once might have had as a principle of unity against the West.

The reality of ethnic tensions within Asia made the demand for a new understanding of "what a nation is" an urgent one. To meet that demand, Matsumoto introduced a new approach to understanding the formation of ethnic nations that relied less on biological and natural scientific claims about past origins and more on consciousness of the nationals themselves as expressed in the present. New psychological theories were seen as offering an advantage over the old racial studies approaches that, at best, had introduced "composite" nations, but which were seen as mired in an old-fashioned way of thinking about nations at a time when a multitude of new nations seemed to be exploding out of the present, rather than the past. To explain this new phenomenon, Matsumoto introduced Wilhelm Max Wundt's *Elements of Folk Psychology* as the most recent development in scientific understanding of the formation and function of national identity. Given this assumption that nations were mainly a matter of consciousness, Matsumoto proposed a new theory of national identity built around religion. The constructivism of his approach is evident in his suggestion that the religion needed to hold Japan's empire together was not State Shintoism, but a new composite religion that would weave together the shard and patches of native Shintoism, Buddhism and even Christianity.[26]

Needless to say, Matsumoto's proposal for a newly constructed religion for the empire went unheeded. But his introduction of psychology as the best hope for a scientific understanding of *minzoku* was a watershed event. The immediate effect of this approach was to call attention to the difference between the institutional reality of the state and the cultural and psychological force of national identity. With a world war underway that was reinforcing the claims of an ethnic identity, an identity that was not always easily mapped out spatially, the distinction between the nation (conceived in ethnic terms) and the political state was a growing feature of Japanese discourse on *minzoku*. In what may have been an indirect rejoinder to Matsumoto, the historian Tanaka Suiichirō (who established the Mita Historiographical Institute which would produce many of the important theorists on *minzoku*) drew from Rudolph Springer to reinforce the argument that the nation (*minzoku*) and the state (*kokka*) were distinct entities and should be kept "as separate as religion and politics."[27] Tanaka may not have appreciated Matsumoto's effort to shift Japanese national identity toward a new, composite religion, but both men were in agreement that Shinto, as a state religion, was unlikely to succeed in raising national consciousness in most Japanese people's minds. It was simply too closely associated with the state.

Liberal and leftist intellectuals were quick to seize on this theory of the nation as a form of consciousness, as they saw in it a way to break free of the determinism of the older, racial theory of the nation. Abe Jirō was one such liberal who was attracted to this new form of ethnic nationalism. One of the most influential intellectuals of the time, he wrote in 1917 that there was no contradiction between the individualism of liberals and ethnic nationalism; indeed, he argued that only by assimilating oneself to "the ethnic national spirit that is alive and well" could the individual truly thrive. His worry was that the state might suppress the unique identity of ethnic nations and reduce

---

26   Matsumoto Hikojirō, "Minzoku kenkyū to kojiki," *Shigaku* vol. 25 (1914): 228–34

27   Tanaka Suiichirō, "Minzokushugi no kenkyū," (1916); cited in Kevin M. Doak, "Culture, Ethnicity and the State in Early Twentieth-Century Japan," 189.

them all to some generalized, universal human nature. The greater threat to international justice, he concluded, was not ethnic nationalism but "imperialist statism" (*teikokushugi-teki kokkashugi*).[28] Two years later, his support for ethnic nationalism was echoed by the leading "Taisho democrat" Yoshino Sakuzō who waxed exuberantly in the pages of the influential *Chūō Kōron* that the reorganization of the international world on the basis of ethnic nationalism was simply the completion of the movement towards democracy that began with "nineteenth century civilization."[29] Yoshino's colleague, and later socialist luminary, Ōyama Ikuo joined the chorus, singing the glories of an ethnic nationalism that would not be a "subjugating imperialism" like the old nationalism built around the state, but would usher in a new era of "international harmonism."[30] What animated this liberal support for ethnic nationalism was a broad consensus that it was not "blood" nationalism, but an identity that rested on the consciousness of individuals to embrace their own forms of identity. It was, therefore, democratic.

If this new psychological approach to national consciousness emphasized the difference between nation and state, it also encouraged diverse ways to think about the nation itself. One of the most remarkable texts to express this way of thinking about the nation was Nakamura Kyūshirō's *The Nations of the Far East*. The text is interesting for many reasons. It was part of a series published by the *Min 'yūsha*, so it had a historical connection with one of the groups that had originated the discourse on *minzoku* in the late nineteenth century. It came with two glowing introductions: one by Tokutomi Sohō and another by Yoshino Sakuzō, both among the most influential intellectuals of that time writing on issues of populist nationalism. But it also was unusual in its effort to reach a broad audience. The text provided *furigana* throughout, so that even those who were only marginally literate could understand what was written. This consideration, along with the topic itself, suggests a serious effort to reach readers in Taiwan and Korea who may not have been native Japanese speakers, in addition to native Japanese of limited literacy but unlimited interest in the problems of nationalism. Anyone who is inclined to follow Yoshimoto Taka'aki's postwar theory that the nationalism of intellectuals never reached the nationalism of the masses should first pay careful attention to this text.[31] Nakamura's work faithfully reflects both the broader intellectual world's concern with coming to a proper conceptual understanding of the problem of nation as *minzoku*, and the growing turn from racial concepts in favor of a sense of the nation that was distinct from the state but formed through the usual factors: common ancestral lineage, historical unity, common culture, common religion, common language and customs, shared economic interest, and a common state structure. The repetition of the familiar recipe for a nation is as important as Nakamura's insistence that a *minzoku* was not the same thing as race (*jinshu*), political nationhood (*kokumin*) or a state (*kokka*).[32] In short, Nakamura's text reveals how widely diffused this burgeoning discourse on *minzoku* as a mode of cultural consciousness was, as well as how much this discourse was mobilized to intervene in the political realities of the Japanese empire.

---

28   Abe Jirō, "Shisōjō no minzokushugi," *Shichō* 1: 99–120, at 116–9.

29   Yoshino Sakuzō, Sekai kaizō no riso: minzoku-teki jiyō byōdō no riso no jikkō kanō, *Chūō Kōron* 367 (1919): 87–91, 90.

30   Ōyama Ikuo, "Shinkyū nishu no kokkashugi no shōtotsu," *Chūō Kōron* 367 (1919): 74–86, 82–83.

31   See Yoshimoto Taka'aki, "Nihon no nashonarizumu."

32   Nakamura [Nakayama] Kyūshirō, *Kokutō no minzoku* (Tokyo: Min'yūsha, 1916), 6–10. For further analysis of this text in its historical milieu, see my chapter, "Narrating China, Ordering East Asia: The Discourse on Nation and Ethnicity in Imperial Japan," in Kai-Wing Chow, Kevin M. Doak and Poshek Fu, eds., *Constructing Nationhood in Modern East Asia* (Ann Arbor: University of Michigan Press, 2001.)

The end of the First World War and the convening of the Paris Peace Talks in 1919 brought the issue of this new, populist nationalism to the attention of journalists, intellectuals and politicians around the world. Japan was no exception. The basic question this new nationalism raised was how to set uniform conditions for recognition as a nation. The old rules, under which any government that could demonstrate exclusive authority over a certain territory could be recognized as a sovereign entity, no longer sufficed, as the war had witnessed the ravages of a new, bloody nationalism that had brought down empires rather than shoring up existing power structures through indoctrinating loyalty among its people. Suddenly, the world was awash with claims of national identity, nationality, nationhood, and thus demands for recognition and political independence of countless new groups. It was impossible to recognize all these groups as sovereign nation-states, and it was left to a handful of diplomats at Versailles to decide who had a "right to self-determination" and who did not. Most of the claims raised at the time did not concern Japan. But the outbreak of Korean and Chinese nationalism in March and May of 1919 was not unrelated to this surge in populist, ethnic nationalism and did require a response from Japanese government officials. The problem of who constituted a nation under the new, post World War I rules was, in the end, also an urgent matter for Japan.

Masaki Masato was one of the first to address directly the problem of identifying this new principle of national "self determination in the postwar years. He did so by introducing William McDougall's 1920 book, *The Group Mind* which promised to bring the certitude of science, psychology to be exact, to resolve the thorny problem of who constituted a nation and who did not. Masaki's article "What is a *Minzoku*?" went beyond a mere review of McDougall's book as it surveyed the field of liberal theories of national identity, introducing many of the theorists whose work would continue to inform Japanese debates on *minzoku* for the next ten to fifteen years. Chief among them were, in addition to McDougall, Karl Lamprecht, G.P. Gooch and Ramsey Muir. Together, their work reinforced the idea that the nation (*minzoku*) is not equivalent to the state, nor is it the same thing as race (*jinshu*); rather, the nation is defined by the ties of affinity that people conceive with one another on the basis of a variety of grounds.[33] Masaki's article was explosive, and both conservatives and Marxists responded quickly to the liberal claim that the nation was in essence a form of collective consciousness, or "group mind."

To counter Masaki and defend the empire, Uesugi Shinkichi employed the rhetoric of restatement in his article published the same year on "The Source of the State's Powers of Unification." Uesugi rephrased Masaki's question as "what is the state (*kokka*)?" Uesugi latched on to the psychological approach's recognition of the open definition of a *minzoku* to reappropriate the concept for the service of the imperial state. Since, as Uesugi repeated, "a nation (*minzoku*) is not the same as race" there could be no objection to conceiving even an imperial state like Japan as a "nation-state." Korean identity, for example, was merely a contingent form of group consciousness that can, and would, change over time.[34] Not to be left behind, socialists and Marxists also tried to appropriate *minzoku* nationalism for their agendas. For them, the main attraction of the concept was the demonstrated ability of *minzoku* movements to break up empires. Ōyama Ikuo emerged as one of the leading leftists to contribute to the *minzoku* project when, in 1923 he published a book-length study, *The Social Foundations of Politics*, that built on his earlier argument that *minzoku* had unleashed a new kind of nationalism that was on a collision course with statist imperialism. He drew on the Austrian social democrat Otto Bauer, particularly Bauer's distinction between the socialist nation and the capitalist state, as a pre-condition for positing *minzoku* as the preferred

---

33   Masaki Masato, "Minzoku to wa nani zo?", 151.

34   Uesugi Shinkichi, "Kokka ketsugō no genryoku," *Chūō Kōron*, no. 36 (1921): 15–37, at 24.

social imaginary, a proletarian agency that would rise up against capitalist imperialism. Like the liberals, Ōyama accepted that *minzoku* was the effect of a group consciousness and not an effect of racial or natural ties, but he preferred Bauer's mode of explanation: nations, he argued, were products of history rather than of nature and this meant that nationality (*minzoku*), like the state, was the result of struggle, war and conquest. In short, he accepted the liberals' view that without an adequate definition of the nation, the formation of nations would be a matter left to sheer power politics. But he turned the problem around and argued that power was ultimately all there was to the matter: no rules, however carefully crafted, could or should restrain the violence unleashed by *minzoku* movements.

Although Ōyama did not share the liberals' belief that a better theory of nationality might reduce, if not completely prevent, wars fought for national independence, he did agree with them that the concepts of nation, nationality and nationalism were fraught with confusion and required clarification. His own effort to define these terms is worth citing at length:

> What I would like to add here is a reflection on how such terms as ethnic nationalism (*minzokushugi*) and nationalism (*kokuminshugi*) are generally understood in their actual usage. The insistence on liberating one or more nationalities from the statist domination of another nationality usually is expressed through the term *minzokushugi*—"principle of nationality" [Ōyama's own English gloss]. In contrast, when a nationality [*minzoku*] that occupies a dominant position within a state attempts to realize its desire to express its existence in the form of an independent nation-state by carrying out assimilation policies or oppressing weaker nationalities at home, while manifesting hostility in various ways toward other nationalities or foreign states, we usually call the guiding principle behind such efforts *kokuminshugi*—"nationalism" [Ōyama's English]. This is because a nationality that is under the dominance of another nationality is usually simply called a *minzoku*—"a nationality" [Ōyama's English], but a nationality that either has already formed its own state. or that occupies the center of superior dominance and power within a state-a nationality that has made a state-is therefore called a *kokurnin* "nation" [Ōyama's English]. We must pay careful attention to the fact that in Japanese common usage, the original word "nation" is often used in a highly indiscriminate way, and its direct Japanese translation as *kokumin* is also used in a very thoughtless manner. In Japan, there are many cases where the word *kokumin* is used as a direct translation of the German *Staatvolk* to express collectively the general members of the object of sovereign power. Before we use such terms as *minzoku* and *kokumin*, we should first be prepared to distinguish these points.[35]

What is striking about Ōyama's terminology is his negative view of *kokuminshugi* and his valorization of *minzokushugi*. This valorization can only be explained as the influence of the Versailles principle of "self-determination" as the right of ethnic groups to their own nation, and his own Marxist commitment to undermining imperial Japan, which was nothing more than an elitist, capitalist state that had suppressed the ethnic nations of Asia. There still were two forms of nationalism at war with each other, as he had argued in 1919. But now he argued that, in addition to Japan's oppression of other ethnic nations, the polarization of politics in Japan suggested that this

---

35 Ōyama Ikuo, *Seiji no shakai-teki kiso* (1923); reprinted in *Ōyama Ikuo zenshū* (Chūō Kōronsha, 1947), 1:217–237, at 232–3.

war between nationalisms also could be found within the same country, that there was, in effect, something like "internal colonization" in Japan.

If it is true, as Hashimoto Mitsuru has argued, that by the beginning of the Showa era (1926), *minzoku* first became a major feature of Japanese political debate, it is not because, as he claims, Japanese society had begun to coalesce around a *minzoku* identity.[36] Just the opposite. From 1925 to 1935, *minzoku* discourse was more diverse than at any other time in Japanese history. This development can be explained as a result of the appeal *minzoku* still had for various people, parties and political agendas across the spectrum: from right to left, everyone, it seemed, wanted a piece of the action. The effect of this broad interest in *minzoku* was not an enhanced national unity in Japan, but a dispersed, contested discourse over what *minzoku* meant, both conceptually and in practice, and a broad disagreement over how Japanese people should respond to its appeal. Through that decade, advocates of the liberal psychological approach continued to present their case. Kamikawa Hikomatsu summarized their arguments in his 1926 essay in the *Kokka gakkai zasshi*, which reviewed McDougall, Hayes, Muir and Pillsbury, and sought to provide what Hayes had announced was urgently needed: a systematic theory of nationality and nationalism. Kamikawa's theory merely admitted race had some influence on the formation of a nation, but ultimately he concluded that a nation was formed most through the subjective factors of culture, history and tradition.[37]

The following year, former Diet member and Tokyo Imperial University professor Nakatani Takeyo drew from the same theorists to once again seek in *minzoku* a fusion of self and society that would not extinguish the liberal hopes for a culture of personalism. He rejected Carlton Hayes's effort to separate *minzoku* (nationality) and nationalism (*minzokushugi*), arguing such an effort was not consistent with the lessons of social psychology: if the nation was the effect, not the cause, of national consciousness, then there can be no significant time lag between the emergence of national consciousness and nationalist movements. Since *minzoku*, in contrast to the state, was a mode of consciousness that existed simultaneously in the mind of the individual and in the minds of those who shared his national identity, *minzoku* consciousness was in fact the mediation between individual and the group. Consequently, nationalism, which completes the individual, and is therefore a liberal movement, can be called a kind of "national personalism (*minzoku-teki jinkakushugi*), or social individualism (*shakai-teki koseishugi*)."[38] This theory of *minzoku* as a form of subjective consciousness had a deep and broad influence on liberal political thinkers of the early Showa period, including Yanaihara Tadao, Tanaka Kōtarō, and Hasegawa Nyozekan.[39]

At the same time, those further to the left continued to assert their preference for *minzoku* nationalism as the best hope for a revolutionary subjectivity. Nagashima Matao played a significant role in making *minzoku* acceptable to Japanese Marxists. His 1929 article on "The Nation and Nationalist Movements," published in the journal *Under the Banner of the New Science*, was essentially a response to Ōyama's interest in the nationalism theories of Otto Bauer. Nagashima explored Bauer's writings on the nation in depth, but he also cited heavily from Stalin's "The

---

36   Hashimoto Mitsuru, "Minzoku—Ninon kindai o tōgō suru chikara," in Senjika Ninon Shakai Kenkyūkai, ed., *Senjika no nihon*, 6.

37   Kamikawa Hikomatsu, "Minzoku no honshitsu ni tsuite no kōsatsu," 1851.

38   Nakatani Takeyo, "Minzoku oyobi minzokushugi," 127. Nakatani is responding to the arguments Carlton J.H. Hayes made in *Essays on Nationalism*.

39   For more on liberal views on *minzoku* during this time period, see my chapter on "Culture, Ethnicity and the State in Early Twentieth-Century Japan"; on Tanaka Kōtarō's views on *minzoku*, see my "What is a Nation and Who Belongs?: National Narratives and the Ethnic Imagination in Twentieth-Century Japan."

National and Colonial Question." This *minzoku* turn among Marxists was made possible by the shift within the Marxist movement towards a reconsideration of cultural and national issues in the late 1920s that lay behind the establishment of the journal *Under the Banner of the New Science*.[40] In addition, Sano Manabu and Nishi Masao had just translated Stalin's work on the "National and Colonial Question" as "*Minzoku Mondai*" in 1928, drawing their comrades into the already vigorous debate over the meaning and politics of *minzoku*. Following Stalin's writings closely, Japanese Marxists contributed to the discourse on *minzoku* by, paralleling their analysis of class struggle, positing a national struggle (*minzoku tōsō*) with "dominant nations" (*shihai minzoku*) and "dominated nations (*hi-shihai minzoku*), or sometimes "oppressor nations" (*appaku suru minzoku*) and "oppressed nations (*hi-appaku minzoku*).[41] These distinctions were of course unstable, and allowed Sano himself (along with Nabeyama Sadachika) to abandon Marxism in 1933 in order to remain loyal to his own *minzoku*.[42] Sano had come to believe, not merely that national struggles paralleled class struggles, but that in fact national struggles were the fundamental ones.

Sano and Nabeyama's abandonment of Marxism was a watershed event for many on the left. Both held key positions on the Central Committee of the Communist Party, and their turn from Marxism toward a closer embrace of the nation made support for *minzoku* even more controversial among Marxists. Tosaka Jun was the loudest voice against an intoxication with *minzoku* identity, warning that it would always lead to reactionary politics and undermine the struggle against capitalism.[43] Not all Marxists agreed. Matsubara Hiroshi (Suga Hirota) published his own outline of Stalin's ideas on *minzoku* in 1935 as study material for his comrades who were planning a conference on ethnic nationalism. Matsubara emphasized that Stalin's definition of the nation "is a most accurate, principled critique … of the confusion we find in our 'everyday' consciousness of ethnicity [*minzoku*], tribe [*shuzoku*], and race [*jinshu*], or of the ethnic nation [*minzoku*], the state [*kokka*], and the political nation [*kokumin*]."[44] Matsubara's memo on Marxist *minzoku* ideas was vigorously debated by Tosaka Jun, Izu Tadao, Ōta Takeo, Hirokawa Hisashi, Utsumi Takashi, Kojima Hatsuo and Mori Kōichi at the conference. Their views ranged widely, but their responses to Matsubara, published in the 49th issue of the journal *Studies in Materialist Theory*, revealed that most accepted *minzoku* as a useful tool, even as they stressed that it was a product of history, and therefore was both real and contingent.[45] Although their politics were different, Marxist and liberal intellectuals shared a broader conceptualization of the ethnic nationality as a matter of consciousness ("ideology") and as a historical reality that was forged through culture and history, rather than through organic, racial ties.

---

40   See my article, "Under the Banner of the New Science: History, Science and the Problem of Particularity in Early 20th Century Japan." *Philosophy East and West* vol.48: no.2 (April 1998): 232–256.

41   Cf. Nagashima, 30–31.

42   Sano Manabu, "Nihon minzoku no yūshūsei o ronzu," (February 1934); reprinted in *Sano Manabu chosakushū* (Tokyo: Sano Manabu chosakushū kankōkai, 1958): 945–61, 945.

43   Tosaka Jun, *Nippon ideorogii ron* (1936); reprinted in *Tosaka Jun zenshū* (Tokyo: Keisō Shobō, 1966); vol. 2: 223–438, at 316–7.

44   Matsubara Hiroshi, "Minzoku no kiso gainen ni tsuite-kenkyū sozai," *Yuibutswon kenkyū*, no. 30 (April 1935); reprinted in Bandō Hiroshi, ed., *Rekishi kagaku taikei 15: minzoku no mondai*, 9.

45   Bandō Hiroshi, "Rekishi ni okeru minzoku no mondai ni tsuite," in Bandō Hiroshi, ed., *Rekishi kagaku taikei 15: minzoku no mondai*, 313–314.

Minzoku and War

During the ten years from 1925 to 1935, when the influence of liberal and leftist discourse on *minzoku* was at its zenith, the emphasis of this discourse gradually shifted from political theory to cultural theory. It is tempting to attribute this shift to an internal development of the discourse itself: the force of conceptualizing the nation in terms of psychology and consciousness, artifice and contingency, history and tradition which ultimately drew theorists to culture as the ground of such identity-making practices. And there may be some truth to that analysis. But contingency was not only a theory, as specific events and particular individuals did make a difference. For example, in 1935 Yasuda Yojūrō founded a new journal *Nihon Rōmanha* that spawned an influential literary movement that lasted throughout the war. The Romantic School writers were not inclined to theoretical articulation of the nation, nor did they connect with the earlier efforts to keep up with the latest writings on nationalism coming from the West. Rather, drawing on late eighteenth century German romantics, they condemned such "intellectual" activities as modern scholarship and sought to actually re-present the ethnic nation itself through the creation of aesthetic and literary works that spoke less to the intellect than to the heart. Along with Kamei Katsuichirō and Hayashi Fusao, among others, Yasuda sought the core of Japanese national identity in an ethnic or *Völkisch* cultural identity which he traced back to the sixth century, before Korean, Chinese (and certain Western) cultures had influenced Japan.[46] Needless to say, this poetic archaicism was not easy to reconcile with the reality of the modern Meiji state, and part of the fascination of the Romantic School writers is the variety of ways in which they tried to reconcile these two, the nation and the state.

From the middle of the 1930s, Japanese literary and philosophical works were awash with *minzoku* impulses. In 1935, Watsuji Tetsurō wrote an influential tract, *On Climate*, that sought to explain the Japanese national character as a function of Japan's unique climate. While he situated Japan within a broader monsoon climate that included other Asian nations, ultimately he argued that Japan's climate was a unique blend of monsoon and temperate climates which yielded the unique ethnic character of the Japanese people. Indeed, Watsuji's argument on climate was in fact anti-nature in a manner that paralleled the emphasis on *minzoku* as a cultural or spiritual principle that contrasted with the nature of biological race. When applied to explaining Japan's unique climate and its role in shaping Japan's particular culture, Watsuji's argument was an effort to isolate Japan both from the claims of Westernizers and from Orientalists who would relocate Japan in Asia. Watsuji's approach blended literary and philosophical ideas with social scientific concerns. There was a sense that the social sciences (other than psychology) were lagging behind the humanities, particularly in terms of responding to the appeal of *minzoku*. Indeed, Hashimoto Mitsuru has concluded that the discourse on *minzoku* in the social sciences merely followed the initiative of philosophy and sought empirical evidence to support the ideas of *minzoku* philosophies through fieldwork.[47]

If political science, philosophy and literature had quickly gravitated to the concept of *minzoku* as a product of culture rather than nature, anthropology was taking a bit longer to accept this idea. As a discipline, it was still recovering its footing in the aftermath of the subjectivist challenge from psychology, and was moving away from an emphasis on the "objective" approaches of physical

---

46   On the Japan Romantic School and their contribution to *minzoku* discourse, see my *Dreams of Difference: The Japan Romantic School and the Crisis of Modernity* (Berkeley. University of California Press, 1994); also "Ethnic Nationalism and Romanticism in Early Twentieth-Century Japan," *Journal of Japanese Studies*, vol 22. no. 1 (1996): 77–103.

47   Hashimoto Mitsuru, "Minzoku: nihon kindaika wo tōgō suru chikara." 8.

anthropology and its emphasis on race in favor of new appreciation of the impact of culture and consciousness. There were earlier hints of this new direction, particularly in 1925 when Yanigita Kunio and Oka Masao founded a new journal *Minzoku* to shift the focus of anthropological research from race studies to a more culturally informed ethnological approach. But Yanagita's influence on professional anthropologists was limited, as he mainly worked outside the professional discipline, drawing as much from the mythological streams that fed Yasuda as from cutting-edge anthropological scholarship. And Oka left for Vienna in 1929, not to return until 1935, a pivotal year in *minzoku* discourse.

Consequently, the anthropological turn to ethnicity was spurred in large measure by the work done by sociologists. Many of the future ethnologists in Japan were trained in sociology, as it was in sociology that they focused on developing an adequate theory of the people as the national body (see Chapter Four). A key barometer of the sociological interest in ethnicity is the 1934 *Annals of the Japanese Society for Sociology*. All six of the essays carried in that volume were explicitly concerned with the problem of *minzoku*. Since they were treated above in Chapter Four in some depth, here I merely want to focus on how some of these key arguments continued to shape the formation of ethnology and wartime discourse on *minzoku*.

Watanuki Tetsurō's article called "Nationality" (*minzokusei*) followed Usui Jishō's article on "The Concept of Nation" (*kokumin no gainen*), and implicitly raised the question of what the distinction between *kokumin* and *minzoku* is. And, in fact, that question was the fundamental one that his article addressed. Watanuki did not build his argument around a theoretical response to the difference between *kokumin* and *minzoku* so much as a historical analysis of different *minzoku* within the Japanese nation. He explicitly drew his conceptions of what a *minzoku* (nationality) is from the liberal, psychological vein, citing Muir, McDougall, Fouilée, and Le Bon, among others, to make the point that what constitutes a sense of nationality is not so much "consciousness" (*ishiki*) as "mind" (*kokoro*).[48] His reliance on McDougall's concept of nationality as "group mind" allowed him to distinguish his approach to nationality from the Marxist theory that transferred class consciousness to nationality consciousness. Instead, Watanuki was interested in how sub-groups (what today we would call "ethnicities") within a given state or national arena develop distinctive cultural styles that yield distinctive ethnic identities, or nationalities. What made his argument most provocative was that it emphasized different "national mores" (*kokufū*) within Japan, specifically the different cultures of Tosa people and Nagasaki people. Watanuki skillfully employed subjectivist theories of nationality as a form of "group mind" to conclude that Nagasaki and Tosa represented two particularly strong examples of the variety of nationalities (*minzokusei*) that existed within Japan proper. Ultimately, Watanuki concluded that, as revealed by the example of Nagasaki and Tosa as particular cultural styles that co-existed within the Japanese state, current efforts to reorganize global politics based nationality as the fundamental unit of political society failed to reflect the continuous dynamic change in these social identities called *minzoku*.[49]

Watanuki's article was provocative and influential. A shift was underway within sociology and it bore fruit when the Japanese Society of Ethnology was formed in 1934. The members of the Society read like a "who's who" of *minzoku* theorists during the wartime: Uno Enkū, Ishida Kannosuke, Koyama Eizō, Shibusawa Keizō, Shinmura Izuru, Kuwata Yoshizō, Utsurikawa Nenozō and Furuno Kiyoto, with Shiratori Kurakichi as the Chairman of the Society's Board of

---

48   Watanuki Tetsurō, "Minzokusei," *Shakaigaku* no. 2 (Tokyo: Iwanami Shoten 1934): 99–150, at 139.

49   Watanuki, 150.

Directors.[50] All these men (but Ishida, Koyama and Shinmura in particular) would make substantial contributions to the wartime discourse on *minzoku* and, at least initially, all started with the belief that the cultural, subjective nature of *minzoku* required a specific discipline distinct from the natural orientation of anthropology and the institutional formalism of sociology.

But in fact, sociology in Japan was changing under the impact of *minzoku* theory. No one did more to push the discipline into a serious engagement with ethnology that the senior sociologist Takata Yasuma who joined his theory of "total society" to the new work being done on *minzoku* with revolutionary results. In 1934, the same year that Watanuki's article appeared, Takata published his major work on *Class and the State* which sought to refute the theory put forth by Marxist social scientists that posited a deterministic relationship between class and the state. In the process of building a pluralistic theory of political structures, Takata argued that the concept of *minzoku* held an independent value that could not be reduced to the political state in all cases.[51] In that work, Takata's main concern was with demonstrating the pluralistic nature of the state; he was not yet focused on the problem of *minzoku* and he strongly rejection the notion that he supported ethnic nationalism (*minzokushugi*)[52] But it immediately became the central concern of his work to the end of the war.[53] Between 1935 and 1939, Takata mainly developed a theory of *minzoku* that situated it within both modernist and subjectivist approaches, rejecting blood as the primary factor and also criticizing "climate" theories (Watsuji's?) for relying too much on natural causes and not enough on culture (see the discussion on Takata's sociology in Chapter Four above).

Takata's 1939 *A Theory of East Asian Nationality* made a major, original contribution to both *minzoku* discourse and imperialist ideology by offering the concept of a single, culturally determined East Asian nationality (*kō minzoku; tōa minzoku*).[54] This idea of a new, East Asian nationality drew from the subjectivist theory that nationality was a matter of consciousness or "mind" and thus was relatively open in possibilities. If nationality was largely a subjective sense of identity, then why could not socialization result in a singular sense of loyalty among all East Asian peoples to the Japanese empire? The key, however, remained the necessity of a state to raise the level of identity to a true consciousness, thereby yielding a modern nation (*kindai minzoku*). Until they developed such a consciousness, other East Asian nationalities would remain at a pre-modern stage of development and would have to rely on the imperial Japanese state to provide them with organization and structure. In this way, Takata transformed and extended a theory of a pluralistic state to a theory that justified Japan's multi-ethnic East Asian empire.

---

50   See my "Building National Identity through Ethnicity: Ethnology in Wartime Japan and After," 18–9.

51   Takata Yasuma, *Kokka to kaikyū*, (Tokyo: Iwanami Shoten, 1934): 15.

52   In a October 1934 issue of *Keizai Ōrai*. Takata published a rebuttal of Shimmei Masamichi's claim that Takata had converted to a *minzokushugi* position, describing his own position as that of a cosmopolitan (*sekaishugisha*). Cited in Seino Masayoshi, "Takata Yasuma no *Tōa minzoku ron*," 29–59 in Senjika Nihon Shakai Kenkyūkai, ed., *Senjika no nihon: shōwa zenki no rekishi shakaigaku*, 32. But as Seino goes on to demonstrate, "But by 1942 ... Takata had converted into one of Japan's leading ethnic nationalists." (33).

53   The centrality of *minzoku* in Takata's wartime work can be gleaned from a quick list of some of his major publications: *Minzoku no mondai* (Tokyo: Nihon Hyōronsha, 1935); *Tōa minzoku ron* (Tokyo: Iwanami Shoten, 1939); *Minzoku to keizai*, vol. 1 (Tokyo: Yūhikaku, 1940); *Minzoku ron* (Tokyo: Iwanami Shoten, 1942); Minzoku to keizai, vol. 2 (Tokyo: Yūhikaku, 1943); and *Minzoku kenkyūjo kiyo* (Tokyo: Minzoku kenkyūjo, 1944), which he edited.

54   On Takada's theories on *minzoku*, see Hashimoto Mitsuru, "Minzoku: nihon kindaika wo tōgō suru chikara," 16–19; Doak, "Building National Identity through Ethnicity."

Takata had begun to outline a theory of ethnic nationality that could reconcile the two countervailing pressures in *minzoku* discourse up to that time: on the one hand, *minzoku* appealed as a cultural theory of identity that was not invested in regional or racial identities; yet at the same time, it was deeply implicated in post World War I political movements for nationalism and a right to self-determination. For Takata, and for those who sought to legitimize the Japanese empire, the problem was how to embrace this new concept as a cultural theory without losing their right to govern other ethnic nationalities. The solution Takata found was a dual notion of *minzoku*, one that was temporally and spatially inflected: not all *minzoku* were at the same stage of historical development, and not all *minzoku* identity claims were narrow in scope. But it was Oka Masao who came up with the most powerful articulation of this concept. Having spent the years from 1929 to 1935 in Vienna, where he watched the development of ethnology, he returned to Vienna again that year and stayed, impressed with the Nazi support for ethnology. When he returned to Japan in 1940, he brought with him a new idea. Within Takata's horizontal community of an East Asian ethnic nationality there had to be a "hierarchy of ethnic nations (*minzoku chitsujo*) that reflected the different historical stages of development of each member *minzoku*. And since Japan was the only ethnic nation to have developed its own independent state, it was accorded the top position, the *Herrenvolk* (*shidō minzoku*) with the moral responsibility to develop the other ethnic nationalities to their own, eventual political independence.

Oka not only provided intellectual support for imperial ethnology, he was also the motivating force behind the creation of the Japan Ethnic Research Institute (*Minzoku Kenkyūjo*) in 1943. Takata was named the Director of the Institute. Oka had many valuable contacts in the military, as well as in companies with close connections to the military and civilian powerbrokers. He received substantial help from Furuno Kiyoto who was working for the East Asian economic research department of Mantetsu and had strong ties to people in the Ministry of Education and in the Imperial Navy. Once it became clear that *minzoku* ideas were not limited to the Marxist agenda, pragmatic imperial bureaucrats, bankers and high level military offers were eager to use the fruits of this discourse both to suppress Marxism and to shore up imperial rule. Ishiwara Kanji is a case in point. Drawing on the idea of Kyoto Imperial University Professor Sakuda Shōichi that the ideals of ethnic national harmony and integration within the political state were compatible goals, Ishiwara founded Kenkoku University (National Foundation University) in Manchuria in May 1938, placing Sakuda effectively in charge of the University. At that university, ethnic harmony was not only an idea, but enacted through admissions policies that yielded a remarkable ethnic balance among the students enrolled. According to research done by Naka Hisao, a member of the last class of Kenkoku University, the first class enrolled 65 Japanese, 59 (Han) Chinese, 11 Koreans, 13 Taiwanese, 7 Mongolians and 5 White Russians, a proportion that was maintained until the university closed in 1945.[55] But Tōjō Hideki thought Ishiwara's belief in ethnic national harmony was quixotic at best, and he never warmed to Ishiwara's social reorganization plans for Manchuria. In fact, he finally recalled Ishiwara to Tokyo and placed him on inactive service.[56]

Oka's contribution to wartime Japanese *minzoku* discourse revealed a new shift in the way that discourse placed the people in relation to the Imperial state. The concern no longer was limited to a shift from race to ethnicity through the mediation of culture. Rather, cultural and political issues began to merge more frequently, particularly under the influence of the Nazi model that the State

---

55   Naka Hisao, "'Minzoku kyōwa' no risō: 'manshūkoku' kenkoku daigaku no jikken," 81–100 in *Senjika Nihon Shakai Kenkyūkai*, ed., *Senjika no nihon*, 90–91, 83–84.

56   Cf. Miyazawa Eriko, *Kenkoku daigaku to minzoku kyōwa* (Tokyo: Fūma Shobō, 1997).

itself could be reconceived as a *Volk-Staat*. This mode of taming the force of ethnic nationalism to serve an expansive wartime state was providing Imperial Japan's state bureaucrats with hopes that they might be able to overcome the Wilsonian liberal theory of *minzoku* as a form of nationalist self-determination, an anti-imperialist movement. This was a marked shift from the negative assessment of *minzoku* that was characteristic of imperial state apologists from the days of Fukuzawa Yukichi, Katō Hiroyuki and Uesugi Shinkichi.

From the late 1930s, the emphasis within Japanese *minzoku* discourse turned toward ways the state might appropriate *minzoku* for its own purposes. This was no simple matter. First, the state had to adopt the liberal theory that *minzoku* was not an objective, racial identity but a matter of consciousness. Second, it had to make a persuasive case that such ethnic consciousness could be transformed, and transformed in a way that would align *minzoku* identity with what was institutionally, historically, and legally a multi-ethnic Empire. And finally, it had to find methods that would successfully accomplish this goal, transforming *minzoku* consciousness from a potentially anti-imperial movement into one that would further invest the loyalties of various peoples throughout Asia in the Japanese Imperial State. What made this agenda particularly difficult was it had to be accomplished without completely alienating ethnic nationalists within Japan who had been opposed to the modern, bureaucratic empire that had, in the words made famous in Japan by J.A. Hobson, become a "debasement of … genuine nationalism by attempts to overflow its natural banks and absorb … reluctant and unassimilable peoples."[57] At the same time, the incorporation of *minzoku* into official ideology had to proceed without transforming the very nature of the constitutional Imperial state. Few of the state bureaucrats who were now turning toward *minzoku* discourse wanted Japan to change its constitutional system as Germany had. And fewer yet were interested in overthrowing the monarchy.

Domestically, the extreme positions were marked out by conservative ethnic nationalists like Yasuda who sought in *minzoku* a principle of overcoming all traces of modernity, including the modern Japanese imperial state, and "reform bureaucrats" inspired by Nazi Germany who sought to push the limits of the imperial state as close to the Nazi model as possible. In between these two extremes were legal theorists like Yanaihara Tadao and Tanaka Kōtarō who incorporated *minzoku* discourse into their writings but with the goal of resisting both the anti-modernity of romantics like Yasuda and the totalitarianism of the "reform bureaucrats." Significantly, in the context of a rising State Shintoism, both men were Christians. Yanaihara was a *mukyōkai* ("non-affiliated," i.e., in Uchimura Kanzō's tradition) Christian, and was inclined to see institutions like church and state as secondary to ideals which, transcendent, must be employed to guide institutions. He brought this idealist philosophy to bear on the problem of *minzoku* in two books *Minzoku to Heiwa* (1936) and *Minzoku to Kokka* (1937), the latter based on a series of speeches he had delivered in Nagano between 31 August and 02 September 1937. On the basis of these works, Yanaihara developed a theory of national identity that accepted ethnic nationality (*minzoku*) as the foundation of national identity, and he saw the state as an artificial institution that needed to be guided by the ideals of a nation (*minzoku*). In practice, he was offering a critique of the Imperial States efforts at assimilating Koreans and at the war in China that had just started in July. When he published this moral critique of the Japanese state in *Chūō Kōron* in September, he attracted the attention and ire of the rightwing ideologue Minoda Muneki who attacked Yanaihara for his pacifism, and ultimately

---

57   J.A. Hobson, *Imperialism: A Study* (New York: James Pott & Co., 1902), 4. The quote is from Hobson's introductory chapter, "Nationalism and Imperialism" which was widely cited by the liberal theorists of nationalism discussed above. It was particularly influential on Yanaihara Tadao.

Yanaihara was forced to resign his chair at Tokyo Imperial University.[58] While the precise reasons for Yanaihara's removal from teaching at the Imperial University are in dispute, what is clear is that he argued that the state must be accountable to the *minzoku*, not the other way around. And this view directly contradicted what statists had been trying to do with the concept of the *minzoku* since the outbreak of the second Sino-Japanese war: subordinate *minzoku* claims to the imperial structure of rule.

In any event, Yanaihara was neither persecuted for advocating *minzoku* ideas nor for being a Christian liberal. That much is clear from the example of Tanaka Kōtarō, a liberal, Catholic professor of law at the same university. Conceptually, Tanaka agreed with Yanaihara that the nation (*minzoku*) had developed out of race but had matured into a concept distinct both from race and from the state.[59] The real question from the perspective of international law, or what Tanaka called "global law," was to determine whether a state was the by-product of a nation, or whether a nation could be engineered by a state. Tanaka rejected the idea put forth by radical conservatives that the Japanese state was an expression of the Yamato nation. But he also rejected the notion that ethnic nationality was merely a tool, either to overthrow the state (Marxists) or to be used to support the multi-ethnic state (authoritarian imperialists). Staking out his position in the moderate middle, Tanaka argued that the relationship between nation and state was one of mutual influence, or what we might today call "overdetermination." His main point, from a perspective grounded in the transcendental principle of natural law, was to limit the state's activities to regulating the objective forms of social life: the state should simply stay out of national issues, as the nation was, ultimately, a spiritual reality.[60] This argument was not only a defense of the right to be both Christian and a loyal Japanese—as outlined by Maeda and Linguel forty years earlier—it was also a defense of Article 28 of the Meiji Constitution that guaranteed freedom of religion. At the same time, it did not completely reject empire as a viable and potentially just political system. Like Yanaihara, Tanaka's approach was not a structuralist, deterministic one, but a human, practical one: how might moral men exercise power in imperfect institutions to achieve the most just and humane result possible? But unlike Yanaihara, Tanaka did not adopt a pacifist position, either in principle or in regard to the second Sino-Japanese war. And, even though he was an active and devout Christian throughout the war, he never suffered any persecution.

There were, however, many social engineers who were eager to make the principle of *minzoku* subordinate to the raw political interests of Japanese imperialism. From the late 1930s, it became an increasingly common feature of *minzoku* discourse that morality ultimately rested in the state, and thus *minzoku* identities could, and should, be manipulated to suit the interests of the Japanese state.[61] One way this argument was put forth is evident in the collection of essays called *Minzoku*

---

58   In fact, Yanaihara was only removed from the classroom and had his writings on *minzoku* and the state suppressed. At the same time, he was allowed to stay on as librarian at Tokyo Imperial University and was never imprisoned. As Susan C. Townsend has noted, "the Japanese authorities, although they persecuted and harassed Japanese Christians, were reluctant to imprison them" (267–8). See her *Yanaihara Tadao and Japanese Colonial Policy: Redeeming Empire* (Richmond, UK: Curzon Press, 2000): esp., 235–251. On Yanaihara's *minzoku* discourse, see my "Colonialism and Ethnic Nationalism in the Political Thought of Yanaihara Tadao (1893–1961)," *East Asian History* (July 1997): 79–98.

59   Tanaka, *Sekai hō no riron*, I, 162–166.

60   Tanaka, *Sekai hō no riron* I, 212–6.

61   The scope of this *minzoku* discourse from the late 1930s is truly impressive and of course there are individual variations within it. But a representative sample of the influential works would include: Komatsu Kentarō, *Minzoku to bunka* (Tokyo: Risōsha, 1939); Izawa Hiroshi, *Minzoku tōsō shikan* (Tokyo: Sangabō, 1939); Takata Yasuma, *Tōa minzoku ron* (Tokyo:

and *War* published by the Young Japanese Foreign Relations Association in 1939. This volume, with essays by leading *minzoku* theorists Shimmei Masamichi, Kada Tetsuji, Shimizu Ikutarō, Nagata Kiyoshi and Maehara Mitsuo, placed ethnic nationality at the center of Japan's war in Asia, arguing from a variety of perspectives that Japan had a moral mission to rectify the political instabilities in the region that resulted from a failure to resolve the claims of ethnic nationalism. The purpose of the book, which was addressed to young men of draft age, is best captured in the title of Shimmei's article, "The Role of War in Establishing Ethnic Societies [*minzoku shakai*]." It provided a bibliography, which illustrated the enduring influence of liberal national theories and established the writings of Takata, Yanaihara, Kada, Koya Yoshio, and Komatsu Kentarō as canonical works in the Japanese discourse on *minzoku*.[62] But most importantly, the authors had learned the lessons of the failure of the liberal theorists to establish a definitive theory of who or what constituted a nation. Ultimately, they concluded, the liberal effort to seek an adequate theory of the nation had failed, and the only solution was to be found through the effects of war.

This approach to resolving the *minzoku* issue through force became most salient after 7 (8 in Japan) December 1941, when the attack on Pearl Harbor offered the chance to reinterpret the overtly imperialist war in Asia as a war for the liberation of Asia from the West. The war could not be presented effectively as a war of liberation of Asian nations without a compelling case for what nationality was and how it could be liberated by an outside state-Japan. Yet, as we have seen, the effort over several decades to establish a definitive theory of nationality had met with little success. Even so, the failure of political theorists to establish a theory of nationality for the empire did not lessen the need for a philosophy of nationality, a normative outline for how nationality, properly understood, could provide a justification for Japan's war. And there was no shortage of philosophers in Japan ready to provide just that.

Kōsaka Masa'aki, a leading philosopher in the Kyoto School tradition, emerged as the most influential of such philosophers when he published a book called *The Philosophy of Minzoku* in April 1942. In that book, he drew from the liberal theory of *minzoku* as a contingent product of history, as well as conservative views of those like Yasuda that there was no transcendental moral principle beyond that of the *minzoku*. He argued that the true subject of world history was neither the individual nor class but the *minzoku*, and he drew from Muir and others to emphasize that *minzoku* was distinct from both race and the state. But Kōsaka offered something new. He emphasized that the ultimate goal, "a world historical nation" was a "state-nation" (*kokka-teki minzoku*):

> Of course, the world is not going to be changed solely through *minzoku*; the *minzoku* must be mediated by culture. And even if the world itself can be seen as a kind of negative universal (*mu-teki fuhen*), there must be within the historical world a species-subject (*shu-teki shutai*). And that is the state-nation.[63]

Iwanami Shoten, 1939); Tanase Jōji, *Tōa no minzoku to shūkyō* (Tokyo: Kawade Shobō, 1939); Matsuoka Jūhachi, *Shina minzokusei no kenkyū* (Tokyo: Nihon Hyōronsha, 1940); Kamei Kan'ichirō, *Dai tōa minzoku no michi* (Tokyo: Seiki Shobō, 1941); Koyama Eizō, *Minzoku to jinkō no riron* (Tokyo: Hata Shoten, 1941) and *Minzoku to bunka no shō-mondai* (Tokyo: Hata Shoten, 1942); Kaigo Katsuo, *Tōa minzoku kyōiku ron* (Tokyo: Asakura Shoten, 1942); the 12 volume *Minzoku* series published by Rokumeikan in 1943, Ogawa Yatarō, ed., *Nihon minzoku to shin sekaikan* (Osaka: Kazuraki Shoten, 1943); Hirano Yoshitarō, *Minzoku seijigaku no riron* (Tokyo: Nihon Hyōronsha, 1943); and *Minzoku kenkyūjo kiyo* (Tokyo: Minzoku Kenkyūjo, 1944).

62   Nihon Seinen Gaikō Kyōkai, ed., *Minzoku to sensō* (Tokyo: Nihon Seinen Gaikō Kyōkai, 1939): 211–244.

63   Kōsaka Masa'aki, *Minzoku no tetsugaku* (Tokyo: Iwanami Shoten, 1942); 3.

Kōsaka's fusion of nation with the state, *minzoku* with *kokka*, through the process of mediation, was a new, original contribution to the moral discourse on *minzoku*. He was not proposing a nation-state (*minzoku-kokka*), which would have contradicted the multi-ethnic empire, but the need for all *minzoku* in the region immediately to associate themselves with a state (the only effective option being the imperial Japanese state). Even while recognizing the distinction between the two concepts, he subjected that conceptual distinction to his historicist philosophy that was more interested in offering creative assertions about new realities than the more modest goal of reflecting what was traditionally seen as limitations to what the nation and the state could demand of the individual.

This was no mere philosophical game. Kōsaka made it clear that his interests were practical and involved specifically offering a rationale for the policy of the Greater East Asian Co-prosperity Sphere. The key to resolving the national question within the empire, he felt, lay in the grand concept of a co-prosperity sphere. Once the pluralistic and artificial ("historical") character of *minzoku* was grasped, Kōsaka believed there would be no barrier, certainly not nature (he spent a great deal of energy distinguishing and discounting natural scientific concepts like race from the historical subject of nation), to the reconstruction of *minzoku* in a new relationship of co-prosperity. It was "not simply a matter of liberating nations in East Asia, but of a new discovery of them and an establishment of them." Sounding very much like Takata Yasuma, he argued that

> the Greater East Asian Co-Prosperity Sphere does not simply mean that existing states and existing nations will enter into a new relationship of co-prosperity. Rather, it means the construction of their own states, the beginning of their own history, for those nations that are non-autonomous, that lack their own history, and in this way, a new East Asian world will open a new stage in world history.[64]

Such a grand constructivist project was possible, Kōsaka maintained, because a *minzoku* was an on-going social construct (*gen ni dekitsutsu aru*). But from a world historical standpoint, the most important consideration was how such non-historical nations would become historical state-nations. The answer was quite predictable. "Through the leadership of our nation, new states will arise from among the other nations and appear on the stage of world history. But this will also mean that our nation's mode of existence will be fundamentally enlarged and become capable of mediating the process toward a new world."[65] While this 1942 defense of the co-prosperity sphere placed Kōsaka squarely among those on the political right, his philosophy of *minzoku* could not have taken shape without the contribution of liberal and leftist theories of *minzoku* that had sought to overcome the constraints of nature and of race in particular.

By the late 1930s, imperial *minzoku* discourse had taken shape around two distinct conceptual approaches. Kōsaka and Takata represented the corporatist approach that insisted that the plasticity of the concept of *minzoku* provided the grounds for the creation of a new, single East Asian identity that would provide the basis for the construction of a New Order in Asia. Takata's student Nakano Seiichi gave this theory its strongest articulation as a policy position in his 1944 article on "An Unfolding of the Nationality Principle in East Asia" published in the *Bulletin of the Ethnic Research Institute*. Nakano recognized Oka's call for an "ethnic national hierarchy" in the region, but

---

64   Kōsaka, 193, 194–5.

65   Kōsaka, 196, 197.

he added Takata's notion of a "broader ethnic nation" as the foundation for a sense of community within the hierarchy of ethnic ations in the East Asian region. He noted that

> the basis of all East Asian ethnic nations is to be found in the position of a single East Asian Ethnic Nation (Dr. Takata). Once we accept this fact, then it is clear that the position of an East Asian ethnic nation is also basis of the position of ethnic national complementarity (*minzoku hokan no tachiba*). Moreover, this means that what appears as a complementary relationship among the ethnic nations is, when seen from a different angle, merely each ethnic nation making manifest its own special job. So, we can call this position of ethnic national complementarity the position of ethnic national duty. In time, as this complementarity progesses, disarray might arise in the relationship between ethnic nations and their specific duties. If we are to avoid such a development, there will need to be a hierarchy among the ethnic nations. Thus, the position of ethnic national complementarity is tightly linked to the position of an ethnic national hierarchy.[66]

Nakano's synthesis was not a very successful one. It is most valuable as an example of how far the social theory of constructed identity could go in providing justification for imperialism as a project that would "overcome" the limitations to national formation history had recorded, and which were seen in the last years of the war as a problem of modernity, or the West.[67]

If Nakano had sought his synthesis largely from within the corporatist approach to nationality in the empire, those who believed that unity in East Asia could best be formed on the basis of a league of separate ethnic nationalities remained unconvinced by his policy recommendation. Kamei Kan'ichirō still asserted that the life of the empire depended not on some dubious social experiment in engineering unprecedented forms of ethnic identity, but in strengthening existing ethnic identities in East Asia. Kamei had been deeply impressed by the ethnic nationalism he found in Nazi Germany, and he drew from that experience to argue that something analogous was possible in East Asia and would lead to unity under the Japanese empire. His league approach had been favored by many activists since the early 1930s, including Ozaki Hotsumi and Ishiwara Kanji.[68] But after Pearl Harbor and the shift in ideology to emphasize the war as a war against modernity, the league approach began to lose influence to the corporatists, who had an easier time connecting their image of a new East Asian *minzoku* with the effort to overcome modernity and its emphasis on the state as the privileged unit of modern political life. But the debate continued down to the end of the war, preventing any final consensus on a nationality policy for the empire.

The unresolved tensions between these two approaches informed the massive "A Study of Global Policy with the Yamato *Volk* as the Core" composed in 1943 by bureaucrats in the Ministry of Social Welfare's Research Office Department of Population and Nationality. The report reflected the same tensions that existed in the broader public discourse on *minzoku* which pitted Takata's new, single East Asia *Volk* against Kamei's vision of a Greater East Asia Co-Prosperity Sphere

---

66   Nakano, p. 54.

67   For a more detailed treatment of Nakano's ethnic nationality policy, see my chapter on "Nakano Seiichi and Colonial Ethnic Studies" in Akitoshi Shimizu and Jan van Bremen, eds., *Wartime Japanese Anthropology in Asia and the Pacific*, Senri Ethnological Studies no. 65 (2003): pp. 109–129.

68   On the East Asian League (*Tōa remmei*) and the East Asian corporatist (*Tōa kyōdōtai*) approaches to nationalism in the empire, see my chapter on "The Concept of Ethnic Nationality and its Role in Pan-Asianism in Imperial Japan" in Sven Saaler and J. Victor Koschmann, eds., *Pan-Asianism in Modern Japanese History* (London and New York: Routledge, 2006).

built around the particular ethnic identities in the region.[69] In the end, wracked with internal contradictions and multi-vocal arguments, the report could only conclude that the Japanese state needed to establish a nationality policy that would bring these various *minzoku* into an organic unity.[70] Yet, there was to be no reconciliation of these two approaches. In a sense, the failure to establish a nationality policy was most likely the result of intractable differences of opinion within the department over what a *minzoku* is and how far it could be molded into something new. But, at the same time, it may simply be that these bureaucrats found themselves confronted with the fundamental problem of Asian regionalism, as Yamamuro Shin'ichi has expressed it: the impossible dilemma of trying to hammer unity out of the plurality that has always been the reality of Asia.[71]

Minzoku and the Postwar Nation

It is often assumed that the devastation of Japan's cities in the final years of the war and the humiliation of defeat and occupation cleansed the Japanese people of any attraction to nationalism. Alternatively, it is claimed that during the seven years of military occupation, certainly during the early stages, any overt expression of nationalism was censored or punished by SCAP. Evidence offered in support of this view is principally the ease of the Occupation and the rarity of any retaliatory attack on the foreign soldiers in Japan. Nationalism must have been worn out by the long war, it is presumed, or there would have been more resistance to the Occupation. Nothing could be further from the truth. There was a wide ranging and very public expression of nationalism from the immediate postwar days throughout and beyond the period of occupation, and it came from all points on the political spectrum: right, left and center. Why did occupation officials allow this open expression of nationalism? Why have so many historians of Japan in the past failed to recognize the vigorous nationalism in the early postwar period? And how has this failure to recognize and restrain nationalism during the years of occupation subsequently shaped the political discourse on national identity and nationalism throughout the postwar period?

To understand why a free expression of nationalism was permitted under military occupation, it is necessary first to recognize that appeals to *minzoku* and *minzokushugi* are indeed forms of nationalism. The most common expression of nationalism in the immediate postwar period was made in *minzoku* terms. American observers of Japanese political thought from the occupation period up until quite recently have not always understood that appeals to the *minzoku* were inherently forms of nationalism; instead they have often swept the problem of *minzoku* under the rug of "race." This tendency to believe that a reference to the Japanese *minzoku* identity was simply a de-politicized (if somewhat morally disreputable) way of referring to race was encouraged by anthropological studies of the Japanese, the most important of which was Ruth Benedict's *Chrysanthemum and the*

---

69   Indeed, one section of the report urges cultural assimilation of other East Asian *Völker* by Japan, *Yamato minzoku* ☒ *chūkaku to suru sekai seisaku no kentō* 7, 2351; another section argues against any single policy for all the *Völker* of Asia, and particularly warns that assimilation efforts would merely cause a backlash against the Japanese (7, 2364–5). On the public debate between proponents of a single *Tōa minzoku* and those who insisted on a plural interpretation of *Tōa (sho-)minzoku*, see my "Narrating China, Ordering East Asia," 102–105, 112, n. 57. It is easy to suspect Kamei's hand behind the anti-assimilation sections of the report, due to his influence in governmental circles, familiarity and support for Nazi nationality theories, and the parallels in the report's arguments and in Kamei's published works.

70   *Yamato minzoku o chūkaku to suru sekai seisaku no kentō* 7, 2197.

71   Yamamuro Shin'ichi, "'Ta ni shite ichi' no chitsujo genri to Nihon no sentaku" In Aoki Tamotsu and Saeki Keishi, eds., *'Ajia-teki kachi' to wa nani ka* (Tokyo: TBS-Britannica, 1998).,43–64

Sword, a work widely read among occupation officials and even translated into Japanese as early as 1948.[72] In short, there was a curious kind of mirror-effect, in which Americans who had been encouraged during the war to view the Japanese as a "race" different from themselves, reflected their own racial interpretation of the Japanese onto discussions of *minzoku* identity among the Japanese. The irony was that the postwar Japanese were not talking about race as the Americans understood it, of course, but were continuing a discourse on nationalism that had been quite vibrant during the wartime and prewar years. But in seeing this discourse as one about "race" rather than about nationalism, American Occupation officials could easily conclude that it was a politically harmless, if somewhat distasteful, topic for Japanese intellectuals to indulge. The imperial Japanese discourse on *minzoku* that separated *minzoku* claims from the right to an independent state only augmented this predilection for seeing *minzoku* discourse as politically harmless.

There were also structural reasons for the resurgence of *minzoku* discourse in the immediate postwar years. Oguma Eiji has summarized the structural changes that made *minzoku* so attractive after the war. As he points out, a key condition for the rise of this myth of *minzoku* identity was the transformation of Japan from the multi-ethnic Meiji Imperial State to a mono-ethnic nation through the process of de-imperialization. In short, the "liberation" of such territories as Taiwan and Korea from the Japanese empire meant that the claims of ethnic nationalism there now resonated with a sense of ethnic purity within Japan. Koreans and Taiwanese were no longer automatically "subjects" or citizens of the Japanese nation (Okinawans were not to be Japanese again until 1972), and this ethnic cleansing of the empire encouraged among the Japanese people a sense of being a mono-ethnic nation. Moreover, drawing from both prewar Marxist and liberal theories that idealized the *minzoku* and criticized the state, this early postwar *minzoku* nationalism found it easy to imagine the *minzoku* as a peaceful nation in contrast to the prewar, militaristic, multi-ethnic state.[73] And, equally important, the earlier liberal distinction between the nation as *minzoku* and the state (*kokka*) provided a sense of legitimate national identity through *minzoku* for the seven years of foreign occupation when an independent Japanese state did not exist. The theoretical distinction between nation and state seemed to be borne out by the political realities of occupied Japan.

One of the most remarkable continuities between wartime and postwar Japan is the way this *minzoku* discourse continued on, unchallenged by either occupation officials or by liberal or leftist Japanese. In recent years, Nishikawa Nagao described the spell *minzoku* has continued to have over the Japanese people as the preferred form of national identity, even while they have largely distanced themselves from the state.[74] It may be tempting to conclude that this continuity, one of many historians have depicted across the prewar–postwar divide, represents the retention of rightwing, even "fascist," elements in postwar democratic Japan. Yet, on closer inspection, the continuity in *minzoku* discourse proves to be, not an exclusively or even largely conservative ideology, but also an extension of the liberal and leftist *minzoku* discourse of the prewar period. Certainly, rightwing ethnic nationalists tried to express their views, but they had the most difficulty getting their ethnic nationalism in print under the occupation. It was not their ethnic nationalism that raised objections, but simply their identities, past associations with wartime pro-government parties, or other extraneous, often personal, reasons that led them to be blacklisted by the occupation

---

72   Aoki Tamotsu, '*Nihon bunka ron' no hen'yō* (Tokyo: Chūō Kōron Shinsha, 1999), 31.

73   Oguma, *Tan'itsu minzoku shinwa no kigen*, 339–40.

74   Nishikawa Nagao, "Two Interpretations of Japanese Culture," (trans. Mikiko Murata and Gavan McCormack) in *Multicultural Japan*, 247–8.

censors. Kageyama Masaharu has detailed was he sees as a history of oppression that "rightwing" ethnic nationalists suffered at the hands of the occupying forces.[75] But he also points out that, as a rightwing ethnic nationalist, he took considerable solace in reading the nationalist appeal of the Christian Yanaihara Tadao that was permitted to appear in the pages of the leftist journal *Sekai* (although Kageyama distanced himself from Yanaihara's Christianity).[76] While the extreme right was prevented from expressing their views through the occupation censors, *minzoku* nationalism was able to thrive through liberals and leftists who led the way in rehabilitating it in the context of post-imperial, occupied Japan.

One of the earliest instances of *minzoku* nationalism in the postwar period was a lecture given on 11 February 1946 by Nanbara Shigeru, president of Tokyo University. Nanbara was an expert on Fichte, and he drew on his knowledge of Fichte in his speech on the "Creation of a New Japanese Culture" in arguing that the *minzoku* is "the site for the creation of the spirit of freedom." The war and all the horrible things Japanese had done to others—and had been victims of themselves—all this could be laid at the feet of the state. States go to war, but *minzoku* were just people, and people were by nature peaceful. Nanbara may have drawn inspiration from Fichte, but he was also implicitly rehashing arguments that had been raised under Wilsonian idealism around the time of the First World War: the hope that if the world map were only redrawn along the lines of ethnic nationalism, true world peace might be attained at last. Nambara's investment in this *minzoku* form of national identity, and his belief that such a national identity would be the foundation for a more just postwar world order is evident in his statement that, "although our *minzoku* has made mistakes, we nonetheless rejoice that we were born into this *minzoku* and we have unending love for this *minzoku*. It is precisely for that reason that we seek to punish our *minzoku* ourselves and so recover its honor before the world."[77] When the president of Tokyo University makes such an appeal to the concept of *minzoku*, others are bound to follow. And follow they did. But what is most striking about the flood of articles and books on *minzoku* nationalism in the early postwar period is that it came largely from liberals and leftists, not from rightwing nationalists like Kageyama.

Nanbara's 1946 speech may have signaled that it was socially and politically acceptable to discuss *minzoku* identity in postwar Japan. But it was Shimmei Masamichi's 1949 *Theory of Historical Minzoku* that provided the clearest connection to prewar and wartime *minzoku* discourse, while at the same time charting the future direction for many *minzoku* theories. Shimmei of course was an active *minzoku* theorist during the wartime: he was one of the contributors to the 1939 *Minzoku and War* volume discussed above. Indeed, the chapters of his 1949 book had been composed originally as lectures given at Tōhoku Imperial University between 1943 and 1945. As such, they provide *ipso facto* evidence of the transwar nature of this *minzoku* discourse. But they also allow us to see how the ideas of the earlier liberal theorists were used, not only to legitimate Japanese imperialism, but after the war to provide a foundation for a Japanese national identity in the absence of a state. Shimmei not only built his argument on wartime Japanese theorists like Takata Yasuma, Komatsu Kentarō and Kōsaka Masa'aki; he also went back to the liberal theorists Hobson, Muir and McDougall to emphasize that the core of national identity lies in this sociological sense of community forged through such elements as a common language, historical experience, and shared

---

75 Kageyama Masaharu, *Senryōka no minzoku-ha: dan'atsu to chōkoku no shōgen* (Tokyo: Nihon Kyōbunsha, 1979).

76 Kageyama, 103–8.

77 Nanbara Shigeru, cited in Oguma, *Minshu to aikoku: sengo nihon no nashonarizumu to kōkyōsei* (Tokyo: Shin'yōsha, 2002): 139

fate.[78] Like the liberal theorists after World War I, he emphasized the importance of the sentiment of the people as determining whether or not they constituted a nation (*minzoku*). And like them, too, he also drew a sharp distinction between race, nation, and the state.

In the two and a half years since the end of the war (the book was written in early 1948), Shimmei had time to consider how these ideas about the nation, articulated during the wartime empire, applied to Japan's new situation as an occupied people. In revising the context and significance of his argument—if not the literal terms he employed—he was able to apply his earlier argument that *minzoku*, which captured the essence of a society and did not depend on the political form of the state for its existence, was the key form of national identity. As during the war, however, the relationship of *minzoku* to the state remained of crucial importance:

> Yet, while it is true that the state has an intimate role in the establishment of a nation (*minzoku*), it is not necessarily correct to think that the state precedes the nation and creates it. ... The nation does not always depend on the state to create it, but may be thought of as coming into being in a spontaneous form. Of course, as the state's political unification progresses, the nation's formation will also progress necessarily. ... But rather than saying this is the creation of the nation, it is better to understand this process as the completion of the nation. In this sense, the state is not the creator of the nation but that which fosters the nation. ... In this way, the nation may be called a *Kulturnation* (*bunka minzoku*). But the fact that the *Kulturnation* is fully established apolitically, without any direct mediation by political unification, is sufficient proof that the political unification of the state does not necessarily constitute an absolute precondition for the nation.[79]

Shimmei's was a nuanced argument with high stakes for postwar nationalism, and it deserves a careful reading. He explicitly termed his theory of the nation a "historical one", thus aligning it ostensibly with the earlier Marxist theories of the nation that reduced the nation to historical determinism. But his ultimate objective was in asserting a sense of the nation, rooted in *minzoku*, as the real foundation of national identity. Here he found an unexpected bonanza in imperialist national theory. During the empire, the theory that *minzoku* was the essence of national identity was offered to deny subjected peoples their own independent state. But now it was re-packaged as proof that the Japanese had not lost their nation and national identity, even though they had no state of their own.[80]

Shimmei's postwar ethnic nationalism provides telling evidence of a continuity between wartime and postwar efforts to place the people as an ethnic nation that was distinct from—indeed substituted for—an independent political state. His argument is a powerful articulation of a conclusion that many others had come to in the early postwar years, even those who had to revise much of their wartime theories to make them fit Japan's new circumstances. A key example of such a revisionist is Wakamori Tarō. Wakamori was an active participant in the wartime ethnological discourse associated with Takata Yasuma, Oka Masao and others. In 1942, he legitimated Japanese imperialism

---

78   Shimmei Masamichi, *Shi-teki minzoku riron* (Tokyo: Iwasaki Shoten, 1949): 36–68.

79   Shimmei, *Shi-teki minzoku riron*, 55–6.

80   For a different view of the relationship of state and nation in Shimmei's work, see Fujita Kunihiko, "Senjika nihon ni okeru kuni no hon'shitsu," *Senjika no nihon*, 61–79, esp, 67–68. I am not able to tell whether Fujita's conclusion (that the state and nation were always connected) is due to his prior theoretical conviction or whether it is because he relies on a 1980 anthologized version of Shimmei's *Shi-teki minzoku riron*.

in China with an argument that the Chinese people traditionally did not invest their nationality in a political state as the Japanese did. But in his *Theory of the Japanese Minzoku* published in 1947—when Japan no longer had an independent state to boast of—he reversed himself, arguing that any national identity promoted by or invested in a state was inauthentic. And to give context to this anti-statist *minzoku* nationalism, he added that it was Westerners—not the Japanese themselves—who seemed unable to understand the difference between Japan's true nationality based in ethnic culture and the false national identity propped up by the state.[81] Wakamori's revisionism did not stop there. He laid the foundations for a particular brand of conservative ethnic nationalism that asserted a moral difference in the two sets of characters used to write the word *minzoku* (民族、民俗), with preference going to the latter set. Wakamori thus was one of the earliest ethnologists to argue that there was a similar distinction between an acceptable form of "folklore," associated with Yanagita Kunio, that was derived from this preferred *minzoku* called *minzokugaku* (民俗学) and that was morally superior to the old, discredited wartime ethnology (民族学). The problem with Wakamori's revisionist effort was that Yanagita himself rejected such orthographic distinctions, arguing that all *minzoku* referred to ethnicity and thus preferring himself the characters (民族) to capture the subject of his ethnological studies.[82] Yanagita's epigones have uniformly ignored his warning on this point, and a postwar discourse of *minzokugaku* (民俗学) continues to this day to promote a form of ethnic national identity that masquerades as merely "folklore."

Shimmei's historical approach to *minzoku* was significant for another reason. Even as Wakamori was joined by wartime ethnologists Oka Masao, Ishida Eiichirō, Egami Namio and others in asserting a new national identity determined by ethnic culture, Marxists were re-asserting their historically determined *minzoku* theories that had been silenced for ten years during the war. Although Shimmei did not join with them, his effort to present his theory as a "historical" one testified to the prestige that the Marxist *minzoku* theories enjoyed in the early postwar years. Kubokawa Tsurujirō was one of the first of the Marxists scholars to revive the prewar leftist ethnic nationalism in the postwar period. His 1948 *Literature, Thought, Life* was, like Shimmei's book, a republication of earlier work, essays that first had been written between 1936 and 1941 and published in earlier volumes that had appeared in 1940 and 1942. Kubokawa had been a member of the Communist Party until his conversion to nationalism in 1933, and he was most active as a literary critic from then until the end of the war. In 1945, he rejoined the Communist Party and played a leading role in the New Japanese Literature group. His experience, both in converting to nationalism and then back to Communism in the postwar period gave him an unusually flexible perspective on ethnic nationalism.

Kubokawa was critical of *minzoku* cultural theories in the early postwar period because he saw how liberals and conservatives were embracing *minzoku* culture as a surrogate for the political state, when his own goal was political independence from the American-led occupation. Given the employment of *minzoku* culture during Imperial Japan as a tool for preventing political independence of nations within the Japanese empire, it is not surprising that he would argue that

the danger of Japan being colonized today comes from nothing but a spirit of anti-foreignism and ethnic nationalism. The reason is that ethnic nationalism and anti-foreignism

---

81   Wakamori Tarō, *Nihon minzoku ron* (Tokyo: Chiyoda Shobō, 1947); cited in my "Building National Identity through Ethnicity: Ethnology in Wartime Japan and After," at 33–34.

82   Yanagita Kunio, "Minzokugaku kara minzokugaku e: Nihon minzokugaku no ashiato o kaerimite," *Minzokugaku kenkyū* 14:3 (February 1950): 1; cited in my "Building National Identity through Ethnicity," 34.

are, as we all know, simply tools by which a certain group enslaves the people for their own interests. But the present danger of being colonized also arises because a certain group pursues its own interests by sacrificing the people, and through subordination, seeks to rely on a foreign country.[83]

Drawing from his knowledge of how *minzoku* was used in the imperial period as a cultural substitution for political independence by Japan's colonies, Kubokawa was working toward a theory of internal colonization that would explain how some Japanese elites had betrayed the Japanese people through a similar ideology of *minzoku* as a substitution for political independence from the United States. The key point is that he did not reject ethnic nationalism *ipso facto* but was merely critical of its exploitation by certain elites who sought to prevent its inherent goal: political independence. The larger point of Kubokawa's argument reveals that he was not opposed to all forms of anti-foreignism (here, his complaint seems directed at those wary of Soviet influence in the Communist Party of Japan). In his short essay on "The Conditions of Ethnic National Culture", Kubokawa decried, not so much ethnic appropriations of national identity, but the "formalistic" and "abstract" nature of ethnic nationalism that left it devoid of any significant response to the demands of the day. In language quite reminiscent of Kōsaka, he argued that this national theory should not be rejected but merely needed to be articulated in "world historical," rather than in particularistic, terms.[84]

Kubokawa wrote as a literary critic for literary scholars. But his call for a more "historical" approach to *minzoku* that would connect ethnic national culture to a critique of anti-colonization directed at the United States was answered by leading members of Japan's historical profession. These historians were mostly Stalinists affiliated with the Japan Communist Party, the Party that had just announced a series of positions at its Sixth Conference that included a commitment to ethnic national independence (*minzoku dokuritsu*). While party members presented this turn to ethnic nationalism as a response to the Occupation of Japan by the capitalist side of the Cold War, it is clear from Curtis Gayle's recent work that this appeal to *minzoku* could not be divorced from the prewar Marxist *minzoku* discourse that had been derailed during the wartime.[85] Of course, there were difference emphases. There were, to start with, differences of context: the postwar Marxist historians benefited from a more open society, from a retrospective sense throughout society that the war was morally wrong and thus everyone who opposed it (Marxists figured prominently) were moral heroes, and from the affront of military occupation to national dignity. Thus, one finds a resounding theme in Marxist historical writing from the late 1940s through the early 1950s that emphasized interpreting the Japanese people as an ethnic nation oppressed by their own imperial state, betrayed by their postwar elites, and crushed under the rule of foreign military occupation. Ishimoda Shō, Toma Seita and Matsumoto Shinpachirō were leaders in the "*minzoku* faction" of Marxist history, but the influence of *minzoku* as a way of conceptualizing the Japanese people was broadly and deeply felt: the 1951 and 1952 annual meetings of the Japan Historiographical Research Association were focused on the problem of

---

83   Kubokawa Tsurujirō, *Bungaku shisō seikatsu* (Tokyo: Shinseisha, 1948): 241–2.

84   Kubokawa, 26.

85   Curtis Gayle, *Marxist History and Postwar Japanese Nationalism* (London and New York: RoutledgeCurzon, 2003): 52–57.

minzoku as the true subject of national history.[86] Leftist historians all agreed that the *minzoku* was "a product of history" but beyond that formulaic expression there was little agreement as to how far back in history its origins were to be found. Ishimoda's "*minzoku* faction" sought to explain that historical production internally, as a precapitalist, organic development going all the way back. In contrast, Inoue Kiyoshi, Eguchi Bokurō and Tōyama Shigeki's "modernization faction" argued that the Japanese *minzoku* was a product of capitalism and the advent of the West in the mid-nineteenth century.[87] In spite of this difference, both wings of the Marxist *minzoku* movement shared a negative view of modernity, seeing postwar history not as a liberation of the nation from fascism, but as only further ensconcing the people in fascism under liberal democratic cover.[88]

The Left was not the only part of the political spectrum in postwar Japan that was outraged at foreign occupation and that turned to *minzoku* as the preferred form of nationalism. Conservative ethnic nationalists who had been prominent during the war were often silenced by occupation censorship, but some continued to write under pseudonyms. Yasuda Yojūrō, one of the most influential of this group, was purged in 1948. Yet, he continued to find ways to express himself: in print through poetry and essays published under other names, and in social gatherings where he influenced the thinking of fellow conservatives who were not purged. Yasuda's influence was especially pronounced in the journal *Sokoku* (1949–55). During this period, he found various ways to present his argument that the Japanese *minzoku*, an agrarian people, had remained largely unchanged in their commitment to ways and mores that were distinctive from the Western forms of life introduced during and after the Meiji Restoration.[89] In curious ways, Yasuda's conservative ethnic nationalism echoed aspects of the ethnic nationalism of the leftist historians: an appeal to Asia as an alternative to the modernity promoted by the occupation, a sense that *minzoku* was a preferred alternative social identity to that of citizenship in the postwar liberal state, and a romantic appeal to pacifism as grounded in Asia as the "third way" beyond the Cold War polarities of the United States and the Soviet Union.

Of course, there were serious political differences that separated Yasuda from the likes of Ishimoda and Inoue. But even within their appeal to ethnic nationalism, there were significant differences. While the leftwing ethnic nationalists intoned Asianism and a critique of modernity, what they meant by "Asia" was a political principle of resistance to capitalist imperialism and what they meant by "modernity" was simply bourgeois class culture. In contrast, to Yasuda "Asia" was a thoode of being prior to and outside of modernity, and by "modernity" he meant the entire culture of the world as he

---

86   Doak, "What is a Nation and Who Belongs? National Narratives and the Ethnic Imagination in Twentieth-Century Japan," at 302–3.

87   Gayle, *Marxist History and Postwar Japanese Nationalism*, 86–87. Gayle quite correctly notes the similarity between Ishimoda's faction and the primordialism of Anthony D. Smith's theory on the historical origins of ethnic nations. One might also add that Inoue and the "modernization faction" reflect arguments on the connection between modern capitalism and national formation that have been raised more recently by Benedict Anderson and Ernest Gellner.

88   Cf. Kubokawa, "Here I believe is the essence of this tendency that, in contrast to the fascism of militarism we had in the past, now spreads fascism under the name of "democracy ... our only true way to live is to make every effort to protect the peace, freedom and independence of Japan from the dangers of a new fascism and war; I believe that is the only way we can discover the true historical image of Japan at this current moment." *Bungaku shisō seikatsu*, 242.

89   The best summary of Yasuda's postwar ethnic nationalism is Oketani Hideaki, *Yasuda Yojūrō* (Tokyo: Kōdansha, 1996), 136–217.

experienced it in his day. Modernity included the United States, Japan, the Soviet Union, and the communism of Mao Zedong. Perhaps because of the depth of Yasuda's anti-modernity at a time when much of Japanese society was convulsed with celebrations of modernity, his writings (even after he was freed from censorship) never garnered the attention and influence of his wartime work. But he remained one key anchor of conservative, anti-state *minzoku* nationalism for many postwar intellectuals.

Yasuda's influence was also diminished by the attack on him by Marxists and other leftists in the immediate postwar period. His high school classmate and friend Takeuchi Yoshimi was able to avoid criticism for "war responsibility" and bring to the public's attention many of Yasuda's ideas about Asia and ethnic nationalism. As a Sinologist, Takeuchi saw Asia less as a projection of Japan's own resistance against the West, and more in terms of China as both victim of Japanese aggression and as offering a way outside of modernity (which he equated with Westernization). But even for Takeuchi, the core of this alternative to modernity was, as imperialists had argued during the war, the national concept of *minzoku* as an alternative to the modern state. Takeuchi's first impulse was to resist the postwar modernists who sought to move beyond ethnic nationality and invest Japanese national identity in the new postwar sovereign nation-state. In his 1951 essay on "Modernism and the Problem of the Ethnic Nation," he argued against the notion that Yasuda and the Romantic School were responsible for everything that was wrong with the war. While he explicitly decried the invasion of China and other parts of Asia, he celebrated the Pacific theater as a war against the West and suggested that postwar Japan should be built on a *minzoku* consciousness as the foundation for a pan-Asian, anti-Western regionalism. Many aspects of Takeuchi's embrace of ethnic nationalism make him easy to confuse with the Marxist ethnic nationalists: especially, his critique of modernity, his expressed solidarity with "Asia", and his antipathy toward the American Occupation. The belief that he was really on "the left" was encouraged further by his 1959 essay "Overcoming Modernity" which was seen as providing a rationale for the "progressive" riots against the LDP and the United States over the handling of the revision of the US-Japan Security Treaty (*Anpo*) in 1960. Here, "the left" really meant those who were "anti-America." But, regardless of whether one characterized the *Anpo* riots as "leftist" (and there is ample evidence of participation by those on both ends of the political spectrum), Takeuchi was no Marxist (he included Marxism in the modernity that he rejected) and was in fact politically and personally close to Yasuda and the conservative ethnic nationalist movement.

The decade of the 1960s saw the rise of populism in Japan, as elsewhere, and this populism had a decisive if complex impact on *minzoku* nationalism. As mentioned above in Chapter Five, as a resurgent state tried to regain the people's respect and allegiance under Prime Minister Ikeda's economism and income-doubling plan, rising affluence and an assertive youth culture combined with the protest culture to make the relationship between state and *minzoku* a more estranged one. Takashima Zen'ya is perhaps the best example of how the 1960s transformed the debate over *minzoku*. In a series of articles and books, most notably his 1970 *Minzoku and Class*, Takashima offered a new theory that would synthesize the Stalinist approach of Ishimoda with liberal *minzoku* theories of Watsuji Tetsurō and Imanaka Tsugimaro and the conservative nationalism of Hayashi Fusao and Mishima Yukio. To Takashima, the key point in understanding Japanese nationalism was the distinction between state and nation. Nationalism held that the nation was the purpose of the state's existence, and by "nation" Takashima really meant the *minzoku* conceived as a natural mode of existence prior to the institutions of politics and culture. His pet formula was "*minzoku* as mother, class as master" (*botai to shite no minzoku, shutai to shite no kaikyū*).[90] Takashima explained that *"minzoku* as mother" was a literary expression (a gesture toward conservative literary nationalists like Takeuchi Yoshimi, Mishima Yukio and Hayashi Fusao?) and "class as master"(or "subject") was a philosophical expression (a gesture toward Marxists like Ishimoda, Inoue and Eguchi?). The precise meaning of Takashima's poetic argument is elusive, but as metaphor it quite clearly was attempting a synthesis of *minzoku* theories as well as a synthesis of the nation itself that had split between right-wing and left-wing ethnic nationalists. Significantly, Takashima saw class as a sub-category of *minzoku*, emphasizing that the bourgeoisie and the proletariat were equally members of the Japanese *minzoku* and each had valuable contributions to make to the *minzoku*. Takashima's goal was a laudable one. He argued that by first separating nation (*minzoku*) from the state, the crisis that confronted Japanese nationalism could be resolved by building a civil society that would tame the state to serve its own purposes. But his democratic theory was fatally flawed by his equation of the nation with an ethnic body and by his dismissal of *kokumin* as a national identity that was not moored to the natural claims of ethnicity. Rather than to democracy, his national theory brought him closer to national socialism.

National socialism, even understood as ethnic nationalism in proletariat packaging, remained marginal to postwar Japanese political culture. In part, this was because *minzoku* was increasingly discussed in isolation from the state, as a form of *Nihonjinron* that sought to imbue the Japanese people with a distinctive identity not determined by what was seen as a bureaucratic postwar state run by the LDP for their American masters. As the postwar state receded into managerial and technological bureaucratism, national identity, if not quite nationalism, became even more closely associated with *minzoku*. But *minzoku* was increasingly intoned as an ostensibly benign cultural theory of how the people in Japan really are: their identities, values and traditions. As Peter Dale has summarized it,

> the curious thing about the *nihonjinron* is that while they express, beneath a bewilderingly diverse range of ideas, a coherent ideology of nationalism, they at the same time deny that they have anything to do with ideology or politics. A key theme of the literature distinguishes the ostensibly ideological, power-fixated character of Western discourse from the putatively aesthetic and sentimental expressionism of the Japanese. ... Postwar *nihonjinron* merely attempts to salvage this discourse [of prewar nationalism] by detaching it from the more overly imperial-political idiom.[91]

If Takashima had hoped to move *minzoku* away from political theory toward a more culturally inflected nationalism, he had succeeded in ways he surely had not intended. The relationship this cultural theory had to nationalism may not always have been clear, but *minzoku* certainly had retreated from the kind of overtly political stance that leftists like Ishimoda and Inoue, or conservatives like Yasuda and Hayashi, or liberals like Yanaihara or Nanbara, had given it in the early postwar period. It provided the people with a coherent identity of a people set apart, but the degree of identity thus achieved was also a measure of its distance from the institutions and organizations that shaped political life. Nation and state were indeed separate and distinct.

By the early 1980s, nationalism had left the realm of ideas and intellectuals and was becoming a central concern of mainstream politicians. This "neo-nationalism" has often been attributed

---

90   Takashima Zen'ya, *Minzoku to kaikyū* (Tokyo: Gendai hyōronsha, 1970): 29–53.

91   Peter N. Dale, *The Myth of Japanese Uniqueness* (New York: St. Martin's Press, 1986), 38–39.

both to Japan's rising economic prosperity and to increasing frictions with Japan's major trading partners, notably the United States. But personalities played a role too. The most important individual in reviving a political theory of *minzoku* was Nakasone Yasuhiro. When Nakasone became prime minister in 1982, he brought with him the long aspirations of the Democratic wing of the LDP to overturn the "abnormal" nationalism of Yoshida Shigeru and the Liberal faction's emphasis on mercantilism as a sufficient national purpose for postwar Japan. At an LDP seminar in Shizuoka in 1986, Nakasone proposed a new "liberal" nationalism that would reconcile the people with the postwar state. Tragically, he articulated this project the following year as the need to "reconcile internationalism with correct nationalism" which he explicitly identified with *minzokushugi*.[92] Nakasone's emphasis on ethnic nationalism as the "correct" or "healthy" form of nationalism, along with a series of pronouncements on Japan's ethnic homogeneity, offended those Japanese who had begun to think beyond ethnic nationalism, as well as many who simply were not ready to see their ethnic national identity associated by political elites with the postwar state. To simply write off Nakasone as an ethnic nationalist is to miss a good deal of what he was trying to achieve. He was one of those postwar Japanese political elites who, as Kenneth Pyle noted a few years after the controversy, "more often seek to contain, if not to suppress, political nationalism."[93] Nakasone was trying to associate the appeal the Japanese people felt for a cultural theory of ethnicity with the state so that the Japanese state might be able to act more resolutely, with broader popular support, in the international arena. This project of reconciling the ethnic nation and the state was a good part of his much ballyhooed "final accounting" of the postwar period. That he confused ethnic nationalism with liberal nationalism is easy to understand, given the long history in Japanese political discourse, dating back to the First World War, that sought to embrace ethnic nationalism for liberal and even Marxist agendas. That his effort to reconcile the ethnic nation with the state met with such stiff resistance tells us as much about Japanese attitudes toward the state as it does about antipathy toward ethnic nationalism.

By the turn of the century, support for ethnic nationalism by the Japanese public, as well as among intellectuals, was fading. This turn of events is surprising, especially since nationalism was a growing feature of intellectual and political discourse. Part of the reason for this new devaluation of ethnic nationalism can be attributed to the shock effect of seeing a leader of the postwar democratic state reverting to a discourse that was deeply implicated in the wartime empire (many critics immediately brought up Nakasone's wartime connections with the imperial state). Another part of the reason, however, can be attributed to the fall of the Soviet Union in 1991 and the general demise of Marxism around the world that followed in its wake. The two main supports of postwar ethnic nationalism—a Marxist theory that found in ethnicity a foundation for an anti-capitalist nationalism and conservatives who had accepted ethnicity as a pacifist substitute for a nationality invested in the postwar state—had been seriously undermined. But ethnic nationalism was not only falling of its own accord. Increasingly, it was being challenged by an alternative nationalism, a liberal nationalism that was grounded in political membership in the postwar state and which was more concerned with integrating the people's loyalties into the state than with proclaiming their ancient ethnic lineages. This new nationalism (*kokuminshugi*) did not always escape the tugs of ethnicity, especially when articulated by older intellectuals who had been influenced by the

---

92   Nakasone Yasuhiro, "Minzokushugi to kokusaishugi no chōwa o," *Gekkan jiyū minshu* (October 1987): 44–61, at 44–45.

93   Kenneth B. Pyle, *The Japanese Question: Power and Purpose in a New Era* (Washington, D.C.: The AEI Press, 1992): 63.

postwar *minzoku* discourse.[94] Yet, the very fact that this neo-nationalism more often preferred to be known as *kokuminshugi* rather than *minzokushugi* is a significant departure from the dominant appeal enjoyed by ethnic nationalism in Japan for most of the twentieth century. How significant this change will be for the future of Japanese nationalism, and whether ethnic nationalism will eventually give way to a more civic nationalism, only time will tell.

---

94   Representative of this rising *kokuminshugi* which, alas, did not always escape from elements of ethnic nationalism is Matsumoto Ken'ichi, '*Hinomaru, kimigayo*' *no hanashi* (Tokyo: PHP Kenkyūjo, 1999).

THE NATIONALIST MOVEMENT
BEFORE 1931

Richard Storry

I N his published lecture on Japanese Fascism[1] Professor Maruyama of Tokyo University suggests that for the beginning of what he describes as the preparatory period of fascism, lasting up to the Manchurian Incident, we need look back no further than 1919. "It was in 1919–20 and thereafter that we have the rapid development of near-fascist groups. The *Genyosha* and *Kokuryukai* may be regarded as exceptions."[2]

Up to about 1920, indeed, the number of extremist organisations was small by comparison with the multitude of such groups which came into being in the years that followed. The early societies, despite some pretended concern for the issue of "popular rights", were chiefly interested in the overseas expansion of Japan. They were composed of samurai, mainly from Kyushu, who had failed to adjust themselves to the revolutionary effects, in every field, of the introduction of Western thought and techniques. After the collapse of the Shogunate the more rabid patriots discovered that the new government, while dangerously bold in the application of disturbing innovations at home, was reluctant to embark on an immediate campaign of expansion abroad. Dissatisfaction led to a series of revolts, of which Saigo's in 1877 was the culmination. The energy of the irreconcilables among the survivors of these rebellions found an outlet in the early nationalist societies, notably the *Genyosha*.

The *Gényosha* was founded in 1881 in the town of Fukuoka by Hiraoka Kotaro, a mine-owner and former samurai who had taken part in the Saigo Rebellion.[3] The name of the society was taken from the *Genkai nada*, the "Black Sea Straits" between Kyushu and Korea. The society was an

---

1 *Nippon Fasshizmu no Shiso to Undo* ("The Movement and Thought of Japanese Fascism") in a collection called *Sonjo Shiso to Zettai shugi* ("*Sonno joi'* Thought and Absolutism") (Tokyo University, Toyo Bunka Kenkyujo, Hakujitsu Shoin, 1948).

2 *Ibid.*, p. 104.

3 *Vide* E. H. Norman, "The Genyosha" (*Pacific Affairs*, Vol. XVII, No. 3, September, 1944). Dr. Norman's study is based on Japanese language material, particularly the *Genyosha sha-shi*, the society's history published by the society in Tokyo, 1917,

amalgamation of certain existing patriotic associations in Fukuoka and never lost a characteristic Kyushu flavour; its leaders were invariably natives of Fukuoka, which was notorious, like the Mito district north-east of Tokyo, for extremely violent nationalist feeling. Spiritually the *Genyosha* was heir to the ideas of the dead Saigo, who had pressed for an invasion of Korea and whose revolt had been an attempt to rescue the Imperial House from "unfaithful ministers."

The declared aims of the society were three: "to revere the Imperial Family"; "to respect and honour the fatherland"; "to guard strictly the rights of the people." The last suggests that the *Genyosha* was concerned with the *Minken ron* (advocacy of people's rights) which was the war-cry of such political figures as Itagaki Taisuke and Goto Shojiro in their agitation for an elected national assembly. The *Genyosha*, of course, was scarcely interested in any principle of political democracy as understood in the West. The inclusion of "people's rights," however, among its original aims was not entirely opportunistic or insincere. The *Genyosha* ideal—Japanese expansion overseas—was popular; and opposition to it came from conservative realists, who appreciated that time was needed for the country to build up adequate industrial capacity before an aggressive foreign policy, with the risk of war, could be undertaken.[4] An intense national consciousness was growing fast, due largely to the introduction, in 1872, of compulsory elementary education with its rigorous inculcation of patriotic ethics. An increasingly literate public sought not only the right of suffrage but also international recognition of their country as a leading power in Asia.

The *Genyosha* was a terrorist organisation, and a school for spies. It made no attempt to become a political party, to be represented in due course in a national parliament. Its membership remained small, and its participation in home politics was characterised by its rôle in the General Election of 1892. The leaders of the *Genyosha* were assured by the Matsukata cabinet that the administration would pursue a strong foreign policy and greatly increase the budget for the armed forces. Accordingly the society exerted itself to terrorise anti-government candidates in the Fukuoka area. Shinagawa Yajiro, the Home Minister, had instructed the police to intervene actively on the side of the government in the Election, which was conducted with considerable bloodshed.[5] This unofficial agreement between the Home Minister and the *Genyosha* is of interest; for it was the first notable example of the close, unavowed co-operation, over a limited period and for a special purpose, between the Home Ministry and the most powerful nationalist organisations.

The first decade of the *Genyosha*'s existence coincided with what the Japanese call the "Rokumeikan era." The *Rokumeikan* was a building in Tokyo in which government hospitality on a Western scale—including dances—was dispensed; and it became symbolic of the craze for Western ideas, clothes, food and customs which developed among the wealthy, especially in Tokyo. It was a time when many sophisticated Japanese appeared to reject their own culture, exchanging native art treasures for tasteless Western importations; when there was talk of abandoning the

---

and the *Toa Senkaku Shishi Kiden* ("Biographical Memoirs of Pioneer Patriots in E. Asia") by Kuzuo Yoshihisa (Tokyo, Kokuryukai, 1933).

4   "With some writers on political affairs it has become axiomatic that liberalism is inimical to a policy of expansion. Historically this is very difficult to prove, either in the case of Japan or of other nations. It will be recalled that between 1871 and 1873 great pressure was brought to bear upon the government by a group favouring a campaign against Korea. … It was not a liberal group which blocked this premature attempt at military adventure, but on the contrary the more conservative and cautious leader Okubo." E. H. Norman, *Japan's Emergence as a Modern State* (New York, Institute of Pacific Relations, 1940), p. 201.

5   Twenty-five persons were killed and 388 injured in this Election. The result, nonetheless, was unfavourable to the government, whose successful candidates numbered 137, against 163 for the opposition parties.

Japanese script for the alphabet, and of the permanent adoption of European dress for both men and women. The *Rokumeikan* had its place in the diplomatic strategy of the government; for it was partly an attempt to prove to foreign nations that Japan had become a civilised modern state, and therefore entitled to secure the revision of the unequal treaties—those agreements, granting foreigners extra-territorial rights, which had been forced on the Shogunate at the time of the opening of the country to Western commerce. But in the provinces there was a strong hostile reaction to the *Rokumeikan* craze; particularly as the government could show no success in negotiations for treaty revision. For its Toyama Mitsuru, so often described as head of the *Kokuryukai* by Western writers, was not even a member.[6] Nonetheless, his name is very rightly associated with the society. If not technically a member, he was its patron, protector and mentor. The truth, perhaps, is that operations were directed by Uchida, policy by Toyama.

The *Kokuryukai* was founded in the first place to repeat in Manchuria the work of the *Genyosha* in Korea; an aim well concealed beneath the generalities which comprised the official programme of the society. This referred only to five vaguely expressed ideals, which may be summarised as: harmony between the civilisations of the East and West; eradication of weakness and inefficiency in the political system; expansion overseas and the solution of problems affecting capital and labour; promotion of the martial spirit in accordance with the Imperial Rescript to the armed forces; and fundamental reform of the educational system, replacing imitation of the educational ideas of Europe and America by the establishment of schools based on the national structure (*kokutai*).

A Japanese police manual, dated January 1936, speaks of the *Kokuryukai* as having been "active behind the scenes, particularly in the Russo-Japanese War, the North China Incident and in the frequent Chinese disturbances."[7] Certainly the activities of the *Kokuryukai*, before the Russo-Japanese War, were on a more extensive scale than those of the *Genyosha* ten years earlier. The prestige of the armed forces had risen greatly, as a result of the quick, successful struggle against China. Despite the humiliation suffered from the Three Power Intervention of 1895, the nation had gained rich rewards as a consequence of victory. It became clear that war paid dividends, and was the sure road to international recognition as a potential equal in the family of civilised states. The most powerful financial interests in Japan were prepared to back the ambitions of the army and navy; and the *Kokuryukai* received funds from such business houses as Yasuda and Okura, as well as from the army; which indeed took the society under its wing as an intelligence organ. The society sent agents to Siberia as well as to Manchuria.[8] When war came Uchida organised Chinese guerrillas to harass the Russian forces, while *Kokuryukai* volunteers from Japan were attached to the army in the field as interpreters.[9]

At home, before the war, the *Kokuryukai* established a school in Tokyo for the study of Russian, and conducted a good deal of anti-Russian propaganda; but many of the society's publications, including Uchida's *Russia Going to Ruin* (1903), were suppressed. In the midst of military preparations the government was concerned to maintain a strictly "correct" attitude towards the probable enemy. Furthermore, the still considerable influence of Ito—*genro* and President of the Privy

---

6   For a list of over a hundred of the prominent members, *vide* Appendix I *(infra)*.

7   Shigematsu Koei, *Shiso Keisatsu Tsuron* ("Introduction to Thought Police"), Japan Police Society, 20th January, 1936; supplement, p. 5. "The N. China Incident" is probably the Tanaka government's Shantung adventure in 1928.

8   According to Tanin and Yohan (*op. cit.*, p. 45) these numbered hundreds; some were sent as far west as the Lake Baikal area.

9   At least some of these were not taken very seriously by Japanese war correspondents, who called them "deaf and dumb interpreters." Byas, *op. cit.*, p. 187.

Toyama Mitsuru, ultra nationalist

Council[10]—was on the side of an understanding with Russia.

It has been claimed that the *Genyosha* converted Ito to the belief in the necessity of war with China, and that the *Kokuryukai*, by direct pressure amounting to the threat of assassination, persuaded him to abandon his moderate attitude towards Russia.

In this connection an account should be given of a celebrated interview between Ito and Toyama.[11]

Leaders of the *Kokuryukai* had asked Toyama for his help with regard to Ito. With three of his closest associates—well versed in the art of judo—Toyama paid an uninvited call on Ito at his home. Just as they arrived Viscount Aoki was leaving the front door, where Ito was still standing. As Aoki passed Toyama he whispered: "Well, I see you have come at last. Is there going to be any beating-up?" In a voice pitched loud enough for Ito to hear, Toyama replied: "I don't know whether there'll be any beating-up or not." Toyama was dressed only in *yukata* (informal summer kimono), and Ito received him coldly. Toyama sat in the place of honour and launched into a harangue on the desirability of war with Russia. Ito replied that as diplomacy was a confidential matter, he was not prepared to discuss the issue. Toyama: "Diplomacy, which you call secret, is something which everybody knows about. The real trouble lies in ignoring public opinion and making government a private affair. I think it right that the trend of public opinion should be given leadership. At one time Your Excellency performed many meritorious services for the state; but you have also committed many errors. In case there should be some fatal blunder in the present crisis it is not unreasonable for the people to express anxiety over such a terrible prospect." Toyama then rose and, coming close to Ito, looked him full in the face and asked: "*Ito-san*, who is the greatest man in Japan to-day?" Ito was so startled by this question that he hesitated to reply; whereupon Toyama declared: "If I may say so, that place belongs to His Majesty the Emperor." After a pause he added: "However, who is the first man among His subjects?" Ito still remained silent, and Toyama said: "You are the one." He then repeated it slowly, and went on: "If you do not hold fast at this moment we are in danger of falling into a grave predicament." Ito replied in a tone of frankness: "If that is your purpose then bear with me. Rest assured that Ito will be responsible for your wish." Toyama was satisfied with this reply and departed with a polite expression of gratitude and appreciation.

---

10   The *genro* were particular elder statesmen, who had been prominent in the Meiji Restoration and in the early period of constitutional history. All together there have been ten *genro* since 1868, of whom Prince Saionji was the last. The institution grew out of custom; it was not formally created. *Vide* Takeuchi, *War and Diplomacy in the Japanese Empire* (London, Allen and Unwin, 1936), pp. 2 0–2, for a short, authoritative account of the *genro* system.

11   This account of the Ito-Toyama interview is based on Norman, "The Genyosha" (*op. cit.*), pp. 27 1–2. His version refers to Aoki as being Foreign Minister at the time. This seems to be an error. Aoki was then a Privy Councillor; but he had been twice Foreign Minister in earlier years.

This account has been related in detail because it is an excellent example of the type of interview in which Toyama specialised. It will be noticed that his tactics were a combination of effrontery, indirect threats and flattery.

That meeting probably occurred in the summer of 1903.[12] Public opinion was almost unanimous in pressing for war against Russia. The newspapers, with the exception of the semi-government Tokyo *Nichi-Nichi*, were extremely bellicose. Although certain of the intelligentsia were involved in the anti-militarist opposition of the infant socialist movement, the great majority of educated people were caught up in this warlike fever. Leading professors of the law department of Tokyo Imperial University demanded war in the press and at public gatherings. Most significant of all, Oyama, the Chief of the Army General Staff, presented a memorial to the Emperor, early in the summer of 1903, urging a quick solution of the Manchurian question, as Japan had a strategic advantage which would be lost within a few years.[13]

The position of the *Kokuryukai* before the Russo-Japanese War was altogether stronger than that of the *Genyosha* before the war with China. In the course of twenty-five years Uchida and Toyama contrived to raise a provincial group of adventurers into an advance guard of popular nationalism.

Yet it would be untrue to suggest that pressure from Toyama and the *Kokuryukai* had a decisive influence on shaping government policy towards Russia. The Russians in the negotiations at St. Petersburg were intransigent to the point of provocation. Japanese public reaction to the Russian stand was reflected—not created—by the *Kokuryukai*. The edifice of Meiji government was still controlled very firmly by the survivors of those Clan statesmen and generals who had been its architects. The indiscipline which thirty years later was to be prevalent among the junior officers of the army did not exist at this time. If the makers of policy—the *genro*, cabinet and General Staffs—had decided against war with Russia, they would still have been able to ignore pressure from any quarter, however powerful.

The point is illustrated by what happened in 1905. Impressive victories on land and sea led the public to believe that Russia was thoroughly defeated and that very substantial territorial and monetary concessions could be obtained from her, including the surrender of the Maritime Province of Siberia—in which, of course, the *Kokuryukai*, as "The Amur River Society," was particularly interested. But the responsible rulers of Japan, military no less than civilian, knew that the country was in no position to secure such terms. Military and financial opinion alike favoured an early peace; and President Roosevelt's offer to mediate—which had been sought by the Japanese Minister in Washington—was welcome news to the government.[14] The self-assurance of popular chauvinism,

---

12 This seems a legitimate guess, judging from the fact that Toyama was in *yukata*, which is worn only between May and September. It was during the summer months of 1903 that public feeling was noticeably roused against Russia. Japan's diplomatic offensive opened in St. Petersburg in June. War started in February, 1904.

13 Takeuchi, *op. cit.*, pp. 13 6–9.

14 "Soon after the Battle of Mukden (10th March, 1905) General Kodama, chief of staff of the Manchurian expeditionary forces, made a secret return to Tokyo and told military and civilian leaders that those who started the war should know when to stop it, and urged them to seek an early opportunity of ending it." Takeuchi, *op. cit.*, p. 149.

There is evidence that at the Imperial Conference of 4th February, 1904, immediately before war broke out, it was decided that the U.S. be asked to intervene to end the war. From an extract from Prince Konoye's Diary for 1941, quoted by the Prosecution at the Tokyo Trial. I.M.T.F.E. (International Military Tribunal for the Far East) Transcript, p. 10260. Konoye was told of this by Count Kaneko. Konoye commented in his Diary: "In other words they were thinking of ending the war at the time of beginning it."

however, rested on the belief that Japan possessed exceptional spiritual advantages, outweighing more material factors not in her favour;[15] and Toyama organised an association, the *Konwa Mondai Rengo Doshikai*, to protest against the "weakness" shown by the Japanese delegation to the peace conference. When the treaty was signed and its terms made public, this association engineered a mass meeting of protest in Tokyo. This led to mob violence on a scale which compelled the government to place the city under martial law. One of the chief objects of the agitation was to overthrow the Katsura cabinet. That this was not achieved was due to the fact that the General Staff, aware of the true condition of Japanese national strength, supported—however reluctantly—the peace settlement negotiated by the government.[16]

The critical, indeed rebellious, attitude of the *Kokuryukai* at this juncture was not to the detriment of the society's reputation. Tokyo after the Russo-Japanese War occupied in the regard of Asiatic revolutionaries the place held later by Moscow. Toyama appeared to be the opponent of all established governments in Asia, including that of his own country. Chinese, Indian and Filippino dissidents visiting Tokyo tended to gravitate to his home in Shibuya. This of course was not a new phenomenon; but the trend was accelerated by the victory over Russia. Japan, so it seemed, was now the champion of Asiatic nationalism. This interpretation of Japan's rôle in world affairs was not necessarily that of the government at the time.[17] But it was welcomed and propagated by Toyama and his associates.

The *Kokuryukai* gave particular assistance to Chinese revolutionaries; the *Yurinkai*, reminiscent of the *Tenyukyo*, being created in 1911 to assist Sun Yat-sen. Chiang Kai-shek and Wang Ching-wei also came for a time under the influence of Toyama; who after 1937 was to claim on this score special qualifications for the tasks of negotiating peace with the one and of controlling the other.[18]

In 1908 Toyama founded a small society, the *Roninkai*. Its exact purpose was not clearly stated, but it is reasonable to suppose that it concentrated initially on strengthening Japanese influence in Mongolia. Leading members of the *Roninkai* included two prominent experts on that region, Sasaki Yasugoro and Viscount Miura, already mentioned as the Minister in Seoul who had helped to organise the murder of the Queen of Korea.[19] The *Roninkai*, with the *Genyosha* and *Kokuryukai*,

---

15   This emphasis on morale is of course a familiar theme, and was much in evidence during the Pacific War. Lt.-Gen. Kawabe Masakazu, Director of Kamikaze Operations at Okinawa, told U.S. interrogators: "I wish to explain something which is a difficult thing and which you may not be able to understand. The Japanese, to the very end, believed that by spiritual means they could fight on equal terms with you, yet by any other comparison it would not appear equal. We believed our spiritual confidence in victory would balance any scientific advantages. …" *Mission Accomplished* (H.Q. Army Air Forces, Washington, 1946), p. 35.

16   Its unpopularity did eventually force the cabinet to resign; but not until January, 1906.

17   The government preferred the view that Japan was a world power—"Great Britain of the Far East"—rather than an entirely Asiatic power. A remark made many years later by Prince Saionji to his secretary, Baron Harada, illustrates the point.

      "Since the time of the Meiji Restoration it has been an accepted fact not to use terms such as 'Orient' and 'Occident' in opposition to each other. In spite of the dissolution of terms contrasting East and West by the honourable intentions of the Emperor Meiji it is unpleasant to see the Right-wing elements and militarists use them." Saionji-Harada Memoirs, Part XIX, Ch. 326, (23rd May, 1939).

18   For an excellent account of *Kokuryukai* activities in China both before and after 1911, *vide* Marius B. Jansen, *The Japanese and Sun Yat-sen* (Cambridge, Mass., Harvard University Press, 1954).

19   In 1916 Kawashima Naniwa, who was close to Toyama and a member of the *Kokuryukai*, organised a small group known as the *Kanzan So* ("Mountain of Sweat Society") for the purpose of setting up a "Manchurian-Mongolian Empire." Kawashima's daughter, Yoshiko, got married to a guerrilla leader in Manchuria and gained some fame at the time of the

The fathers of Kokushikan: Front row, from left, nationalist Mitsuru Tōyama, Rep. Utarō Noda, financier Eiichi Shibusawa, author Sohō Tokutomi; back row far right is the founder of Kokushikan, Tokujirō Shibata.

formed the core of the politically active, extra-parliamentary nationalist movement up to the end of the First World War. There were, however, three other important nationalist organisations during this period. They were the *Zaigo Gunjinkai, Dai Nippon Butokukai* and *Dobunkai*. Strictly speaking they were non-political. Their founders and leaders were men of high social or official standing. Two of these societies—*Zaigo Gunjinkai* and *Butokukai*—had a national membership.

The *Zaigo Gunjinkai*, the society of ex-servicemen, was instituted in 1910 as a result of the work of Generals Terauchi and Tanaka Giichi, who reorganised for this purpose the existing *Teikoku Gunjin Gojikai* ("Imperial Association of Aid to Ex-Servicemen"). Soldiers and sailors on discharge from active service automatically joined the *Zaigo Gunjinkai*. The society was very much more than a Japanese version of the British Legion. For its organisation was based on that of the regular army. The head of the divisional district of the *Zaigo Gunjinkai* was always the major-general, second-in-command of the army division of that district. The district was divided into regimental associations, and lower down the scale were the town sections and the village, railway and factory sub-sections. These units frequently undertook some form of military training.

Manchurian Incident (imaginative journalists called her "The Joan of Arc of Manchuria"). She was of help to the Kwantung Army when she escorted Pu Yi's wife from Tientsin. The *Roninkai* was the parent of the *Kanzan So*.

Zaigo Gunjin may be translated as "military men in their homes," and the society represented in the lives of many Japanese peasants an influence almost as persuasive as that of their own families.[20] This very large and socially active organisation did not take part in nationalist politics until the London Naval Treaty, of 1930, created a ferment of agitation, leading to growing political intervention by military groups in the decade before the Pacific War.

The *Butokukai* ("The Society of Military Virtues") was founded in 1895 in Kyoto, at the same time as the inauguration of the Heian Shrine. The aim of the *Butokukai* was the promotion of the samurai spirit. Its headquarters—the *Butokuden*, close to the Heian Shrine—became a centre for the practice of judo, fencing, archery and other traditional martial sports. In the course of time branches were established throughout the country, and by 1912, at the end of the Meiji era, the society claimed a membership of over a million and a half. Its leaders were eminent military figures. The society did not engage in political activity before the nineteen-thirties; and until that time, at least, it appears to have had no connections with the *Genyosha-Kokuryukai* groups.

In 1898 Prince Konoye Atsumaro founded the *Dobunkai* with the object of promoting the "same language" between Japanese and Chinese. The society established a college, the *Dobun Gakudo*, in Shanghai and schools in Hankow and Tientsin. The Konoye family maintained close ties with the society until the end of the Pacific War. The society on the whole represented the respectable, genuinely cultural, side of Japanese penetration in China.[21]

Until the end of the First World War, then, there were very few important nationalist associations. These, as have been seen, belonged to one or the other of two broad categories—namely the reputable, non-political type (for example, the *Zaigo Gunjinkai*), and the conspiratorial (such as the *Kokuryukai*).[22] But from about the year 1919 the number increased steadily. It was the measure of nationalist reaction to a series of events wounding to patriotic self-esteem and very damaging to the reputation of the parliamentary political parties which were in the ascendancy between 1918 and 1930.[23] These events, in popular patriotic opinion, were little less than national misfortunes.

They were the failure, at the Versailles Conference, to secure the inclusion of the racial equality clause in the League Covenant (a clause implying the right of emigration); the termination by England of her alliance with Japan; the Nine Power Treaty (anathematic to the nationalists, as it put restraints on interference in Chinese affairs); the evacuation of Siberia, in 1922, with nothing to show for a four-year occupation except the retention of North Saghalin (to be surrendered three years later); the United States Congress "exclusion" legislation of 1924; the reduction of the strength of the standing army by twenty per cent (the disbanding of four divisions, in 1925, out of a total of twenty-one); the abortive military adventure in Shantung, 1927–9; the ratification of the Kellogg Pact (regarded widely as an encroachment on the prerogatives of the Emperor); and the conclusion of the London Naval Treaty of 1930.

Neither the disastrous Kanto earthquake of 1923 nor the banking crisis three years later did more than interrupt, though seriously, the general tendency towards industrial and commercial expansion. But the world depression struck Japan with alarming force. In 1930 there was a

---

20   Some typical activities of the *Zaigo Gunjinkai* in the countryside are described in J. F. Embree, *op. cit.*, pp. 124 and 14 6–8.

21   Nevertheless Japanese students from *Dobun* colleges sometimes made long journeys into the interior of China, penetrating far to the West and making political and topographical investigations.

22   Certain nationalist societies which have not been mentioned in the text appear in Appendix III *(infra)*.

23   Landmarks at the beginning and end of this ascendancy are the fall of the Terauchi cabinet in September, 1918 and the attack on Hamaguchi at Tokyo Station on 14th November, 1930.

catastrophic fall in agricultural prices—quotations for rice and silk fell to the lowest figure since 1897—and a famine in the north-east of the country.

At the same time there was the phenomenon in the years immediately following 1918 of what might be called a second *Rokumeikan* era. Western democracy, which had triumphed in the First World War, became fashionable. And Western thought, ranging from feminism to the Marxist dialectic, exercised a growing appeal, for the urban intelligentsia in particular.[24]

The Crown Prince's European tour in 1921 and Yamagata's death in 1922 were symbolic of the advent of a new world and the passing of the old. Prince Yamagata was the most powerful surviving representative of the Clan hegemony which ruled political life in Japan for half a century after the Meiji Restoration. In his old age, as the leading *genro*, he constituted a strongly conservative force, resisting change of any description, particularly in the army; which he dominated through his leadership of the Choshu Clan. The young Crown Prince—he was to be Regent in November, 1921—represented the modern generation, scientific, liberal and, it seemed, relatively democratic. His visit to England and France was a drastic break with tradition. Indeed it caused much anxiety among rabid nationalists. They were apprehensive, no doubt, not only of the physical risks of the long journey, but also of the possibility of a young mind being influenced by the very un-Japanese ideas of modern Europe.

The First World War enriched the business classes and greatly increased their numbers. Their political energies found expression in support, or manipulation, of the parties in the Diet. War profits exacerbated differences between rich and poor—wages by no means kept up with rising prices—and made possible an unprecedented public display of wealth by a section of the *nankin*, the newly enriched capitalists of the time.[25] Under the circumstances, and considering the impact of the Russian Revolution, it is not surprising that all in positions of authority should have feared the appearance of a robust socialist movement.

This anxiety gave rise to that unattractive phrase "dangerous thoughts," in condemnation of all radical ideas. The first socialist party had been formed in 1901 but was soon suppressed. Though it reappeared in 1906 a mortal blow seemed to have been dealt the party, and the movement generally, when Kotoku Denji, a pioneer socialist, and eleven others were executed for an alleged plot against the life of the Emperor. That was in 1911. But by 1918 new vigour inspired Japanese socialism as a result of economic tensions inside the country, not to mention such events abroad as the Russian Revolution. Yet even at this stage the Left-wing movement showed a tendency to divide into a state socialist wing, nationalist in essence, and a Marxian socialist wing, some fraction of which looked to Moscow for guidance.

The prevailing mood of the time, however, could be called one of optimistic, bourgeois moderation, suspicious of military adventures abroad and radical experiments at home. The first party cabinet, under Hara, seemed to be the promise of a gradually broadening political democracy. For the time being this appeared to be a substantial advance. An American scholar has given point to the argument in these words:

---

24   In this context it may be remarked that Tokyo had perhaps the largest student population in the world. The city contained within its boundaries at least fourteen universities, with a student population of some 43,000. To these must be added the pupils, aged from eighteen to twenty-one years, of Higher Schools.

25   There is a short, astringent account of some features of this war boom prosperity in A. Morgan Young, *Japan under Taisho Tenno* (London, Allen & Unwin, 1928), pp. 110–18.

Japan entered the First World War apparently under the control of a small oligarchy, and then, as the war ended and Japan entered the post-war world, it suddenly became evident that there was no longer a small, clear-cut ruling group but instead, thousands of bureaucrats, military leaders, business men, and intellectuals, all contending for control of the government. There was even a growing demand that all classes be allowed to participate in politics.[26]

This clash of interests and opinions—the very life-blood of a healthy political democracy—was looked upon by believers in *Nihon Shugi* ("Japanism"[27]) as nothing but deplorable confusion. The point is important. Harmony between Emperor and people, ruler and the ruled—like the unity of religion and politics—was a deeply felt nationalist ideal. This essentially Confucian concept of the state was implicit in the opening words of the Imperial Rescript on Education (1890):

> Our Imperial Ancestors have founded Our Empire on a basis broad and everlasting and have deeply and firmly implanted virtue; Our subjects ever united in loyalty and filial piety have from generation to generation illustrated the beauty thereof. This is the glory of the fundamental character of our Empire, and herein also lies the source of Our education.

It is difficult to exaggerate the compelling power, for Japanese, of such words. To the Western mind they convey little more than the sentiments associated with legitimate national pride. To the Japanese they represent more than an idealised version of their country's history. Except to the sophisticated and critical the words carry the authority of absolute truth. They suggest to the Japanese a well-regulated social order, pervaded by a spirit of unruffled harmony, entirely excluding the possibility of bitter political dissensions; for the people have had virtue "deeply and firmly implanted" in them, and are "united in loyalty and filial piety."

By contrast, the strikes,[28] the political party and financial scandals, the "dangerous thoughts" of the nineteen-twenties were chaos and degeneracy.

Occurrences which in the West would hardly be regarded as suggestive of any particular trend in national morals were interpreted by many Japanese as pointing to a general deterioration in the loyal, patriotic spirit of the country. Mention has been made of the diplomatic setbacks and economic troubles of the period. Each of these was associated to some extent—in the minds of nationalists—with the deplored tendencies of the day, the liberal and Left-wing thought prevalent

in the universities, the impact of modern Western books, music and social customs. Even the great Kanto earthquake was interpreted by some as a kind of supernatural punishment for the frivolity and individualism of the times.[29]

---

26 Edwin O. Reischauer, *Japan Past and Present* (London, Duckworth, 1947), p. 145.

27 The translation is ungainly but no better exists. *Nihon Shugi* implies the cultivation, to the exclusion of foreign ideas, of all the native concepts, institutions and genius of Japan.

28 In 1919 there was even a soldiers' strike, at Matsuyama. A. Morgan Young, *op. cit.*, p. 168.

29 Before the Pacific War the Earthquake Commemoration Museum at Yokohama displayed posters and cartoons, etc., illustrating this point of view. According to vulgar superstition, dating from ancient times, earthquakes were caused by the motions of a giant catfish which lived beneath the surface of the land. Some of the cartoons showed this creature angrily heaving its back in irritation at the frivolity and confusion prevailing above it.

RESTORATION AND REPRESSION

Herbert Bix

When Japan recognized Manchukuo and withdrew from the League of Nations, most Japanese felt that something fundamental had changed. Youthful, ancient Japan had fought another war of "self-defense," and in the process scored an armed victory over Chinese warlordism and a spiritual one over "Western moral decadence." By its own efforts, the nation had opened a new road to modernity and put forth a claim to becoming greater and more respected in the world than it had been.

For General Araki and other politically active officers of the army, the rhetoric of "crisis," "Shōwa restoration," "Anglo-Saxon encirclement," and so on was simply a mobilizing device too effective to let go. They prolonged the euphoria of victory and took advantage of it by continuing the Imperial Way theme, using it to strengthen army influence in politics and to reshape the emperor's image. The pleasant view of an indestructible and virtuous Japan confronting morally inferior, devilish foreign states spread widely. So too did notions of "national defense state," "empire," and "holy mission" to spread the "emperor's benevolence." These ideas led people to invest the military's expansion abroad with notions of goodness. They also strengthened their desire to overcome the West in every field of endeavor and, in that way too, structured a new, more exclusionary sense of collective identity.

Under Meiji, Japan had superficially "escaped from Asia" (*datsu'A*), assimilating certain concepts, as well as the technology, and in certain ways even the identity of the leading Western societies. The practical consequence was a kind of hopeful, shallow, often resentful sense of solidarity with the white Western communities in Asia, including the adoption of their racist attitudes and epithets toward Chinese and other Asian peoples. Now, however, Japan was on the rise, independently striving, building, renewing its role as the—rightful—leader in Asia. Therefore many ideologues now discovered that Western political thought was essentially exploitative, hegemonistic, and aggressive—in short, a contagious plague that for a time had infected insular Japan and caused it to threaten the interests of fellow Asians. Henceforth Japan should act not so much in "self defense," as to spread the Shōwa emperor's virtues by establishing a morally superior society in Manchukuo, where the "five races" would live in hierarchical "harmony" in accordance with the "principle of the 'kingly way.'"

Japan's Manchukuo-vindicating new national image, as well as some characteristics of its worship of the state, resembled aspects of German Nazism and Italian Fascism. (The latter developed partly out of an Italian search for a counterpart to Japan's national political religion of emperor worship.) With the arrest in 1933 of eighteen thousand dissidents, and the forced recantation of many left-wing leaders, the communist movement in Japan was all too easily suppressed. Between 1934 and 1936, what remained of Taishō democracy and the institutions of constitutional liberalism were similarly enfeebled by intimidation and assassination. Although racial intolerance and bigotry never became a state policy as in Nazified, anti-Semitic Germany, racial discrimination against other Asians was habitual for many twentieth-century Japanese, having begun around the time of the Sino-Japanese War of 1894–95, with the start of Japanese colonialism. The Anti-Comintern Pact made with Germany and Italy in November 1936 brought in Nazi ideologues who gained many Japanese supporters and injected Nazi-style anti-Semitic arguments into mainstream public discussion—where defamation of Jews was already widespread. Thereafter all Japanese governments shamelessly manipulated the popular image of the Jews, not so much to persecute them as to strengthen domestic ideological conformity.

Ethnological studies of the rural areas from which the army recruited most of its troops during the 1930s suggest, however, that despite the best efforts of the Ministry of Education, many country people were relatively unaffected by official propaganda. To them emperor ideology was neither so meaningful nor so valid as their own nativism. Family and village considerations still took precedence over state considerations. Indeed, down to the start of the China war in mid-1937, many villagers displayed only the shallowest acceptance of the emperor's authority. Knowing this, the army always acted on the premise that soldiers were rooted, above all, to their families and villages. The army's Field Service Code (sen-jinkun), issued on January 8, 1941, emphasized that "[t]hose who fear shame are strong. Remember always the good reputation of your family and the opinion of people of your birthplace." And: "Do not shame yourself by being taken prisoner alive; die so as not to leave behind a soiled name."

Significant exceptions to rural ignorance of the emperor's authority were persons in posts of responsibility in local society. Village officials, schoolteachers, policemen, Buddhist and Shinto priests—the foot soldiers of Japanese nationalism—invoked the authority of the emperor and the power of the state to strengthen their local authority. Their loyalty to and veneration of the emperor often seemed spontaneous and deeply felt. But most villagers did not occupy positions of public responsibility and probably were not devout believers in the emperor. Their patriotism was of a different order.

In 1935, for example, anthropologists John and Ella (Lury Wiswell) Embree interviewed farmers in the remote agricultural village of Suye Mura on Kyushu Island. When Ella Wiswell's book, *The Women of Suye Mura*, appeared many years later, it described a world of hard-drinking, outspoken farm-women, who laughed at the emperor's pretensions. Wiswell recorded a conversation with a literate woman of the village:

> Having stopped by for a chat, I asked her, "You worship the Emperor like a god (*kamisama*) don't you?" indicating the hanging scroll portraying the Imperial couple in the *tokonoma* [ceremonial alcove in the main room]. "Yes, when we make a ceremonial offering to the gods, we make it to the emperor too. When we pray in front of the gods, it is also in front

of the emperor, and to him we offer flowers," she said. "Why?" I asked. "Well, I suppose it is because he is head (*taisbō*) of the country," she replied. Then she described the figures in the scroll. "There on the left is Jimmu-tennō", the very first ... and on the right is his wife. Then come Taishō-tennō and the Empress. Below them is the palace, then the three princes, Chichibu, Mikasa, and Takamatsu-sama. Below, there behind the flowers (she had a tall vase in front of the scroll) are the present Emperor and Empress. They are all great people. ..." "And who is above them all?" I asked. "That is Amaterasu-Ōmikami. ... She is the number-one goddess." "So, but why are they all in the picture together? What is the relationship between Amaterasu and the present Emperor?" "I don't know, but they are both there most probably because she is the greatest *kamisama* and he is the head of the country, the greatest person in Japan." "Then the Emperor is not a *kamisama?*" "No, he is just worshiped like a god ..., but he is not a real god. He is human, a very great man." ... "If the policeman were to hear us, he would tie me up and throw me in prison. But he can't hear, can he?" I said I thought we were safe. I left her on the balcony, dusting and drying her lacquer-ware. So much for Emperor worship.

Even allowing for Wiswell's leading questions, this interview, which occurred at the height of the "*kokutai* clarification movement," suggests that the effort to prepare the populace for war had not penetrated deeply or widely. Life in the countryside was not yet geared to the political objectives of the army and navy. Nonideological irreverence for the throne and ignorance of, or disbelief in, the foundation myths were realities behind the effort to pump up state Shintoism, and they were hard to overcome.

By the eve of all-out war with China, Japanese public schools, under orders from the Ministry of Education, were inculcating Shinto mythology as if it were historical fact; emperor ideology had become fused with anti-Western sentiment; and a conceptual ground had been prepared for the transformation of Hirohito into a benevolent pan-Asian monarch defending not only Japan but all of Asia from Western encroachment. Emperor Meiji's image as a Western-style monarch defending Japan (alone) from Western imperialism was thereby enhanced—and stood on its head. From this time one can see a deepening conflict in official ideology between an emphasis on the absolute uniqueness of divine Japan, and the pan-Asian ideal that stressed a fundamental identity shared by the Japanese and their fellow Asians.

I

In the spring and summer of 1933 Hirohito faced discipline problems in his military and attacks on his court entourage from within the military, from the Seiyūkai, the privy council, and civilian right-wing organizations. Hirohito's military critics faulted him privately for "obstructing the army." They called him an incompetent "mediocrity" who was manipulated by his advisers. Others complained, privately, that he gave less importance to affairs of state than to his recreations—marine biology, tennis, golf, and even mah-jongg. Young staff officers in Manchuria were irritated by his alleged dislike of war. Members of the imperial family were also critical. His brother Prince Chichibu and Princes Higashikuni and Kaya frequently reported that younger officers were unhappy with Hirohito's expressions of dependency on his entourage.

The year before, in 1932, Prince Chichibu, next in line to the throne and the brother with whom Hirohito was least intimate, had repeatedly counseled him to implement "direct imperial rule"—even if that meant suspending the constitution. At that time the emperor told Nara of his intention to transfer Captain Chichibu out of the Third Infantry Regiment because he had "become very radicalized" there. The regiment, commanded by Gen. Yamashita Tomoyuki [Hōbun], was home to many populist young officers including Nonaka Shirō, who, two and a half years later, would help plan and carry out the mutiny of February 1936. Acting as head of the imperial family, Hirohito had Chichibu reassigned to Army General Staff Headquarters in Tokyo, then to a regional command in distant Hirosaki, Aomori prefecture.

In April 1933 Hirohito had tried to curb the young officers' movement by pressing Nara to have the inspector general of military education, Hayashi Senjurō, an opponent of Army Minister Araki, take appropriate "educational measures" against extremism in the army. It was yet another example of rule by three-cushion indirection. Araki, however, was not easily deterred from his support of the young officers. He proceeded to undermine the emperor by calling for pardons for the army cadets, naval lieutenants, and ensigns who (together with one civilian) had been indicted for the unsuccessful coup on May 15, and the murder of Prime Minister Inukai.

Through the summer newspapers and radio covered the separate army and navy trials of the indicted. As support mounted for these "true believers in the *kokutai*," military reservists throughout Japan and the colonies gathered more than seventy-five thousand signatures on a petition calling for a reduction of their sentences. On September 11, 1933, a navy court-martial sentenced Koga Kiyoshi and three other naval perpetrators to death, but later reduced their sentences to fifteen years' imprisonment. An army court-martial handed down even lighter sentences (four years' detention) to eleven young army officers who had taken part in the coup. The lone civilian conspirator, tried in a civilian court without the benefit of a huge and popular bureaucratic organization behind him, received imprisonment for life. At this time the Japanese judicial process invariably gave perpetrators of mutiny and assassination lenient treatment if they claimed to have acted purely out of patriotism. Ordinary civilian criminals, tried under civilian jurisdiction, rarely got off so lightly.

Two weeks after the navy court-martial, Prince Takamatsu, who had served aboard ship with some of the criminals, wrote in his diary that their "act of violence" had been:

> … purely motivated. … As military men they wanted to end the corruption of the political parties, the selfishness of the *zaibatsu*, the paralysis of the farming villages, the decadence of social morals, and the attitude of the nation's statesmen … But social problems were not their immediate objective. Rather their primary aim was to convert dissatisfaction and distrust toward the leaders of the navy into perfect order. Many [navy] people regard social reform as secondary. … Since such a thing has happened once, there is a possibility that naval personnel might generate a second May 15 incident. … [R]ight now we must restore discipline and order in the navy.

Restoring discipline and order in the military became the primary concern of Hirohito and his palace advisers after the formation of the Okada cabinet in July 1934. On the surface the problem appeared two sided: Abroad, the Kwantung Army and the small China Garrison Force in the Peking-Tientsin region had begun plotting to establish Japanese influence in North China, and it was unclear in Tokyo whether they would succeed. Meanwhile radical army officers impatient for reform were fomenting civil discord and extremism at home as a way of gaining power for themselves. The need to impose strong central control became clear during 1935 but both the palace and the Okada cabinet were slow to respond. Officers implementing national policy in the field often disagreed with General Staff officers in Tokyo who participated in drafting policy, while policy planners on the General Staffs feuded with their counterparts in the Army and Navy Ministries and in the Foreign Ministry. The emperor's task was to stand above this dissension and, without becoming directly involved, foster unity. In 1935 he was still groping for a way to achieve this.

More particularly, small incidents of anti-Japanese resistance in the demilitarized zone separating Manchukuo from northern China led the field generals to demand that Chiang Kai-shek withdraw his forces from the Peking-Tientsin area. Chiang yielded, and in June 1935, the Chinese side approved the demands of the Japanese army by signing the Ho Ying-ch'in-Umezu Yoshijirō Agreement. Five months later an Autonomous Committee for Defense Against Communism in Eastern Hepei Province was established in the demilitarized zone under Kwantung Army supervision. Intelligence agencies in the army soon followed up this diplomatic "success" by inaugurating a second pro-Japanese puppet regime, the Kisatsu Political Affairs Committee in Tungchow, under Yin Ju-keng a Chinese graduate of Waseda University in Tokyo, whose wife was Japanese.

Hirohito's reaction to this arbitrary conduct of diplomacy by military field commanders was to propose to eighty-eight-year-old Makino that an imperial conference conduct a full-scale reexamination of policies toward China. According to Makino's diary entry of June 15, the emperor said, "Even if you question the *genrō* [Saionji] concerning the North China problem, he is far from Tokyo and far from the [government] authorities. I doubt he can provide us with good ideas. It will be effective to have an imperial conference depending on the circumstances [at the time of defining fundamental policy]." Yet because of deep divisions among the political elites, not to mention the opposition and chronically poor judgment of Saionji and Makino, no such conference was convened.

II

The premeditated efforts of the Kwantung Army and the China Garrison Force to separate North China further hardened Chinese opposition. Japan's "Monroe Doctrine" for Asia became an immediate source of conflict with the United States and Britain. While this was occurring, domestic debate on the *kokutai* rekindled, gradually resulting in popular distrust of the nation's ruling elites. For nearly a decade the court group had initiated efforts to "clarify" the national polity—that is, counter antimonarchist thought and impart rationality to the tangle of statements and intellectual arguments pertaining to the nature of the state. The leaders of the army, frustrated by the slowness of political reform, now launched their own campaign to promote an ideal of Japanese nationhood within the concept of the *kokutai* and the myth of the emperors' divine ancestry.

The campaign began in the House of Peers on February 18, 1935, with an attack on Minobe's "organ theory" of the emperor's position as the "traitorous thought of an academic rebel." The speaker was Baron Kikuchi Takeo, a retired general and member of the Imperial Reservists Association as well as the Kokuhonsha—a radical rightist organization that was part of the mainstream of Japanese politics. Kikuchi demanded that the Okada government ban Professor Minobe's books. A week later Minobe spoke in his own defense, while outside the Diet right-wing groups associated with the Imperial Way officers demonstrated against him.

In early March, reserve Maj. Gen. Etō Genkurō charged in the House of Representatives that at least two of Minobe's books—*Kenpō satsuyō* [Compendium of the constitution] and *Tsuiho kenpō seigi* [Additional commentaries on the constitution]—fell within the purview of the crime of lèse-majesté. Shortly afterward, on March 4, Prime Minister Okada yielded to the hysteria by declaring in the Diet that "No one supports the emperor organ theory."

Emperor Hirohito at his coronation in 1928

The following month, after the Diet went into recess, Okada and his cabinet ministers asked Minobe to resign his imperial appointments and initiated administrative measures against his writings. The entire government bureaucracy was instructed not to refer to the emperor as an "organ" of state. Officials of the Education Ministry directed prefectural governors and heads of institutions of higher learning to participate in clarifying the meaning of the august *kokutai*, following up by initiating investigations of books, articles, and lectures by law professors in the nation's universities. Bureaucratic ministries and offices throughout the nation soon began holding seminars on the meaning of the *kokutai* and the national spirit. To deliver the lectures and teach the new courses, they enlisted specialists in Japanese racial thought, academic opponents of liberalism, and advocates of Nazi theories of law.

In effect, in order to counter the unauthorized, radical movement denouncing Minobe's constitutional interpretation, Okada generated a government-sponsored, national *kokutai* clarification campaign, which also declaimed against Minobe's teachings and banned some of his books and articles. It was this official campaign that Hirohito supported. To control the radicals within the armed forces and resist the *kokutai* indoctrination movement from below, which aimed at overthrowing Okada, he lent his authority to a government campaign that fostered unbridled fanaticism.

On April 6, 1935, Superintendent of Military Education General Mazaki, a member of Hiranuma's Kokuhonsha and a dispenser of secret army funds to right-wing newspapers, had issued an instruction to the army on "clarifying the *kokutai*." In it Mazaki reminded one and all that Japan was a holy land ruled over by sacred emperors who were living deities. At that point right-wing civilian groups allied with the army formed a League to Destroy the Emperor Organ Theory and "accomplish the clarification of the *kokutai*." Member journalist Ioki Ryūzō and law professor Nakatani Takeo espoused totalitarian ideas of remaking Japan in the image of Germany. The league's immediate goals, however, were to remove Ichiki Kitokurō from the presidency of the emperor's privy council and to eliminate the influence of Makino and Saionji. The opposition Seiyūkai, hoping to overthrow the Okada cabinet, began cooperating with the League.

Nationwide antigovernment agitation on the *kokutai* issue continued throughout the spring, summer, and autumn of 1935. Senior officers of the army and navy, the army-dominated Imperial Reservists Association (with branches in all the prefectures), and an alliance of many small and some large right-wing groups, led the agitation, while religious sects that outwardly had subjugated themselves to the state, such as "Imperial Way Ōmotokyō," also joined the campaign. In August, when public procurators dropped the lèse-majesté charges against Minobe because his intent had not been criminal, the antigovernment movement against his theory rekindled. Thereafter the demand grew that there be no dissent from the truth that Japan was a "peerless nation" led by a divine, precious, august ruler, and also that there be no public criticism of military budgets.

Behind these attacks lay the ideological desire to discredit not a particular interpretation of the Meiji constitution but all constitutional interpretations, whether Minobe's or his opponents', that differentiated the emperor from the state. The leaders of the "League to Destroy the Emperor Organ Theory" were fighting to abolish the advisory powers of ministers of state, and to return to a more flexible process of governance in which the voice of the military could be freely translated into national policy. At their head stood the Imperial Way generals Mazaki and Araki, Vice President of the Privy Council Hiranuma, certain Seiyūkai politicians, and rightwing agitators outside the government, such as Ioki. Their underlying demand was for very radical reform, captured in Ioki's slogan of a "Shōwa restoration," and it made the campaign against Minobe a threat to the Okada cabinet and, indirectly, to Hirohito. When the army and navy ministers mounted the rostrum at a convention of the Imperial Reservists, meeting in Tokyo in late August 1935, and publicly expressed solidarity with this radical anti-Minobe movement, the Okada cabinet realized that a crisis was at hand and it had to act.

To control the agitation, Okada was forced to issue a second statement clarifying the *kokutai*. Based on a draft prepared by the Army Ministry and revised by civil officials after discussions with the vice ministers of the army and navy, this statement declared: "In our country ninety million subjects believe absolutely that the emperor exercises the sovereign powers of the state. On this point no one in government holds the slightest difference of opinion. Consequently the emperor organ theory, which is incompatible with this belief, must be eliminated." In effect Okada twice officially proscribed Minobe's constitutional theory as an alien doctrine. After his second statement was issued, senior army leaders withdrew their support from further attempts to overthrow his cabinet. By this time the Ministry of Education had initiated the development of a new system of ethics based on Confucian social values, Buddhist metaphysics, and Shinto national chauvinism. A united front of the leading right-wing organizations formed, dedicated to saying "Out!" to American and European thought, and "In!" to the reformation of Japan's institutions on the basis of Imperial Way principles.

Doctrinally, one of Minobe's main crimes in the eyes of militarists and political opportunists was his (correct) assertion that the emperor's right of supreme command was not a responsibility of ministers of state. Its "sphere of application," therefore, had to be carefully circumscribed by the Diet if Japan was not to have "dual government," with laws and ordinances deriving from separate sources. In extreme cases, he warned, military power could "control the government and there would be no end to the damage caused by militarism."

Minobe did not stop with only admonishing the military for interfering in national affairs. He also interpreted Article 3 of the Meiji constitution ("The emperor is sacred and inviolable") to mean simply that the emperor was not by law required to suffer judgment for his actions in affairs of state. If the emperor could freely conduct politics of his own volition, "then he could not hope to be nonaccountable, and the unavoidable result would be to harm the dignity of the imperial house." In other words Minobe assumed that in Japan the constitution imposed limits on the power of the monarch even though he alone was personally nonaccountable. Not wanting the emperor to be an "absolute" ruler saddled with political accountability, Minobe took a stand against the notion of direct imperial rule and the dictatorship that the army leaders were then advocating. Minobe further argued that imperial rescripts issued in matters of state were not "sacred and inviolable" but could be criticized by the Diet and the nation. Only those that pertained to moral issues and were unsigned by ministers of state were immune to criticism.

Many of the army's leaders, wanting to have things entirely their own way, opposed Minobe by resurrecting a constitutional theory of divine right that sharply counterposed "sacred" and "inviolable." They found the explanation of Article 3 that they were seeking in the writings of Uesugi:

> [Our] emperor is the direct descendant of the gods and rules the state as a living god. He originally dwelt with the gods and was inherently different from his subjects. ... That being so, it is obvious indeed that Article 3 of our constitution has a nature completely different from the same article in the constitutions of other countries.

Uesugi's interpretation triumphed because it neither assumed Western-style constitutional monarchy nor infringed on the army's independence of command authority. Moreover, his view, which highlighted the emperor's absolutist position, was much closer to the truth of the 1889 constitution than Minobe's, which sought to justify the transition from rule by the Satsuma-Chōshū oligarchy to rule by party cabinets.

However, many extreme rightist believers in "*kokutai* clarification" were really seeking to abolish the practice of constitutional interpretation per se. While Minobe was suffering for not succumbing to the lunacy of this *kokutai* debate, and campaigns against him and Okada (considered to be too moderate because he too was unwilling to implement radical reform) were spreading, demagogic attacks on the court entourage also increased. Earlier, anonymous allegations of improper behavior by high court officials had forced the resignations of Imperial Household Minister Ichiki and his secretary, Sekiya. Kawai had also resigned his post and assumed the job of chief of the Imperial Household Accounts Office. Kido, the most politically competent member of the palace entourage, had stayed on as Makino's secretary and in August 1933 had assumed the additional post of president of the Board of Peerage and Heraldry, with jurisdiction over the imperial family. Now the two "*kokutai* clarification" movements, one from above and the other from below, precipitated a further reshuffling. Makino resigned at the end of 1935; a few months later Hiranuma obtained his wish of succeeding to the presidency of the privy council in place of Ichiki. Ultranationalists, however, were not contented with this shakeup of the palace entourage and weakening of the Okada cabinet. Until the army's voice in national affairs was further strengthened, and the use-value of the emperor pushed to its peak, they refused to allow the situation to stabilize.

When Chief Aide-de-Camp Honjō informed Hirohito of the spreading attacks on the Okada cabinet and the Diet debates on constitutional theories, the emperor—then thirty-four—made no attempt to intervene and end the crazy furor in which he personally was never mentioned. Privately he told Honjō that "the monarchical sovereignty argument" was "better." But in a country like Japan, "the emperor and the state are, generally speaking, the same. So it doesn't matter which [theory] prevails." Decades of effort to define a system of parliamentary governance under the Meiji constitution were at stake in this "debate," yet Hirohito was indifferent to its implications. On the other hand, Honjō also alleges in his diary that Hirohito told him: "[I]n dealing with international matters such as labor treaties and debt problems, the organ theory is convenient."

These inconsistent statements reveal Hirohito's attitude: protect members of the entourage, such as Ichiki Kitokurō, but avoid commitment to specific constitutional interpretations of his role in governance. After the war, when discussing the attack on Minobe's rationalist interpretation of the Meiji Constitution, Hirohito observed that:

> Under the Saitō [*sic*; Okada] cabinet [in 1935], the emperor organ theory became a topic of public discussion. I once told my chief military aide-de-camp, Honjō, to tell Mazaki

Jinzaburō that I liken the state to a human body in which the emperor is the brain. If we use the words "bodily organ," instead of "organ" in a social sense, then my relationship to the *kokutai* is not in the least affected. … In addition there was the question of the "living god." I am not sure whether it was Honjō or Usami [Okiie] who held that I am a living god. I told him it disturbs me to be called that because I have the same bodily structure as an ordinary human being.

In fact the state was not for Hirohito an entity with an independent life of its own, capable of meeting the needs of ruled and rulers alike. It had to have an emperor who functioned as its "brain." In this respect Hirohito always stood midway between the modern, rationalist theory of the state propounded by Minobe and the absolutist theory of Uesugi, which, under army pressure, became the official orthodoxy from 1935 onward. Hirohito also found the myth of the living god to be helpful for amplifying his voice in the policymaking process and for strengthening loyalty to himself in the military. Moreover, banning Minobe's theory was a way of checking any further attempt to revise the Meiji constitution by reinterpretation. So he allowed Minobe—who had denied the absoluteness of the imperial will and taught that the Diet could freely criticize laws and ordinances sanctioned by the emperor—to be purged from public life. And the Japanese people were encouraged to behave as if they thought the emperor was a living deity.

Yet Hirohito was by no means personally comfortable with a movement that sought to deprive him of his freedom. He realized, too, that the participation of commoners in antigovernment debates on the clarification of the *kokutai* could undermine faith in the nation's privileged elites and diminish his own charismatic authority. Nevertheless he did nothing to stop the chattering cult that surrounded the throne from reaching new levels of fanaticism. If Hirohito ever thought his military rightists were thinking and acting wrongly, he never let them know it. What his sardonic exchanges with Honjō mainly showed was his eclecticism, his irritation with the army's attacks on his entourage, and his belief that the constitutional order contrived under his grandfather was compatible with any form of authoritarian government. He had been educated to play an active role in political and military decision making; he intended to do so, and he knew that many of the people denouncing Minobe's theory wanted to deny him precisely that.

Honjō, a stubbornly persistent fanatic, repeatedly pressed the emperor to change his thinking regarding his deification. "Because we in the military worship your majesty as a living god," Honjō opined on March 28, 1935, "it is extremely difficult in military education and command to treat your majesty as only a human—which is what the organ theory [of Minobe] requires." Hirohito tried to enlighten Honjō somewhat the next day. Addressing the text of the constitution, he pointed out that "[a]rticle 4 says that the emperor is the 'head of state.' That says precisely what the organ theory says. If you wish to reform the organ theory, you must inevitably reform the constitution."

Hirohito's view of the constitution had been shaped by Shimizu Tōru, who opposed the "emperor organ theory" yet also found fault with Uesugi. Like Shimizu, Hirohito straddled these two main interpretations. That he refrained from coming out in defense of Minobe, thereby allowing Uesugi's absolutist theory to triumph, was only to be expected. Essentially Hirohito stood for protecting and strengthening the imperial house, drastically reducing the importance of elected professional politicians in making policy, and allowing limited reforms only as needed to meet crises. Because he equated himself with the state, and hence the state of the state, as it were, he tended to view all who opposed the established order as standing in opposition to him, and a threat to his sovereignty.

On this last point he was not wrong. Many advocates of direct imperial rule rejected the very notion of a state based on law and sought a dictatorship unrestrained by any constitutional interpretation. Hirohito was never prepared to go that far. The irony is that, in sacrificing Minobe, he and the Okada cabinet sanctioned a war against heresy that not only wiped out academic freedom but also abetted the very military radicalism they sought to control.

III

In late 1934, several Imperial Way officers at the Army Cadet School were arrested on suspicion of plotting a coup. No punishments were imposed in this incident, but the following year two of the same group—Isobe Asaichi and Muranaka Takeji—were again arrested, for having distributed a document charging that officers of the Control faction, such as Maj. Gen. Nagata Tetsuzan, had once authored plans for coups d'état against the government. This time the highest echelons of the army reacted. The accusations by Isobe and Muranaka were condemned as disloyalty, and both officers lost their commissions. Other officers of the Imperial Way targeted for retaliation a stalwart of the Control faction, Military Affairs Bureau Chief Nagata Tetsuzan, who was rumored to be planning a major purge to rid the army of factionalism.

In August 1935—six months into the populist movement to denounce Minobe's interpretation of the constitution—Lt. Col. Aizawa Saburō of the Imperial Way entered Nagata's office and used his samurai sword to slash him to death. At that point the struggle within the military over reform of the state and the demand for increased military spending, which lay in the background of the movement to denounce Minobe, took a more dangerous turn.

The anti-Okada forces in the army, still using the slogans "*kokutai* clarification" and "denounce the organ theory," now stepped up their attacks on the emperor's entourage and the hereditary peers. Senior Imperial Way generals arranged to give Aizawa a public court-martial under the jurisdiction of the First Division, a hotbed of Imperial Way officers based in Tokyo. When Aizawa's show trial opened on January 12, 1936, his lawyers quickly turned it into an emotional indictment of the Okada cabinet, the court entourage, and the constitutional theory of Professor Minobe. They not only won popular support in many parts of the country but even in such unlikely places as the palace, where Hirohito's own mother, Dowager Empress Teimei Kōgō, now a woman of strongly rightist views, became an Aizawa sympathizer. Before the trial could run its course, however, it was disrupted by a military mutiny in the capital. Army Minister Hayashi's earlier dismissal of Imperial Way General Mazaki as superintendent of military education, and the issuing of orders for the transfer of the entire First Division to Manchuria, had triggered the largest army uprising in modern Japanese history.

Around five o'clock on the morning of February 26, 1936, the word storm over the *kokutai*, which had raged throughout 1935, burst into rebellion. Twenty-two junior-rank army officers, commanding more than fourteen hundred fully armed soldiers and noncommissioned officers from three regiments of the First Division, plus an infantry unit of the Imperial Guards, mutinied in the center of snow-covered Tokyo. They seized the Army Ministry and the Metropolitan Police Headquarters and proceeded to attack the official and private residences of senior statesmen and cabinet ministers. The rebels—1,027 were recruits who had just entered the army in January—assassinated Lord Keeper of the Privy Seal Saitō Makoto, Finance Minister Takahashi, and the new Inspector General of Military Education, Gen. Watanabe Jōtarō, a known supporter of Minobe's constitutional theory. They also killed five policemen and wounded Grand Chamberlain Suzuki, among others. While the assassinations were in progress, other mutineers raided the newspaper offices of the *Asahi shinbun* and *Tokyo nichi nichi shinbun*. Shouting, "Traitors!" at the journalists, they overturned type trays and fired their weapons into the air.

Yet within the first few hours the insurrection began to go awry. The rebel officers killed Prime Minister Okada's secretary, but Okada and Privy Seal Makino escaped; they failed to secure the Sakashita Gate to the palace, so allowing the palace to continue communicating with the outside; and they made no preparations to deal with the navy. In Yokosuka, naval base commander Rear Adm. Yonai Mitsumasa and his chief of staff, Inoue Shigeyoshi, ordered marines to guard the Navy Ministry building and gathered warships in Tokyo Bay in preparation for suppressing the rebels. On the morning of February 28, after fruitless negotiations through sympathetic officers in central army headquarters, the martial-law commander in the occupied area transmitted an imperial order to disperse. Most of the troops returned to barracks, one officer committed suicide, the remaining leaders surrendered, and the uprising collapsed without further bloodshed. Martial law in Tokyo, however, continued for nearly five months.

The rebel officers had originally planned to have the army minister, General Kawashima, who was associated with the Imperial Way faction, report their intentions to the emperor, who would then issue a decree declaring a "Shōwa restoration." Despite their radical aim—overthrowing of the political order—the mutineers (like other military and civilian extremists of the 1930s) assumed the legitimacy and intended to operate within the framework of the imperial system and the *kokutai*. They saw the emperor as the puppet of his advisers and, in effect, devoid of a will of his own. Once the lord keeper of the privy seal and the grand chamberlain were out of the way, they believed, the emperor could be counted on to bestow the mantle of prime minister on General Mazaki, the hero whom they trusted to strengthen the military and resolve the China problem.

At the beginning of the insurrection they had a chance of success. The Tokyo military police commander, Gen. Kashii Kōhei, was an Imperial Way sympathizer; the emperor's chief aide, General Honjō, was the father-in-law of rebel officer Capt. Yamaguchi Ichi-tarō; and supporters of the mutineers could be found at military bases throughout the country.

According to the historian Hata Ikuhiko, the rebels contacted General Honjō both by phone and written message prior to the attack on the Okada cabinet. Honjō, the first of the entourage to learn of the mutiny, could have warned the intended targets of their danger if he had been so inclined. He did not. By the time Honjō came to court at 6:00 A.M. on the twenty-sixth, however, Chief Secretary Kido, Imperial Household Minister Yuasa Kurahei, and Vice Grand Chamberlain Hirohata Tadakata already knew that Saitō had been murdered and Suzuki seriously wounded. So too did the emperor. At 5:40 A.M. the chamberlain on night duty, Kanroji Osanaga, had awakened Hirohito and informed him that his old ministers and advisers had just been attacked and an uprising was underway.

From the moment Hirohito learned what had happened, he resolved to suppress the coup, angered at the killing of his ministers but also fearing that the rebels might enlist his brother, Prince Chichibu, in forcing him to abdicate. He put on his army uniform, received Honjō in audience, and ordered him to "[e]nd it immediately and turn this misfortune into a blessing." Honjō departed, and Hirohito embraced a strategy devised by Kido and presented by Imperial Household Minister Yuasa. Kido had taken swift action earlier that morning when Honjō arrived at court, demanding that the chief-aide-de-camp immediately determine how the Imperial Guard Division would respond in the event the mutineers marched on the Palace. Kido's plan was to prevent the formation of a new, provisional cabinet until the mutiny had been completely crushed. At 9:30 A.M., Army Minister Kawashima, who in January had met with Isobe, one of the main energizers of the rebel officers, came to court and performed the role that the rebels had scripted for him: He urged the emperor to form a cabinet that would "clarify the *kokutai*, stabilize national life, and fulfill national defense." Taken aback at his army minister's obtuseness, Hirohito scolded Kawashima and ordered him to give priority to suppressing the mutiny. Hirohito also vented his anger that morning on Chief of the Navy General Staff Prince Fushimi, a supporter of the Fleet faction, who came to the palace to learn the emperor's intentions on forming a new cabinet and was told, in effect, to get lost.

Later that day Kawashima met with the Supreme Military Council, an informal group of high-ranking army officers, most of whom were sympathetic to the rebels. Among those in attendance and controlling the meeting were the Imperial Way generals Araki, Mazaki, and Yamashita and their supporters, including Prince Higashikuni Naruhiko and Lt. Gen. Prince Asaka Yasuhiko. The council decided to try persuasion on the rebel officers before conveying the emperor's order to them, which was precisely the opposite of what Hirohito had demanded. According to the historian Otabe Yūji, "the army minister's instruction" was issued from the palace to the rebel officers at 10:50 A.M., five hours and fifty minutes after the start of their mutiny. It declared that "(1) Your reason for rebelling has reached the emperor; (2) We recognize your true action was based on your sincere desire to manifest the *kokutai*. ... 5) Other than this, everything depends on the emperor's benevolence." This "instruction," expressing informal upper-echelon approval of the uprising and intimating to the rebels that the emperor might show leniency, was conveyed to the ringleaders by Tokyo martial law commander General Kashii.

On the evening of the first day of the uprising, when the ministers of the Okada cabinet came to court to submit their resignations Hirohito again refused to permit it, telling them to stay on without their prime minister until the mutiny ended.

Early on the morning of the second day, February 27, Hirohito declared "administrative martial law" on the basis of Article 8 of the Imperial Constitution, pertaining to emergency imperial ordinances. Formally he was invoking his sovereign governmental power to handle the crisis. In reality he was backing his orders to suppress the rebellion in his capacity as commander in chief by freeing himself from any obligation to obtain the consent of any cabinet ministers for his actions.

Hirohito displayed unusual energy in working to crush the rebellion. At short intervals throughout the second day and into the early morning hours of the twenty-eighth, the third day, Hirohito sent chamberlains scurrying down the long corridors of the Meiji Palace to summon Honjō for repeated audiences. Each time he demanded to learn whether the rebels were being suppressed. When he did not like Honjō's replies, he threatened to lead the Imperial Guard Division himself. But (as Hata notes) Honjō was equally stubborn in his defense of the rebel's actions: Indeed, Honjō's own diary account of this period shows him a virtual traitor to the emperor.

During the uprising Hirohito met Prince Chichibu, who had just returned from his post in distant Hirosaki and with whom his relations were not always amicable. After their meeting Chichibu is alleged to have distanced himself from the rebels and ended his relations with the young officers and the Imperial Way generals. Nevertheless, rumors of the prince's sympathy for them never ended, and two years later Prince Saionji twice revealed (to his secretary, Harada) his fear that sibling rivalry in the imperial family could someday lead to murder. Also on the second day two senior naval officers distinguished themselves by their show of loyalty to the emperor: Rear Admiral Yonai and his chief of staff, Inoue.

By the morning of the fourth day of the uprising, February 29, the emperor had firmly maintained his authority, the troops were returning to their barracks, and most of the ringleaders were in custody. Court-martialed in April, secretly and without benefit of defense lawyers, seventeen of them were executed in July by firing squad. Shortly afterward, around the time of the Buddhist *obon* festival for the spirits of the dead, Hirohito is alleged to have ordered one of his military aides (who happened to have been on night duty at the Palace when the mutiny occurred) to secure seventeen *obon* lanterns. The aide later hung them somewhere in the palace. Hirohito said no more about the lanterns, which had to be kept secret because he could not be perceived as condoning mutiny. Perhaps this action made him feel more at ease with himself. Even after having sanctioned death sentences in order to extinguish threats to his entourage, he could still feel that he was living his belief in compassionate concern for his subjects.

When the military investigated the February uprising, it discovered that the rebels' sense of crisis had been magnified by the general election held on February 20, in which voters had expressed antimilitary sentiments by supporting left-wing candidates. Further, despite the rural roots and populist rhetoric of the ringleaders, most had not become revolutionaries because of the agricultural depression, and their ultimate goals had little to do with agrarian reforms, as many contemporaries imagined. The aim of the insurgent leaders was to further the good of the *kokutai*, as they understood it, by accelerating Japan's rearmament. The military portion of the national budget had increased steadily since the start of the Manchurian Incident, going from 3.47 percent of GNP in 1931 to 5.63 percent in 1936. During that period the navy had steadily increased its tonnage; both services had begun to develop air forces; but the army had not expanded significantly and still totaled about 233,365 officers and men organized in seventeen divisions. The insurgent officers blamed the political system, not economic conditions, for limiting military budgets in a time of national emergency.

Interestingly, in their concept of total war the thinking of the ringleaders and their senior commanders in the Army Ministry and the Army General Staff was strikingly similar: Both wanted state control of industrial decision making and production in order to fully mobilize the nation's resources. Beyond their common ignorance of what "total" war really required, the rebel leaders were as disunited in their thinking as they had been in their actions throughout the uprising. Only the idea of a "Shōwa restoration" to reform the management of the state seems to have been widely shared. Notions of what such a "restoration" would mean in practice varied from individual to individual. For Isobe, perhaps the most deranged of the ringleaders, it denoted "[s]tate consolidation of the economy together with completing the Meiji restoration and developing it into a world restoration."

The February mutiny confirmed Hirohito's belief in the constitution's importance for securing his powers of military command. So rigidly did he heed that lesson that when General Ishiwara Kanji later drafted a plan to establish a separate, independent army air force, Hirohito would not even consider it for fear that an air force, not provided for in the constitution, might elude his control. Ultimately the entire experience strengthened his sense of the enormous power he had when performing as a military commander. He seems to have resolved never to appear indecisive when confronted with decisions to act; and he began to move closer to the Control faction of the army, and to feel justified in sanctioning large military spending increases. Yet he never overcame the memory of this incident, and tended to infer from it that the throne was more insecure than it really was.

After World War II, when Hirohito was particularly concerned to play down his role as supreme commander, he offered a deliberately distorted account of the February mutiny:

> I issued an order at that time for the rebel force to be suppressed. This brings to mind
> Machida Chūji, the finance minister. He was very worried about the rebellion's adverse

effect on the money market and warned me that a panic could occur unless I took firm measures. Therefore I issued a strong command to have [the uprising] put down.

As a rule, because a suppression order also involves martial law, military circles, who cannot issue such an order on their own, need the mutual consent of the government. However, at the time, Okada's whereabouts were unknown. As the attitude of the Army Ministry seemed too lenient, I issued a strict order.

Following my bitter experiences with the Tanaka cabinet, I had decided always to wait for the opinions of my advisers before making any decision, and not to go against their counsel. Only twice, on this occasion and at the time of the ending of the war, did I positively implement my own ideas.

Ishiwara Kanji of the Army General Staff Office also asked me, through military aide Chōjiri [Kazumoto], to issue a suppression order. I don't know what sort of a person Ishiwara is, but on this occasion he was correct, even though he had been the instigator of the Manchurian Incident.

Further, my chief military aide, Honjō, brought me the plan drafted by Yamashita Hōbun, in which Yamashita asked me to please send an examiner because the three leaders of the rebel army were likely to commit suicide. However, I thought that sending an examiner would imply that they had acted according to their moral convictions and were deserving of respect. …

So I rejected Honjō's proposal, and [instead] issued the order to suppress them. I received no report that generals in charge of military affairs had gone and urged the rebels to surrender.

When Hirohito ordered the immediate suppression of the rebels on the morning of February 26, he was angry at them for having murdered his closest advisers, and at his senior army officers for procrastinating in putting them down. On the second day Minister of Commerce and Industry Machida assumed the additional post of finance minister, and fear of economic panic and confusion became a reason, though not the main one, for the emperor's action. Thereafter Hirohito felt that every hour of delay harmed Japan's international image.

Repeatedly since the Manchurian Incident, the emperor had clashed with the military over infringements of his authority but never over fundamental policy. Occasionally, in step with the army's rise to power, he had impressed his own political views on policy making, just as he had done earlier under the Hamaguchi cabinet. The February 26 mutiny taught him and Yuasa—his privy seal from March 1936 to June 1940, and the very first lord keeper of the privy seal to come to court daily—the importance of exercising the emperor's right of supreme command to the full whenever circumstances required. Even with Honjō acting against him, Hirohito had received support and gotten his way by taking a firm stance. His decisiveness abruptly ended the period in which alienated "young officers" had tried to use him as a principle of reform to undermine a power structure they could not successfully manipulate. Hirohito however, had learned precisely how to manipulate that establishment in most situations and circumstances.

The decision-making process had built into it secrecy, indirection, lack of clear lines of communication, vagueness in the drafting of policy statements, and manipulation of information networks-m short, confusion, misunderstanding, and perpetual intrigue to negotiate elite consensus. That was the way things worked in Tokyo. It was how the emperor worked. Now, once again, he had reminded all the close-knit elites that *he* was *the reason* the system worked.

IV

On May 4, 1936, in his rescript at the opening ceremony of the Sixty-ninth Imperial Diet, while Tokyo still lay silenced under martial law, Hirohito had finally closed the curtain on the February mutiny. For a short time he considered sending the military and the nation a strong message of censure of the army, but after much thought and procrastination over a three-month period, he settled for one terse, utterly innocuous sentence: "We regret the recent incident that occurred in Tokyo." Many in his audience of Diet members and military officials responded with startled "awe," and privately some were disappointed. Once again, at a crucial moment, Hirohito declined an opportunity to rein in his military publicly through his constitutional role. Nevertheless, owing to his actions behind the scene, the drifting and yawing in domestic policy that had characterized Japan since the Manchurian Incident now ended, and over the next fourteen months, the emperor and most of his advisers concurred with the demands of the army and navy for accelerated military buildup and state-directed industrial development.

The Hirota Kōki cabinet, formed immediately after the February 26 mutiny, following Privy Seal Yuasa's recommendation, is remembered for having furthered military influence in politics while allowing interservice rivalries and jealousies to affect national goals. In May 1936 Hirota, on the advice of his army and navy ministers, revived the practice of appointing military ministers only from the roster of high-ranking officers on active duty. He professed to believe the measure would prevent officers associated with the discredited Imperial Way faction from someday regaining power. By narrowing the field of candidates and increasing the power of the army vis-à-vis the prime minister, Hirota's action paved the way for army leaders to use this weapon to overthrow the cabinet of Admiral Yonai in July 1940.

In policy toward China, Hirota spurned cooperation based on equality and supported the army's plans to separate the five provinces of North China, with a population estimated at more than eighty million, from the Nanking government. Hirota had been foreign minister when the Japanese commander of the China Garrison Force, based in the port city of Tientsin, and the chief of the Mukden Special Agency had signed local agreements with Chinese Nationalist minister of war, Gen. Ho Ying-ch'in, by which Chiang Kai-shek withdrew both his political organs and his Central Army from North China. Like the emperor, Hirota had thereafter done nothing to counter statements by the commander of the China Garrison Force and other generals publicly suggesting that the coal- and iron-rich northern provinces be split away from the rest of China and, in effect, incorporated into the Japanese continental holding.

Also like the emperor, Hirota shared an assumption that many Japanese officers considered self-evident: China was neither a nation nor a people but merely a territorial designation, and Japan was entitled to rearrange that territory and take whatever parts it wished. Emperor Hirohito, on April 17, 1936, sanctioned the army's request for a threefold increase in the size of its small China Garrison Force from 1,771 to 5,774 troops. He also approved the establishment of a new military base at Fengtai, a rail junction in the southwest suburb of Peking, not far from the historic Marco Polo Bridge. Strong Chinese protests ensued, but the expanded garrison went ahead with the construction of its Fengtai barracks. Japanese troops were soon conducting training exercises with live ammunition, in close proximity to Chinese military facilities, setting the stage for repeated clashes with Chinese troops.

Hirohito should have known that Japan needed time, capital and more industry—in short, needed years of at least relative peace, if it was going to profit from its new territories on the continent and the industrial development already in place. And the Army General Staff also ought to have appreciated the dangerous animosity and distrust Japan had stirred up within China's educated public of workers, students, and intellectuals, and especially among such Manchurian exiles as Chang Hsueh-liang and his officer corps, who identified strongly with the northeastern provinces and were determined to go on resisting Japan.

Hirohito and his strategists were more concerned with protecting their overlong (and exposed) northern lines of supply and communication from possible Soviet interruption than with the "united front" that Chiang Kai-shek and his archrival Mao Tse-tung were forming throughout the first half of 1937. Japanese contingency planning under the Hirota cabinet focussed on defense against the Soviet Union. A major war with China was neither expected, desired, nor prepared for. Japanese relations with Moscow deteriorated as the Kwantung Army reinforced and expanded its activities in Inner Mongolia, and strengthened its positions along the northern border with Outer Mongolia.

The Hirota cabinet responded favorably to Nazi Germany's policies of rapid rearmament on a gigantic scale, anti-Sovietism, economic autarchy, and racial and religious bigotry and intolerance. The signing of the Anti-Comintern Pact with Germany in November 1936 was preceded by the growth of military ties between the Imperial Army and Navy and the German military command, and came on the heels of a series of foreign policy coups by Hitler that destroyed the post-World War I settlement in Europe. A secret protocol to the pact committed the signatories not to assist Moscow in the event of war between one of them and the Soviet Union. A year later Italy joined the pact. Having aligned internationally with the rising Nazi and Fascist dictatorships, imperial Japan could now be expected to act together with them in the future. For the democratically elected governments of Britain, France, and the United States, the Anti-Comintern Pact united the looming crises in Europe and Asia.

Hirota adopted his most important foreign policy measures in mid-1936, in four- and five-member ministerial conferences that departed from the practice of full cabinet meetings envisioned under the Meiji constitution. The "Criteria for National Policy," and the "Foreign Policy of the Empire," both decided on August 7, 1936, set forth a grandiose, provocative and unrealistic array of projects and goals, which, if they came to be concurrently attempted, would quite exceed Japan's national power. Manchukuo was to be built up; the resources of North China were to be secured for the empire through puppet regimes; preparations would be made for future war with the Soviet Union; control of the western Pacific and Southeast Asia was to be brought about, which would require new naval construction in competition with the United States, as well as the building of air bases and radio stations on Taiwan, the Marianas, and the Carolines (in the Central Pacific)—and, at the same time, there would be an increase in military and naval manpower and logistical support structures.

The "Criteria for National Policy" registered the tendency of Japan's bureaucratic elites to line up their respective positions, side by side, in vague official texts that could be interpreted to suit the convenience of their drafters. This was to be the pattern of decision making for all later stages of the crisis of Japanese diplomacy. That this tendency made its appearance on the eve of war with China was significant, for it meant that the prime minister, foreign minister, army and navy ministers, and the two chiefs of staff had abandoned the task of thrashing out their disagreements in reasoned argument. Rather than struggle to reach genuine consensus, they adopted a simpler, easier procedure. They enscribed their respective positions in "national policy" documents that postponed reckoning over the resources needed to accomplish their goals, and also left unclear whether force or diplomacy, or both, would be employed.

The drafters of the national policy equated their first criterion—to "eliminate the hegemonistic policies of the Great Powers in East Asia"—with "manifest[ing] the spirit of the imperial way" in foreign policy. Henceforth foreign policy would become more expansionist and radical, for the "imperial way" implied, internationally, that the emperor's "benevolence" be extended until Japanese overlordship was established throughout Asia. The second yardstick of sound foreign policy required Japan "to become the stabilizing force in East Asia in both name and reality" by building up armaments. The third and fourth "criteria of national policy"—and the core of the document—were "to secure our footing on the East Asian continent, and to advance and develop in the Southern Oceans by combining diplomacy and national defense."

The reference to the "East Asian continent" met the wish of the army to advance north with a view to countering the Soviet Union; the "Southern Oceans," an elastic geographical term, denoted the navy's goal of moving southward and preparing to achieve supremacy over the United States and Britain in the vast western Pacific. Neither service was happy with the goal of the other; neither trusted the other. By posting their plans side by side, thereby avoiding a clear decision as to which one should prevail, they prevented the pluralistic system of advising the emperor from breaking down.

Japan was now only a year away from all-out war in China, but the inability of its constitutionally mandated imperial advisers and the chiefs of staff to agree on a unified national policy was more than ever an endemic feature of the political process. And complicating these disagreements and splits between "the government" and "the military," under both Hirota and his successors, was continuing discord between the Army General Staff in Tokyo and officers in the field charged with implementing policy.

Once Japan entered a serious war emergency, with the prestige of the throne exalted far beyond the limits of ordinary times, this multitiered structure of bureaucratic conflicts created increasing room for Hirohito to maximize his influence in policy making. Constantly becoming more experienced in playing his designated political and military roles, Hirohito would watch as his advisers developed their policies, note their disagreements, and finally insist that they compose their differences and unify their military and political strategies. As it was impossible for them to do so, the pressure he exerted complicated the already confused decision-making process. His "unity" card would become Hirohito's special wedge for driving home *his* views, ensuring that those of "middle stratum" officers did not prevail in national policy making, and that the process itself remained primarily "top-down" in nature.

And the more Hirohito pressed "unity" upon the representatives of his chronically divided "government" and "high command," the more they papered over their differences in policy texts that virtually impelled expansion abroad and, soon, war without end. It was not just the Japanese military provoking aggression in China during the middle and late 1930s; the religiously charged monarchy was also driving aggression, while offering a shield from public criticism to those who acted in its name.

On August 25, 1936, the Hirota government announced that slightly more than 69 percent of the government's total 1937 budget (or nearly 33 billion yen) would be allocated to the military. This amounted to almost a threefold increase in the 1936 military budget of approximately 10 billion yen, or 47.7 percent of government spending. To pay for all this, taxes would be raised and inflation tolerated, armaments manufacturers and the great *zaibatsu* enriched and the patriotism of ordinary wage earners fanned up while their wages were held down.

These policies of the Hirota cabinet reflected and to some degree were impelled by backlash within the navy over the army's unilateral actions at home and abroad. On March 27 1936 the

Third Fleet commander, Adm. Oikawa Koshirō, had offered to the navy minister and the chief of the Navy General Staff his "Views on National Policy Centering on China." Writing from his flagship *Izumo* in Shanghai Harbor, Oikawa pointed out that the Kwantung Army was rushing "political machinations" to "separate the Five provinces of North China from the authority of the Nanking government and so form a buffer zone between Manchukuo and China."

After urging the navy not to permit the Kwantung Army to act unilaterally in so grave a matter, Oikawa recommended a policy of expanding southward into Southeast Asia and the southwest Pacific, while also moving north. Although this should be done peacefully, Japan had to prepare and be ready someday to free itself of tariff and other obstacles to economic growth "by using military force." Therefore, even if war against the Soviet Union should be decided on and "preparation for a war on land" made the immediate national goal, the navy still should prepare for war at sea. Oikawa also stressed the need to exercise care and prudence so as not to provoke the Great Powers and induce them "to unite against us."

The reply to Admiral Oikawa by the navy vice minister and the vice chief of the Navy General Staff was later formally adopted as the Hirota cabinet's "Criteria for National Policy" and "General Principles of National Policy," approved in August. The latter document spoke of making Japan the "stabilizing force in East Asia" while it expanded southward. At this time, however, the navy's senior commanders clearly recognized the irrationality of separate army and navy advances, fearing that this would exceed Japan's national strength and "ultimately lead to war with more than two countries." They recommended a policy of "gradual and peaceful expansion" in both the north and the south.

This was indeed the rational strand in the otherwise wildly ambitious strategy pursued by the cabinets of Hirota and his successor, General Hayashi. That influential groups in the navy, army, Foreign Ministry, and imperial court were still capable of lucid evaluations of Japan's problems during 1936 and the first half of 1937 is undeniable. Nevertheless, these same leaders were already beginning to be carried by the momentum of their choices. Sooner or later their policy goals—military expansion on the continent, naval control of the western Pacific and Southeast Asian sea lanes, and equalization of relations with the Great Powers—would provoke military clashes with China—and even more serious clashes with the United States and Britain.

Significantly, in the fall of 1936, after several incidents involving attacks on Japanese nationals living in central and south China, the navy began to study ways to improve its policing capabilities in south China. The air power theories of the Italian Maj. Gen. Giulio Douhet were then in vogue among navalists, and the resulting contingency plan included a punitive air campaign against the civilian population of China's major cities as well as preparations for conducting a coastal blockade should one ever be needed.

Hirota's tenure as prime minister ended on January 23, 1937. He was followed on February 2 by General Hayashi, whose cabinet lasted only four months. Prince Konoe then organized his first cabinet on June 4. He was a descendant of the famous Fujiwara family of court nobles, whose women had for centuries regularly intermarried with imperial princes and during the Heian period (794–1185) had ruled Japan. Personal cleverness, charisma, and high lineage, as well as good connections with the navy and willingness to cultivate the army and the civilian right wing, all combined to propel him to the top.

V

Following the February 26, 1936, uprising, under the prime ministerships of Hirota and Hayashi, the emperor and his entourage became more supportive of reinforcing his theoretically unassailable power from below. In this context the Ministry of Education accelerated efforts to further the nation's spiritual mobilization for a possible protracted war, and on May 31, 1937, published and distributed for school use an estimated three hundred thousand copies of *Kokutai no hongi* (The Fundamentals of the national polity). Eventually more than two million copies were sold nationwide.

Kokutai no hongi was a discourse on the *kokutai*, and on the emperor's ideological and spiritual role as the exemplar of national benevolence and morality. A transitional ideological tract, it did not completely reject Western thought and institutions, but went beyond merely emphasizing Japanese cultural distinctiveness. Extolling the "bright," "pure," and selfless "heart" of the Japanese, and counterposing the *kokutai* to modern Western individualism and "abstract totalitarianisms," it stressed the absolute superiority of the Japanese people and state over all other nations. "We loyal subjects differ completely in our nature from so called citizens of Western nations. … We always seek in the emperor the source of our lives and activities."

Kokutai no hongi also emphasized the centrality of the family-state, home, and ancestors, and reminded readers that the "divine winds" (*kamikaze*), which had twice saved Japan from Mongol invasions in the late thirteenth century, proved indisputably Japan's divinity and indestructibility. Above all the pamphlet implanted the image of the emperor as a military ruler and "a living god who rules our country in accordance with the benevolent wishes of his imperial founder and his other imperial ancestors." All Japanese subjects had the duty to give Hirohito their absolute obedience. In practice that meant "to live for the great glory and dignity of the emperor, abandoning one's small ego, and thus expressing our true life as a people." Here, in essence, was that peculiar amalgamation of Shinto, Buddhist, neo-Confusian, and Western monarchist ideals, known as *kōdō*—"the imperial way," that powered Japanese aggression, and was used by army leaders to browbeat critics and by right-wing thugs to justify their terrorist actions. For Hirohito the chief merit of the pamphlet was the possibility it offered of producing a stronger spirit of devotion to his person, thereby enhancing his influence over the military.

The myth of Japan as a tightly unified, monolithic state and society, which *Kokutai no hongi* perpetuated, was reaffirmed four years later in July 1941 in yet another hysterical Shinto-Buddhist tract published and distributed by the Ministry of Education. By this time Hirohito had become the symbol of Japan's "escape" from the West, and had begun the process that would lead to the momentous decision to declare war against the United States and Britain. He needed more than ever the strongest possible political influence over the entire nation. The country had taken on the identity of a fascist state and had even adopted the haunting rhetoric of fascism; its people labored under the burdens of food rationing and a total war economy; policies were in place designed to increase war production by lowering living standards; in the emperor's name all open dissent had been squashed.

Against this background *Shimmin no michi* (The Way of the subject) called for overthrowing "the old order based on the dominance of individualism, liberalism, and dialectical materialism," and building a new order in East Asia based on the principle of allowing "all nations to seek their proper places." The pamphlet demanded that "a structure of … unanimity" be established in all realms of national life so that Japan could perfect its total war state and establish "a world community based on moral principles." With every subject involved in serving the emperor, it called upon all Japanese to purge egotism from their souls and practice daily a relation to the state in which nothing is "our own," and "even in our private lives we always remember to unite with the emperor and serve the state."

BORYOKUDIAN REDUX:
YAKUZA AND THE CONSERVATIVE NEXUS

Eiko Maruko Siniawer

Although prewar-style *sōshi* and *ingaidan* were pushed out of postwar politics, yakuza did not meet the same fate. Instead, they became an integral part of a conservative nexus that was a reincarnation of the prewar nationalist version discussed in the previous chapter. That yakuza were a part of this network helps explain their resilience and continued presence in politics—why the public impatience with the use of physical force did not spell the end of these particular violence specialists. Conservative political leaders and fixers determined that the need for, and utility of yakuza and their violence outweighed the negative effects of any criticism, at least in the initial postwar decades. And, perhaps, it was hoped that forming loose alliances with yakuza might seem marginally less offensive than institutionalizing *sōshi-like* figures into the political parties; it did at least, allow slightly more room for denial and obfuscation.

To understand the postwar emergence of conservative politicians and the political right, we need to go back to the late 1940s, after the iron curtain was said to be descending in Europe and the United States had expressed its concern about Soviet expansion in the Truman Doctrine. Heightened anxieties about the spread of communism in Japan, the rambunctious character of some labor unions, and other seemingly unruly popular movements provoked a "reverse course" in occupation policies whereby anticommunism eclipsed democratization as the Americans' primary concern. Earlier, from 1946 to 1948 the occupation authorities had carried out purges to prevent the resurgence of the prewar right and help protect the democratizing project. Among those targeted along with militarists and political leaders were "influential members of ultranationalistic, terroristic or secret patriotic societies," including the likes of the Gen'yōsha (Dark Ocean Society). In the initial phase of the occupation, more than 100 organizations were dissolved. At the same time, the occupation had granted labor the freedom to unionize and had legalized the Japan Communist Party, helping to spark leftist movements. But in 1949 and 1950, the occupation did an about-face, removing Japan Communist Party members, unionists, and other leftists from their positions in the public and private sectors, from heavy industry to education and communications; this "red purge" cost 21,000 people their jobs At the same time, the occupation depurged some prewar militarists and nationalists. Together, the red purge and the depurge facilitated the development of a conservative hegemony in politics and jump-started the postwar reemergence of right-wing organizations.

Among those given a chance for a new political life was Kishi Nobusuke, who was released from Sugamo Prison in 1948 where he had been held for over three years as a suspected Class A war criminal. Kishi had been a bureaucrat in Manchuria in the late 1930s, where he formed a network of political connections and allegedly filled his own pockets with both legal and illegal profits from the opium trade and the trafficking of capital. From 1941 to 1944, he served as the minister of commerce and industry for Prime Minister Tōjō Hideki and managed the wartime economy. And around that time, Kishi rallied his political allies to form the Kishi New Party (Kishi Shintō), which consisted of Diet members, Japanese businessmen with whom he had worked in China, and nationalists who had been responsible for the attempted coups d'état of 1931. Once released from prison in 1948, Kishi set to work on constructing a conservative political party that could dominate postwar politics. His first attempt, a recreation of both his prewar Kishi New Party and the Association for Defense of the Fatherland (Gokoku Dōshikai), was known as the Japan Reconstruction Federation (Nippon Saiken Renmei); but it failed in its electoral debut. Kishi managed to work his way into the conservative Liberal Party, was elected to the Diet in 1953, was thrown out of the party the next year for trying to undermine it from within, and was taken in by the rival conservative Democratic Party. All the while, Kishi had his eye on the consolidation of conservative power. And in November 1955, he helped orchestrate the merger of the Liberal and Democratic Parties into the LDP, the party that would dominate Japanese politics until the early 1990s. Kishi (brother of future prime minister Satō Eisaku and grandfather of twenty-first-century prime minister Abe Shinzō) became secretary-general of the LDP and served as prime minister from 1957 to 1960. (After 1960, he remained in the Diet until retiring from his seat in 1979.)

What helped the feuding conservatives—and, eventually, the conservative nexus—coalesce was a shared fear of the socialists. The electoral gains enjoyed by some socialist subgroups in the early 1950s and, most immediately, the reunification of the two main factions of the JSP in October 1955 were deeply frightening to the rival conservatives. Along with this antisocialist stance, what held the conservatives together was a dislike of labor union activism, support for business interests, and, for many, the desire for Japan to rearm.

Antipathy toward the left may have brought conservatives together, but what greased the wheels of conservative politics and fueled the construction of LDP hegemony was money. To trace the financing of the LDP and its politicians is to connect many of the nodes of an expansive and powerful conservative web. Some of the contributions to the LDP were technically legal, even if they could be viewed as the buying of influence on party policy. One representative of big business known as the Keizai Dantai Rengōkai (Federation of Economic Organizations, hereafter Keidanren) donated huge sums of money, mainly to conservatives. In January 1955, the federation established a system whereby political contributions from various members would be pooled by an administrative body, the Keizai Saiken Kondankai (Economic Reconstruction Council), and then distributed. The intent behind the creation of this mechanism was to make political financing more transparent by eliminating the many separate transactions that individual corporations and industries had previously been conducting with politicians, political factions, and parties; it was hoped that the attempt to be more open would prevent the public from losing trust in Japanese industry, which had already been tainted by a political bribery scandal the previous year. The money doled

Class A war criminal

out by the council was thus clean, and one of the main administrators of the system, Hanamura Nihachirō, expressed pride that all corporate donations adhered to political finance laws and that the council was scandal free. Nonetheless, the extent of Keidanren's financial power raises questions about the place of big business in democratic politics. It is quite clear that Keidanren played a key role in financing the consolidation of conservative power. In the council's first year, it collected approximately one billion yen, the majority of which went to the two conservative parties. After the establishment of the LDP, which Keidanren had hoped for, Hanamura worked to build the financial foundation of the party, ostensibly to ensure the continued existence of a liberal economic system. In a postwar version of the prewar ties between *zaibatsu* and the major political parties, Keidanren played a crucial role in forming a financial bond between big business and the LDP. From 1955 to 1960, the council distributed ¥2.5 billion; for the election of 1960, it collected ¥800 million, of which ¥770 million was given to the LDP. Keidanren did dole out money to all political parties, except for the communists, but 90 percent of its giving was to the LDP. More telling of Keidanren's influence was the size of its contributions relative to those of other funders—by 1960, the council's donations constituted about 60 percent of all reported political contributions. And as political scientist Richard Samuels has pointed out, this stream of money from the council accounted for only a portion of all financial donations from business to the LDP.

Another strong supporter of the LDP was the U.S. Central Intelligence Agency (CIA), alleged to have provided covert funds to the party and specific conservative politicians. Declassified documents unequivocally reveal that the U.S. government wanted to see a conservative government in Japan. In August 1955, Secretary of State John Foster Dulles spoke of the importance of acting in concert with the conservatives. And several years later, Ambassador to Japan Douglas MacArthur II reported that it was in the best interests of the United States for Kishi Nobusuke to win what was seen as a crucial election in May 1958. When Kishi proved victorious, the State Department commented that the political climate in Japan was "favorable to the interests of the United States in the Far East" and predicted that "Japan will become an increasingly valuable ally in the Far East." American support for the election of Kishi included financial backing, according to CIA documents and former intelligence officers. And the funding of Kishi in the 1958 election was part of a larger strategy of financing the LDP. According to Alfred C. Ulmer Jr., head of the CIA's Far East operations from 1955 to 1958: "We financed them. We depended on the LDP for information." And Roger Hilsman, who led the State Department's intelligence bureau during the administration of John F. Kennedy, described funding of the LDP and its politicians in the early 1960s as "so established and so routine" that it was accepted as a given and important aspect of U.S. foreign policy toward Japan.

Others in the conservative nexus helped not only with fundraising, but also with organizing support for the LDP. Political fixers, usually acting behind the scenes, leveraged their prewar connections and leadership skills to reinvigorate conservative politics and right-wing groups. It was these men who helped bring yakuza into the conservative fold. One of the most influential political fixers was Sasakawa Ryōichi, who had been imprisoned in 1945 alongside Kishi Nobusuke as a suspected Class A war criminal. In the prewar period, Sasakawa had been a fervent nationalist and supporter of war. He had discontinued his education after completing elementary school (because of family fears that he would turn socialist if he continued his studies, Sasakawa claims), served as a pilot in the Imperial Navy, and then became involved with various nationalistic endeavors. In September 1931, he was installed as president of the Kokusui Taishūtō (National Essence Mass Party), an organization with 23 branches and more than 10,000 members who, following the Italian fascist model, wore black shirts. In 1932, he constructed an air field in Osaka for the purpose of training fighter pilots. The hangar at this facility had space for 70 fighter planes and 20 training planes; ownership of the property eventually passed to the army. From 1935 to 1938, Sasakawa sat in prison, having been arrested for various crimes including extortion and bribery and the planning of violent political crimes, including one against the prime minister—newspapers at the time dubbed him the "don of Japan's violent groups" (*Nihon no bōryokudan no don*). And in 1939, after his release, Sasakawa went to Rome to visit Mussolini.

Kodama Yoshio prison photograph

It was in the 1930s that Sasakawa came to know a fellow nationalist who, like him, would become a postwar political fixer: Kodama Yoshio. Kodama had developed a disdain for leftist ideologies fairly early in his life. Although he had worked as a laborer in various factories and mills and was sympathetic with the difficulties of working life, he vehemently opposed the communist tint of labor unions and the labor movement. In his diary he recalled, "It was difficult for me to understand why the Soviet Union should have to be called our motherland and why Marxism should be forced upon a Japan differing fundamentally in conditions from Russia, in order just to solve the labor-capital dispute." He became enamored with nationalism and in 1929 joined the anticommunist Kenkokukai (National Founding Association) which was led by nationalist leaders Akao Bin and Ue-sugi Shinkichi. Over the next eight years, Kodama became involved with various nationalist groups and was imprisoned a number of times; he served his longest sentence for planning to assassinate cabinet members. While in prison, Kodama met

Fuji Yoshio, a close associate of Sasakawa. Through this connection, Kodama eventually served as East Asia division chief of Sasakawas Kokusui Taishūtō.

The tie between Sasakawa and Kodama grew stronger in 1941 when Sasakawa was asked by Navy Air Force Headquarters to recommend a colleague who could head up a special purchasing and procurement agency. Sasakawa chose his junior, Kodama, who reluctantly left a part-time arrangement with the army to establish the Kodama Kikan (Kodama Agency) in December 1941. Two years after its founding, Sasakawa's right-hand man, Fuji Yoshio, became vice president of the agency; Sasakawa himself took credit for helping to found the Kodama Kikan and has been described as one of its major supporters. Headquartered in Shanghai, the Kodama Kikan received millions of yen from the navy for its establishment and proceeded to acquire war material for Navy Air Force Headquarters. Kodama's operatives in this endeavor, numbering in the hundreds, were said to consist mainly of "professional criminals, right-wing thugs, and members of the *kenpeitai* (military police)"—making Kodama and his staff a kind of *tairiku rōnin* (continental adventurer). Although Kodama began with the modest duty of providing copper and airplane parts, over time he expanded his reach to include raw material, food, clothing, and vehicles. He also ran mines in China, some of which yielded rare metals such as tungsten and molybdenum. It has also been speculated that Kodama dealt in gold, diamonds, and opium. According to CIA and Army Counterintelligence Corps reports, much of this material was acquired illegally through expropriation and theft or was obtained at costs lower than those reported to the navy so that operatives could pocket greater profits. In addition to illegal revenue, Kodama was paid ¥3.5 billion by the navy between 1941 and 1945, and by the end of the war, he was worth the equivalent of $175 million. In the closing weeks of the war, the property and money of the Kodama Kikan were sent back to Japan; some of this material was allegedly stored in warehouses rented by Sasakawa.

Immediately after the war, Sasakawa and Kodama drew on their financial resources and organizational savvy to back the founding of Hatoyama Ichirō's Liberal Party. It has been suggested by many that money from the sale of some of the Kodama Kikan's spoils directly funded Hatoyamas efforts. The oft-quoted, but unsubstantiated, figure for this donation is ¥70 million. In addition, Sasakawa and Kodama recruited supporters for the party—including yakuza. When Sasakawa attended the ceremony for the Liberal Party's establishment, he was accompanied by a group of *tekiya* (itinerant merchants and a kind of yakuza). It has also been suggested that Kodama solicited campaign contributions from *tekiya* bosses in the first postwar general election of April 1946. So it seems that neither Kodama nor Sasakawa experienced any kind of postwar apostasy, either in style of politics or ideology. Sasakawa, for one, gave numerous speeches immediately after the war arguing that the West had provoked Japan into war by threatening its survival and that Japan's expansion into Taiwan, Korea, and Manchuria was not an invasion but a blessing for these areas.

The political careers of these two fixers were temporarily put on hold when they were jailed as suspected Class A war criminals. But like Kishi Nobusuke, both were eventually released. It has been assumed that Kodama and Sasakawa were set free in December 1948 because of their anticommunism and perhaps because of promises that they would gather information for either the occupation or the CIA. The latter claim seems questionable. Kodama did approach occupation authorities to offer his intelligence services. But his actual connection to American intelligence was more indirect—Kodama's aid was enlisted by Arisue Seizō, former chief of intelligence at Imperial General Headquarters who, after the war, was recruited by the occupation's intelligence arm (G-2) to establish a clandestine intelligence section within it. Kodama and his old Kodama Kikan connections on the continent were involved in a number of Arisue's projects. Although American money was finding its way to Kodama, however indirectly through Arisue, Kodama's attentions were not focused on working for the United States. One of his other pursuits at the time, for example, was blackmailing the Mitsui Corporation out of one billion yen. By 1953, when the CIA had replaced G-2 as the foremost American intelligence organ in Japan, it had become clear that the vaguely shared goal of anticommunism was not always enough to maintain strong alliances. Of Kodama, the CIA determined he was too unreliable to make for a good intelligence operative: "He is a professional liar, gangster, charlatan, and outright thief." Kodama was also described as "a distinct menace, and because of his manipulations of the Japanese underworld, is widely feared and his favor is sought by weak men in high positions."

In the decades that followed, Sasakawa backed right-wing organizations as he had in the prewar period. He served as an adviser to a number of groups and spoke against communism, comparing it to cholera and the plague, and rallied people to put their lives on the line to fight its spread. He also continued to work with Kodama and Kishi to further his next profitable venture: motorboat racing. Sasakawa used their help to secure Diet passage of a law that gave him a monopoly on the enterprise. And about 15 percent of the revenues from related gambling ventures went to the Zenkoku Mōtābōto Kyōsōkai Rengōkai (Motorboat Racing Association), which Sasakawa founded with seed money from Kodama and the Zaidan Hōjin Nippon Senpaku Shinkōkai (Japan Shipbuilding Industry Foundation), of which Sasakawa assumed the chairmanship in the early 1960s. Included on the staffs of both organizations were former members of his prewar Kokusui Taishutō. Sasakawa also benefited from the revenues of the Tōkyō-to Mōtābōto Kyōsōkai (Tokyo Motorboat Racing Association), which had Kodama at its helm. At about this point, Sasakawa began to take up philanthropic causes and contributed substantial funds to the United Nations and to the World Health Organization in particular—for his efforts, a bronze statue of Sasakawa stands in the European headquarters of the UN. Sasakawa also made a concerted push to be awarded the Nobel Peace Prize. Although this commendation proved elusive, he did win the Martin Luther King Peace Prize, the U.N. Peace Prize, and the Linus Pauling Award for Humanitarianism.

Kodama too backed right-wing causes in the postwar period. Though banned from "taking open part" in politics as a condition of his purged status, he was free to pursue political agendas so long as he stayed out of the limelight. So he resumed an active political life after his release from Sugamo Prison and seems to have revived some version of his prewar agency (which U.S. intelligence, at least, continued to call the Kodama Kikan). This network was said to be engaged with the elimination of communist influence from Asia and the construction of Japan as the foundation of an anticommunist league. In keeping with these aims, the agency had a branch in Hokkaidō, for example, from which Kodama allegedly engaged in anti-Japan Communist Party activities. Fund-raising was conducted out of a trading company based in the Marunouchi district of Tokyo. In addition to this particular company, a number of others were considered affiliates of the Kodama Kikan. The agency also garnered the cooperation of various prewar military men and nationalists, such as Ōkawa Shūmei and Miura Giichi. Many of those associated with the Kodama Kikan were rumored to have been part of a larger plan to smuggle supplies to the Chinese Nationalists and to recruit Japanese youth into a volunteer military corps to fight on the anticommunist side. Kodama, however, denied any connection to such efforts.

Over the course of his postwar career, Kodama continued to use and build his various political connections. He and Kishi, for example, seem to have remained collegial even after their years in Sugamo Prison, when they had played the game of *go* together and eaten their meals at the same table. Kishi admits that during his years as prime minister, Kodama would attend meetings at which Kishi was present. And their relationship seems to have been friendly—they would occasionally get together for *go*, Kodama shared whatever he caught when fishing, and they allegedly golfed, once. Kodama also had close ties with Ōno Ban-boku, discussed in Chapter 3 for his recruitment into the Seiyūkai *ingaidan* in the 1910s. Ōno's political career flourished in the postwar period, despite implication in a major political scandal in 1948. He became speaker of the House of Representatives in 1952, minister of state in 1953, and then served as vice president of the LDP until his death in 1964. Ōno was rumored to have a rough demeanor akin to that of *bakuto* and "kyōkaku." One journalist, in an article with a tabloid-esque quality, chastised him for continuing his fighting ways even after he had become a prominent politician. It was normal for boys to brawl, the reasoning went, but Ōno should not still shake his clenched fist and get into heated scuffles. More to the point, Ōno did not shy away from association with yakuza groups. Even when he was vice president of the LDP, he was photographed at a gathering of big yakuza bosses from the Kansai area, including Honda Nisuke and Hirata Katsuichi—Honda and Hirata were the first and second presidents, respectively, of the yakuza organization Hondakai (Honda Association). The Kobe-based group was originally established in 1938 as the Honda-gumi, changed its name in 1946 to the Hondakai, and had just under 2,000 members in the early 1960s. Included among its enterprises was management of its construction company (Honda Kensetsu Kōgyō).

Kodama himself fostered direct ties with yakuza. At one party that he hosted in September 1956, for example, among the 40 in attendance were about a dozen bosses from various yakuza "families" along with professional wrestlers, officers of a right-wing organization, and Minister of Agriculture and Forestry Kōno Ichirō from the cabinet of Hatoyama Ichirō, another Kodama connection.

Like the postwar resurrection of Kodama and Sasakawa, the rebirth of nationalist organizations is a story of resilience and the strength of old political connections. The right-wing groups of the 1950s most known for their violence were typically hybrids—part yakuza, part political organization—not unlike the Dai Nihon Kokusuikai (Greater Japan National Essence Association) and Dai Nihon Seigidan (Greater Japan Justice Group) of the prewar era. Yakuza, who had been so scarce during the war, managed to rebuild and survive the late 1940s by making money in the black markets that proliferated soon after the end of the war. As early as October 1945, approximately 17,000 such markets had popped up to peddle necessities such as food, toiletries, and clothing, as well as amphetamines. In big cities, yakuza bosses staked out territories in which they managed vendors. In Tokyo, for example, the Matsuda-gumi was in charge of the Shinbashi district, the Shibayama of Asakusa, the Ueda of Ginza, the Sekiguchi of Ikebukuro, and the Ozu and Wada of Shinjuku. And the heads of the yakuza organizations viewed themselves as maintaining order in a rough environment. One such figure was a Morimoto Mitsuji who took control of the Umeda market in Osaka, extolling the virtues of protecting the weak and defeating the strong while keeping everyone in line, armed with a knife and a pistol. Yet the yakuza presence often did not discourage violence but encouraged it, especially as territorial disputes led to physical clashes. In one incident in June 1946, a gunfight between thousands of yakuza resulted in seven deaths and 34 injuries.

When the economy began to show signs of recovery and black markets became less necessary, yakuza organizations took financial advantage of economic growth by shifting more of their attention to the burgeoning entertainment industry. Gambling, *pachinko* (pinball), bars, restaurants, and prostitution provided opportunities for the extraction of protection money. These revenues were supplemented by supplying labor for the construction and docking industries, a niche that yakuza had occupied in the prewar period and had begun to fill again during the occupation. All of these enterprises brought money into yakuza coffers and funded their development into large organizations and, eventually, powerful mafia syndicates.

When these yakuza organizations took on a political tinge, it was that of the right rather than the left. This remains true to the present day, so much so that the notion of leftist yakuza is laughable. There are some general reasons for this political orientation. It was strategically wise not to upset the ruling conservative hegemony so as to maintain a cordial relationship with the police and others who had the authority to crack down on the yakuza's financial lifelines. Conservatives also tended to stand behind company management in labor disputes. As in the prewar period, it was more lucrative for yakuza to ally with management, who had the funds to pay them for intimidating striking laborers.

At least one yakuza group not only cooperated with right-wing organizations but also became one itself. The Sekine-gumi was a yakuza "family" that managed black markets in the Asakusa, Honjo, and Mukōjima areas of Tokyo. When the head of the Sekine-gumi was arrested by occupation authorities in 1948 on a weapons possession charge, the group was ordered to dissolve. The defunct Sekine-gumi then remade itself into a (legal) political organization, building a reputation as a right-wing group around 1953 and officially establishing itself as the Matsubakai (Pine Needle Association) in September 1959. The Matsubakai platform articulated the organization's desire to prevent the invasion of communist thought into the minds of youth and to bring about the collapse of teachers' unions and other groups that embraced "dangerous ideas." The group also professed views vaguely reminiscent of the prewar period, such as respect for the emperor as a symbol of the nation and hope for the construction of a "Greater Asia" in the future. By 1960, the Matsubakai had six offices in Tokyo and branches in nearby Chiba, Ibaraki, and Gunma Prefectures. The membership of 2,000 to 3,000 people was described by at least one newspaper as consisting mainly of yakuza—*bakuto*, *tekiya*, and *gurentai* (street gangsters) in particular.

Other right-wing organizations drew heavily on the recent past, making connections with prewar groups and appropriating their ideologies. After the end of the occupation, it seems that former members of the Kantō Kokusuikai, a splinter group of the Dai Nihon Kokusuikai, had maintained or reestablished contact and were planning to convene a "countrywide national essence meeting" (*zenkoku kokusui taikai*) in Tokyo in March 1953. Umezu Jinbei, of the Kantō Kokusuikai, was also approached for advice and help in mobilizing yakuza for the anti-Soviet and anticommunist causes. The man who called on Umezu was politician and lawyer Kimura Tokutarō, who served as minister of justice in two Yoshida Shigeru cabinets. Together, Umezu and Kimura were among those who helped rally *bakuto* and *tekiya* to form the Gokokudan (National Protection Corps) and its subsidiary Gokoku Seinentai (National Protection Youth Corps) in 1954. Also central to the group's founding was Inoue Nisshō who, in the prewar period, had founded the Ketsumeidan (League of Blood) that carried out assassinations in 1932. And among the financial contributors to the Gokokudan were Kodama Yoshio and Sasakawa Ryōichi. Like the Matsubakai, the Gokokudan spoke highly of the emperor but in even stronger terms, describing him as the center of the blood relationship that bound the race together; using ideas from the prewar period, Japan's racial society (*Nihon minzoku shakai*) was also presented as a family.

The prewar legacy was also strong in the case of the Nihon Kokusuikai (Japan National Essence Society, hereafter Kokusuikai), a reorganization of the Dai Nihon Kokusuikai which had dissolved at the end of the war. The Kokusuikai adopted the language and platform of the prewar group, describing itself as an organization of the chivalrous, linking itself not only to the Dai Nihon Kokusuikai but also to an ideal dating back to the yakuza of the Tokugawa period. In addition, it purported to foster love for the fatherland, to absolutely oppose the left, and to protect the "beautiful customs" of Japan's national essence that were a proud part of the country's history and tradition. At the same time, the Kokusuikai adopted language that would be more palatable in a postwar context, claiming not to be rightist and speaking of members' devotion to the eradication of, among other things, "cruel violence" that oppresses the lives of the nation's people. Despite these stated aims, the group did not refrain from using violence and included *bakuto* among its ranks as well as those affiliated with the Gokokudan. Officially established in July 1958, the Kokusuikai was headquartered in Tokyo and had 250 members around 1960.

According to the Metropolitan Police, 28 such organizations claimed to be right-wing political groups but were more like "bōryokudan," to use the police's terminology. Of this number, only a handful—the Matsubakai, Gokokudan, and Kokusuikai prime among them— were repeatedly involved in violent, political incidents. In one such event in October 1958, three men disrupted a meeting of Nikkyōsō at Kudan Hall in Tokyo. The commotion began when one of the intruders set off a smoke bomb,

Yakuza Shrine in Asakusa Tokyo. In Japanese law, yakuza, or Japanese mafia is not allowed to show their tattoos in public except for Sanja Matsuri (festival).

then tried to cause panic by holding up a placard that read: "this is dynamite." His accomplices followed suit, igniting two more smoke bombs that darkened the entire room. Two of the three suspects were arrested and found to be members of the Kokusuikai's Seinen Teishintai (Youth Corps). The young man who had set off the first smoke bomb was a 26-year-old leader of the Seinen Teishintai; he was held under suspicion of forceful interference and trespassing. In a similar incident from late March 1959, about 60 members of a dozen right-wing organizations—including the Gokokudan and the Gokoku Seinentai—disrupted a JSP speech meeting by distributing leaflets, heckling speakers, and throwing smoke bombs on the dais.

In the late 1950s, these violent incidents and the seeming consolidation of right-wing organizations worried leftists and others fearful of the resurgence of a violent right wing. The Gokokudan and Kokusuikai were among a dozen or so groups that in March 1959 came together as the Zen Nihon Aikokusha Dantai Kyōgikai (All-Japan Council of Patriotic Organizations), for which Sasakawa and Kodama served as advisers. Not only was the council a federation that included hybrid yakuza and right-wing groups, but many of its other advisers and some of its leaders were connected to violent incidents of the prewar period: Sagōya Tomeo of the Gokokudan had received the death penalty, later reduced to life imprisonment, for his attack on Prime Minister Hamaguchi in November 1930 but was released in 1940; Inoue Nisshō was mentioned above for his connection to the League of Blood and its assassinations of 1932; Miura Giichi was, among other things, involved in the attack on Seiyūkai president Nakajima Chi-kuhei in 1939; Tachibana Kōzaburō was a key instigator of the May 15 Incident in 1932; Amano Tatsuo had been arrested for the Shinpeitai Incident in 1933 and was implicated in the attack on politician Hiranuma Kiichirō in

1941; and Ōsawa Takesaburō was involved in the failed assassination attempt on former prime minister Wakatsuki Reijirō in 1933. Another right-wing federation that coalesced in 1959 was the Aikokusha Kondankai (Meeting of Patriots), founded on July 11 by 30 heads of 16 right-wing organizations including the Gokokudan and Matsubakai.

As in the prewar period, right-wing organizations were not isolated political entities but part of a more encompassing political nexus—in the immediate postwar decades, there were connections at the highest of levels between violent right-wing groups and politicians. The political ties of the Matsubakai became apparent, for example, through the funeral of the president's wife. The former mayor of Tokyo sent flowers, and many other figures attended, including an ex-superintendent-general of the Metropolitan Police, a previous minister of education, 17 LDP Diet members, and 50 local parliamentarians.

Yakuza thus managed to survive and even thrive, entirely unlike *sōshi*, because of the resurgence of the political right and the mutually beneficial ties they (re)formed with various conservatives. Conservative politicians who were anti-labor and anticommunist could gain from the activities of yakuza groups, who profited financially so long as they were protected by the conservative hegemony. And political fixers like Sasakawa and Kodama were the influential brokers who ensured, and benefited from, the continuation of this arrangement. With a secure place in the conservative nexus, yakuza also operated in an immediate environment that did not fault them, indeed valued them, for their violence—within this part of the political world, prewar-style connections and tactics were still considered assets. And the utility of yakuza was especially beneficial in the political war between the right and the left that was being fought on a number of fronts.

THE POLITICIAN AS ENTREPRENEUR

Jacob Schlesinger

That was, however just one side of the Tanaka story: Tanaka was also the most powerful person in Japan to keep so little distance between the pursuit of public good and his own personal enrichment—and with such blatant disregard for the commonly accepted ethical and legal boundaries separating the two. In the early 1970s, the Japanese people were so desperate for a "contemporary hero," as that same *Yomiuri* front-page story labeled the new premier, that they were willing—for a while—to overlook his faults. But Tanaka's attempt to juggle two such contradictory personae—the idealistic torchbearer of Japanese democracy and its mocking, cynical profiteer—was an extremely precarious stunt.

In reality, politics was just one part of the complex, interlocking empire of power and money that Kakuei Tanaka had built between 1945 and 1972. As he climbed steadily to the premiership, Tanaka had also become president of several different companies and taken advisory roles and ownership stakes in others. In his district's biggest city, Nagaoka, he had converted some of the choicest real estate along the Shinano River into a sprawling compound of Tanaka-related firms.

Tanaka's personal lifestyle took on all the opulence that usually accompanies such business success. Beginning in the 1950s, he started to build a sprawling estate that eventually was valued at more than $8 million and covered two acres in the tony Tokyo neighborhood of Mejiro. The compound was graced with landscaped gardens, a tulip field, and a pond filled with carp worth $3,000 each. He acquired three villas in the wealthy resort town of Karuizawa, the Nantucket of Japan, and in the early 1960s "purchased" a beautiful geisha, buying her a large house and supporting the two sons he fathered by her. The year Tanaka became prime minister, he reported a total income of 86 million yen (well over $200,000), five times the official premier's pay. Critics said that his spending habits indicated a much higher unreported total.

It would be impossible to separate "public servant Tanaka" from "tycoon Tanaka." Each relied heavily on, and contributed handsomely to, the other. Tanaka's construction company, after all, had opened the door to politics for him in the first place, since he had used the profits to curry favor with conservative bigwigs and had then had his employees run his first campaigns. Soon after, he had found an even better confluence of his political and business interests when he became president of a struggling local train company. The Nagaoka Railroad, as it was known, was one farming community's lifeline to urban markets. Its failure would be a severe economic blow to Tanaka's district; whoever saved it, therefore, would be a hero.

That tiny railroad became the foundation of Tanaka's local power base. As the company's dynamic, youthful chief executive, he rallied his executives to work long hours at reduced pay to build a new, modern rail system. When five of the six new trains broke down in tests just hours before the system's planned public opening in late 1951, Tanaka pushed the glum company to take its last chance. At two a.m., the sixth train successfully chugged down the line. Meanwhile, as the railroad's representative in Parliament, Tanaka secured the crucial funds to pay for the project from the national government's Japan Development Bank. When the new electric-powered train made its maiden journey, large crowds, heedless of dark clouds above, thronged every crossing along the twenty-five-mile track, waving Japanese national flags and cheering as the cars sped by. The company sponsored "Tanaka Cup" baseball games and fishing contests to spread his name. In the 1952 parliamentary election campaign, stationmasters and ticket punchers urged passengers to vote for their boss. Tanaka handily won, boosting his vote total by 50 percent over the previous election.

Over the next decade, he and some cronies bought control of another railroad and did a hostile takeover of a bus company. In addition to helping Tanaka expand his operations into a major new transportation service, the bus company was a desirable acquisition because its ousted chairman had backed a rival Niigata politician and had taken to hanging anti-Tanaka posters. Tanaka consolidated the businesses into a company called Echigo Kotsu, or Echigo Transport, which developed into the dominant public transportation network in Tanaka's constituency. He then engineered an informal union between Echigo Transport and his political support group, the Etsuzan-kai, which ran, among other things, his local campaigns and his district constituent services. The two organizations had the same executives and shared a headquarters, as if both were wholly owned subsidiaries of a sort of Tanaka Inc.

As he assembled this politico-business conglomerate, Tanaka would profess that his role models were two of Niigata's most beloved politicians: Mitsugu Okamura, who, on entering Parliament in 1894, had owned mountains, forests, and acres of rice fields; and Kan-ichi Otake, who had also become an MP in 1894 and who headed a family that had ruled sixty communities for thirty-two generations. Japan had adopted a limited parliamentary government a few years earlier, and these men were part of a class of politicians, especially common in the countryside, who filled the role of the old feudal system's domainal lords, taking personal responsibility for the well-being of their subjects. Okamura used his fortune to try to build a railroad that could alleviate the isolation of the snow country; Otake personally planned and paid for the damming and dividing of a river to prevent destructive floods. Such men were called "well-fence politicians," because a well and a fence were said to be all that was left of their clans' once-vast properties. At the end of Okamura's life in 1922, according to local legend, his holdings had dwindled to a few paintings, and those remained only because his family, fearing starvation, had hidden them from the railroad-obsessed patriarch. Otake died heavily in debt, unable to fix the leak in his roof.

In 1961, the people of Niigata erected a commemorative bust of Okamura at a train station, and it was Tanaka who was invited to inscribe the plate and deliver the evocative dedication. "Both men [Okamura and Otake] endeavored devotedly for the development of our home province, taking no account of their own interests ... nay, throwing away all their property," he recalled. "Once I became a politician, I aspired to be like my great predecessors." But Tanaka managed to invert the Okamura-Otake formula: The more he did for the people of Niigata, the richer he got.

Tanaka tended to concentrate his entrepreneurial energies in fields such as construction, building supplies, transport, and real estate that benefited from the public works he was channeling, as a politician, into Niigata. The new roads he lobbied for proved a boon to his bus company, while the construction boom increased the value of the Niigata property he owned. Tanaka's firms also relied heavily on government contracts—and, apparently, on inside information about future national budgets. In 1953, he used his position as an MP to help bring a large-scale government-funded hydroelectric power project to his district and, separately, secured national monies to rebuild a train line. That same year, one of his companies just happened to begin producing gravel. Parliament Member Tanaka got votes for enriching the district, while supplier Tanaka monopolized the lucrative gravel contracts for both projects. Tanaka also won passage of a popular law requiring the government to clear the heavy snows from highways—and then set up a road-clearing service that won much of the work.

In the 1960s, "Tanaka Inc." moved heavily into Japan's thriving real estate market, this time working through a series of "ghost companies," mysterious firms with no phone numbers, staff, or offices, and often no formal link to Tanaka. But the ties were obvious: the registered executives and owners were his close friends and relatives—even his chauffeur—while the listed headquarters of one such venture, called Tokyo New House, was smack in the middle of a garden on Tanaka's compound. Whoever ran them, the companies had an uncanny knack for snapping up cheap Niigata property that, unbeknownst to the old landowners, was about to soar in value, thanks to soon-to-be-announced public works projects. In 1961, a "Tanaka family" company bought some undeveloped swampland; then the government decided to build a school on that very location, paying 20 percent above the total purchase price for just a small portion of the land. In the mid-1960s, Tanaka's associates offered farmers what seemed, at the time, a good price for a worthless, flood-prone riverbed. Shortly after they secured all the property, the national government disclosed plans to build a dike, then a highway, right through the plot. In less than a decade, the acquisition appreciated in value two hundred times. The Tanaka team hit jackpots again with the bullet train and the nuclear power plant that came to the region. It was, as one observer put it, "modern alchemy."

Tanaka's frequent accomplice in such wizardry was the murky mogul Kenji Osano, who, like Tanaka, had overcome humble roots to win the grudging acceptance of the Establishment. The son of a tenant farmer, Osano had made a killing selling auto parts to the Japanese military during the war, and then to the American forces in peacetime, and was a main fixer in the currency black markets that thrived under both. In the days following Japan's surrender, when many people were scavenging the ruins of Tokyo for sustenance, Osano ostentatiously kept piles of cash in his house. "This is the time for land," he told an associate, flashing a grin. "I will buy every hotel, inn, and summerhouse in Japan." Just two weeks after Japan's surrender, he snapped up his first luxury inn. He then bought his way into the destitute aristocracy, paying a 4-million-yen dowry to marry the daughter of a former earl. Osano suffered a temporary setback in 1948, when the U.S. Occupation jailed him for embezzling scarce gasoline. But by the mid-1980s, he had gone on to amass a conglomerate with stakes in seventy companies from airlines and bus lines to hotels and golf courses, with total assets estimated at more than $18 billion. He cornered the Waikiki Beach hotel business in the 1970s, becoming one of the first in a line of Japanese real estate investors to draw American protests of "economic invasion." When Osano died at age sixty-nine in 1986, he left an estate of 16 billion yen, or $100 million, the fourth largest ever recorded in Japan. (Experts suspected that, as a cutthroat strategist to the end, he had hidden trillions more to spare his heirs inheritance taxes.)

Osano's ruthless tactics and gruesome countenance—sunken eyes, fleshy nose, swollen lips, and protruding bald pate—earned him the tabloid sobriquet "Monster." Tanaka, though, referred to him as a "sworn friend." They had met as young men in 1947, when a prophetic mutual acquaintance decided to introduce "the biggest politician in Japan" to "the biggest businessman in Japan." "We'd go drinking" was how Osano described their relationship years later. But their ties developed much further than that. Osano was a frequent investor, lender, adviser, and purchaser in Tanaka's complicated financial schemes. Tanaka, meanwhile, was a valuable friend in a high place. When Tanaka was finance minister in 1963, Osano secured a special waiver to Japan's strict capital-export limits, allowing him to buy his first Hawaii hotel. Tanaka's ministry also sold government-owned Tokyo real estate to Osano for a pittance. Osano, who reaped a handsome profit reselling the land on the open market, returned the favor, buying a near-bankrupt company from businessman Tanaka at far above the market value.

Osano was a heavy donor to Tanaka's political campaigns. During his summit meeting with Nixon in Hawaii, Tanaka stayed in an Osano hotel, and later he gave his pal a plum spot on the management committee of the national telephone monopoly. Wags snidely referred to Tanaka's premiership as the "Tanaka-Osano Trading House."

Associates often warned Tanaka that he was risking political—and legal—trouble by so blithely blurring the line between doing good and doing well. "Tanaka is somebody who walks on the fence of prison," Shigeru Yoshida, the doyen of early postwar politics, quipped. Tanaka himself never seemed perturbed by such perceptions, once telling a group of legislators, "You can't be called a man if you are afraid of going to jail once or twice."

He had, in fact, landed there in 1948—during his first parliamentary term—for taking a bribe from the coal industry to oppose state control of the mines. At least, that's how prosecutors had seen things when they had charged him. Tanaka did not deny the facts: he had voted against the bill and taken the money. But he maintained his innocence, arguing that the two actions were unrelated. "The one-million-yen check I accepted from the mine operator was an advance payment on construction work [by Tanaka Construction]," he told the authorities. Refusing to concede even the appearance of an ethical problem, Tanaka unapologetically filed his reelection papers from the Tokyo Detention House. Upon his release ten days before the vote, he told constituents, "My conscience is perfectly clear." He won the election and, though convicted by one court in 1950, won his appeal the following year.

Over the next twenty years, Tanaka and his Etsuzankai support group had, by one estimate, nearly a dozen more "brushes with the law," most involving "misuse of public office." In 1955, two Tanaka underlings were arrested for embezzlement and misappropriation from the public railroad Tanaka had saved with such fanfare a few years back. In the early 1960s, clouds appeared over contract awards for a new highway and a series of dams that Tanaka had brought to the district, once again landing close Tanaka backers in jail. In each case, Tanaka himself was also investigated personally, though he was never charged with any crimes.

As he rose to national prominence, suspicion of wrongdoing trailed Tanaka like a shadow. In 1966, he was forced to resign as national secretary-general of the Liberal Democratic Party over accusations of cronyism in the bargain-price sale of public lands. Even at the peak of the "Tanaka boom," rumblings arose about his business ethics. In late 1972, the opposition parties managed to turn Prime Minister Tanaka's geisha turned mistress into a miniscandal—not because of his marital infidelity but because she was apparently serving as a front for some of his funny-money land deals. A few months later, a Communist MP alleged during parliamentary proceedings that

Tanaka had leaked advance information about government projects to land-investing friends, drawing a furious outburst from the red-faced Tanaka.

Each of these "incidents," as the Japanese press calls scandals, blew over quickly, slowing Tanaka's skillfully navigated power drive only slightly. Many of the charges were dismissed in their time as reckless rhetorical grenades from the Left; instead of investigating the Communist's suspicions, for example, Parliament suspended the accuser for twenty days for spreading malicious slander. The lesson Tanaka seemed to derive from that long experience of dodging allegations was that he would always beat the rap. But he was wrong. Those scandals were the persistent early-warning symptoms of a serious, career-threatening ailment.

The nitty-gritty of governing is always more formidable than the heady promises of campaigning, as Tanaka learned shortly into his term as prime minister. The centerpiece of his domestic agenda—the grand scheme to redirect industry—quickly collapsed under the weight of short-term economic crises. In 1973, business conditions, policy missteps, and then the Arab oil embargo pushed Japan's annual inflation rate to 30 percent, among the worst in the industrialized world. The "crazy prices" touched off the first widespread consumer panic since the dark days just after the war, as housewives, fearing shortages, stampeded stores for everything from heating oil to detergent to toilet paper. The bright neon lights of Tokyo's Ginza shopping district, an emblem of the nation's thriving commercial culture, were dimmed to conserve scarce energy. A communal gloom settled in over the nation; the hottest novel of Tanaka's reign, turned into a blockbuster movie, was *The Sinking of Japan*.

The times called for austerity. But Tanaka had built his whole career around the simple formula of winning votes by showering constituents with government largess, and he clung stubbornly to his sanguine pledge for more and better growth. He exacerbated inflationary pressures by pushing through a giant increase in public spending and a deep tax cut. His blind obsession with "archipelago remodeling" turned irritating. The people wanted a "firm determination to put down inflation and control disruptions of their economic life," one newspaper editorial pleaded after yet another oblivious policy speech by the prime minister; they certainly didn't want "another lecture, no matter how well intentioned, about why the construction of more bullet-train lines and three ... bridges is necessary to sustain Japan's economy and population ten years from now." By early 1974, Tanaka's grandiose "remodeling" brainchild was widely derided as "the grand illusion of economic development," and he was forced to drop it.

The hopes Tanaka stirred for a more independent, Asian-oriented diplomacy were also soon dashed. Barely a year after his warm welcome in China, he was disgraced in Southeast Asia, where smoldering anti-Japanese sentiment—the aftermath of Japan's World War II military invasion, stoked by recent economic incursions—mixed dangerously with unstable politics. In Thailand, a mob paraded his effigy, labeled "Tanaka, Ugly Economic Imperialist," outside his hotel. In Indonesia, he was a virtual prisoner inside the Presidential Palace for three days as demonstrators outside smashed Japanese cars, pushed them into canals, and torched the Toyota distribution center. The Indonesian police killed eleven rioters during the visit, which the Japanese leader had to cut short by fleeing Jakarta early one morning by helicopter.

Japan's domestic politics, too, proved far more sticky than Tanaka had imagined. Despite his popularity, he was unable to stanch the conservatives' early-1970s decline. In elections for the lower house of Parliament in December 1972, Tanaka's stumping tours drew unusually large, enthusiastic throngs. But his Liberal Democratic Party still suffered heavy losses and fell to its lowest strength since its founding; the Communists, meanwhile, who kept promising more social services, especially for urban small businesses, continued their surge, nearly tripling their legislative power. In the 1974 elections for Parliament's upper house, the LDP clung to a bare three-seat majority. Squabbles also flared up within the party. A group of young right-wing politicians, furious about Tanaka's continued overtures to Communist China, formed the "Blue Storm Society." Members joined the group by taking a gangster-style blood oath, and they sometimes acted like mobsters—in one intraparty debate, the upstarts toppled desks, smashed glasses, and hurled sushi.

Tanaka did not handle these stark realities of office well. His temper grew short. "Some call him mini-Hitler now," one newsmagazine reported. He got easily flustered in parliamentary debates and frequently made embarrassing gaffes requiring retraction. Unable to boost the LDP's strength through elections, Tanaka rashly tried to overhaul the entire electoral system. So blatant a power grab drew protests even from within his own party; after the ensuing commotion virtually shut down Parliament for a month, he was forced into a humiliating retreat. Under the strain, Tanaka's health deteriorated. An ear infection sent him to the hospital for a week in December 1973. He came out with a bad case of facial neuritis that left his right cheek frozen for three months. When he spoke, his words were slurred and his face twisted into grotesque contortions. Many people saw more than a medical explanation: "His face shows the uneasy state of his mind," a housewife was quoted as saying, "which is the result of his policy failures."

Popular disappointment was especially perilous for a politician such as Tanaka. He had, after all, ridden to power on mass expectations that his commoner's touch, combined with the no-nonsense efficiency of a self-made businessman, would succeed where distant bureaucrats had failed. His spotty record after two tough years in office inevitably led to a reassessment of that image.

The turning point came in the summer of 1974. At the time, industry leaders were extremely worried about the Left's electoral advances and the implications for Japan's fundamentally probusiness stance. Tanaka's advisers proposed what seemed like a logical, mutually convenient solution: just as Tanaka's Echigo Transport conglomerate ran his campaigns back in Niigata, corporations should "buy" candidates, then "sell" them to the voters. Major banks, automakers, and steel producers, even cosmetics companies, signed on to sponsor specific conservative politicians. In one instance, the twenty-seven companies of the large Mitsubishi group rallied to raise funds and votes among its 300,000 employees for one LDP candidate, while the seventy-five-year-old chairman of Mitsubishi Electric Corporation personally jetted around the country, coordinating the campaign.

The strategy backfired. The brazen collusion between big business and top politicians provoked an outpouring of denunciation against "money-power politics" gone too far. The Mitsubishi stooge lost. Furthermore, the outrage alerted Tanaka's rivals to the force of the issue—as well as to his vulnerability on that score. One of the first to pick up the cudgel was Takeo Fukuda, who was still sore about losing, two years earlier, the premiership he considered his entitlement and eager to unseat the man who had swiped it. During the 1974 national parliamentary election campaign, Fukuda seemed less intent on helping the LDP than on undercutting the party president. "The trend of money-based politics is too strong," he taunted at one campaign stop. "Politics must be conducted cleanly." Fukuda and two other senior politicians quit Tanaka's cabinet with much fanfare after the election, claiming shock at the premier's free-spending political style and raising a new banner: "Reform the LDP." This time, the charges started to stick. The attacks intensified through the summer, until Tanaka's name became all but synonymous with "money-power politics." America's Watergate scandal, which forced Richard Nixon from office that August, invited Nixon-Tanaka comparisons and fueled the crusade by heightening sensitivity to corruption in high places.

Inspired by the investigative journalism that had toppled a sitting U.S. president, a respected Japanese intellectual magazine called *Bungei Shunju* assembled a crack team of twenty researchers to get to the bottom of Tanaka's "gold-studded background." The detailed exposé, published in early October under the title "A Study of Kakuei Tanaka: His Money & His Men," ran an exhaustive forty pages. The articles provided intricate details of Tanaka's properties, his past scandals, his "ghost companies," his constant conversion of power into profit. Much of the report was actually a rehash of old allegations or unconfirmed innuendo—the authors typically cited "standard rumor" on reports that "Tanaka spent as much as 25 million yen to completely renovate his house in Niigata with precious cypress wood." But it was the first time any publication had presented the whole rather incredible record in one account, and it effectively cast Tanaka in a new, harsher light, arguing that his political career had been one long confidence game. "Was there a connection," the magazine suggested at one point, "between his political enthusiasm and his passion for more land?"

Tanaka's response only worsened matters. The first time he was cornered into commenting on the magazine exposé—at a luncheon speech to foreign journalists—he turned pale and stormed out of the session. He seemed genuinely unable to understand why his behavior might be considered improper. He did not—could not—dispute most of the facts that had been published. But as with his run-in with the prosecutors over the 1948 coal bribery case, he insisted that somehow his two careers should be judged separately—even though he himself clearly ran them together. "It is regrettable that the article mixed up my business dealings with my politics," he grumbled at a press conference devoted to answering the charges. Echoing Nixon's "I am not a crook" refrain, he repeated over and over, "I have done nothing illegal."

Those were hardly reassuring words. Merely "to stay out of legal prosecution is not enough," the *Mainichi* newspaper retorted. "Moral integrity is a key for political leaders to gain people's confidence." "He should have been critical enough of himself to realize that, for a politician at the pinnacle of power, the public and private phases of his life were the same," the *Yomiuri* newspaper lectured.

A couple of years earlier, Tanaka's protestations might have gotten a sympathetic public hearing, but in 1974 the Japanese people were no longer in a tolerant mood. Two years of rampant inflation had done more than erode incomes; they had undermined the common assumption that the fruits of Japan's postwar growth were being divided fairly. The conviction that Japan was a "lantern-shaped society" with its 90 percent middle class had been a crucial foundation of support for the LDP. Now the middle-class housewives who had been reduced to brawling with neighbors for an extra roll of toilet paper resented the sectors that were profiting—the large trading companies, for example, that were widely suspected of jacking up prices, even when shortages did not exist, to reap a windfall from the panic buying.

By failing to slam a lid on prices, the man chosen as the "people's prime minister" now seemed to side with the LDP's fat-cat contributors. When Tanaka promised during one parliamentary address "to conduct the affairs of government so that social justice will be attained—so the honest will not be cheated," he was hooted down with jeers. Then the mob turned on Tanaka's personal wealth. Protesters outside his Tokyo home wielded papier-mâché knives and chanted, "Let's kill Tanaka's [$3,000] carp and eat them."

The thing that really stuck in the collective Japanese craw was Tanaka's extensive real estate portfolio, laid bare in great detail in the *Bungei Shunju* report. The early-1970s hyperinflation had hit the land market particularly hard, making homeownership all the more unthinkable for millions of Japanese. It was bad enough when people realized that Tanaka's "archipelago-remodeling" plan, by touching off a speculative stampede in anticipation of major new government projects, had been a major cause of the skyrocketing real estate prices. But, as the magazine exposé pointed out, it was altogether unforgivable that the prime minister and his pals had profitably played that market. Tanaka was no longer the "commoners' premier"; he was just another member of the odious nouveau-riche cabal of parasitic speculators. Because Tanaka had raised hopes so much, this was more than disappointing; it was betrayal. His public support rating, once a record-high 62 percent, plunged to a record-low 12 percent.

By November 1974, events were spinning completely beyond Tanaka's control. "Tanaka's money veins" dominated the front pages. Opposition politicians trooped to Niigata to conduct an investigation of his ill-gotten lands. Tanaka faced open mutiny in his own party: an LDP "League for Party Reconstruction" openly clamored for a formal inquiry, while, behind the scenes, Fukuda and other Tanaka rivals were actively scheming to bring the premier down. Amid the mayhem, Tanaka had no choice but to accept the scheduling of embarrassing parliamentary hearings on his personal finances; a date was set for later that month with a close Tanaka aide slated to testify first.

Tanaka tried to divert attention with a two-week diplomatic foray, but he himself was plainly rattled by the growing din at home. During a state banquet in Australia, he drank glass after glass of wine; in between his numerous trips to the bathroom, he lectured the Australian prime minister with wild gesticulations, forcing his rattled host to dodge Tanaka's flailing fork and knife. Tanaka was exhausted, his aides said. His blood pressure and his sugar count shot up, while his eyes often seemed to bulge out of his head.

First thing on the morning of Tuesday, November 26, Tanaka went to the Buddhist altar in his Tokyo home and told his ancestors he was going to make "an important decision" later that day. Outside, he encountered dozens of reporters, some of whom had been waiting since five a.m. "I am in a serene state of mind," he told them. After a cabinet meeting, Tanaka's spokesman read to the press a brief statement titled "My Determination." "I have not rested even a day since I left my hometown without a single yen in my pocket," the pronouncement said. As a politician, "I did my best to … improve the people's livelihood with a sense of decision and action." But "political confusion … has resulted from my personal problems," he acknowledged. There was no choice: "I have decided to resign as prime minister and president of the Liberal Democratic Party."

"I must have been possessed by some evil spirit," he told associates that night. "There is an evil spirit you cannot control." It was a demon that would haunt Tanaka for the rest of his life.

ARRESTED

Jacob Schlesinger

For a time, though, Tanaka apparently thought he could exorcise the demon. An old Japanese proverb states that no scandal lasts longer than seventy-five days, and indeed, barely two months after his ignominious resignation, reports surfaced of a planned comeback. He kept his seat in Parliament and his membership in the party, and the various official investigations into the scandals were all petering out without punishment—without his even being questioned by the authorities. The probe into one suspicious land deal was dropped after the relevant documents mysteriously disappeared from the Construction Ministry's files. A criminal case, meanwhile, did lead to the conviction of two Tanaka business associates in late 1975, but they pleaded guilty without a trial, a move widely suspected as being an attempt to end the matter quickly and protect the boss. In the end, the only penalty Tanaka faced for all the fuss was a bill, reportedly for 40 million yen, in back taxes.

The disgraced leader and his backers started openly wielding influence again, advising the new prime minister, Takeo Miki, on parliamentary strategy and helping smooth over various crises such as a public workers' strike. Japan's political commentators, as if they were Kremlinologists, sought a deeper significance in Tanaka's every move. Some saw signs, for example, of rehabilitation in his appointment as chair of the funeral committee for former Prime Minister Eisaku Sato in mid-1975, one of Tanaka's first public appearances since his fall. "He is still young," a politician loyal to the charismatic Niigata politician crowed, noting that the fifty-seven-year-old Tanaka was eleven years younger than Prime Minister Miki and thirteen years younger than archenemy Fukuda, who was still angling for the top job. "The day will again come when his vitality and ability will be needed to get things done."

Then "Tanaka's money veins" sprang a new scandal, one far more serious than the manipulation of provincial marshland—graver, in fact, than any postwar political corruption case.

The "Lockheed Incident," as it is now called in Japanese history books, first surfaced in Watergate-obsessed Washington, where investigators wading through the records of Nixon's slush funds stumbled on evidence that U.S. corporations had given shady contributions to foreign politicians as well. By the time the inquiry was through, more than five hundred U.S. companies had admitted making questionable payoffs to win business all over Asia, Europe, and the Middle East. One of the most active was the Lockheed Aircraft Corporation, America's biggest defense contractor and a major civilian manufacturer. Lockheed's confession of having paid $55 million in such overseas "donations" single-handedly touched off political upheavals in the Netherlands, Germany, and Italy. But nowhere did the revelations stir up as much turmoil as in Japan.

In February 1976, Lockheed president A. Carl Kotchian told a U.S. Senate committee hearing that he had personally arranged for bribes to "high government officials" in Tokyo to win a hotly contested contract, worth $430 million, to sell wide-bodied jets to a leading Japanese commercial airline. He did not name names or provide much detail. But that was enough to launch a public frenzy in Tokyo. Within two weeks, Parliament was holding special hearings that drew huge national television audiences. By month's end, nearly four hundred government agents had raided twenty-nine locations seeking evidence. The U.S. government, wary of fomenting political instability in a close ally, declared it would keep crucial documents related to the matter confidential—until March, after Prime Minister Miki wrote an emotional personal letter to President Gerald Ford pleading that, if the scandal were covered up, it would destroy democracy in Japan.

In late June, the Japanese authorities started rounding up the perpetrators. In *one* day, four executives from two corporations involved in the affair were arrested. Two weeks later, two more suspects were detained. By July 20, a dozen men, mainly corporate officials, were behind bars for their alleged involvement in the complex scheme. But the country was still waiting for the other shoe to drop—no politician had yet been touched.

At 6:30 a.m. on July 27, the dragnet finally reached the wooden front gate of the Tokyo estate of a "high government official": former prime minister Tanaka. He said he had not slept well that night, waking four hours earlier with a premonition that something bad would happen that day. Now two representatives of the Tokyo prosecutors office were politely presenting themselves to one of his servants, saying they would like to escort Mr. Tanaka to their office for a few questions. He put on his standard dark blue suit with a light blue necktie and sat between the two men in the backseat of their black sedan.

Upon arrival, the tanned politician offered a wan smile and wave to the gathered reporters. The session lasted barely more than an hour. The interrogators were deferential but resolute: "We are very sorry to have to investigate a person who was once prime minister of Japan, but we must ask you to tell the truth in order to find out the truth," one prosecutor began. Tanaka denied any involvement in the matter. "Please take care of yourself," an inquisitor said gently as the interview ended. "Thank you," replied Tanaka with a wave. "Thank you. Thank you." He was then formally arrested and ignominiously dragged to the same dreary Tokyo Detention House where he had been incarcerated twenty-eight years earlier in the coal bribery affair. That day, he was charged with violating the Foreign Trade and Exchange Control Law by taking money illegally from foreigners. The bribery indictment came a few days later; if convicted, Tanaka would face a five-year jail term. While Tanaka sat in the "pig-box," as Japan's criminals call a detention cell, a team of prosecutors spent eleven hours scouring his home and carting out box upon box of documents.

If it hadn't been for the gravity of the matter, the case would actually have seemed somewhat humorous, like an amateur production of a cloak-and-dagger B movie. The sordid affair, prosecutors charged, had started in August 1972, just six weeks after Tanaka had become prime minister. Hiro Hiyama, president of the Marubeni Corporation general trading company, which Lockheed had hired as its official sales agent in Japan, had come calling early one morning to congratulate the premier on his recent victory. As the new head of the government, Tanaka had a lot on his mind: he was leaving the next week for a summit with President Nixon to try to patch up the fraying alliance, planning his historic trip to China, and starting to implement his daring economic reconstruction plan. But Hiyama wanted to take just a moment of his time with a more mundane matter: if Tanaka could just make sure that All Nippon Airways (ANA) bought Lockheed planes, he'd get a cut of 500 million yen, worth $1.6 million at the time. Tanaka supposedly gave his trademark reply of approval, "*Yossha, yossha,*" and it was agreed. The entire meeting lasted but a few minutes.

U.S. President Richard M. Nixon (right) with Prime Minister of Japan Kakuei Tanaka (left) outside the White House.

Tanaka is said to have called the ANA president later that month to urge the Lockheed purchase. In a particularly shameful twist, the prosecutors charged, he dragged in U.S.-Japanese tensions to earn his bribe, claiming that Nixon had personally requested that ANA buy Lockheed aircraft as a way of cutting Japan's trade surplus. In October, ANA finally got the message and made the right choice. But after winning the bid, Lockheed president Kotchian had second thoughts about making the payoff. The Marubeni president, through an underling, told him it was "very serious": if Lockheed reneged on the deal, it would never sell so much as another monkey wrench in Japan again. And Marubeni's Hiyama would have to leave Japan for good.

Lockheed delivered the cash in four installments in 1973 and 1974. Each time, the company's Tokyo manager handed over to a Marubeni official a cardboard box stuffed with piles of yen. (One Japanese commentator scoffed that the box was a typically uncouth American touch; a Japanese briber, he said, would surely have wrapped the money carefully in a tasteful cloth bundle.) In return, Marubeni would give Lockheed a typed receipt, signed by a trading company executive, saying "I received 150 pieces" or, one time, "I received 100 peanuts"—a "piece" or "peanut" being the not-so-subtle code for one million yen. A Marubeni man would then take the valuable box to a prearranged rendezvous spot—one time a street behind the British Embassy, other times a public phone booth or a hotel parking lot—where Tanaka's waiting limousine would pick up the package.

"The nation was shocked," the *Yomiuri* newspaper blasted the day after the arrest, "to learn that a man of his rank had accepted dirty money from a foreign business corporation. ... Kakuei Tanaka has the dubious distinction of being the first prime minister in history to sell out the nation for private gain." He was, indeed, the first Japanese premier ever to face criminal charges for abusing his position. Newspapers rushed out extras. When the news broke, trading on the busy Osaka Stock Exchange came to a temporary, stunned halt. Crowds gathered in a downtown park to demand a full airing of the scandal and punishment of those involved. THE PEOPLE OF THE NATION, one handwritten placard declared, CANNOT BE DECEIVED. An unarmed, middle-aged drifter was apprehended after scaling the wall into Tanaka's private garden; he had wanted to personally urge the politician to commit hara-kiri, or ritual suicide. Marubeni, too, drew scorn for its role. Local governments all over the country canceled contracts with the trading house. Marubeni employees complained that their children were being harangued by classmates for having family ties to "the bad, bad company"; one such child got stuck with the schoolyard nickname "Lockheed."

The most bizarre response came from a young porno movie actor dressed in full kamikaze regalia, complete with a rising-sun headband, who dive-bombed a rented Piper-Cherokee airplane smack into the home of a Japanese consultant to Lockheed. The suicide mission was apparently intended to protest the shame the affair had brought upon the nation; the pilot's final words, shrieked over the plane's radio, were "*Tenno heika BANZAI!*" (Long live the emperor!). The target of his attack, a well-known fixer named Yoshio Kodama, escaped unscathed. But when Kodama tried to check into a hospital for treatment of a chronic illness, an angry mob forced him to turn around and go home. Later, four armed ultrarightists took over the headquarters of Keidanren, the national big-business trade group, and held four staffers hostage for more than ten hours. "The Lockheed scandal has rocked the nation's free-society system to its roots," their manifesto protested.

People were furious, not only because of the obvious dishonor of having a prime minister on the take but because the Lockheed affair, as it turned out, had stained much of the Japanese power structure. While Tanaka was at the center of the caper, he was by no means the only one implicated. A total of eighteen men were eventually arrested. Two were respected leaders of the big-business world: the presidents of the Marubeni trading company and All Nippon Airways. Two were conservative politicians who, like Tanaka, were arrested for taking bribes. There were four "gray" politicians—MPs who, Lockheed said, had received money but who were never indicted. (Lockheed's executives, meanwhile, were given immunity from prosecution in Japan in return for their testimony.) The scandal's fallout even forced the president of NHK, Japan's leading television broadcast system, to resign his post; a public uproar ensued after he paid a friendly personal condolence call to Tanaka after the arrest. Then there was the eccentric district judge in Kyoto who somehow came up with the idea of making a midnight phone call to Prime Minister Miki in which, impersonating a prosecutor, he urged a stop to the arrest of politicians. He later offered mental instability as a motive and had to relinquish his position.

One notably disturbing facet of the scandal was the exposure of the clout of Kodama, a notorious underworld boss. The American aircraft company said it had paid Kodama $6 million for his services as a special agent supplementing Marubeni's role. No evidence surfaced that Kodama had ever dealt directly with Tanaka on the issue. But he seems to have been able to pull a number of other important strings in the business and political world in order to, as Kotchian put it, "establish a climate in which our product would be properly received." Kodama had apparently pulled off such fantastic feats as engineering a scandal to oust an ANA executive who favored a competitor over Lockheed. He had also introduced Lockheed executives to magnate Kenji Osano, who was both Tanaka's "sworn friend" and ANA's tenth largest shareholder—and who, after receiving more than a million dollars from Lockheed, was willing to lobby both.

That a man such as Kodama had such valuable connections was a national disgrace. His ideology tended toward ultranationalism and militarism; his modus operandi was blackmail, intimidation, and violence. Before the war, he had been jailed for, among other things, plotting a failed "state massacre" to assassinate a large part of the business and political establishment. After the war, he had been imprisoned again, as a suspected "Class A" war criminal. In between, he had made a fortune procuring strategic raw materials in China for the Imperial Navy—or rather, stealing the minerals, then selling them to his government at a huge profit.

Kodama had used part of his booty to help fund the new postwar conservative parties, thereby gaining pull with politicians. He had been a prison buddy of one future LDP prime minister, Nobusuke Kishi, and a close friend of other party bosses. Kodama also wove into and out of the worlds of *yakuza* gangsters and extreme rightists, serving as a broker between those groups and the mainstream conservatives. He could do useful things that, officially, the government could not. In 1939, Japan's Foreign Ministry had sent him to Hong Kong to round up bodyguards for a Chinese leader collaborating with Japan; in 1960, he had organized a private army of nearly fifty thousand gangsters, rightists, and others to help police a planned state visit by American President Dwight D. Eisenhower. (Despite Kodama's extra security force, leftist riots over the U.S.-Japan security treaty had forced Eisenhower to cancel the trip.) Kodama also managed to frighten anybody, including top political and business leaders, who crossed him—such as the time he sent a messenger to ask an MP, at sword point, to halt a certain line of questions in Parliament. The very night before the Lockheed scandal surfaced, several LDP politicians attended a swank banquet thrown in Kodama's honor, and for a full week after Kodama's name had been linked to the Lockheed affair, his friends in the police supposedly kept his whereabouts a secret.

The implication was becoming clear: perhaps Tanaka was not a monstrous aberration, as many Japanese had liked to believe when his money scandals had surfaced a couple of years earlier. Maybe he was, in fact, a fitting captain for a ship of state rotten to the core. "The whole LDP and its traditional practices are under indictment," a senior conservative MP stated tearfully on the floor of Parliament after Tanaka's arrest. "All of the evils accumulated under the conservative party system during the past 30 years are now out" in the open, the *Mainichi* newspaper moaned. Tanaka's detention, it continued, "warned us to make a soul-searching reappraisal of postwar political history." Americans evidently saw the Japanese power structure as both rigged and buyable. "I think you should recognize," Lockheed's Kotchian told the assembled senators in that February 1976 hearing, justifying his dubious behavior, "that the Japanese establishment, if you want to call it that, is a fairly close-knit group of individuals, both in business and government." To enter that group, he explained, "you need some help." That the revelations had first come out in the United States—Japan's closest ally and its mentor in democracy—only heightened the embarrassment. "I thought [such] rampant bribery was seen only in underdeveloped countries," sneered Senator Frank Church, who was leading the congressional investigation.

It was all the more excruciating, of course, for Tanaka himself. RAGS TO RICHES TO JAIL was how one headline pithily traced his tragic arc. For twenty-one days after his arrest, Tanaka was confined in the detention house, where, like the murderers, bombing suspects, and other common criminals in that holding facility, he was stuck in a six-foot-by-nine-foot concrete cell adorned with collapsible desk and toilet—quite a comedown from his twenty-five-room mansion. He was fed a breakfast of cheap rice mixed with cheaper barley, a meal that "even a beggar hardly eats these days," one press account noted with vengeful glee. He was strip-searched upon incarceration and thereafter denied a watch and a belt to hold up his pants, routine precautions against prisoner suicide. Though famous for his profuse sweating, Tanaka was given only a bamboo hand fan to cut the sweltering Tokyo summer heat in his un-air-conditioned cell and allowed just one bath every five days. After the daily seven a.m. morning roll call, he would roll up his own bedding, then endure hours of prosecution grilling lasting well into the night.

When Tanaka was finally released for a near-record bail of 200 million yen—he managed to raise the money in just ten minutes—he found his world shattered. The press had dropped the honorific "san" after his name, now referring to him either as "Suspect Tanaka" or just plain "Tanaka." His longtime chauffeur, prodded by prosecutors to supply damaging information, had driven into the woods and asphyxiated himself with a hose attached to his car's tailpipe. Tanaka was forced to resign from the LDP. It was widely presumed that he would also relinquish control of the faction of MPs who had followed him and that, though he did not quit Parliament, he would do so soon.

The ritual public humiliation peaked in January 1977, with the opening of Tanaka's trial. A thousand people braved a cold morning rain to compete for the fifty-two spectator tickets assigned by lottery. "Your Honor, I swear that I have nothing to do with this case," began Tanaka's emotional half-hour declaration of innocence. By the last ten minutes, the well-known jut-jawed visage had dissolved into a stream of tears, the rapid-fire voice into halting, choked-up sobs. When the man once dubbed a "mini-Hitler" did manage to see and speak clearly enough to proceed, his hands—famed for their firm, sharp gestures—trembled to the point that he could not read the statement they held. "I am suffering even more than if I were put to death," he wailed. "My terrible misfortune has damaged the reputation of Japan. … I deeply apologize to the people."

Japan, it seemed, would never be the same again. "The foundations of this establishment-oriented society have been permanently shaken," a correspondent for *The New Yorker* magazine argued in a lengthy analysis of the Lockheed case and its fallout. "The case has passed beyond scandal into self-exploration and a search for new answers and motivations." Optimists thought the exposure and prosecution of such blatant corruption would cleanse the system, the *Mainichi* newspaper calling the event a "springboard" to "create a better and healthier political atmosphere." Many forecast the end of two decades of conservative one-party rule. The party started to fracture, with a half-dozen young, popular MPs quitting in disgust and forming their own reform party. At the very least, Tanaka, the figure who had dominated Japanese government since the early 1970s and come to symbolize "money-power politics," was surely crushed.

"This is an opportunity to strengthen democracy in Japan and build a foundation for political reform," declared Prime Minister Miki, who bravely overcame powerful opponents to push full prosecution of the case. The "Lockheed Incident" indeed turned out to be a momentous turning point for Japanese democracy—but not in the ways that anyone had expected or desired.

POLITICAL CORRUPTION IN JAPAN

Eric Messersmith

Corruption Theory

The study of political corruption can be broken down into numerous disciplines, depending on the approach taken. Economics, political science, public administration, sociology, philosophy—each of these approaches would present a different facet of corruption in general and political corruption in particular. Thus, one could theoretically come up with a different definition of corruption to fit each of these fields. One could also come up with different effects for corruption: economic effects, effects on the country's political system, its bureaucracy, its mores and attitudes as a society, and even the general view we have of human beings as creatures who make rational decisions and moral choices (or at least are capable of making such decisions).

Although those who have argued this line are definitely in the minority, there might even be an argument made to the effect that, under some circumstances, corruption is actually a necessary evil or even desirable, under an analysis which considers an action desirable if it produces consequences that are good. For example, if one wished to argue some form of consequentialism or utilitarianism, one could say that there might be positive consequences arising from a bribe payment:

> Positive consequences accruing to the bribe-payer ... may include increased profits, increased employment, and greater security for the bribe-payer's creditors. The bribe-receiver gains the value of the bribe payment itself. In a very corrupt society, the bribe may even overcome inefficient government regulation and provide a more efficient allocation of resources (Hess and Dunfee, 2000, p. 605).

Several authors, including Leff (1964) and Huntington (1960), have extended this notion of personal gain to one which benefits the entire economy. They argue that, rather than lowering economic growth, personal gain might actually raise it in two ways: by enabling individuals to avoid the unnecessary bureaucratic delay of going through normal channels, and by stimulating government employees to work harder in their desire to increase their take from bribes.

Holmstrom and Smith (2000) present another argument, one that is definitely in the minority: Corruption is inevitable in a capitalist society. Using Marx's notion of "primitive accumulation," Holmstrom and Smith try to show that the "gangster capitalism and wholesale corruption in the former Soviet bloc and China should have been entirely predictable to anyone familiar with the historical origins of capitalism in Europe, the United States, and elsewhere" (p. 1).

For the purposes of this chapter, however, the majority opinion will be followed—and that is that the effects of corruption on any given society are not positive, and that corruption is not an inevitable consequence of a political system. What those effects are, how and why corruption comes about, and whether particular nations (areas) have particular types of corruption or share a universal form of corruption (transcending national and cultural boundaries), will be the focus of this chapter.

As pointed out by LaPalombara (1994),

> Corruption ... is not necessarily tied to a particular type of political regime. It may occur in repressive or democratic regimes, in political systems that are ruled by aristocratic elites or by representatives of mass publics, in polyarchies that are open to many organized interest groups, or in corporatist systems that provide access to policy-making or policy-implementation only to certain so-called functional groups (p. 327).

Definitions of Corruption

What, then, defines corruption? Does corruption exist in some absolute form or is it a construction of the society in which it is embedded? Heidenheimer and Johnston (2002) place definitions of corruption in three categories: those having to do with public office, those in terms of market theory, and those centered around the public interest.

In terms of public office definitions, the classic one is by Nye. He defines corruption as

> behavior which deviates from the normal duties of a public role because of private-regarding (family, close private clique), pecuniary or status gains; or violates rules against the exercise of certain types of private-regarding influence. This includes such behavior as bribery (use of reward to pervert the judgement of a person in a position of trust); nepotism (bestowal of patronage by reason of ascriptive relationship rather than merit); and misappropriation (illegal appropriation of public resources for private-regarding uses) (2002, p. 284).

Market-driven definitions are exemplified by those offered by Van Klaveren (2002) and Leff (1964). Van Klaveren states that a "corrupt civil servant regards his public office as a business, the income of which he will ... seek to maximize. The office then becomes a 'maximizing unit.' The size of his income depends ... upon the market situation and his talents for finding the point of maximal gain on the public's demand curve" (p. 83). Leff says that "corruption is an extra-legal institution used by individuals or groups to gain influence over the actions of the bureaucracy. As such the existence of corruption *per se* indicates only that these groups participate in the decision-making process to a greater extent than would otherwise be the case" (p. 8).

The third set of definitions related to the public interest or public good is exemplified by authors such as Friedrich (1974), who argues that:

> The pattern of corruption can be said to exist whenever a power holder who is charged with doing certain things, i.e., who is a responsible functionary or office-holder, is by monetary or other rewards not legally provided for, induced to take actions which favor whoever provides the rewards and thereby does damage to the public and its interests (p. 127).

The detailed analysis of the strengths and weaknesses of each set of definitions will be left for later on. In fact, many of the discussions on political corruption come to a halt due to the inability to come to some consensus on definition. However, it can be stated here that all three definitions encounter problems when it comes to determining who will decide the norms to be used to distinguish between corrupt and incorrupt behavior:

> If the definitions are public-office-centered, then which statement of the rules and norms governing public officeholders is to be employed? If the definitions are public-interest-centered, then whose evaluation of the public's interest is to be operationalized? Definitions couched in terms of market theory appear to bypass this problem, but in fact they do not. They too imply that somewhere there is an authority that distinguishes between the rules applicable to public officials and those applicable to businessmen operating in the free market, or that there are certain characteristics that distinguish a "black market" from the free market (Heidenheimer and Johnston, 2002, p. 10).

Essentialism versus Constructivism

Closely connected to the attempts at defining political corruption are the philosophical underpinnings in the debate between corruption as a universal, cross-national and cross-cultural phenomenon, and corruption as a culturally bound occurrence. In other words, is corruption identifiable as such wherever it is found (the essentialist argument), or does such an identification have to rely on the particular circumstances within a particular culture (constructivist)? Or is it a combination of both with some essential features common to all corruption, while other features are relative to the particular forms it takes in the particular country or region in which it is occurring?

For our purposes, we will assume that some general elements of political corruption can be identified across national boundaries and cultures (i.e., universally), while the particular instances of these universal elements are open to interpretation. As an example, bribery is typically considered corrupt behavior. However, the construction of boundaries (gift-giving versus bribery, for example) is problematic in that what might constitute gift-giving in one society might be seen as bribery in another. Therefore, rather than begin with an essentialist definition of political corruption that will fit across all national and cultural boundaries, it seems more practical to approach the situation through corruption effects and results—on the political system, on the economy, on social conditions. Thus, it becomes important to establish linkages between these effects and the source(s) of these effects.

In his analysis of corruption in Japan and why the country was able to develop for so long despite pervasive bribery and other forms of government graft, Werlin (2000) uses his theory of "political elasticity," which he feels allows him to examine a situation through the lenses of both political science and public administration. According to Werlin, the theory consists of five propositions, including:

- Effective government entails integrating and alternating "soft" forms of power (incentives and persuasion) with "hard" (punishment and coercion).
- This integration and alternation produces an "elastic" form of government, whereby it can delegate power when needed and at the same time draw in as many people as possible into its circle of influence.
- Political hardware (organizations, rules, technologies) and software (policies which create a bond between leaders and citizens) are both needed to make this elasticity work.
- Political software is effective proportionately to how well governance is achieved: goals acceptable to the majority, employing qualified people, delegation of responsibility and duties, two-way communication flow, established procedures to resolve conflicts, etc.
- The ability to balance the struggle between competitive advantage (primary politics) and consensus (secondary politics) improves political software.

Within this framework, Werlin identifies two types of corruption—primary (related to primary politics) and secondary (related to secondary politics). His basic argument is that primary corruption, which is subject to official punishment, does not necessarily prevent development, while secondary corruption, whose practitioners have little fear of punishment, hampers development. Thus, while it is generally acknowledged that bribery was part and parcel of Japanese politics and there still remains an intricate system of political gift-giving (Iga and Auerbach, 1977; van Wolferen, 1989), the country was, until the recent recession, "one of the fastest growing industrial economies ever known" (Johnson, 1995, p. 202).

Does Werlin's theory explain the effects (or lack thereof until recently) of corruption within the Japanese political system and economy? Werlin argues that what Japan suffered from was a form of primary corruption and that, as long as it remained that way, the economy was able to survive. However, the danger occurs when the corruption penetrates into the secondary sphere. For example, MacDougall (1988) noted that, while the Japanese are exceptionally tolerant of some gray area political activity, something like the Lockheed scandal of the late 1970s showed that "clear violations of the law, personal enrichment through dishonest behavior, bureaucratic corruption, and unseemly behavior by national leaders … are seen by the public as detrimental to legitimate government" (p. 227). If the effects of corruption are now being felt in Japan (through a prolonged recession, bank collapses and scandal involving politicians, bureaucrats, and members of organized crime), then according to Werlin, this corruption has moved into its more virulent and dangerous secondary stage.

Statement of the Problem

Japan's economy, a model for booming efficiency and progressive principles and the envy of the West throughout the 1970s and 1980s, has been in a deep slump for more than a decade. This is true even though other, considerably weaker and less broad-based Asian economies have managed to climb out of the downturn, including the effects of the "Asian Flu." During this time, and even amid the renewed boom years of the late 1990s for most of the world's economies, the Japanese economy has stubbornly remained stagnant, refusing to emerge from that decade-long slump. What had been double-digit advances in the 1980s in the Gross National Product had become a minus 2.6 percent shrinkage by 1998. Presently, with the world economies slowing down once more, Japan faces even greater struggles to right itself.

Of course, the reasons behind a nation's economic slump are multifarious and complex, and these slumps are often cyclical in nature—having to do with natural boom-and-bust periods, overproduction, shrinkage of export markets, loss of consumer confidence, etc. However, when a nation's economy does not recover on the cyclical up curve, such as the one experienced in the mid- to late-1990s by most of the industrialized world, then one must start to look for more specific and particular reasons: internal government policies, mismanagement of the economy, errors in decision making, and outright corruption.

The danger is even more keenly felt within an economy such as Japan's, where the private and public sectors are so interwoven as to be practically indistinguishable or inseparable in some cases, and where the direction taken by the economy is very carefully planned (a result of the continuation of pre–Second World War policies when the Japanese government saw the positive results of the Soviet experiments in planned economies). It is also an economy that still runs on family or group dynamics rather than the rule of law and one in which most disputes are settled on a personal level because of the lack of trust in the judiciary. This makes the notion of "rooting out" corruption problematic and very much reliant on one's definition. For example, is political corruption in Japanese society a cancer to be cut out (with all the potential damage such an excision might cause), or is it a symbiotic relationship? This can be further connected to a similar question about corruption in political systems in general. At first glance, and using an essentialist definition, one would assume the former—that what we call corruption must be expunged. However, it might be that what has been labeled corruption is simply one step along a spectrum of behaviors involving reciprocity in relationships. Or it might have different connotations for Japanese society than it does in North America, for example. If that is the case, then the situation becomes much more complex.

For example, seen in this way, Japan's organized criminal elements, the *yakuza*, become more than simply leeches and extortionists: they become an integral part of the political and economic structure of the country, and any attempts at eliminating them will alter the fabric of Japanese society in ways which are not entirely predictable. The *yakuza*—at one time content with confining their activities to gambling (from which the word originated—signifying 8-9-3 or ya-ku-sa in Japanese, the worst possible result in a medieval card game resembling blackjack), extortion, construction sites, etc.—expanded rapidly into real estate, the stock market, banking, and even national politics during the boom economic days of the mid-1980s. The *yakuza* also do not perceive themselves as simply gangs but rather as business enterprises:

> In terms of operating style, the *yakuza* are not back-alley outfits; they function like large corporations. Like any major business enterprise, the crime groups maintain offices that

prominently display each group's logo. Members sport lapel pins and carry business cards identifying their positions in the syndicate ("More Eyes," 1992, p. 2).

In fact, the *yakuza* are proud of their role in Japanese society and trace their roots back to the mid-to-late 1700s. Originally known as the *machi-yakko*, townspeople who banded together to fight roving gangs of unemployed samurai (the *hatamoto-yakko*) who had turned into bandits, they developed a Robin Hood–like quality about them and even had stories and legends written about them. Some were considered folk heroes and had stories and songs written about them. But once the threat of the pillaging samurai ended, the proto-*yakuza* themselves turned into gangs of petty criminals, street peddlers, and gamblers.

They remained this way until after the Second World War, when a group known as the *gurentai* (hoodlums) entered the picture. This group got involved in extortion, protection rackets, prostitution, and drugs. Then, when the Japanese economy started to boom, they found themselves in a perfect position to use their wealth to infiltrate so-called legitimate business and government affairs.

One of the major reasons for the success of the *yakuza* is the result of their "management" model. By creating family-like bonds among gang members (with *oyabun* as "fathers" and *kobun* as "children"), the organization developed unswerving loyalty and following orders unquestioningly. As well, any disobedience or betrayal called for swift retribution—from the severing of the top joint of the little finger (*yubitsume*) for minor offenses to more pronounced maiming and even death for major crimes against the organization. This assured loyalty in one way or the other and made it very difficult for anyone to infiltrate the gangs or to get the gang members to talk against others.

The fact remains that, while few question the influence *yakuza* activities have had on Japan and its economy (especially following the Second World War), there is some argument as to the mechanisms that led to the current decade-long recession. After all, the *yakuza* gangs were there while the economy was booming.

This chapter is designed on several levels to examine a group of questions surrounding the notions of political corruption and organized crime, and the effects these may have on a nation's political system, economy, and social structure. Underlying these questions is the idea of "definition" and how we come to have knowledge about a particular subject—in this case, that of corruption within a political system. Some of the background material includes:

- A brief look at the debate between essentialist and constructivist versions of notions of corruption (absolutist versus relativist; moral versus cultural);
- The results of studies on the effects of corruption on political systems in general and the applicability of such results to one particular system (or to any particular system);
- The transportability of notions of corruption between moral systems and cultures;
- The role of organized crime within societies (once more in general and within particular societies).
- The connections between organized crime, legitimate business, and government departments;
- The feasibility of severing corruption and organized crime elements from government operations and what the potential results of that might be on the economy.

Using some of this material as background, the chapter will attempt to find the connection between Japan's *yakuza*, government corruption, banking scandals, and the prolonged recession.

The field of study will include an examination of the role corruption and organized crime play in Japan's economy in general and in the recent recession in particular, as seen through the prism of a comparative study of political corruption and organized crime around the world. This will include: an examination of whether the corruption/organized crime pattern in the Japanese political system is part of a reasonably definable universal phenomenon or peculiar to Japanese government and economic styles; an examination of whether, in either case, something can be done to reverse, negate, or at least mitigate the effects on the economy. The main questions we will attempt to answer in this chapter are

+ Does the situation in Japan call for a new paradigm that takes into account a government system where corruption/organized crime are essential characteristics and cannot be extricated or separated from "legitimate" patterns without destroying the entire fabric?
+ Does this new paradigm involve a new set of rules—neither wholly essential nor wholly constructivist?
+ Could the recent economic woes in Japan be the result of a shift from primary corruption to secondary (Werlin's Hypothesis) rather than simply the result of corruption per se? In other words, is there a point where the balance is tipped from an economy that is functioning despite (because of, in concert with) corruption/organized crime to one that is in danger of collapse within the same general framework?

This chapter proposes a series of hypotheses to be built up from these questions and this field of study, based on the following assumptions:

+ Assumption 1: Corruption and organized crime have been part of Japanese government and political life throughout its history and more specifically after the Second World War.
+ Assumption 2: These forces—the acceptance of bribes, gifts, sinecures, and the influence of the *yakuza*—have been there even when the economy was at the height of its powers.
+ Assumption 3: The nature of Japanese governance and its political party system has not changed significantly following the end of the American Occupation of the country.
+ Assumption 4: Corruption within Japan has not changed to a significant extent, judging from the reports of indictments and trials.

Ergo, if these assumptions are correct, we have the following hypotheses to be explored:

+ Hypothesis 1: There must be other factors involved in what is occurring within the economy, factors that helped facilitate the initial conditions for the recession (even if they did not create them), and that are making it much more difficult for Japan to escape the recession than other parts of the world.
+ Hypothesis 2: Among those factors was the movement and involvement of organized crime into the upper echelons of the banking system in Japan, leading to the ease with which *yakuza* and/or *yakuza*-fronted entities received billions in loans during the real estate boom.
+ Hypothesis 3: Once the boom ended and the bubble collapsed, the banks were left holding billions in nonperforming loans, the majority of which were due from companies with *yakuza* ties and connections.

- Hypothesis 4: Because of the nature of the Japanese banking system, the banks did not act quickly enough to (a) reveal the extent of the nonperforming loans; and (b) to take action in dealing with them until the situation had become untenable.
- Hypothesis 5: The situation in Japan and the reasons behind its prolonged recession are unique to that country, even given an essentialist reading of the definition of corruption.

Limitations/Delimitations

While the literature pertaining to corruption and organized crime (both universally and in Japan) is fairly extensive and a strong, qualitative analysis of this literature can be achieved, there is one area where this will hit a natural limitation. That is in the capacity to gather direct information related to political corruption in Japan (for example, the difficulty of conducting surveys of and interviews with businesspeople, political officials, bureaucrats, and bankers). As well, there is the same type of limitation when it comes to direct information from members of Japan's organized crime gangs. While some of the activities of these gangs have been well documented (in fact, they allow many to be written about so as to spread greater awe among the general population—to the point where some of the gangs have their own newspapers and newsletters), when it comes to government and banking institution connections, the information is more tenuous and speculative.

Thus, while there is plenty of background historical material on the *yakuza* and predecessor gangs leading to the modern version, direct and documented information on present-day activities is hard to come by. Several books have been written on the subject, including Kaplan and Dubro's *Yakuza: The Explosive Account of Japan's Criminal Underworld* (1986) and Christopher Seymour's *Yakuza Diary: Doing Time in the Japanese Underworld* (1996). These books speculate on the role played by the *yakuza* in Japan's postwar era but they do not offer any direct proof of that involvement. That is only natural, considering the secret nature of such societies and the dire consequences for anyone who reveals those secrets to outsiders.

Even more difficult to uncover for a fact is the spread of the *yakuza* into legitimate business (much like the American Mafia has tried to legitimize itself by fronting businesses which claim to be clean)—and its infiltration of government and banking spheres through bribery, blackmail, intimidation, or straightforward expenditure of large sums of money. The web of business and financial dealings is hard to trace back to the source, given disclosure and competition laws designed to protect private business—not to mention off-shore accounts and the establishment of head offices in other jurisdictions. In Japan, this is combined with even further traditional secrecy on the operation of the government at high levels, and the unwillingness of officials to admit their mistakes or involvement for fear of public embarrassment and dismissal.

Thus, at this level, we will have to rely on indirect sources. As well, a comparison can be made between the activities of the *yakuza* in this arena and those of other organized crime groups around the world in order to draw useful parallels on how organized crime operates to infiltrate both businesses and governments. Finally, an example of how difficult it is to extricate the group without causing even more severe damage to the economy comes from the years immediately following the Second World War. At the time, American occupying forces in Japan immediately identified the *yakuza* as the major threat to their reconstruction efforts. They thought they had the threat under control—until they realized, in 1950, that several *oyabun* (notably Kodama Yoshio and Sasagawa

Ryoichi) were being supported by high-level government officials (Kishi Nobusuke), and that eradicating the *yakuza* might have meant plunging the country into economic chaos once more.

Nevertheless, efforts were made to carry out anonymous questionnaire surveys and interviews with a cross-section of Japanese society, including ordinary citizens. It is felt that the prospect of anonymity will help the response rate.

Philosophical and Sociological Underpinnings

The essentialists and the constructionists represent the latest incarnation in a long philosophical battle between those who believe that knowledge is vested in objects (innate) and those who argue that knowledge is "constructed" by humans through the particular circumstances in which they find themselves and the social framework under which they labor. One particular type of constructionism is "social constructionism," a concept first put forward by Thomas Kuhn (1962) in his seminal *The Structure of Scientific Revolutions*, and Berger and Luckmann's *The Social Construction of Reality* (1966). Kuhn's well-known thesis was that the notion of scientific fact as a collection of newer and better discoveries and facts was not the way scientific theories were constructed. Scientific research was conducted within what he called a paradigm, and a paradigm shift could make previous research useless and the facts no longer valid. Kuhn argued as well that much scientific discovery was actually a result of agreement within the scientific community.

Berger and Luckmann (1966) took this a step further in their argument that this sociology of knowledge could not work within epistemology:

> To include epistemological questions concerning the validity of sociological knowledge in the sociology of knowledge is somewhat like trying to push a bus in which one is riding … these questions are not themselves part of the empirical discipline of sociology (p. 13).

Essentially, they were saying that one cannot attempt to find absolute answers within the sociology of knowledge, as this is a self-defeating exercise and serves only to reintroduce essentialist elements into the picture. However, they did have to find a way around the criticism that this sociology of knowledge seemed simply a relativistic, anything-goes, no-holds-barred type of knowledge that would quickly lead to either anarchy or total skepticism. Thus, they came up with commonsense knowledge as understood by the general public:

> Society does indeed possess objective facticity. And society is indeed built up by activity that expresses subjective meaning … The central question for sociological theory can then be put as follows: How is it possible that subjective meanings become objective facticities? … An adequate understanding of the "reality sui generis" of society requires an inquiry into the manner in which this reality is constructed. This inquiry, we maintain, is the task of the sociology of knowledge (p. 18).

According to Berger and Luckmann (1966), the key to this inquiry is the use of language, which allows humans to free themselves from the purely subjective and to evolve more abstract meanings. As a result, you have two sets of realities—the subjective (socialization and identity) and the objective (institutions and legitimacy)—constantly in a dialogue and actually making up the fabric of social meanings.[1]

In terms of understanding what has been happening in Japan with respect to government and corruption, the argument could be set thusly: (a) a strictly essentialist interpretation argues that there are absolute terms by which corruption can be measured; and (b) a constructivist approach works more closely with people's perceptions of what is taking place.

The implications of this are quite obvious: if one accepts the constructionist view of knowledge, then one has to drop any idea that knowledge could have absolutist or essentialist qualities—or that there is some truth out there just waiting for us to pluck. Any views we "discover" are actually our own views, which we project upon the world. According to Putnam, "The world is not going to impose" any particular view upon us (1993, p. 150).

However, Schmidt (2001) points out that philosophy and sociology do not pursue the same goals when it comes to the study of knowledge—and therefore the two should not make overly ambitious claims in the other's domain. One cannot use philosophy to refute the claims made by sociology and vice versa.

Risse (2000) distinguishes between social constructivist and rational choice theories in the fields of international relations and comparative politics. The first uses a "logic of appropriateness" in decision making, while the latter emphasizes a "logic of consequentialism." In keeping with constructivism, the logic of appropriateness stresses a rule-guided behavior where "human actors are imagined to follow rules that associate particular identities to particular situations, approaching individual opportunities for action by assessing similarities between current identities and choice dilemmas and more general concepts of self and situations" (March and Olsen, 1998, p. 951). On the other hand, the logic of consequentialism assumes that the interests and preferences of actors in an interaction are fixed for the most part, and that the goal is to maximize those interests and preferences: "Rational choice is instrumental: it is guided by the outcome of action. Actions are valued and chosen not for themselves, but as more or less efficient means to a further end" (Elster, 1989, p. 22).[2]

Hopf (1998) provides a list of what he feels constructivism is better able to do in international relations when compared to neorealist approaches. This includes:

- The ability to better understand the involvement of nationalism, ethnicity, race, gender, religion, and sexuality in world politics;
- The ability to make sense of the tendency of states to assume different identities, depending on the situation and conditions;
- The ability to uncover features related to culture and domestic politics;
- The ability to collaborate with other approaches to get a fuller account of international relations.

In a famous televised discussion, which took place in the Netherlands in 1971, Noam Chomsky and Michel Foucault outlined the fundamental differences that separated Chomsky's essentialist

---

1 For a more detailed discussion on the themes running through constructivist thought, see Gergen (1985); for the consequences to knowledge, see Schmidt (2001).

2 See Hopf (1998) for the use of social constructivist principles in practical politics.

view of human nature and, by extension, politics, and Foucault's constructivist vision of what it is like to be a human being.[3]

For our purposes, we employ elements of the constructivist viewpoint in a sociological, but not an epistemological, sense: that is, while notions of corruption may be socially constructed, that does not preclude a universal continuum along which what is and what is not corruption are ultimately judged. In other words, while the particulars of any individual act might be considered either corrupt or not within a certain society, the general parameters of what constitutes corruption are known across cultures.

Corruption Theories, Models, and Effects

Definitions

There are numerous definitions of corruption (Nye, 1967, 2002; Van Klaveren, 2002; Leff, 1964; Friedrich, 1972). That by no means exhausts the set of definitions. Hess and Dunfee (2000) set limits on corruption by defining it as "coarse bribery," which is "the promise or payment of a benefit that induces a public official to breach a duty pertaining to a significant community interest" (p. 593). LaPalombara (1994) defines it as

> Behavior by a public servant, whether elected or appointed, which involves a deviation from his or her formal duties because of reasons of personal gain to himself or herself or to other private persons with whom the public servant is associated. Corruption, however, requires two or more parties to a transaction, at least one of whom holds a position of public trust and/or exercises a public role, and another (or others) of whom acts in a private capacity. The latter may be, of course, individual persons, legal persons in the private sector (such as banks, corporations, trade unions, or formal associations), or collectivities, such as a tribe, ethnic group, extended family, political party or club, and so on (p. 327).

Tanzi (1998) breaks acts of corruption down into various categories, including:

+ Bureaucratic (petty) or political (grand);
+ Cost reducing (for the briber) or benefit enhancing;
+ Initiated by the briber or the person being bribed;
+ Coercive or collusive;
+ Centralized or decentralized;
+ Predictable or arbitrary;
+ Involving money or not.

Macrae (1982) defines corruption as "an arrangement involving an exchange between two parties (the 'demander' and the 'supplier') which (i) has an influence on the allocation of resources either immediately or in the future; and (ii) involves the use or abuse of public or collective responsibility for private ends" (p. 678).

---

3   For a detailed discussion of the Chomsky-Foucault argument, see Wilkin (1999), and Donaldson (1997).

Other definitions of corruption include:

Huntington (1968): "Behavior of public officials which deviates from accepted norms in order to serve private ends" (p. 59).

Senturia (1931): "The misuse of public power for private profit" (vol. iv).

Andreski (1968): "The practice of using the power of office for making private gain in breach of laws and regulations nominally in force" (p. 92).

The common factor in all these definitions seems to be the reliance on the existence of a public domain that is separate from the private one, as well as the existence of the kind of bureaucracy which is run on fixed principles of an objective nature: a Weberian legal-rational bureaucracy, in other words. There have been several objections raised to these kinds of definitions, including:

- The notion that this idea of public office is a Western concept and that, in many countries, what the West would consider corruption—nepotism, patronage, bribery in the form of gift giving—are actually socially approved in certain cultures.
- The notion that a government itself sets the norms and standards for those in public office, leading to situations where the definition might actually condone oppressive regimes. For example, there is the famous example given by Rose-Ackerman (1978) in which she asks: Does a policeman in a regime where torture is part of the criminal law act corruptly if he accepts a bribe from a suspect so as to torture him or her less severely?
- The notion that bureaucratic rules and regulations are so clear-cut as to be completely transparent when, in fact, there is much ambiguity even in the most well-ordered bureaucracies.
- The problem with elected officials who have no formal rules, procedures, or qualifications: "Whereas the behaviour of civil servants, particularly in relation to outside interests and the acceptance of gifts, is usually quite circumscribed, politicians need to endure few restraints. In Britain a member of parliament may accept regular retainers or lavish hospitality from commercial interests, foreign governments or trade unions" (Theobald, 1990, p. 4).
- The problem of the very recent appearance, historically speaking, of the difference between public and private sphere, while corruption existed even during those periods when it was simply the monarch and his favorites. For example, "Two thousand years ago, Kautilya, the prime minister of an Indian kingdom, had already written a book, *Arthashastra*, discussing corruption" (Tanzi, 1998, p. 559). And Davis (1910) noted: "In the last days of the [Roman] Republic, the trading in votes rose to such a height that … in 55 BC a new law struck at what was probably the most flagrant form of corruption, namely, payments made to *interpretes* on the basis of how many votes they were able to deliver to the interested candidates" (p. 13).

In light of these objections to the public office concept of political corruption, some writers have opted for a less essentialist definition, one more closely connected to public interest (Friedrich, 1966, p. 74; Hurstfield, 1967, p. 19). Rogow and Lasswell (1963), for example, rely on "responsibility" and "common interest" to define corruption:

A *corrupt act* violates responsibility toward at least one system of public or civil order and is in fact incompatible with (destructive of) any such system. A system of public or civic order exalts common interest over special interest; violations of the common interest for special advantage are corrupt (p. 132).

Tarkowski (1989), writing at the time when Poland and the USSR were about to undergo extreme political transitions, tried to reconcile the reemerging interplay between societal interests and official institutions in his definition:

> Corruption … is any activity motivated by interest, violating the binding rules of distribution, the application of which is within one's responsibility. Rules of distribution … refer not only to the letter of the law, but also to norms recognized as binding by society and/or to the system's "official" norms and operational codes. Also "corrupt" are those activities regarded by society as illegitimate or seen by the power elite as contradictory to the logic of the system (pp. 53–54).

The question quickly arises, however: What exactly is this "common" or "public" interest? Where do we find it in a modern, complex society with a variety of special interest groups or blocs? And what about "national interest?" Is that the same as public interest? A second problem with these types of definitions is that some authors (including Friedrich, 1966, 1972; Leff, 1964; Huntington, 1968; Lui, 1985; Graziano, 1980; Tullock, 1996; and Becker and Stigler, 1974) have argued that corruption itself can be in the best public interest under some conditions. Among the arguments for the positive benefits of corruption:

+ Institutionalized corruption is better than random corruption, in that a person knows exactly where to go to pay for services;
+ Corruption improves efficiency by helping to remove government-imposed regulations which might interfere with investment and growth;
+ The promotion of efficiency in bidding competitions where those who can afford the highest bribes are by definition the most efficient;
+ The economizing of time and effort by allowing those whose time is valuable to jump the queue;
+ Allows politicians to gather funds to help keep a country together and promote growth;
+ The use of bribes to supplement low wages and thus allow the government to maintain lower tax levels, which, in turn, is supposed to promote growth.

While all these arguments can be countered, it does throw a wrench into any clear-cut definition of corruption that relies on public or common interest.

The last type of definition is perhaps the most anti-essentialist, if not quite constructivist: that of relying on "public opinion." In this definition, "corruption then is simply what public opinion in a given society deems to be corrupt" (Theobald, 1990, p. 7). When it comes to public opinion and what that might mean under these circumstances, Heidenheimer (1978, 2002) proposes three types of corruption: white, gray, and black. Black corruption is the type which both elite opinion and mass public opinion would condemn; gray is where some (usually elite) want to see it punished, but mass opinion is ambiguous; white is where neither the majority of mass nor elite opinion would see the need for condemnation or punishment. Alongside these, Heidenheimer postulates ten types of behavior within four types of political or cultural systems, examining everything from minor forms of nepotism to criminal extortion. The four types of political obligation systems are (see Table 2.1 below):

- Traditional Familist- (Kinship-) Based System: loyalty to the nuclear family is all that counts;
- Traditional Patron-Client-Based Systems: ties to strong protectors, weak ties to the rest of the community;
- Modern Boss-Follower-Based System: control is through machine politics with a more flexible economic model than traditional patron-client;
- Civic-Culture-Based System: ideally with highly developed community norms with political exchange relations being diversified and indirect.

Characteristic	TRADITIONAL Familist-Based: Within	Between	Patron-Client	MODERN Boss-Follower	Civic-Culture
Archetypal protector	Family head		Patron saint	Political boss	State
Prototype for political exchange relations	Family obligation	Economic exchange	Social and economic exchange	Economic and social exchange	Social (indirect) exchange
Strength of community-regarding norms		Nil	Weak	Weak	Strong
Denotation of "patron"			Moral ideal, protector, intermediary	Protector, intermediary	Benefactor of community
Strong reciprocal basis of obligations between patron and client	No		Yes	Yes	
Kinship-friendship network open enough to permit independent "contacts" by clients	No	Yes	No (depends)	Yes (depends)	Yes
Collective obligation for favors to its members		Yes	Yes	Yes (depends)	No
Clients directly follow patron-chief in political behavior	Yes		Yes	Yes	
Family obligations perceived as having primary claim on officeholder	Yes		Yes	No	No

Table 2.1: Types of Community and Political Exchange (Heidenheimer, 2002, pp. 144–145).

Table 2.2 below lists the ten types of behavior that someone in the modern Western tradition would consider corrupt according to present-day administrative norms and rules. Heidenheimer provides a code to classify the frequency of the behaviors within each of the four political exchange systems, as well as how these behaviors are perceived within the particular system. These codes are:

- ◆ SOP: Standard Operating Procedure
- ◆ FI: Frequent Incidence
- ◆ OI: Occasional Incidence
- ◆ OO: Rare Incidence, Without any regular pattern of incidence
- ◆ B: Black Corruption
- ◆ G: Gray Corruption
- ◆ W: White Corruption

As well, the types of corruption are divided into three categories: petty, routine, and aggravated.

Type of Behavior	Familist System		Patron-Client		Boss-Follower		Civic-Culture	
	Incidence	Evaluation	Inc	Eva	Inc	Eva	Inc	Eva
Petty Corruption								
Officials deviate from rules in minor ways for benefit of friends	SOP	W	SOP	W	SOP	W	FI	G
Routine Corruption								
Gifts accepted by public officials (or parties) for generalized good will	SOP	W	SOP	W	SOP	W	OI	B
Nepotism practices in official appointments and contract awarding	SOP	W	SOP	W	SOP	G	OI	B
Officials profit from public decisions through sideline occupations (clean graft)	SOP	W	SOP	W	FI	G	OI	B
Clients pledge votes according to patron's direction	SOP	W	SOP	W	FI	G	OO	B
Aggravated Corruption								
Clients need patron intervention to get administrative "due process"	SOP	W	FI	G	OI	B	OO	B
Gifts (kickbacks) expected by officials as prerequisite for extending "due process"	SOP	W	FI	G	OI	B	OO	B
Officials tolerate organized crime in return for payoffs	FI	W	FI	G	OI	B	OO	B
Activists suddenly change party allegiance for pecuniary reasons	FI	W	OI	B	OI	B	OO	B
Officials and citizens ignore clear proof of corruption	FI	W	OI	B	OI	B	OO	B

Table 2.2: Incidence and Evaluation of Corrupt Practices (Heidenheimer, 2002, pp. 148–149).

A series of surveys (Gardiner, 1970; Peters and Welch, 1978; Atkinson and Mancuso, 1985; and Johnston, 1986) seems to indicate that Heidenheimer's categories and criteria generally correlate to public opinion in a broad sense. Respondents were more likely to label something as corrupt if it involved larger amounts of money; if those involved were public officials rather than private citizens; if it involved the direct taking of a bribe rather than something indirect; if it involved keeping the money rather than passing it on; and if it involved a prominent person as opposed to an average citizen.

Philp (2002) lays out what most people would consider a clear case of political corruption where:

1. A public official (A),
2. in violation of the trust placed in him by the public (B),
3. and in a manner which harms the public interest,
4. knowingly engages in conduct which exploits the office for clear personal and private gain in a way which runs contrary to the accepted rules and standards for the conduct of public office within the political culture,
5. so as to benefit a third party (C) by providing C with access to a good or service C would not otherwise obtain" (p. 42).

Of course, the problem rests with the fact that very few cases are this clear-cut. As well, even in cases where all five criteria are fulfilled, the notion "is intelligible only against the background of a political culture in which there are clear, shared norms and rules governing the conduct both of public officials and of members of the public in their dealings with these officials" (p. 42). The same problem arises with Alatas (1990) and his ninefold breakdown of the characteristics of corruption. Alatas also covers one area that others do not—and that is the notion of "autocorruption," where only one person is involved. For example, the legislator who has advance knowledge of a zoning change and who supports the bill so that he can then profit from it because of his foreknowledge (p. 2).

For our purposes, the definition supplied by Philp (2002) seems to best cover both the general notion of corruption and the detailing of instances of corrupt acts. Because it speaks of "the accepted rules and standards for the conduct of public office within the political culture," it escapes some of the arguments against universal morality-based definitions or the tendency to "translate" one country's or region's notions to another's.

Corruption Effects

With all the difficulty in coming to a consensus definition of corruption, it comes as a bit of a surprise that the vast majority of researchers and authors seem to agree on the deleterious effects of political corruption (with the exception of those mentioned above who made an argument that on occasion, corruption could actually help an economy—even if only in the short term). Hess and Dunfee (2000); Mauro (1995, 1997); Shleifer and Vishny (1993); Tanzi (1998); Tanzi and Davoodi (2001); Theobald (1990); Rose-Ackerman (1997, 2002); Johnston (1997); Elliott (1997); Nichols (1997); Hillstrom (1996); and Alatas (1990) all present arguments outlining the damage corruption can cause to: an economy, political system, and a people's moral compass.

Tanzi (1998) breaks down the effects of corruption on an economy in two: qualitative and econometric. Under the qualitative list, he includes: reduced public revenue and increased public spending; increased income gaps; market distortion; reduction of economic efficiency and growth. According to Mauro (1995, 1997), the econometric results of corruption include reduced investment, and reduced spending on education and health. For Tanzi and Davoodi (2001), corruption spurs public investment because these types of projects are most easily manipulated by high-level officials to get bribes, while at the same time it reduces the productivity of any public investment.

According to Hess and Dunfee (2000), any positive effects from corruption under certain conditions are more than balanced by the negatives, including "an overall inefficient allocation of resources where decisions are based on personal benefit to the bribe-receiver, not political rules or markets. Further, the secrecy of bribery may reduce the value of price information" (p. 605). Shleifer and Vishny (1993) also stress the necessarily secret nature of corruption, causing a shift in investments from key sectors such as health and education and into those areas where there are better opportunities for corruption—such as defense and infrastructure. Theobald (1990) adds the dissipation of capital, squandering of natural resources, weakening of administrative capacity, and undermining of democracy. Aside from inefficiency and unfairness, Rose-Ackerman (1997) points to the danger that corruption can undermine the political legitimacy of the state: "Corruption is also evidence that deeper problems exist in the state's dealings with the private sector. The most severe costs are not the bribes themselves but the underlying distortions they reveal—distortions that may have been created by officials to generate payoffs" (p. 42).

Elliott (1997) focuses on the political consequences of corruption and indicates that, in developed nations, "the primary cost of influence-peddling 'corruption' is increased cynicism among voters and the alienation of citizens from their government" (p. 197). In developing countries, while some have argued that corruption may be beneficial, "its undemocratic and detrimental nature causes moral decay, social discontent and political alienation" (Hillstrom, 1996, p. 4). Nichols (1997) finds similar results and concludes that corruption is not simply a matter of economics, but one of public ethics and morality, arguing that bribery takes away from the people's happiness, reduces their confidence in the government, and stimulates lawlessness.

Have the negative effects of corruption been proved without a doubt? According to Theobald (1990), there are linkages, but no smoking gun:

> Having outlined the main costs and benefits of corruption it has to be admitted that it is extraordinarily difficult to balance one against the other in any concrete situation. This is primarily because corruption is frequently claimed to bring about diametrically opposed effects … Whilst it is certainly conceivable that corruption may do all of these things, unless we can specify the point which benefits become costs such claims are relatively meaningless. To date no writer has been able to do this mainly because there are so many unknown and unquantifiable elements which interrelate in a variety of highly complex ways with basic variables such as economic growth and political development (p. 131).

Models and Theories of Corruption

In an effort to put current anticorruption campaigns into some sort of historical perspective, Ala'i (2000) cites two main approaches or models that have dominated studies of corruption—the pre-1960s moralist and the post-1960s revisionist. According to the moralist perspective, corruption is the result of moral failings within either individual human beings or particular societies. A corollary of the moralist approach was that Western Christian societies were morally superior to the rest of the world. The rejection of this approach by social scientists coincided with the loss of essentialist and absolutist theories in sociology and anthropology:

> The most striking feature of the revisionist definition is that it is intended to be amoral. The revisionists used concepts from economics, sociology, anthropology, and other social sciences to make two arguments: (1) the definitions of corruption and bribery varied with societal values and inherited cultural and religious traditions, and (2) an increase in the incidence of corruption and bribery was a necessary and inevitable part of the modernization process (Ala'i, 2000, p. 887).

It is the second revisionist argument that has caused the most problems, and according to some scholars, has actually brought back a version of the moralist thesis in the form of so-called "geographical morality." This is where the so-called inevitableness of a corrupt stage for developing countries leads to a double standard. As put by Caiden and Caiden (1977), the revisionist thesis amounted basically to this attitude:

> [P]oor countries for cultural and historical reasons have a propensity toward corruption, seen as a violation of Western norms. To this propensity may be added a breakdown in the allocative mechanisms of society, or economic, political, and administrative reasons, so that corruption steps in to fulfill the missing functions. Corruption is thus legitimized in terms of its prevalence, and of its functionality: indeed, given the inappropriateness of Western norms and inadequacy of Western institutions, corruption does not really exist at all—it is simply a different way of doing business (p. 304).

The analysis of the causes of corruption is also an area that has led to divergent and sometimes contradictory conclusions, depending on the approach taken: be it the examination of economic, political, cultural, or psychological factors. The majority of the studies have focused on economic theory and how it is that rational, self-interest-seeking individuals decide to become involved in corruption. Among these theories can be included public choice (Rose-Ackerman, 1978), game theory (Macrae, 1982), psychological profiling (Rogow and Lasswell, 1963), and transaction-cost economics (Husted, 1994). However, as Husted (1999) points out: "The usefulness of these studies is limited to the countries in which they originated because the recommendations fail to take into account the variety of cultural contexts in which corrupt activities occur" (p. 339). Husted uses four of the five work-related cultural values originally set up by Hofstede (1997)—power distance, individualism, masculinity, and uncertainty avoidance—in combination with the level of economic development to come up with a comparative model of corruption. These values are defined as:

+ **Power Distance:** The extent to which the less powerful expect and accept the unequal distribution of power;
+ **Individualism:** The extent to which decisions in a person's life are determined by the individual or by an in-group of family, friends, and peers;

- **Masculinity:** The extent to which the focus is on material success instead of quality-of-life concerns;
- **Uncertainty Avoidance:** The extent to which members of a culture feel threatened by uncertainty or unknown situations.

Husted (1999) found that, while "the most significant correlate of corruption is the level of economic development as measured by the purchasing power parity estimate of GNP per capita … three of the four cultural variables are positively correlated with corruption at a significant level. On the basis of these results, we can tentatively describe a cultural profile of a corrupt country as one in which there is high uncertainty avoidance, high masculinity, and high power distance" (p. 351).

Corruption in Asia

In the specific context of corruption within one country or area, several authors (Alatas, 1990; Vittal, 2001; Quah, 1999; Chan, 2000, 2001; Pharr, 2002; and Mitchell, 1996) have made contributions to the literature of corruption in Asia in general and Japan in particular.

Alatas points out that some of the Western theories on the causes of corruption in developing societies—such as kinship solidarity and gift-giving—do not hold water under proper analysis: "Appointing relatives to public office against the rules of appointment, ignoring merit and qualification, is rejected by traditional society. Throughout history, the traditional societies in Asia have always made the distinction between the public and the private, between corruption and non-corruption … A phenomenological analysis of corruption will reveal that the constituent elements of corruption are cheating and stealing … Traditional societies do not condone stealing and cheating" (1990, p. 95). Alatas concludes that the rise of corruption in these societies can be explained better through historical conditions and special circumstances than by any cultural traits which might be unique in the area.

Chan (2001, 2000) develops a macro-micro model of corruption and applies it to post-Mao China and Hong Kong. Integrating macro theories (functional, political-institutional, revised modernization, and cultural approaches) with micro models (frequency of corrupt opportunities, stakes involved, external control such as legal penalties, internal control, or moral restraints), Chan determines that, given the macro conditions, the increase in corruption occurred because there were more opportunities for corruption and because both internal and external controls failed. Chan's model is based on the "principal-agent" analysis and the thick rational-choice framework which Klitgaard (1988) uses in describing a potentially corrupt agent: "This decision model considers the probability of being caught and punished, the size of the penalty, the utility of corruption and the moral cost of taking a bribe" (Chan, 2000, p. 509). Therefore, if the agent decides against the corrupt act, he or she gets the reward of a regular pay plus moral satisfaction; if the agent decides to act corruptly, he or she gets the extra money involved in the bribe but at the expense of moral satisfaction, and, of course, the danger of being caught. According to Klitgaard (1988), the decision depends on a whole series of factors including "her own ethical, cultural, and religious standards … on what her peers and colleagues are doing … on how big a bribe she gets for how large a deviation from her responsibilities to the principal. For an unscrupulous person in a corrupt subculture, the moral cost of being corrupt may approach zero" (p. 71). Chan (2001) also discusses the "social learning" aspect of corruption. In effect, if someone observes behavior around him or her which is identifiably corrupt but which goes unpunished or which is accepted as normal practice, that person is likely to accept those favorable ideas of corruption as well. In these cases, "corruption is a result of a social exchange in which the words, responses, presence, and behavior of other persons directly reinforce corrupt behavior, providing line setting for reinforcement, or serving as the conduit through which other social rewards and punishers are delivered or made available" (p. 911).

Both Mitchell (1996) and Pharr (2002) deal with corruption with direct reference to Japan. In his book, Mitchell speaks of "structural corruption" and the entrenchment of money politics into the Japanese political system from the very beginning of representational government in that country, which extends back to the middle of the 19th century. He says:

> Scholars writing about Japan use the term "structural corruption," meaning that the structural nature of corruption is built into the political system to the point that to survive, politicians are forced to exchange favors with businessmen in return for funds to pay members of their faction and to use for elections. Furthermore, because structural corruption is so deeply embedded in the political system, reform programs are doomed to failure unless the entire system is destroyed (pp. xv–xvi).

How does this structural or institutional corruption work? Ironically, Mitchell argues that, despite dominating the elections for almost four decades, Japan's Liberal Democratic Party did not exert as much power as it theoretically could—and the titular head of the party (the prime minister) was even more powerless. As described by Van Wolferen (1989):

> There is, to be sure, a hierarchy, or, rather, a complex of overlapping hierarchies. But it has no peak; it is a truncated pyramid. There is no supreme institution with ultimate policy-making jurisdiction ... The bureaucrats tinker with the economy ... The politicians and almost everyone else keep out of their way. Parliamentary representatives ... attend mainly to the business of getting re-elected ... The industrialists continue to expand their foreign market shares ... They are kept in line by their peers; and they pay the politicians. Nobody is boss, but everybody, in some way or other, has leverage over somebody else, which helps ensure an orderly state of affairs (p. 41).

Having examined the role that the policy performance of leaders (economic conditions) and/or the store of social capital (vibrant versus low civic society) play on the level of trust citizens have in their government, Pharr (2002) concludes that the key indicator for this trust is neither of these factors. Rather, it is the perceived level of corruption the population sees in its governing bodies, a dimension associated strongly with "character" or how leaders carry out their duties on behalf of the citizens: "Reported corruption is a far more important cause of citizen distrust in leaders and political institutions than either economic or social capital deficits ... At least for Japan, leaders' reported corruption was by far the single best predictor at any given point in time of confidence in government over two decades" (p. 852).

Despite these studies on so-called institutional corruption within the Japanese government, none have come up with explanations as to why: (a) the Japanese political system was able to resist for such a long time; (b) the Japanese economy was able to function at such a high level for so long; and (c) what occurred in the late 1980s and early 1990s to start the country down the road to recession.

General Studies

Like corruption, attempting to come up with a universal definition of organized crime has proved to be a very difficult task. For example, some have defined it as a set of relations among illegal organizations, while others put the emphasis on the illegal activities performed by a given group of people. The first might be labeled the governance theory of organized crime (or organized crime syndicates as quasi-governmental institutions which often run parallel to legitimate governments); the second describes these syndicates as quasi-firms which produce illegal goods and services for a populace that wants them. Fiorentini and Peltzman (1995) see these two definitions as two sides of the same analytic coin—and the choice depends on the underlying reason for the analysis:

> For instance, if one is interested in the internal structure of a criminal organization, it is perhaps more appropriate to investigate it as a firm where agents at different levels maximize their objective functions. The analogy ... holds even more tightly if one is interested in the analysis of the investment decisions of the criminal organizations or their competitive behavior with respect to rivals in the output market. On the other hand, the analogy with a governmental structure is much more useful when the analysis focuses on racketeering activities or the management of military conflicts against other organisations (pp. 6–7).

Fiorentini and Peltzman further offer a set of characteristics by which organized crime can be recognized. These include:

+ Economies of scale and exploitation of monopolistic prices on the supply of illegal goods and services;
+ Practice of violence against other legal and illegal business;
+ Criminal hierarchy with internalization of negative externalities and management of a portfolio of risky activities;
+ Avoidance of resource dissipation through competitive lobbying and corruption;
+ Easier access to markets.

Godson and Olson (1995) cobble together a definition of organized crime as:

> [A] more or less formal structure that endures over time, is directed toward a common purpose by a recognizable leadership operating outside the law, is quite often based on family or ethnic identity, and is prepared to use violence or other means to promote and protect common interests and objectives (p. 22).

How gangs originate is another question that is open to a multitude of answers. Godson and Olson (1995) note that a large number of what are now considered organized crime groups may have started as societies, which actually helped disenfranchised members of ethnic or political groups. However, they also indicate that other gangs may have started from gangs of thieves or others operating outside the law. Interestingly enough, as indicated in the section on the history of the *yakuza*, both these elements are present in discussions as to the origins of this group in Japan: the

Robin Hood/oppressor syndrome. Volkov (2000), in analyzing the rise of violent criminal gangs in Russia following the collapse of communism, gives an example of the typical evolution of one of these gangs. At the same time, he argues that this has been the favored evolution of most states:

> Specialists in violence—former sportsmen—create an organization, a violence-managing agency that allows them to extract tribute from the local business by offering protection. Having established a kind of territorial control, the agency wages a war with competing violence-managing agencies … Having attained the monopoly position … [the gang] makes a conscious choice of economic policy of reasonable taxation and reliable protection of property … In the longer run, protection rents and reputation result in the growing capital accumulation and further economic expansion. [The gang] turns into a "financial-industrial group." Parallel to that, it concludes an informal pact and then establishes institutionalized relations with the legitimate regional government. Finally, it makes an effort to legalize its political and economic power by registering as Social-Political Union (OPS) … and seeks to achieve legitimacy with and support from the local population (p. 728).

Milhaupt and West (2000) link the emergence of organized crime groups with the "mismatch between property rights and enforcement mechanisms" (p. 50) following eras of great social upheaval—post-feudal Japan or Italy, for example, or postcommunist Russia. They explain the apparent success of the Japanese economy (at least until the early 1990s) thanks to the development of a "highly workable set of rules to govern economic exchange that held up without heavy reliance on formal enforcement mechanisms" (p. 53).

The link between organized crime and corruption has always been assumed and made explicit by a number of authors, among them Gardiner (1970); Tanzi (1995); and Grossman (1995). Of course, there can be corruption without organized crime, and theoretically, organized crime without corruption, but the odds are fairly high that the two sets will intersect at some point.

Gardiner's famous study of the fictional American town of Wincanton, home to a crime syndicate for more than four decades and a place where most of the city officials were hand-picked by crime syndicate bosses, revealed some interesting facts about how the citizens felt about corruption:

> A survey of city residents did not show that they wanted corruption per se, or that they opposed law enforcement efforts, but the survey clearly showed … that substantial numbers of respondents were tolerant of minor forms of corruption such as conflicts of interest and accepting gifts from companies doing business with the city (1970, pp. 55-56).

Tanzi (1995) emphasizes the close relationship organized crime has with the community in which it exists and interacts. His analysis of Sicilian gangs could very well be used to describe their Japanese equivalents: (a) come from the same region; (b) speak the same dialect; (c) often intermarry; (d) direct a portion of their criminal activities outside the area where they live; and (e) are often an integral part of the society in which they operate. It is under these conditions that corruption can flourish. Speaking of Sicilian crime syndicates but once again transferable, he says:

> The corruption of bureaucrats who hold power in local decisions allows the mafia to operate with relative impunity and to expand its power, especially if that power brings a

lot of money with which to compensate the bureaucrats (and sometimes the local politicians) for their assistance (p. 176).

Grossman (1995) discusses the idea of organized crime and governments (the *kleptocratic* state) competing for the "total rent" to be extracted from taxpayers. In his analysis, given that neither organized crime nor governments can be completely eliminated, this sort of competition is good for the taxpayers because they then have alternative means of getting their goods and services. The worst scenario, according to this analysis, is the possibility of collusion between crime syndicates and governments, whereby they share these "rents" and are thus able to fix the prices through a joint monopoly situation. This is effectively the same as saying that the worst possible result of an organized crime/government axis is the corruption of government officials by the syndicate so that they both hold the general public hostage.

The *Yakuza*

As indicated in Chapter One, the *yakuza* claim a long and colorful history in Japan, and it is often difficult to distinguish between mythology and reality. One of the most persistent is that of the romantic outlaw, the Robin Hood type who, for some reason or other, found himself outside society's pale. Modern *yakuza* like to see themselves as a combination of the *hatamoto-yakko*, samurai warriors who found themselves unemployed when Japan was united under the first shogunate, and the *machi-yakko*, townspeople who came together to resist the incursions of the *hatamoto-yakko*. These romantic outlaws became the favorite heroes of 18th-century popular Japanese novels and plays, as well as folk tales and songs (Kaplan and Dubro, 1986).

Yakuza Background

No matter whence they trace their ancestry, one thing stands out for the modern-day *yakuza*: they have set up one of the most effective organized crime operations in the world. In the late 1980s, it was estimated that more than 86,000 gangsters belonging to 3,200 gangs roamed Japan (Chua-Eoan, 1988; "In The Land of The Rising Gun," 1989), with annual revenues in the $50-billion range (Ormonde, 1992). But this was nothing compared to the early 1960s, when police estimated 184,000 in 5,200 groups (Kaplan and Dubro, 1986). Table 2.3 below lists the major syndicates between 1981-1984.

Syndicate	Sphere of Influence (prefectures)	Affiliated Groups	Mem-ber-ship	Head-quarters	Year Formed	Syndicate Boss
Yamaguchi-gumi	29	400	10,400	Kobe/ Osaka	1915	Kazuo Nakanishi
Sumiyoshi-rengo	20	113	6,723	Tokyo	1958	Masao Hori
Motokyokuto Aioh Rengo-kai*	22	105	4,416	Tokyo	1930	Haruo Tanaka

Inagawa-kai	12	119	4,347	Yokohama	1945	Kakuji Inagawa
Ichiwa-kai	30	140	2,800	Kobe/ Osaka	1984	Hiroshi Yamamoto
Matsuba-kai	12	41	2,147	Tokyo	1953	Eisuke Sato
Nippon Kokusui-kai	10	22	943	Tokyo	1958	Kyo Koo-soo
Dai Nippon Heiwa-kai	13	51	914	Kobe/ Osaka	1965	Katsuyoshi Hirata
Toa Yuai Jigyo Kumiai	NA**	none	796	Tokyo	1966	Chong Gwon Yong

*Officially Disbanded
**Not Available

Table 2.3: Major Yakuza Syndicates (1981–1984) (Kaplan and Dubro, 1986, p. 139)

The police divide the *yakuza* into three types, according to criminal occupation: the *bakuto* (traditional gamblers); *tekiya* (street peddlers); and *gurentai* (hoodlums). Table 2.4 lists the occupational backgrounds of *yakuza* and their numbers as of 1980. It should be noted that the totals are greater than the number of estimated *yakuza* because of the intermingling of the various gangster elements. For example, many listed as *bakuto* also act as *sokaiya*.

Occupation	Full-status Members	Marginal-status Members	Total
Bakuto (gamblers)	26,960	5,148	32,108 (31%)
Tekiya (peddlers)	21,438	2,570	24,008 (23%)
Gurentai (hoodlums)	9,861	1,639	11,500 (11%)
Seaport racketeers	3,221	0	3,221 (3%)
Sokaiya (corporate racketeers)	47	2,417	2,464 (2%)
Scandal sheet extortionists	41	803	844 (1%)
Prostitution gangsters	495	74	569 (1%)

Others	39	29,202	29,241 (28%)
Totals	62,102	41,853	103,955 (100%)

Table 2.4: Occupational Background of Yakuza (Kaplan and Dubro, 1986, p. 171)

Although aligned along family lines in much the same way as the American Mafia and with similar oaths binding the members, the *yakuza* show one important difference: they conduct their business in very visible offices with logos, business cards, and brass plates on their doors, and the largest of them, the Yamaguchi-gumi, even prints its own telephone directory ("Honourable Mob," 1990; "Tycoons of Crime," 1992). Members carry pins identifying their gang affiliation and they still maintain a code of conduct, which in its ideal state is closer to the days of the samurai than modern Japan. The closest bond is between the boss, the *oyabun* (literally father), and his sidekick, the *kobun* (literally child). This is an interesting psychological relationship for, as Seymour (1996) points out:

> Blue-collar fathers ... were obliged to work long days that made them non-factors in the raising of their children. The lack of a controlling influence and the discipline of a strong father figure often led to wild uncontrolled boys. Most yakuza have nothing good to say about their fathers. A disproportionately large percentage of yakuza are the products of divorced or separated parents (p. 17).

It seems, however, that some of the romance is starting to wear off as the economy continues to slide. In 2000, police in Osaka issued more than 500 "cease extortion" directives under the 1992 Anti-Organized Crime Law. As well, many major corporations are starting to say "no" when gangsters come calling for "political donations" ("Cops Rap Yakuza," 2000). Perhaps, most importantly, the National Police Agency has reversed a long-standing policy of not releasing information on those associated with organized crime. Now, townspeople who are trying to drive gangsters from their local neighborhoods will be provided information by the police to help them ("Cops to Reveal Data," 2000). Whether this will spur the police force to take more action against the gangsters has yet to be seen, but for the moment, the police seem content with simply keeping an eye on the gangsters.

Yakuza Scams

> The yakuza are an exceptional organized crime group. In the twentieth century, they have often been a major key to political power in Japan ... Organized crime ... has grown remarkably powerful since World War II ... over the past 300 years, the yakuza have become one of the world's most successful criminal organizations, and that whatever the public does, these once honorable outlaws of Japan are apt to be around another 300 years (Kaplan and Dubro, 1986, p282).

The Japanese yakuza constitute a parallel universe running beneath virtually every institution and industry in the nation. It's a mind-numbing thought, considering the already Byzantine nature of Japan's "legitimate" corporate and "democratic" political institutions (Seymour, 1996, p. 19).

The *yakuza* in Japan have come a long way from the days when they were controlling portable booths and stalls at fairs or taking money from those unfortunate enough to become involved in gambling. In fact, they have come a long way from the turn of the 20th century, when they organized day labor for construction and stevedores for docks. By the 1970s, the *yakuza* were also:

- Running protection rackets and forcing local bars and restaurants to pay.
- Organizing political parties and influence-peddling.
- Running nightclubs, massage parlors, geisha inns, and other entertainment centers where prostitutes were provided.
- Involved in boxing, sumo, and other types of wrestling. In 1996, a former wrestler-trainer by the name of Onaruto claimed that 29 of the top 40 wrestlers fixed their matches. Onaruto died under mysterious circumstances shortly before he was to conduct a press conference on corruption in the sumo world. That did not silence him, however, as he had already written a book on the subject, which went on to become a bestseller in Japan. In it, he claimed that "the yakuza are the sport's leading sponsor … that sumo stars sup with crime bosses, use them to procure discreet hookers and ask their help in laundering cash earnings … Onaruto states baldly that it is routine for wrestlers to sell matches for between $5,000 and $10,000" ("Sumo Wrestling," 1996, p. 84).
- In control of hundreds of theater and movie production firms.
- In control of booking and talent agencies.
- Dealing drugs—especially amphetamines.
- Involved in loan sharking, smuggling, and pornography.
- Bidding on huge public works projects through dummy companies. According to a gang expert in the Japan Bar Association, it is estimated that 30-50 percent of public work projects require payoffs to mobsters at a cost of 2-5 percent of construction (Fulford, 1999).
- Rigging sports events and even auctions on foreclosed property.
- Taking control of hospitals, English-language schools, amusement centers, and fortune-telling parlors.
- Managed real estate, video games and parlors, the trucking business, waste disposal, and even security services.
- Making fake stamps and money, including American dollars, and objects such as watches and foods;
- Running one of the world's largest sex slave trades involving some 150,000 women working illegally in Japan (many of them as prostitutes). According to Jesse Gimenez, information attaché at the Philippines embassy: "They are forced into it. After they arrive their passports are taken from them, they're given no money, they're locked up and closely guarded and told that if they don't work as prostitutes they'll be hit, be killed, or their families will be attacked back home" (quoted in "Sex Trade Flourishing in Japan," 1995, p. 42).

The *yakuza* have also managed to turn blackmail and extortion into an art form. In a country where "saving face" is sometimes more important than life itself, the *sokaiya* have extorted millions

from companies simply by promising to stay away from stockholder meetings and not asking embarrassing questions. In one case, the head of Ito-Yokada, the corporation which owns 7-Eleven,
admitted to having paid more than $1 million to *sokaiya* (Seymour, 1996). In 1996, three execu-
tives from Takashimaya, one of Japan's oldest department-store chains, were arrested for paying
$740,000 in *sokaiya* money ("Spare Your Blushes, Sir," 1996). What makes this kind of activity
much easier is that a lot of daily bribery and greasing of wheels is considered just part of doing
business in Japan:

> There is institutionalized payola that flows from parent to teacher, patient to doctor,
> contractors to officials, distributors to suppliers, and within just about any important
> relationship imaginable. All these cash "gifts"—sliding under, over, and around the pro-
> verbial table—softens up the populace for real yakuza exploitation and corruption (p.
> 25).

The *yakuza* are also involved in the activities of extreme right-wing groups, the same groups
who were responsible for the rise of ultranationalism in Japan prior to World War II. These groups
have been implicated in political kidnappings and assassinations, as well as the Sarin gas attack in
the Tokyo subway system. In North American terms, Kaplan and Dubro (1986) describe that this
partnership would be like the Ku Klux Klan and the Mafia forming a long-lasting association. The
yakuza take no sides, however. When a right-wing group was using loudspeaker vans to harass
Noboru Takeshita in his 1987 bid to become prime minister, the Inagawa-kai syndicate was paid
to silence the loudspeakers (with the implication they would then have something to hold over
Takeshita's head once he was in power) ("A Gangster Story," 1992).

Fulford (2000c) argues that the *yakuza* have infiltrated all the way up the political ladder. He
cites the $14 billion Kansai airport project as an example of the "I-scratch-your-back-you-scratch-
mine" world. According to an unnamed gang source, bureaucrats informed the *yakuza* where the
access roads would go. The mobsters then went about intimidating residents along the route to sell.
The properties were then sold back to the government at premium prices with portions ending up
in the pockets of politicians. As well, the same gangster says that politicians use mobsters to either
bribe or intimidate newspapers and other media into suppressing stories which might harm them:
"Or, the intimidation can be more direct. The editor and deputy editor of Uwasa no Shinso ... were
stabbed by gangsters after publishing allegations that Prime Minister Yoshiro Mori was arrested at
a house of ill-repute as a youth ... Reporters for the Asahi Shimbum ... have been receiving death
threats ... and many are living apart from their families for security reasons" (p. 66).

Yakuza and the Banks

> The story is told of a small credit association called Gifu Shogin that had gone belly-up
> in the wake of the four-year collapse of real estate prices. Government officials moved in
> to force a lifesaving merger of Gifu Shogin with another financial institution. Then there
> was a fantastic revelation: Of Gifu Shogin's $110 million in bad loans, about $70 million
> were to organized crime gangs or their front companies ... The well-documented connec-
> tions between yakuza and politicians all pale beside the yakuza's hand in the inflation and
> crash of the most awesome economy in the world (Seymour, 1996, p. 22).

Aside from straightforward business errors, lax regulations and oversight, and scandals involving bureaucrats and financial officials, perhaps the most astounding revelation has been the deep-rooted involvement of the *yakuza* in Japan's banking and monetary system. Even before the bubble economy burst, some banks in the 1980s packaged bad debts to the *yakuza* along with substantial new loans (Delfs, 1991b). Additionally, as land prices soared, banks got into the act and started lending money without proper credit checks: "Once the connections were built with financial institutions, the yakuza ... started to run real estate businesses, develop buildings and golf courses on their own. And financial institutions just kept lending them money" ("Who Got Yakuza into Our Banking System?" 1996, p. 2).

In 1991, Fuji Bank, then the country's fourth largest, admitted to being involved in a scam in which $2 billion worth of forged deposit certificates were issued as collateral for real estate loans—some to clients with mob connections ("Japan's Financial Scandals," 1991). It was also revealed that Nomura Securities and Nikko Securities had loaned Susumu Ishii, then boss of the Inagawa-kai, the fourth largest organized crime family in Japan, $268.1 million to be used for stock marketing trading ("More Eyes on Yakuza's Role," 1992). By 1992, it was estimated by some that more than $3.6 billion in *yakuza* money was invested in the stock market—and the number could go higher if dummy companies were included. Nomura was once again involved in a scandal when, in 1997, it was revealed that Japan's biggest securities firm had paid $340,000 to Ryuichi Koike, a *sokaiya*, or corporate extortionist. At the same time, the Dai-Ichi Kangyo Bank, Japan's second largest, lent Koike millions with little collateral ("Clean-Up Time," 1997). Later that year, officers of Daiwa Securities, Nikko Securities, and Yamaichi Securities were also arrested ("Once There Were Four," 1997). In all, Koike's work as a *sokaiya* led to some 60 resignations and 20 arrests. It also led to the suicide by hanging of Kunji Miyazaki, ex-chairman of Dai-Ichi Kangyo Bank (Hirsh and Takayama, 1997):

> For years, foreign financial advisers have been counseling the Japanese to securitize the non-performing loans—repackage them into bonds to be sold to investors ... But Japan's banks have an even tougher problem: they loaned billions to yakuza-affiliated real-estate speculators. As a result, they're literally terrified to collect on much of the billions in bad debt ... or to foreclose on the collateral. Why? ... When Sumitomo Bank got a little aggressive in collecting loans in Nagoya, its branch manager was killed. More than half of Japan's bad real-estate debt is somehow gang-linked, estimates Teikoku Batabank, a leading compiler of financial stats (p. 44).

If the *yakuza* cannot get into the financial system through bribes and intimidation, they have another weapon, a very potent one in Japan's "save face" moral world. They will set up a high-ranking bank official with a woman, and when the two go to a motel for some indiscretion, they are videotaped and photographed. These are then used to blackmail the official into doing what the *yakuza* want (Fulford, 2000a).

In 1998, as a result of the opening up of the Japanese financial markets (caused in part by the bad debts and scandals), American investors started to snap up bad-loan portfolios in the hope of acquiring real estate very cheaply. However, what these investors were not told at the time was that a large part of those bad loans—some estimate up to 40 percent and to the tune of $235 billion—were in the hands of organized crime (Kaplan, 1998). These gangsters were not happy about what was taking place. Two private investigators checking on a property were beaten up by thugs; a top executive at Cargill, one of the first foreign businesses to buy bad loan portfolios, had his house set on fire:

> One portfolio of 49 loans … found that 40 percent of the borrowers had ties to organized crime. Fully 25 percent … had criminal records … *U.S. News* obtained a similar portfolio of 108 properties … Thirteen … are held by Azabu Building … In early March [1998], Azabu's president … received two years in prison for hiding some $18 million in assets from creditors. Azabu properties … are protected by groups tied to Tokyo's largest crime syndicate (Kaplan, 1998, p. 41).

Local bank officials have not been so fortunate. Among the crimes committed against them are:

- The 1993 shooting and killing outside his home of Tomosaburo Koyama, vice president in charge of problem debts at the now-bankrupt Hanwa Bank;
- The execution a year later of the manager of the Sumitomo Bank;
- The so-called 1998 "suicide" of Tadayo Honma, ex-director of the Bank of Japan called in to clean up the bankruptcy mess left by the collapse of the Nippon Credit Bank;
- A total of 21 shooting attacks as well as assaults and arson on corporate executives in the banking industry.

Unlike the savings and loan scandal in the United States, which was perpetrated mostly by white-collar thieves, the looting of Japan's banks was done mostly by violent organized gangs—and they are not about to return money from loans on real estate which is now worth less than half its original price.

> As pressure mounts to foreclose and sell off the properties, the gangs are employing a black bag of enterprising tricks to profit from the cleanup. Their people are known … as *songiri-ya*, or "loss-cutting specialists"—a shadowy industry of yakuza squatters, extortionists, and investors. In one favorite loss-cutting technique, an indebted owner leases or sells the building to a gang, which then fills the property with mobsters. These underworld squatters use threats and violence to avoid foreclosure, gain a better settlement, or extract huge payoffs to move … Another favorite mob tactic is to file false liens against the property and then demand payoffs to relinquish their claims. Still another technique is to scare off potential buyers, then come in at the last minute and buy the property at a rock-bottom price (Kaplan, 1998, p. 43).

It may be that American investors will have no choice but to deal with elements of the *yakuza* if they wish to become involved in the collection of problem loans and bad-debt property portfolios. This may include payoffs to the mob—or what Ryuma Suzuki, head of the Sumiyoshi-kai, Tokyo's largest crime syndicate, calls a "commission," which may run to 40 percent. According to Suzuki: "On the big discounted properties, you may have to cooperate with organizations like mine. Things can get a little rough out there" (quoted in Kaplan, 1998, p. 44). In fact, bankers have admitted in private that such tactics might have to be employed—and the profit margins are high enough so that there is money to be made even with 40 percent "commissions."

Is this a wise thing to do? The Japanese banks, which in the past have used one set of gangsters to rid themselves of another, have discovered it definitely is not. For one thing, this means that the *yakuza* will be flush with even more money—this time from American investors. And that money could very easily be plowed back into their drug smuggling, extortion, and money-laundering businesses in the United States. Additionally, as many businesses have found (much to their regret), once you form a partnership with a gangster, it is usually for life. According to Harry Godfrey, who ran the U.S. embassy's FBI office in Tokyo for four years: "In the short term, you're getting an opportunity to make a profit. But you're exposing yourself to paying off organized crime, and that could spill over into the rest of your business" (p. 45).

And according to Fulford (2001), these are definitely not the kind of people you want to get on the wrong side of: "Theirs is a world in which victims are visited at night in hotel rooms, forced to write wills at gunpoint, injected with sedatives, and then strangled in a way that makes it appear that they have committed suicide by hanging" (p. 81). It is also a world that is a long way from the glamour of the romantic outlaw who helps right injustice and fights for the poor and the unlucky.

It seems the evidence is fairly overwhelming when it comes to whether the *yakuza* are intimately involved with the Japanese banking system and the nonperforming loan scandal. While no one makes the direct linkage between the *yakuza* loans and the slide into recession, the implications are fairly clear. The nonperforming loans given to *yakuza* may only be one of the reasons for the recessionary pressure, but there is little doubt that they have helped contribute to the prolonging of the recession (along with the very nature of governance and banking in Japan and the almost incestuous relationship between the banks and the institutions which are supposed to regulate them).

The Japanese Economy

The Japanese economy has never recovered fully from the time the real estate and stock market bubble burst in the early 1990s—even though the rest of the world underwent a tremendous surge during this time period. This portion of the literature review attempts to explain in more detail why this happened, and what the economy can expect in the future now that the rest of the industrialized world is itself in danger of recession.

Economic Woes and Their Causes

As early as 1991, when it was first admitted that the Japanese economy was in recession, some commentators were predicting that this recession would be a particularly nasty one (Hillenbrand, 1992; "From Miracle to Mid-Life Crisis," 1993). While government officials and some economists said the recession would be short-lived, just like the others previously experienced in Japan, other experts were saying that it marked the start of a fundamental shift within the country's economy. According to Hillenbrand (1992), some of the causes of the downturn were:

+ The hugely inflated values of the Tokyo Stock Exchange and real estate values between 1985-1989, with the Nikkei stock jumping from 13,136 to 38,915, and land values so high they were routinely more valuable than the buildings on them.

- Vast expenditures for plants and equipment ($3 trillion between 1986 and 1991), research and development ($600 billion), and overseas purchases ($167 billion), which represented capital outlays without immediate returns.

The result of the deflation of the real estate bubble was felt throughout the economy—from banks with $454 billion in outstanding real estate loans to drops in domestic car sales and the electronics industry, from the layoffs of part-time employees to a rise in bankruptcies.

> Historically, Japan has shown a knack for adjusting to external economic crises. But now Japan faces a more complex crisis, emanating from within. The nation must restructure its economy to accommodate not only shareholders' demands for a higher return on their investments but also the wishes of workers eager to enjoy the prosperity they have created (Hillenbrand, 1992, p. 45).

"From Miracle to Mid-Life Crisis" (1993) makes the same point, indicating two reasons why this recession could be seen as different from the previous ones: (1) the nature of the slowdown; and (2) changes taking place in Japanese society. Whether this would lead to long-term problems depended on theories of how Japan got to be the world's second most powerful economic engine in the first place. One argument has it that the economy blossomed on the backs of the workers and consumers and that it was allowed to do so as long as it grew so quickly that living standards were dragged along with it. Now that it has slowed, the standard of living is also endangered. Institutional bribery and other corruption were also tolerated so long as everyone benefited, but were now perceived as having grown out of hand. In the end, the article indicates that Japan has the capacity to pull itself out of the recession because of its "distinctive form of capitalism" and predicts that "in the early years of the next century ... it will still be out-performing the other big industrial economies" (p. J5).

Obviously, this prediction did not come true. In 2001, headlines still read the same way: "Monster Problems: Japan Is Getting Pretty Scary" (*Fortune*, 2001, April 2); "Missing: $3 Trillion" (*Forbes*, 2001, April 30); "The Japanese Economy in Balance Sheet Recession" (*Business Economics*, 2001, April). As Kano (2001) put it:

> The Land of the Rising Sun disappeared behind the dark side of the moon more than a decade ago, and, incredibly, has yet to emerge. To the contrary, it now appears to be floating off helplessly into a deflationary black hole from which no one has a clue as to when it might return (p. 82).

Blecsak (2001) points out that, at the beginning of 2001, the banking system was still in a state of disarray, faced with mounting numbers of nonperforming loans and new ones added monthly as companies continued to go bankrupt. And the two original causes of the recession—the precipitous fall in real estate prices and the stock market—are still there, with real estate at 20 percent of their early 1990s values. At the time, it was argued that the only thing that was keeping the GDP from slipping into negative territory was the strong demand for high-tech materials—and that is no longer true. As well, Japan now carries the highest gross public debt of all the industrialized nations, pegged at 136 percent of the GDP. In the words of Philip Hall, director of equity research at Credit Suisse First Boston: "I don't see what is happening now as anything new, rather the culmination of a long, chronic, slow-motion crisis, stemming from the refusal of successive governments to tackle the underlying problems. Japan is like a giant pyramid scheme in which the whole edifice is moving closer to collapse" (Quoted in Delgado, 2001, p. ITEM01095011).

The warnings today are the same as they have been throughout the 1990s (Schmidt, 1996; Shibata, 1998; Brummer, 1998; Bremner, 1999). For example, by 1996, many Japanese firms were abandoning their long-term practice of not laying off people or eliminating positions, something that went counter to one of the cornerstones of Japanese business practices with its emphasis on harmony, stability, and consensus (modeled after the ideal Japanese family). Shibata (1998) argues that the end of the "Heisei Boom" (1986-1991) resulted from drops in (1) rental housing construction; (2) durable goods consumption; and (3) fixed business investment in nonmanufacturing firms. The reasons behind the continued slump are: (1) slump in fixed business investment; (2) negative contribution of private consumption to the GDP; (3) rapid increase in the public debt ratio to the GDP; (4) negative foreign demand: "The most crucial factor of the Japanese depression of the 1990s was debt deflation ... The main reason for this ... was the instability of the Japanese financial system ... Japanese financial institutions accumulated a huge amount of bad assets and faced a decline in capital asset ratio due to the depreciation of stocks and land ... The Ministry of Finance concealed the real financial positions of the Japanese banks and postponed the disposal of their bad assets" (pp. 416-417).

This last statement perhaps hides the kernel or crux of the situation. The banks were having difficulty disposing of "their bad debts" because many billions of dollars in loans were held by either the *yakuza* or *yakuza*-fronted businesses. It would be like trying to collect a debt from the Mafia in the United States.

Government Scandal

While government corruption and scandal are given as one of the reasons for current problems with the Japanese economy, the truth is that corruption, or *kinken-seiji* (money politics), has been endemic in the country. In 1988, for example, aides to the then prime minister were accused, along with 74 other politicians and journalists, of cashing out illegal insider tips on the Recruit Cosmos real estate company ("How to Make Pals with Pols," 1988; "Murk in Japan," 1988; "You Scratch My Back ...," 1989; "The Scandal Will Not Die," 1989; "Sand in a Well-Oiled Machine," 1989; "Is There No End to Recruits for Japan's Scandal?" 1989). An editorial in the *Economist* at the time said in part:

> Corruption is burrowing deeper and deeper into Japanese political and business life. Japan did not invent it, certainly, but corruption has become more extensive there than in other industrial countries ("Murk in Japan," 1988, p. 17).

How bold and brazen were Japanese politicians? Ken Harada, deputy prime minister and director-general of the Economic Planning Agency continued taking money from Recruit well after the scandal broke—and after he had been appointed head of the parliamentary committee which was investigating Recruit ("Is There No End ...," 1989). By the spring of 1989, the scandal had engulfed Prime Minister Noboru Takeshita himself, forcing him to resign. This was followed in 1989 with the country's new prime minister caught up in a sex scandal, as well as allegations of undeclared political donations ("Once Over Lightly," 1989). Then came the Nomura Securities scandal in 1991, alleging that the firm has loaned $290 million to Susumu Ishii, retired boss of the country's second largest crime syndicate ("While Sleeping Watchdogs Lie," 1991) and the arrest in 1992 of Fumio Abe, senior political ally to the prime minister, for accepting $540,000 from Kyowa Corp., a steel-frame maker ("A Scandal by Any Other Name," 1992).

Among the other scandals breaking in the mid- to late-1990s were

- Sagawa Express: Allegations that the highly profitable trucking company bribed more than 120 politicians (including two members of the then current cabinet and three ex-prime ministers) to the tune of $630 million, while at the same time funneling billions of dollars to gangsters (Eisenstodt, 1992; "Dirty Dozen," 1992; "One Delivery Too Many," 1992; Redl, 1992; "Cash Diet," 1992; "Political Sin," 1993). The scandal spelled the end for Shin Kanemaru, kingmaker for the Liberal Democratic Party. Following Kanemaru's arrest, public prosecutors found more than $51 million in cash, bonds, and gold bars in his offices and homes.
- No Pan Shabu Shabu: In 1998, two high-ranking officials (chief bank inspector and deputy) with the Ministry of Finance were arrested for taking bribes from banks in return for tipoffs on government surprise inspections, thus giving the banks a chance to hide bad loans and real estate investments that had gone sour. This was followed by a third official hanging himself with his own necktie and the resignation of the finance minister (Tashiro and Sakamaki, 1998; Butler, 1998; Sakamaki, 1998a, 1998b; Horvat, 1998). The raid and arrests marked the first time in 50 years that a sitting bureaucrat had been arrested. The bribes included trips to a Tokyo entertainment place, where waitresses take off their underwear for an $80 tip (thus *no pan shabu shabu*, or "hot pot without panties"). According to Richard Hanson, author of a book on the Ministry of Finance: "When the Japanese economy was expanding, people didn't care if bureaucrats had a good time. But during the present, long recession, the semi-corruption that has been part of the Japanese financial industry is no longer seen as acceptable" (quoted in Horvat, 1998, p. 40).
- Central Bank and Dobon: Also in 1998, prosecutors raided the Bank of Japan for the first time in its 116-year history to arrest a senior official accused of providing inside trader information for $33,000 in golf and dining (Tashiro, 1998): "At the central bank, accepting free nights on the town was so commonplace that bureaucrats had their own argot for it ... One code word was *dobon*, literally the sound of a heavy object plopping into the water, which referred to a night out for the bank's heaviest hitters at restaurants where dinner might cost $400 a head and attractive kimono-clad women serve the sake" (p. 35).

While each scandal seemed to lead to one more prime minister resigning (there were eight in all between 1987 and 1998) and promises that the economy would pick up, this has not proved to be the case thus far. Perhaps most indicative of the unclear signals given off by Japan's power brokers came in the "promotion" of Katsuhiko Kumazaki, the prosecutor who led the raids on the Ministry of Justice in the spring of 1998. By the summer, Kumazaki had been sent off to Toyama Prefecture, a rural area on the northwest coast known for fishing and rice production (Clark, 1998).

Banks: Bad Debt and Financial Sector Woes

When 1991 started, the danger of mounting bad debt for Japan's banks was hidden behind the more immediate problems of a collapsing stock market and real estate prices. Yet, by the fall of that year, these bad debt problems were starting to come to the surface ("Bad-Debt Troubles," 1991; "Deep in Bad Debt," 1991; "Overburdened: Japanese Banks," 1992; Garsson, 1992). In the first seven months of that year, there were 5,600 bankrupt companies with more than ¥4 trillion ($29 billion) in bad debts. This did not take into account the companies that had to restructure some ¥15 trillion in debts, the ones who were alive simply because they did not pay the interest on their debts, or the ¥2 trillion in fake deposit certificates used as collateral.

By 1995, it was estimated that the banks were carrying something like $600 billion in bad loans, with some predicting it would rise to $800 billion, or 10 percent of all loans (Morris, 1995). The reason it proved so difficult to determine the amount of bad debt lay in the lenient accounting and lax disclosure rules—and the fact that the banks could pretend to show a healthy balance sheet by shifting bad loans to non-bank affiliates (Sugawara, 1996). In 1997, what the Ministry of Finance said could not happen did—the Hokkaido Takushoku bank, the country's tenth largest commercial bank, collapsed, the largest financial collapse in Japanese history ("Sayonara? Japanese Banks," 1997; "And Then There Were 19," 1997).

In October of 1998, the Japanese government announced a $500 billion bailout ("Japanese Banks," 1998). However, by this time, the estimates on the bad bank loans had reached $1.2 trillion, or some 30 percent of the GDP—and those were just the private banks (Rohwer, 1998; Smith, 1998). Independent Strategy, a London-based investment group, predicted public-sector bad loans would be in the same vicinity (Rohwer, 1998). According to an article in the *Economist*: "Were they obliged to keep realistic accounts, perhaps half of Japan's 19 biggest banks, which between them account for around 70 percent of the country's bank assets, would require either immediate nationalization or a huge injection of fresh capital" ("Empty Package," 1998, p. 92). On December 13, 1998, another of the country's top banks—the Nippon Credit Bank—was nationalized, with the discovery that nearly half of its loans were nonperforming ("Japanese Banks: Hard to Credit," 1998; Zielenziger and Walcott, 1998).

In an analysis of bank systems in general and the Japanese system in particular, Genay (1998) and Peek and Rosengren (1999) listed three major reasons for the problems faced by these banks, including:

+ Sharp declines in stock and land prices in Japan;
+ Collapse of commercial real estate prices in the United States in 1990–1991;
+ The 1998 Asian crisis and problems with asset quality.
+ Because banks are a source of funds for firms, have an important role in the transmission of monetary policy, and are an integral part of the payments system, the social costs of bank failures may be greater than those of other types of businesses. Previous studies on the determinants of bank profitability and the likelihood of bank survival have shown that certain bank characteristics are important in determining future bank performance (Genay, 1998, p. 12).

Unfortunately for Japanese banks, these characteristics included an underperforming economy, growing problem loans and outright bad debts, high credit expenses for these problem loans, and low profitability. Differences between U.S. and Japanese accounting practices when it comes to banks made it easier for problems to be covered up in Japan. These differences included the definition of nonperforming loans, how loan provisions and reserves were handled, the charge-off policy, how securities were valued, and Bank of International Settlements (BIS) capital requirements (Genay, 1998).

Peek and Rosengren (1999) concentrate a part of their analysis on the extremely close relationship between a bank and the *keiretsus*, groups of firms which are closely tied together, both because of natural affinities in the marketplace and in the holding of equity. The bank or banks associated with these firms not only served as their primary source of credit, but often had equity in the firms—and senior positions would flow either way. This meant that Japanese banks had a tough time cutting off credit to customers even when those customers were no longer viable.

By 1999, the banks had written off ¥13.5 trillion ($117 billion) in bad loans ("Japanese Banks Narrowly Avoid Crash Landing," 1999): "The problem is that almost as fast as banks provide against existing bad and doubtful debts, new ones continue to come on to their books as a result of the continuing high level of corporate bankruptcies" (p. 8).

Despite all the government's efforts in trying to deal with the near-fatal collapse of the banking system in 2002, the country does not seem any closer to a resolution of the problem. In fact, many experts are saying that only now are the banks willing to take the drastic measure of cutting off insolvent companies instead of feeding them a lifeline. One of the most dramatic cutoffs was Daiichi Kangyo Bank's pulling away from Phoenix Resorts and its Seagaia ocean park, forcing the company into bankruptcy with debts of more than $2.2 billion (Chandler, 2001). In 2000, it was estimated that the total liabilities of corporations in the country that were seeking protection from creditors had reached a record-breaking $195 billion.

Brief Summary and Analysis

As indicated, the extensive literature review above provides a set of alternative analyses related to the effects of corruption and organized crime on Japan's economy, both in the long term and during its present crisis period. In effect, the literature review "drilled down" from a set of general, overarching theories on essentialist versus constructivist philosophical and sociological approaches through definitions of corruption, and down to the specifics of corruption and organized crime in Japan.

What the literature has shown is that there is normally a tolerance of what might be defined as corruption, provided that the corrupt acts do not seriously damage a nation's economy. In other words, people will tend to turn a blind eye while government departments, regulators, and banks take part in practices which most agree are not ethical—as long as those acts do not hurt the people in a discernible way.

As the literature also indicated, the Japanese banks were more than willing to loan huge sums of money to real estate and stock investors in the mid-to-late 1980s, without being too concerned as to who was actually behind these businesses. Once more, no one made noises about this until the collapse of the Japanese economy. This was followed by the banks using various accounting practices to hide the extent of their nonperforming loans. A large percentage of these loans (the actual amount would be extremely difficult to ascertain given the secrecy of the *yakuza* and the bankers) turned out to be in the hands of Japan's organized crime syndicates. Because both real estate prices and the stock market were a mere fraction of what they had been at the height of the economic bubble, the assets held by both legitimate businessmen and the *yakuza* did not match the amounts of the outstanding loans. There was also the problem of trying to collect these nonperforming loans. The failure to reveal the size of these loans and the inability to collect them have meant the difference between a recovery and a continuing recession.

1. Part One: Philosophical Underpinnings

Berger, P. L., and Luckmann, T. (1966) *The Social Construction of Reality: A Treatise in the Sociology of Knowledge.* Garden City, NY: Doubleday.

Chomsky, N. (1973) *For Reasons of State.* London: Penguin.

_____. (1988) *Language and Problems of Knowledge.* Cambridge, MA: MIT Press.

_____. (1993) *Language and Thought.* London: Moyer Bell.

Davidson, A. I. (1997) *Foucault and His Interlocutors.* London: University of Chicago Press.

Elster, J. (1989) *Nuts and Bolts for the Social Sciences.* Cambridge: Cambridge University Press.

Foucault, M. (1970) *The Order of Things.* London: Routledge and Kegan Paul.

_____. (1980) *Power/Knowledge.* Brighton: Harvester Wheatsheaf.

Gergen, K. J. (1985) "The Social Constructionist Movement in Modern Psychology," *American Psychologist,* 40:266–275.

_____. (1995) "Metaphor and Monophony in the 20th-Century Psychology of Emotions," *History of the Human Sciences,* 8(2):1–23.

Hacking, I. (1999) *The Social Construction of What?* Cambridge, MA: Harvard University Press.

Hesse, M. (1988) "Socializing Epistemology," in *Construction and Constraint* (edited by E. McMullin). Notre Dame: Notre Dame University Press.

Hoffman, M. (1987) "Critical Theory and the Inter-Paradigm Debate," *Millennium: Journal of International Studies,* 6(2):233–236.

Honderich, T., ed. (1995) *The Oxford Companion to Philosophy.* Oxford: Oxford University Press.

Hopf, T. (1998) "The Promise of Constructivism in International Relations Theory," *International Security,* 23(1):171–200.

Hruby, G. G. (2001) "Sociological, Postmodern, and New Realism Perspectives in Social Constructionism," *Reading Research Quarterly,* 36(1):48–73.

Kubálková, V., ed. (2001) *Foreign Policy in a Constructed World.* Armonk, NY: M. E. Sharpe.

Kuhn, T. S. (1962) *The Structure of Scientific Revolutions.* Chicago: University of Chicago Press.

March, J. G., and Olsen, J. P. (1998) "The Institutional Dynamics of International Political orders," *International Organization,* 52(4):943–969.

Putnam, H. (1993) "Objectivity and the Science-Ethics Distinction," in *The Quality of Life* (edited by M. Nussbaum and A. Sen). Oxford: Clarendon Press.

Risse, T. (2000) "'Let's Argue!' Communicative Action in World Politics," *International Organization,* 54(1):1–43.

Schmidt, V. H. (2001) "Oversocialised Epistemology: A Critical Appraisal of Constructivism," *Sociology,* 35(1):135–158.

Shapin, S. (1994). *A Social History of Truth: Civility and Science in Seventeenth-Century England.* Chicago: University of Chicago Press.

Shapin, S., and Schaffer, S. (1985) *Leviathan and the Air-Pump: Hobbes, Boyle, and the Experimental Life.* Princeton, NJ: Princeton University Press.

Taylor, C. (1987) "Interpretation and the Sciences of Man," in *Interpretive Social Science: A Second Look* (edited by P. Rabinow and W. M. Sullivan). Berkeley: University of California Press:33–81.

Wilkin, P. (1999) "Chomsky and Foucault on Human Nature and Politics: An Essential Difference?" *Social Theory and Practice,* 25(2):177–205.

2. Part Two: Corruption Theories, Models, and Effects

Ala'i, P. (2000) "The Legacy of Geographical Morality and Colonialism: A Historical Assessment of the Current Crusade Against Corruption," *Vanderbilt Journal of Transnational Law*, 33(4):877–929.

Alatas, S. H. (1990) *Corruption: Its Nature, Causes and Functions*. Aldershot, England: Avebury.

Andreski, S. (1968) *The African Predicament*. New York: Atherton Press.

Atkinson, M., and Mancuso, M. (1985) "Do We Need a Code of Conduct for Politicians? The Search for an Elite Political Corruption in Canada," *Canadian Journal of Political Science*, 18(September):459–479.

Becker, G. S., and Stigler, G. J. (1974) "Law Enforcement, Malfeasance, and Compensation for Employees," *Journal of Legal Studies*, (January):1–18.

Caiden, G. E., and Caiden, N. J. (1977) "Administrative Corruption," *Public Administration Review*, 37:301.

Cariño, L. V., ed. (1986) *Bureaucratic Corruption in Asia: Causes, Consequences, and Controls*. Quezon City, Manila: JMC Press.

Chan, K. (2001) "Uncertainty, Acculturation, and Corruption in Hong Kong," *International Journal of Public Administration*, 243(9):909–1015.

_____. (2000) "Towards an Integrated Model of Corruption: Opportunities and Control in China," *International Journal of Public Administration*, 23(4):507–532.

Cho, J., and Kimt, I. (2001) "Jobs in the Bureaucratic Afterlife: A Corruption-Facilitating Mechanism Associated with Law Enforcement," *Southern Economic Journal*, 68(2):330–348.

Clarke, M. (1983) *Corruption: Causes, Consequences and Control*. London: Printer.

Davis, W. S. (1910) *The Influence of Wealth in Imperial Rome*. New York: Macmillan.

della Porta, D., and Vannucci, A. (1999) *Corrupt Exchanges: Actors, Resources, and Mechanisms of Political Corruption*. New York: Aldine de Gruyter.

Elliott, K. A., ed. (1997) *Corruption and the Global Economy*. Washington, DC: Institute for International Economics.

Elliott, K. A. (1997) "Corruption as an International Policy Problem: Overview and Recommendations," in *Corruption and the Global Economy* (edited by K. A. Elliott). Washington, DC: Institute for International Economics:175–233.

Friedrich, C. J. (1966) "Political Pathology," *Political Quarterly*, 37:70–85.

Friedrich, C. J. (1972) *The Pathology of Politics: Violence, Betrayal, Corruption, Secrecy, and Propaganda*. New York: Harper & Row.

Gardiner, J. (2002) "Defining Corruption," in *Political Corruption: Concepts & Contexts, Third Edition* (edited by A. J. Heidenheimer and M. Johnston). New Brunswick, NJ: Transaction Publishers:25–40.

_____ (1970) *The Politics of Corruption: Organized Crime in an American City*. New York: Russell Sage.

Girling, J. (1997) *Corruption, Capitalism and Democracy*. London: Routledge.

Graziano, L. (1980) *Clientelismo e Sistema Politico: Il Caso dell'Italia*. Milan: F. Angeli.

Heidenheimer, A. J., and Johnston, M., eds. (2002) *Political Corruption: Concepts & Contexts, Third Edition*. New Brunswick, NJ: Transaction Publishers.

Heidenheimer, A. J., ed. (1978) *Political Corruption: Readings in Comparative Analysis*. New Brunswick, NJ: Transaction Books.

Heidenheimer, A. J. (2002) "Perspectives on the Perception of Corruption," in *Political Corruption: Concepts & Contexts, Third Edition* (edited by A. J. Heidenheimer and M. Johnston). New Brunswick, NJ: Transaction Publishers:141–154.

_____. (1978) "Introduction," in *Political Corruption: Readings in Comparative Analysis* (edited by A. J. Heidenheimer). New Brunswick, NJ: Transaction Books:3–30.

_____. (1970) *Political Corruption: Readings on Comparative Analysis*. New York: Holt, Rinehart, and Winston.

Hess, D., and Dunfee, T. W. (2000) "Fighting Corruption: A Principled Approach," *Cornell International Law Journal*, 33(3):593–629.

Heywood, P., ed. (1997) *Political Corruption*. Malden, MA: Blackwell Publishers.

Hofstede, G. (1997) *Cultures and Organizations: Software of the Mind*. New York: McGraw Hill.

Holmstrom, N., and Smith, R. (2000) "The Necessity of Gangster Capitalism: Primitive Accumulation in Russia and China," *Monthly Review*, 51(9):1–10.

Hillstrom, B. (1996) "Effects of Corruption on Democracies in Asia, Latin America, and Russia," *Woodrow Wilson Center Report*, 8(3):3–40.

Huntington, S. P. (1968) *Political Order in Changing Societies*. New Haven, CT: Yale University Press.

Hurstfield, J. (1967) "Political Corruption in Modern England: The Historian's Problem," *History*, 52:16–34.

Husted, B. W. (1999) "Wealth, Culture, and Corruption," *Journal of International Business Studies*, 30(2):339–357.

_____ (1994) "Honor Among Thieves: A Transaction-Cost Interpretation of Corruption in the Third World," *Business Ethics Quarterly*, 4(1):17–27.

Jain, A. K., ed. (2001) *The Political Economy of Corruption*. London: Routledge.

Johansen, E. (1990) *Political Corruption: Scope and Resources*. New York: Garland Publishers.

Johnston, M. (1986) "Right and Wrong in American Politics: Popular Conceptions in Corruption," *Polity*, 18(spring):367–391.

_____. (1997) "Public Officials, Private Interests, and Sustainable Democracy: When Politics and Corruption Meet," in *Corruption and the Global Economy* (edited by K. A. Elliott). Washington, DC: Institute for International Economics:61–82.

_____. (2001) "The Definitions Debate: Old Conflict in New Guises," in *The Political Economy of Corruption* (edited by A. K. Jain). London: Routledge:11–31.

Klitgaard, R. (1988) *Controlling Corruption*. Berkeley: University of California Press.

LaPalombara, J. (1994) "Structural and Institutional Aspects of Corruption," *Social Research*, 61(2):325–350.

Leff, N. (1964) "Economic Development Through Bureaucratic Corruption," *American Behavioral Scientist*, 8(3):8–14.

Levi, M., and Nelken, D., eds. (1996) *The Corruption of Politics and the Politics of Corruption*. Cambridge, MA: Blackwell Publishers.

Lui, F. T. (1985) "An Equilibrium Queuing Model of Bribery," *Journal of Political Economy*, 93(August):760–781.

Mauro, P. (1995) "Corruption and Growth," *Quarterly Journal of Economics*, 110(3):681–712.

_____ (1997) "The Effects of Corruption on Growth, Investment, and Government Expenditure: A Cross-Country Analysis," in *Corruption and the Global Economy* (edited by K. A. Elliott). Washington, DC: Institute for International Economics:83–107.

Macrae, J. (1982) "Underdevelopment and the Economics of Corruption: A Game Theory Approach," *World Development*, 10(8):677–687.

Mitchell, R. H. (1996) *Political Bribery in Japan*, Honolulu: University of Hawaii Press.

Nichols, P. M. (1997) "Outlawing Transnational Bribery Through the World Trade Organization," *Journal of International Law and Policy*, 28:337–343.

Noonan, John. (1984) *Bribes: The Intellectual History of a Moral Idea*. Berkeley: University of California Press.

Nye, J. S. (2002) "Corruption and Political Development: A Cost-Benefit Analysis," in *Political Corruption: Concepts and Contexts, Third Edition* (edited by A. J. Heidenheimer and M. Johnston). New Brunswick, NJ: Transaction Publishers:281–300.

_____. (1967) "Corruption and Political Development: A Cost-Benefit Analysis," *American Political Science Review*, 16(2):417–427.

Pharr, S. J. (2002) "Public Trust and Corruption in Japan," in *Political Corruption: Concepts and Contexts, Third Edition* (edited by A. J. Heidenheimer and M. Johnston). New Brunswick, NJ: Transaction Publishers:835–859.

Peters, J., and Welch, S. (1978) "Political Corruption in America: A Search for Definitions and a Theory," *American Political Science Review*, 72(September):974–984.

Philp, M. (2002) "Conceptualizing Political Corruption," in *Political Corruption: Concepts and Contexts, Third Edition* (edited by A. J. Heidenheimer and M. Johnston). New Brunswick, NJ: Transaction Publishers:41–57.

Quah, J. S. T. (1999) "Corruption in Asian Countries: Can It Be Minimized?" *Public Administration Review*, 59(6):483–502.

_____. (2002) "Responses to Corruption in Asian Societies," in *Political Corruption: Concepts and Contexts, Third Edition* (edited by A. J. Heidenheimer and M. Johnston). New Brunswick, NJ: Transaction Publishers:513–532.

Rogow, A. A., and Lasswell, H. D. (1963) *Power, Corruption and Rectitude*. Englewood Cliffs, NJ: Prentice-Hall.

Rose-Ackerman, S. (1978) *Corruption: A Study in Political Economy*. London: Academic Press.

_____. (1997) "The Political Economy of Corruption," in *Corruption and the Global Economy* (edited by K. A. Elliott). Washington, DC: Institute for International Economics:31–60.

_____. (1999) *Corruption and Government: Causes, Consequences, and Reform*. Cambridge: Cambridge University Press.

_____. (2001) "Political Corruption and Democratic Structures," in *The Political Economy of Corruption* (edited by A. K. Jain). London: Routledge:35–62.

_____. (2002) "When Is Corruption Harmful?" in *Political Corruption: Concepts and Contexts, Third Edition* (edited by A. J. Heidenheimer and M. Johnston). New Brunswick, NJ: Transaction Publishers:353–371.

Senturia, J. J. (1931) "Corruption, Political," *Encyclopaedia of the Social Sciences*, vol. iv:448–452.

Shleifer, A., and Vishny, R. W. (1993) "Corruption," *Quarterly Journal of Economics*, 108(3):599–617.

Tanzi, V. (1998) "Corruption Around the World: Causes, Consequences, Scope and Cures," *International Monetary Fund Staff Papers*, 45(4):559–588.

_____. (1995) "Corruption: Arm's-Length Relationships and Markets," in *The Economics of Organised Crime* (edited by G. Fiorentini and S. Peltzman). Cambridge University Press:161–180.

Tanzi, V., and Davoodi, H. (2001) "Corruption, Growth, and Public Finances," in *The Political Economy of Corruption* (edited by A. K. Jain). London: Routledge:90–110.

Tarkowski, J. (1989) "Old and New Patterns of Corruption in Poland and the USSR," *Telos*, 80:51–62.

Theobald, R. (1990) *Corruption, Development and Underdevelopment*. London: MacMillan.

Tullock, G. (1996) "Corruption Theory and Practice," *Contemporary Economic Policy*, 14(July):6–13.

Van Klaveren, J. (2002) "Corruption as a Historical Phenomenon," in *Political Corruption: Concepts and Contexts, Third Edition* (edited by A. J. Heidenheimer and M. Johnston). New Brunswick, NJ: Transaction Publishers:83–94.

Van Wolferen, K. (1989) *The Enigma of Japanese Power: People and Politics in a Stateless Nation*. New York: Alfred A. Knopf.

Vittal, N. (2001) "Corruption and the State," *Harvard International Review*, 23(3):20–30.

Wang, H., and Rosenau, J. N. (2001) "Transparency International and Corruption as an Issue of Global Governance," *Global Governance*, 7(1):25–47.

Weber, M. (1968) *Economy and Society*, three volumes. New York: Bedminster Press.

Werlin, Herbert H. (2000) "Linking Public Administration to Comparative Politics," URL: http://www.apsanet.org/PS/sept00/werlin.cfm, September.

Williams, R., ed. (2000) *Party Finance and Political Corruption*. New York: St. Martin's Press.

3. Part Three: Corruption and Organized Crime

(a) Studies

Ames, Walter L. (1981) *Police and Community in Japan*. Berkeley: University of California Press.

Alexander, H. E., and Caiden, G. E., eds. (1985) *The Politics and Economics of Organized Crime*. Lexington, MA: Lexington Books.

Anderson, A. (1995) "Organised Crime, Mafia and Governments," in *The Economics of Organised Crime* (edited by G. Fiorentini and S. Peltzman). Cambridge University Press:33–54.

Befu, Harumi. (1974) "Bribery in Japan: When Law Tangles with Culture," in *The Self and the System*. San Francisco: Chandler Publishing.

Dorman, M. (1972) *Payoff: The Role of Organized Crime in American Politics*. New York: McKay.

Feige, E. L., and Ott, K., eds. (1999) *Underground Economies in Transition: Unrecorded Activity, Tax Evasion, Corruption and Organized Crime*. Aldershot: Ashgate.

Fiorentini, G., and Peltzman, S., eds. (1995) *The Economics of Organised Crime*. Cambridge University Press.

Garoupa, N. (2000) "The Economics of Organized Crime and Optimal Law Enforcement," *Economic Inquiry*, 38(2):278–293.

Godson, R., and Olson, W. J. (1995) "International Organized Crime," *Society*, 32(2):18–29.

Grossman, H. (1995) "Rival Kleptocrats: The Mafia Versus the State," in *The Economics of Organised Crime*. Cambridge University Press:143–156.

Heymann, Philip B. (1985) "Understanding Criminal Investigations," *Harvard Journal on Legislation*, 22 (2):314–334.

Iga, Mamoru, and Auerbach, Morton. (1977) "Political Corruption and Social Structure in Japan," *Asian Survey*, 17 (6):556–61.

Johnson, Chalmers. (1995) *Japan: Who Governs?* New York: W. W. Norton.

Johnson, David T. (1997) "Why the Wicked Sleep: The Prosecution of Political Corruption in Postwar Japan," *Japan Policy Research Institute, Working Paper #34*.

Kaplan, David, and Alec Dubro (1986) *Yakuza: The Explosive Account of Japan's Criminal Underworld*. Reading, MA: Addison-Wesley Publishing Co.

Koh, B. C. (1989) *Japan's Administrative Elite*. Berkeley: University of California Press.

Kpundeh, Sahr J. (1993) "Prospects in Contemporary Sierra Leone," *Corruption and Reform*, 7 (3):237–47.

_____. (1999) "The Fight Against Corruption in Sierra Leone," in *Curbing Corruption: Toward a Model for Building National Integrity*, eds. Rick Stapenhurst and Sahr J. Kpundeh. Washington, DC: World Bank EDI Development Studies.

Martin, B. G. (1996) *The Shanghai Green Gang: Politics and Organized Crime, 1919–1937*. Berkeley: University of California Press.

McDougall, Terry E. (1988) "The Lockheed Scandal and the High Cost of Politics in Japan," in *The Politics of Scandal: Power and Process in Liberal Democracies*, eds. Andrei S. Markovits and Mark Silverstein. New York: Holmes & Meier.

Milhaupt, C. J., and West, M. D. (2000) "The Dark Side of Private Ordering: An Institutional and Empirical Analysis of Organized Crime," *University of Chicago Law Review*, 67(1):41–97.

Mitchell, Richard H. (1996) *Political Bribery in Japan*. Honolulu: University of Hawaii Press.

National Police Agency (1989) "Organized Crime Control Today and Its Future Tasks," *White Paper on Police*, Tokyo.

_____. (1998) *White Paper on Police*. Tokyo: Police Association.

Reynolds, M. (1995) *From Gangs to Gangsters: How American Sociology Organized Crime, 1918–1994*. Guilderland, NY: Harrow and Heston.

Skaperdas, S., and Syropoulos, C. (1995) "Gangs as Primitive States," in *The Economics of Organised Crime* (edited by G. Fiorentini and S. Peltzman). Cambridge University Press:61–82.

Volkov, V. (2000) "The Political Economy of Protection Rackets in the Past and the Present," *Social Research*, 67(3):709–731.

Wilson, J. Q., ed. (1983) *Crime and Public Policy*. San Francisco: ICS Press.

Wilson, J. Q., and Herrnstein, R. J. (1985) *Crime and Human Nature*. New York: Simon & Schuster.

(b) Yakuza: History, Reports, and Statistics

"A Gangster Story: Japan." (1992) *Economist (US)*, 325 (7788):33.

Arahara, Bokusui. (1966) *Dai Uyoku Shi (Great History of the Right Wing)*. Tokyo: Dai Nippon Kokumin To. Trans. David Kaplan.

Castro, Janice. (1992) "A Worrisome Brand of Japanese Investor," *Time*, 139 (16):21.

Chua-Eoan, H. G. (1988) "Thugs Beware: Citizens Rout the Yakuza," *Time*, 131 (11):42.

"Cops to Reveal Data on Yakuza," (2000) *Mainichi Daily News*, September 19:MDN12879200.

"Cops Rap Yakuza over Blackmail," (2000) *Mainichi Daily News*, January 5:MDN8965786.

Cox, Mary-Lea. (1996) "The Dark Side of Japan," URL: http://members.tripod.com/~orgcrime/japdarkside.htm, December.

Delfs, R. (1991b) "Feeding on the System: Gangsters Play Increasing Role in Business and Politics," *Far Eastern Economic Review*, November 21:28.

Fulford, B. (2001) "Buried in the Books," *Forbes Magazine*, January 8:80.

_____. (2000a) "Blackmail," *Forbes*, March 20:132.

_____. (2000b) "Don't Go There," *Forbes*, October 30:66box1.

_____. (2000c) "Japan's Dirty Secrets," *Forbes*, October 30:66.

_____. (1999) "Japan's Cement Shoes," *Forbes*, February 8:82.

Hirotoshi, Ito. (1996) "Yakuza Entrepreneurs Active Behind the Scenes," URL: http://members.tripod.com/~orgcrime/japscenes.htm, December.

"Honourable Mob," (1990) *Economist*, 314 (7639):19–21.

"In The Land of the Rising Gun," (1989) *Economist*, 312 (7617):23–24.

Johnson, Adam. (2001) "Yakuza: Past and Present," URL: http://web.new.ufl.edu/~northrup/dylan/yakuza.html, March.

Jordan, Mary, and Sullivan, Kevin. (1997) "Japanese Fear Mobsters Turning More Violent," *Washington Post*, September 5:A25.

Kaplan, David. (1991) "International Mob Money: Japanese Organized Crime Moves into High Finance," *Journal*, October:52.

_____ (1998) "Yakuza Inc.: American Investors Are Spending Billions of Dollars to Snap Up Portfolios of Bad Loans from Japanese Banks," *U.S. News & World Report*, 124 (14):40.

Landers, Peter. (1997) "Tokyo: Mob Scene," *Far Eastern Economic Review*, 160 (12):58.

Lowry Miller, Karen. (1991) "Goodfellas, Japanese Style: Well-Connected and Twenty Percent Legit," *Businessweek*, August 26:44.

"More Eyes on Yakuza's Role in Japanese Economy," (1992) URL: http://members.tripod.com/~orgcrime/japeconomy.htm, May.

Ormonde, Tom. (1992) "Cracking Down on the Yakuza," *World Press Review*, 39 (5):48.

Reading, Brian. (1998) "Gangster Economy Comes Under Siege," *European*, March 16:54–55.

"Sex Trade Flourishing in Japan," (1995) *WIN News*, 21 (1):42.

Seymour, Christopher. (1996) *Yakuza Diary: Doing Time in the Japanese Underworld*. New York: Atlantic Monthly Press.

—————. (1991) "A Look at the Other Japan: Sanya's Dying Mavericks," *New Leader*, 74 (12):8–10.

Sundara, Miyuki I. (2001) "Yakuza, the Japanese Mafia," URL: http://members.tripod.com/~orgcrime/japgangint. htm, March.

Takayama, Hideko. (1997) "Big Bang or Bust: Mobsters Slow Tokyo's Plan to Join World Markets," *Newsweek, 130* (9):44–45.

"Tycoons of Crime: Japan," (1992) *Economist (US), 322* (7748):36–37.

"Who Got Yakuza into Our Banking System?" (1996) URL: http://members.tripod.com/~orgcrime/yakuzabanking.htm, February.

4. Part Four: Japan's Banks and Economy

"And Then There Were 19: Japanese Banks," (1997) *Economist (US), 344* (8044):87–88.

"A Scandal by Any Name," (1992) *Time, 139* (4):38.

"A Useful Scandal," (1998) *Economist (US), 346* (8052):37.

"Bad Debt Troubles: Japanese Banks," (1991) *Economist (US), 320* (7724):97–98.

"Banks in Never-Never Land," (1997) *Economist*, June 28 (9):S6–7.

Belcsak, Hans P. (2001) "International Insight," *Business Credit, 103* (1):58.

Bremner, Brian. (1999) "A Year of Fresh Disasters," *Businessweek*, January 18:56.

Brummer, Alex. (1998) "Japan's Economy Faces Overhaul," *Airline Business, 13* (4):1.

Butler, Steven. (1998) "Good Life, Bad Loans: A Japanese Scandal," *U.S. News & World Report, 124* (5):47.

Chandler, Clay. (2001) "Taking a Bubble-Economy Bath," *Washington Post*, March 27:E01.

Clark, Tanya. (1998) "Sayonara, Reformer," *Forbes, 162* (1):46.

"Clean-Up Time: Japan's Scandals," (1997) *Economist (US), 343* (8020):78–79.

"Deep in Bad Debt," (1991) *Economist (US), 321* (7731):70–71.

Delfs, R. (1991a) "Clash of Loyalties: Complex Structure Makes for Loose Control," *Far Eastern Economic Review*, November 21:34.

Delgado, Martin. (2001) "Lavish Spending in Tokyo Belies Weak Foundations of Japanese Economy," *Knight-Ridder/ Tribune Business News*, April 5:ITEM01095011.

Desmond, Edward W. (1998) "An Ex-Champ Battles Back," *Fortune*, June 8:8.

"Dirty Dozen," (1992) *Economist, 324* (7775):36–37.

Eisenstodt, Gale. (1992) "Cash on Delivery," *Forbes, 150* (2):140–41.

"Empty Package: Japanese Banks," *Economist (US), 347* (8090):93–94.

"Forgiveness Eases Japanese Woes," (2000) *Banker, 150* (896):8.

"From Miracle to Mid-Life Crisis," *Economist (US), 326* (7801):J3–5.

Garsson, Robert M. (1992) "Japanese Banks Are Poised on a Precipice," *American Banker, 157* (143):10A.

Genay, Hesna. (1998) "Assessing the Condition of Japanese Banks," *Economic Perspectives, 22* (4):12–43.

Greenwald, John. (1989) "You Scratch My Back … : A Stock Scandal Exposes the Cozy Ties Among Japan's Power Elite," *Time, 133* (2):47.

Hillenbrand, Barry. (1992) "Recession, Japanese-Style," *Time, 139* (12):44.

Hirsch, Michael, and Hideko Takayama. (1997) "Big Bank or Bust; Mobsters Slow Tokyo's Plan to Join World Markets," *Newsweek, 130* (9):44.

Horvat, Andrew. (1998) "MOF Fries in 'No Pan Shabu Shabu,'" *Euromoney*, March (347):40–42.

Horvitz, Leslie Alan. (1995) "Telling Bids from Bribes," *Insight on the News, 11* (44):34–35.

"How to Make Friends with Pols," (1988) *Time, 132* (3):45.

"Is There No End to Recruits for Japan's Scandal?" (1989) *Economist*, 310 (7587):29–30.

Jameson, Sam. (2001) "Non-Performing Loans: The Kuroko of Japan's Economy," *Japan Policy Research Institute Critique*, 8 (5).

"Japanese Banks," (1998) *Economist (US)*, October 17:86.

"Japanese Banks: A Funny Sort of Crisis," (1998) *Economist (US)*, October 31:81.

"Japanese Banks Cut Jobs as Reforms Start to Bite," (1999) *Business Asia*, 7 (4):16.

"Japanese Banks: Hard to Credit" (1998) *Economist (US)*, 349 (8099):105.

"Japanese Banks Narrowly Avoid Crash Landing," (1999) *Banker*, 149 (883):8.

"Japan's Bad News on Bad Debts," (1998) *Banker*, 148 (864):13.

"Japan's Economic Red Tide Rises," (1993) *Time*, 141 (10):19–20.

"Japan's Financial Scandals: Now a Big Bank," (1991) *Economist*, 320 (7717):70–71.

Kano, Cindy. (2001) "Monster Problems: Japan Is Getting Pretty Scary," *Fortune*, 143 (7):82.

Koo, Richard C. (2001) "The Japanese Economy in Balance Sheet Recession," *Business Economics*, 36 (2):15.

"Looking Back: Guilty: The Shadow Shogun: Tokyo, October 1983," (2000) *AsiaWeek*, October 9: ASWK13197439.

MacLeod, Scott. (1989) "Sand in a Well-Oiled Machine," *Time*, 133 (19):44.

Matsuda, Keitaro. (2000) "Lessons From Japan's Lost Decade," *ABA Banking Journal*, 92 (9):128.

McGregor, Richard. (1994) "Japan Inc.'s Dirty Secret," *World Press Review*, 41 (12):40.

Morris, Kathleen. (1995) "Meltdown in Tokyo?" *Financial World*, 164 (20):22–25.

"Murk in Japan," (1988) *Economist*, 309 (7578):17–18.

"My Brother, the Middleman," (1991) *Time*, 137 (25):25.

"Once Over Lightly," (1989) *Economist*, 311 (7607):42.

"Once There Were Four: Japanese Securities Firms," (1997) *Economist (US)*, 344 (8036):80–81.

"One Delivery Too Many," (1992) *Economist (US)*, 325 (7779):35–36.

"Overburdened: Japanese Banks," (1992) *Economist (US)*, 324 (7769):77–78.

Peek, Joe, and Rosengren, Eric S. (1999) "Japanese Banking Problems: Implication for Lending in the United States," *New England Economic Review*, January–February:25–38.

"Political Sin: Japan," (1993) *Economist (US)*, 326 (7802):40–41.

"Rebuilding the Banks," *Business Week*, September 6 (3645):48.

Redl, Christopher. (1992) "Cash Diet," *New Republic*, 207 (22):25.

Rohwer, Jim. (1998) "Yikes! Japan's Bank Bad Debt Bomb Is Scarier than You Think," *Fortune*, November 9:124.

Rowley, Anthony. (1999a) "Japanese Banks Take Cold Comfort from NPL Investigation," *Banker*, 149 (876):10.

_____. (1999b) "Japanese Banks Restructure Balance Sheets," *Banker*, 149 (879):12–13.

_____. (1999c) "Performance Anxieties," *Banker*, 149 (881):97–100.

_____. (1998) "From Bad Loan to Worse in Japan," *Banker*, 148 (868):12.

_____. (1996) "Japan's Banks on Life Support," *Banker*, 146 (845):112–114.

"Rush for the Exit: Lending in Asia," (1998) *Economist (US)*, 347 (8064):71–72.

Sakamaki, Sachiko. (1998a) "End of An Era," *Time International*, 150 (24):14.

_____. (1998b) "Death and Golf in Japan," *Time International*, 150 (27):25.

"Sayonara? Japanese Banks," (1997) *Economist (US)*, 342 (8004):73.

Schlesinger, Jacob M. (1998) "Sundown: The Good News from Tokyo," *New Republic*, 219 (5):12–14.

Schmidt, Richard J. (1996) "Japanese Management, Recession Style," *Business Horizons*, 39 (2):70–76.

Seiichi, Takarabe. (1996) "The War for Bad-Loan Recovery Has Started," URL: http://members.tripod.com/~orgcrime/japbadloan.htm, September.

Shibata, Tokutaro. (1998) "An Evolutionary Interpretation of the Japanese Depression in the 1990s," *Journal of Economic Issues*, 32 (2):411–418.

"Silence of the Calves," (2001) URL: http://members.tripod.com/~orgcrime/japecoli.htm, March.

Smith, Charles. (1998) "Auditing a Calamity," *Institutional Investor International Edition,* 23 (10):85.

"Spare Your Blushes, Sir?" (1996) *Economist (US),* 339 (7972):70.

Sterngold, James. (1992) "Japan's Rigged Casino," *New York Times Magazine,* April 26.

Sugawara, Sandra. (1996) "Japanese Banks Shuffled Bad Loans to Affiliates," *Washington Post,* February 8:D09.

"Sumo Wrestling: Ringleaders?" (1996) *Economist (US),* 339 (7971):83–84.

Tashiro, Hiroko, and Sakamaki, Sachiko. (1998) "End of an Era?" *Time International,* 150 (24):14.

Tashiro, Hiroko. (1998) "Ministries of Shame," *Time International,* 150 (30):35.

"The Scandal Will Not Die," (1989) *Time,* 133 (12):58.

"While Sleeping Watchdogs Lie: Japan's Financial Scandals," (1991) *Economist (US),* 320 (7721):70.

Woodall, Brian. (1993) "The Logic of Collusive Action: The Political Roots of Japan's Dango System," *Comparative Politics,* 25 (3):297–312.

Zielenziger, Michael, and Walcott, John. (1998) "New Finance Group Forces Insolvent Japanese Banks to Clean Up Their Bad Loans," *Knight-Ridder/Tribune News Services,* December 23:K1365.

YAKUZA

Jeff Kingston

The yakuza (organized crime syndicates) are Japan's mafia, controlling various illegal and profitable rackets ranging from drugs and prostitution to gambling, blackmail, loan sharking, and extortion based on their core strengths in violence and intimidation. The yakuza have a long and rich tradition in Japan dating back to the seventeenth century, although contemporary gangsters have little in common with their forebears beyond initiation rituals and a penchant for violence. The yakuza are also quite distinct from the mafia. In its heyday the mafia in the US numbered some 5,000 while even the greatly downsized yakuza of the twenty-first century have more than 40,000 core members and as many non-regular members. Another significant difference, until recently, has been the high-level, visible access of yakuza bosses reaching right up to the top of the political and business establishment and a symbiotic relationship with law enforcement. Until the twenty-first century the yakuza, unlike their mafia counterparts, could operate quite openly and maintained cordial relations with police with whom they would frequently share information.

The Lost Decade led to significant changes in Japan and also within the yakuza and in their relations with the establishment. The economic turmoil of the 1990s is often dubbed the yakuza recession because they are blamed for pushing many lenders to the edge of bankruptcy by not repaying large loans, thereby damaging the overall economy. The yakuza, like most other investors at the time, suffered tremendous losses from the dramatic drop in asset values, but unlike other borrowers, they were in a good position to renege on their loans. The scale of non-performing loans linked to the yakuza is stunning, indicating that regulators and bankers could not have been in the dark as to the nature of who was borrowing such extraordinary sums.

The yakuza like to portray themselves as keepers of Japan's traditions men of virtue who help the vulnerable and regulate crime. The reality is quite different. These avatars of tradition are thoroughly adapted to modern ways and conduct their operations ruthlessly with scant compassion for those who do not comply with their demands. They are violence specialists who tap modern niches and constantly reinvent themselves to stay a step ahead of the police and to develop lucrative new business lines. The stereotypical images of the yakuza projected in film, anime, manga, and novels are mostly way out of date. The punch-perm hairstyle has given way to the moussed look, tattoos and missing pinkies are not quite so common, and few wear the flashy clothes of yesteryear.

The yakuza are also adjusting to vastly different operating conditions. Law enforcement has become hostile and is cracking down, forcing the yakuza to adapt accordingly. In addition, the prolonged recession, rapid aging, and labor shortages that are causing havoc in Japan are similarly bedeviling the yakuza. While the yakuza may be experiencing a microcosm of the ills facing all of Japan, they are pioneers in rapidly and effectively adapting to these challenges. Some pundits predict their demise, but as we examine below, it is premature to count the yakuza out.

Flexible Business Model

The yakuza remain at the cutting edge of business, responding nimbly and resolutely to new challenges and constantly reinventing their organizations and methods to deal with those they face and those they anticipate. Their motto, if they had one, would be "by any and all means necessary." They are a lesson in how to successfully adapt to a rapidly changing world. The yakuza, of course, have the added problem of pursuing many dubious if not illegal activities while the state is ratcheting up pressures on them to go out of business. Paradoxically, in a society that values harmony and peace, these violence specialists belonging to very visible crime syndicates have managed to survive by nurturing a symbiotic relation with mainstream Japan. But times are changing.

The yakuza's problems are exactly those of Japan as a whole: they are rapidly aging, have trouble recruiting and retaining a young cadre, face hungry international competitors and an unfavorable regulatory market, are downsizing while merging to gain efficiencies while cutting costs, and are trying to reinvent themselves and adapt their core strengths to new market niches, all amidst a stagnant economy. Like their upper-world counterparts, underworld bosses are pruning their core labor force and relying increasingly on non-regular workers and outsourcing. Harvard Business School is not likely to make them a case study, but it ought to.

The yakuza have long faced adversity since they began operating in the seventeenth century and would have faded long ago if they couldn't respond quickly and effectively. It is worth bearing in mind that the term *yakuza* is derived from the name for a losing hand in cards that requires a player to skillfully judge opponents in order to overcome the odds.

For many yakuza, the odds are steep indeed. They are rapidly aging and their profligate lifestyles are catching up with them. Gambling, prostitution, drugs, public works bid-rigging, and usury—the mainstays for the yakuza—are not as lucrative as they once were and the police are not as tolerant. The police crackdown beginning in the early 1990s has forced the yakuza to diversify, and many operations that were once openly practiced have been driven underground. In the old days the yakuza would hand over criminals to the police and favored knives and swords, but in recent years they have been having shootouts with the cops and even gunned down two mayors of Nagasaki. The cozy and collusive cooperation between the state and the yakuza, always oversimplified and overstated, is not nearly as symbiotic as it once was, one of the many transformations in contemporary Japan.

Like corporate Japan, crime syndicates are worried about attracting and retaining sufficient labor, and both see possibilities in tapping the talents of foreign workers and developing alliances with foreign operators. They also have to contend with a new breed of Japanese who have higher expectations, more options, and less patience about paying their dues to rise in the mob hierarchy.

The reluctance of young Japanese to enter the yakuza means that organized crime is aging even more rapidly than the general populace, a huge problem given that their operations ultimately rely on intimidation and credible threats of violence.

Membership

The police estimate the ranks of the core yakuza at some 43,000 as of 2007, down from 91,000 in 1991 and a peak of 184,000 in the early 1960s. This is still a large number compared to the 5,000 "wise guys" working for the US mafia at its peak. An additional 40,000 gangsters are quasi-members, reflecting the yakuza response to a harsher legal and economic environment that bears some resemblance to the expanding Japanese corporate reliance part-time and temporary workers during the Heisei era. The shrinking numbers of yakuza are a response to the new laws that create incentives for groups to expel members with criminal records (or at least pretend to do so) or run the risk of being designated a "dangerous group" subject to various sanctions. In addition, members who are not performing well or those who fall in arrears on their tribute payments have been expelled.

The three biggest syndicates, the Yamaguchi-gumi, Sumiyoshi-kai, and Inagawa-kai, have between them around 61,100 members, or nearly three-quarters of the total mob population of 84,000. The Yamaguchi-gumi alone employs nearly half of this total. If listed on the stock exchange, the Yamaguchi-gumi would be the Toyota in its sector, a juggernaut besting all its rivals. Robert Feldman, chief economist at Morgan Stanley Japan, calls it the "largest private equity group in Japan."

The yakuza are employers of last resort, employing and imposing discipline on poorly educated, marginal young men prone to violence and crime who have few, if any, other options. Many are juvenile delinquents and some are recruited from motorcycle gangs. Koreans and *burakumin* (a hereditary outcast group subject to persistent discrimination despite legal strictures) are overrepresented in the ranks of yakuza due to exclusion from many other career options. The National Police Agency estimates that some 10 percent of the Yamaguchi-gumi is *zainichi* (ethnic Koreans born and raised in Japan) while 70 percent of its members are *burakumin*.

The new breed of yakuza that has emerged during the Heisei era is not all about brawn and violence. The core strength of yakuza remains "protection" and that depends on a credible threat of violence. However, as yakuza have diversified their interests and moved into legitimate business activities, usually through layers of front companies, other skill sets have become valuable. Yakuza are less concerned about maintaining a flashy image and are more inclined these days to adopt the corporate camouflage of business suits and blend into the world of legitimate business. In the twenty-first century, they also need good computer and management skills, knowledge of the law, and financial savvy. The yakuza's core competence remains rooted in intimidation, ruthlessness, opportunism, and violence, but more than ever smooth, intelligent, and presentable operators are guiding the yakuza through a tough and prolonged period of transition as they reposition operations and adapt to new realities.

The key problem facing the yakuza is a rapidly aging leadership and core membership. Geriatric hoods are just not as intimidating as they need to be. To some extent yakuza are outsourcing, cultivating symbiotic relationships with foreign gangs and bringing in Chinese mobsters to provide the muscle on certain types of jobs such as armed robbery and human trafficking. As legitimate businesses all know, however, there are limits to outsourcing and dangers in nurturing tomorrow's competitors. It is indicative that yakuza groups have resorted to placing classified ads, a sign of desperation that is unlikely to address the key problem: younger people have other options, the marginalized are not so hungry anymore, and few have the patience to put up with the strict discipline and hierarchical structure of the yakuza. Moreover, for new recruits the rewards are less than they used to be and the police are more hostile and more inclined to arrest and imprison gangsters.

Construction State

Japan has an enormous public works budget and the yakuza have earned considerable sums from their involvement in construction projects and bid-rigging, just as organized crime exploits sand and gravel contracts in other nations. The nexuses of massive construction projects, bureaucrats, politicians, businessmen, and yakuza are as revealing about Japan as they are about Italy and Russia. In Japan, the yakuza cut on construction projects is estimated at 3 percent, a vast sum that keeps them afloat, given that during the 1990s the public works budget was on a par with the US Pentagon's budget and remains quite high despite huge cutbacks.

During the bubble era in the late 1980s, yakuza came to provide a crucial service for real-estate developers and construction companies by clearing large plots of land of tenants and small landowners. These *jiage* operations involved thugs intimidating and threatening people living on or adjacent to sites designated for development to sell out, thereby creating a large plot of land needed for some of the expansive real-estate projects that characterized the tasteless excesses of the bubble at its worst. This was a frightening experience for many of the older people living in central Tokyo, and cast yakuza in the role of hoods bulldozing aside the weak and vulnerable at the behest of the powerful, hardly the Robin Hood image the yakuza are keen to promote. Anyone visiting Tokyo these days can see these huge gleaming new shopping centers and condominium projects all over the city where there had once been vibrant neighborhoods and tightly knit communities of mom-and-pop stores, small business operations, and traditional wooden family homes.

For their work, these violence specialists got a 3 percent commission on the value of the land cleared at a time when land values were skyrocketing in the late 1980s. This lucrative business led many yakuza to plow their illicit earnings into land speculation and stock investment, believing like everyone else that asset prices would continue to soar. These significant underworld investments in legitimate enterprises involved them much more extensively in the establishment where their existence has been tolerated because they provided services in demand that others were unable to carry out as effectively. In doing so, the yakuza were setting themselves up as competitors and blurring distinctions, making them increasingly unwelcome in the mainstream, a theme we return to later in the chapter.

Following the crash in land prices at the beginning of the Heisei era, the *jiage* business dried up and the yakuza were bleeding from the implosion in asset values. Their investments had soured big time and they could no longer service loans many had taken out. However, unlike other borrowers, the yakuza could rely on their ruthless reputation to keep creditors at bay while scrambling to find new lucrative business opportunities.

Recession Management

The new businesses were adaptations of old staples: debt collection, bankruptcy management, and protection. In Japan's distressed economy, these were highly profitable growth markets for violence specialists. Yakuza normally charge a 50 percent commission on whatever they collect from debtors, but could easily supplement their earnings by adding expenses and working both sides of the deal. Approaching a debtor, the yakuza could negotiate a favorably low settlement, collect half of it from the creditor, and then also net a handsome "tip" from the grateful debtor for having drastically reduced their debt. The creditors played along because it was better than nothing and only the yakuza had the ability to convince dead-beat debtors, often colleagues, to ensure partial payment. In some respects it is an elaboration of the protection racket where the yakuza sell protection from the threats and inconveniences that only they themselves pose. They were collecting from underworld debtors only they would dare approach and only they could make pay.

Another lucrative market involved obstructing the auction of foreclosed properties. By inveigling in various ways to take some form of possession of a distressed property, or occupy it, the yakuza could make life miserable for the creditor trying to sell the property. By making it clear to potential buyers that buying the property also meant buying into an unwanted connection to the yakuza, the yakuza could drive away buyers and depress the price. They could then turn around and buy the property at a much reduced price or wait for the creditor to make them a generous offer to leave. Either way, they stood to profit. The reason the yakuza manage to survive under adverse circumstances is that they have many arrows in their quiver.

Sokaiya

One of the more lucrative rackets involves corporate extortion by *sokaiya*, professionals specializing in information. *Sokaiya* ferret out, or invent, information about embarrassing corporate or executive misconduct and threaten to expose this to the public unless they are paid large sums of hush money. Police estimate that this has been a key source of yakuza income because firms, including a who's who of corporate Japan, are determined to keep their secrets. Although this extortion is illegal, it persists. Companies are vulnerable and pay precisely because reputation and image translate into financial performance; inconvenient revelations can hammer a company's share price. Society, and perhaps more importantly the market, value good reputation, sound and ethical business practices, decorum, and harmony. These would all be at risk if the yakuza publicized indiscretions, malfeasance, or incompetence.

Clearly this racket depends on the yakuza reading the cards, understanding exactly what corporate executives fear most and what they are prepared to do to make their nightmares go away. There are different permutations of the squeeze, ranging from threats to disrupt annual shareholder meetings by asking embarrassing questions or surrounding corporate headquarters with sound trucks blaring out the juicy details. Alternatively, yakuza might publish their research in special magazines and offer management the opportunity to buy the entire print run to bury the story, or enroll them as subscribers to expensive newsletters as a quid pro quo for not spreading the secrets. Occasionally the yakuza researchers feed some stories of corporate misconduct to the media just to remind "subscribers" about the advantages of keeping up with their subscriptions.

Ironically, *sokaiya* were initially hired by companies to protect them from such threats. One of the most infamous cases involved the Chisso Corporation that hired *sokaiya* for its annual shareholder meetings to intimidate and shout down the questions by victims of mercury poisoning caused by effluent from its factory in the fishing village of Minamata. Savvy *sokaiya* quickly learned just how valuable their intervention and information could be, whether defending corporations or shaking them down. In the booming days of the bubble in the late 1980s, firms flush with cash proved easy and lucrative targets.

As times got tough in the 1990s and paying the *sokaiya* to go away became an apparently dispensable luxury, some companies stopped paying. As a result, executives were threatened with violence and targeted for reprisal. An executive of Fuji Film was stabbed to death on his doorstep, a warning to others about the dangers of not paying. It is difficult to know with certainty about the scope and nature of *sokaiya* activities, but their ruthlessness suggests that the state's determination to limit this practice faces a tough hurdle.

In fact the government initially tried to tackle the *sokaiya* problem in 1982 by prohibiting the use of corporate (but not personal) funds for payoffs, but the *sokaiya* modified their tactics, establishing *uyoku dantai* (fake right-wing groups) who harassed companies with their loudspeaker trucks until paid off. The government also mandated holding annual shareholder meetings on the same day, making it more difficult for *sokaiya* to disrupt them. However, cracking down on *sokaiya* while respecting shareholder rights puts the government in a tight legal bind because ostensibly they enjoy the same rights and legal protections of any citizen.

Close ties with yakuza groups, legal shortcomings, and adaptability have kept the *sokaiya* in business. Not only are they creative in elaborating new scams, they have an ace up their sleeves: executives' reluctance to cooperate with police because they fear exposure of corporate wrongdoing.

Public Image

If it was up to the yakuza, they would try to keep public attention focused on how they set up the first soup kitchens for survivors of the Kobe earthquake in 1995. This stands as their greatest public relations triumph of the Heisei era, one that highlighted the government's dawdling and bumbling response in contrast to their selfless, generous, and timely provision of assistance to ordinary citizens hammered by a massive natural disaster. Nothing could have been more humiliating to the government and more flattering to the yakuza. But a reputation is not made on a single event and overall the yakuza image has taken a well-deserved pummeling during the Heisei era, largely a consequence of self-inflicted wounds.

During the Heisei era, increasing numbers of non-combatants have been caught in the crossfire of gang battles while there have been more citizens victimized by predatory gang operations. This has created a groundswell turning public opinion against the yakuza. As long as gangsters engaged in crimes of a consensual nature such as gambling and prostitution, the police averted their eyes, but as *minbo* (extortion) operations targeting citizens expanded during the 1990s, the yakuza were setting themselves up for a backlash.

One of the more notorious cases involved film director Juzo Itami whose 1992 film *Minbo No Onna* (*The Anti-Extortion Woman*) satirized the yakuza and made them look foolish. In the film, a hotel vying for an important conference contract is targeted for extortion by yakuza that decide it makes a good place to hang out unless they get paid to leave. Naturally their uncouth presence undermines the ambience that the upscale hotel wants to project. The hotel staff is useless in trying to deal with the yakuza until a woman lawyer specializing in such matters begins to advise the hotel on how to get rid of the unwanted guests. In the film the yakuza come across as weak and foolish bullies who are all bark but no bite and, most embarrassingly, no match for this clever woman. In retaliation for all the laughs at their expense, real-life yakuza from the Goto-gumi exacted revenge on Itami by brutally beating him and slashing his face. This violent attack on a popular actor and director shortly after the film's release led to harsh media coverage and calls for action. In that same year, coincidentally, the Diet passed the *botaiho* (anti-yakuza) legislation targeting yakuza organizations and their activities.

Thus in the 1990s the yakuza could only blame themselves for destroying all the glamorous and noble myths they had been promoting for so long with notable success. The myths had power and considerable currency not because they were true, but because people didn't know better. Once people began to understand the seamy and nasty nature of the yakuza and their operations, the cozy image faded rapidly. Yakuza may claim to be agents of social control who keep the streets free of crime, but citizens observe the reality of their ruthless violence increasingly reported in the press and government white papers on organized crime. Based on their track record, they are now seen and depicted as a threat to safety and social harmony rather than as guardians of traditional ethos and values.

The once symbiotic relationship with the police, a lingering image that vastly oversimplifies the situation *pre-botaiho*, was always a partial truth that is fading rapidly. Now that the state has declared war on the yakuza and treats them as a social evil, vestiges of cooperative relations between authorities and gangsters have receded.

Nonetheless, the yakuza do maintain close ties with politicians and until the 1990s saw no reason to hide such relations. Some politicians depend on yakuza campaign donations and support in canvassing, and rumors suggest much more. In return, yakuza are always eager to develop networks of powerful and influential friends who can give them an inside track and put in a timely word. But working with politicians carries the risk of scandal and media attention.

The Sagawa Kyubin scandal that erupted in 1992 revealed the sleazy nexus of ties linking yakuza, businessmen, and politicians. Most attention focused on this parcel delivery company's large illegal donations to Shin Kanemaru, an LDP political heavyweight. A police raid on his home uncovered a stash of gold ingots, cash, and bank debentures worth several million dollars. But this was no ordinary cash-for-favors scandal. Kanemaru, it turns out, had asked executives at Sagawa Kyubin to arrange a meeting with Susumu Ishii, the head of the Inagawa-kai. The purpose of the meeting was to ask for Ishii's help in stopping right-wing sound trucks from harassing Noboru Takeshita as he was campaigning for support to become the Japanese prime minister. The right-wingers were embarrassing Takeshita with effusive and excessive praise (*homegoroshi*), just the kind of support and ties he was not eager to embrace or advertize. Kanemaru persuaded Ishii to intervene, the volume was turned down, and Takeshita became prime minister (1987–9), one who owed the mob.

While many Japanese suspect that politicians' links with mobsters are extensive, never has the highest-ranking politician found himself in the spotlight in such a compromising situation, at least since 1960 when Prime Minister Nobusuke Kishi unleashed yakuza goons on left-wing demonstrators protesting the security treaty with the US. And almost never again, except in December 2000 when the media published an old photo of PM Yoshiro Mori drinking in an Osaka bar with a former top-level gangster. It was one of many good reasons that he was ousted from the premiership, but since then he remains an influential player in the LDP and the Diet. Apparently mobster friends in political circles are not as taboo as some would imagine or hope.

The public, however, is not amused that gangsters seem to have excellent access to the corridors of power, a situation most would believe is a problem in Italy or contemporary Russia. Imagining that the yakuza can pull strings is somewhat different than actually watching them doing so. It appears odd, for example, that Japan still lacks a racketeering law akin to the RICO (Racketeer Influenced and Corrupt Organizations) Act in the US that has been a key to anti-organized crime efforts there, fueling speculation that the fix is in.

One of the key problems is that most yakuza no longer lead the good life because they can't afford to. Budgets no longer stretch to designer clothes, expensive cars, and posh watering holes except for privileged members of the relatively well-off Yamaguchi-gumi and higher-ranking members of other groups. Losing the appurtenances of wealth and power, and leading a less flamboyant lifestyle, have lowered the yakuza's cool quotient and also help explain why fewer youth aspire to join.

Yakuza Recession?

During the economic bubble of the 1980s, the yakuza plunged into legitimate ventures, borrowing from banks and their affiliates with abandon to fund them while often diverting chunks of the loans into other dubious schemes. Banks were desperate to lend money because their established corporate customers were not borrowing and instead were raising easy and cheap money on the frothy stock market. Bankers were thus not as fussy about who they lent to and yakuza could borrow large sums using land as collateral based on madly inflated values. Many yakuza-related loans were channeled through *jusen*, real-estate lending affiliates of the major banks. In 1996 the *jusen* went belly-up under the weight of massive non-performing loans. It is the yakuza connection to Japan's massive bad debt problem in the 1990s, and its role in deepening and sustaining Japan's economic nosedive, that led many commentators to dub this the yakuza recession.

The *jusen* were lightly regulated and not covered by the Ministry of Finance's 1990 belated restriction on banks' real-estate-related lending, issued with impeccable timing just as the bubble was collapsing. The *jusen* were known for lax lending standards and no risk assessment, often lending more money than the collateral was worth. During the early 1990s they were lending into a highly risky market in a tailspin and went bankrupt as a result of this folly. The banks and the Ministry of Finance all knew about *jusen* activities, but chose to look the other way; the banks were trying to make money on higher interest-rate spreads on *jusen* loans and the government wanted to help banks through what was then thought to be a rough patch. It ended in a colossal financial disaster requiring an unpopular bank bailout as the *jusen's* non-performing loans reached some US$81 billion. As a result, in 1996 the government liquidated seven *jusen*.

The large volume of loans to yakuza presented creditors with special challenges and dangers not usually associated with foreclosure. The yakuza had lost heavily in the collapse in asset values while banks faced the unanticipated problem of the land used as collateral guaranteeing the loans being worth a fraction of bubble era values. To the extent that the banks took over the land posted as collateral, assuming they could do so, and sold it off to recover some of their money, they risked sparking a further downward spiral in land prices that would further undermine their already distressed balance sheets. But foreclosing on the yakuza was never going to be easy.

The murders of two bank executives in 1993 and 1994 highlighted the risks of recovering debts owed by yakuza. Sumitomo Bank adopted an aggressive strategy of recovering the loan collateral and in yakuza-related cases hired other gangsters to spearhead such loan collection efforts. The yakuza responded by fatally shooting a Nagoya-based Sumitomo Bank officer involved in these efforts. Subsequently, the Ministry of Finance granted Sumitomo Bank permission to write off some JPY500 billion of yakuza-linked non-performing loans, suggesting that it was not oblivious to institutions under its supervision having mob connections. Other banks also lined up for permission to write off what were euphemistically designated "hard-to-recover" loans, totaling some JPY20 trillion by 1997.

Official estimates of the bad loan problem of banks and non-bank financial institutions were relatively small, but in 2002 Goldman Sachs estimated the total as high as JPY237 trillion. Yakuza exposure, directly and indirectly, was estimated at 40 percent of this bad debt mountain. When the government acted to clean up the mess, it established the Resolution and Collection Corporation in 1999 that purchased non-performing loans to take them off bank balance sheets. By its own reckoning nearly 20 percent of the loans purchased by the RCC were believed to be yakuza linked. Foreign investors buying up distressed assets would often purchase a basket of mortgages at a fraction of their face value. Based on their due diligence they estimated that about 30 percent of the mortgages involved yakuza and priced their offers accordingly. Rather than trying to get the yakuza to pay, they would then forgive their debts and concentrate on the more readily recoverable loans.

It's not every day that you get a riveting post-WWII social history of Japan from the perspective of a yakuza, but Manabu Miyazaki, a former member of Japan's underworld, has risen to the task. Among other things, he seeks to set the record straight on the yakuza recession. Unexpectedly, he waxes philosophical about the hysteria and greed that gripped Japan during the booming bubble era at the end of the 1980s. This all may seem odd coming from a man who made ends meet and then some by busting heads and elbowing in on land speculation. Here, however, he settles scores against the Japanese establishment "wimps" who he accuses of forgetting how to act like men. The crime? Getting in bed with the yakuza to enlist their help and then betraying them. This is not how everyone sees it, but Miyazaki thinks the yakuza have been unfairly blamed for causing the Lost Decade, also known as the yakuza recession.

Miyazaki recalls his life as a *toppamono*, one who bulldozes his way ahead regardless of the consequences. He rescued his family's fortunes, telling his older brother to carry on the legitimate side of the construction business while offering to secure contracts in any way possible. Here we learn about the art of bid-rigging, price-fixing, and the web of corruption in the *doken kokka* involving yakuza, politicians, bureaucrats, and businessmen.

Miyazaki also recounts the artful way gangsters were able to shake down banks for massive real-estate-related loans that they didn't repay. In popular lore, these deadbeat borrowers pushed the financial system to the verge of insolvency. He argues, however, that the real villains were the bankers and that the yakuza became convenient scapegoats. In his version, the bankers were desperately pushing loans to gangsters speculating on real estate, all with the knowledge of the Ministry of Finance.

Yakuza as victims? Well as it turns out when the bubble burst and the music stopped it was the bankers who were without a chair, the nation's best and brightest outmaneuvered and fleeced, mistakenly thinking they could play with the players. Miyazaki has a point in fingering the bankers and bureaucrats for their negligence, but surely the yakuza worked the relationship for all it was worth and did commit crimes in carrying out the dirty work. In Miyazaki's version, the establishment was not amused by the yakuza muscling in on legitimate businesses, although happy to avail of their services when needed. The establishment responded by cracking down on the yakuza, passing new legislation aimed at putting them out of business and in their place.

Miyazaki makes a convincing case that the Iron Triangle of big business, the bureaucracy, and politicians has much to answer for in creating the bubble and prolonging its messy unraveling.

In his view, they shifted blame for the consequences of their incompetence and neglect onto the yakuza, helping turn public opinion against them.

The Tide Turns

Public tolerance of the yakuza was based on the misperception that their activities involved largely victimless crimes of mutual consent such as gambling and prostitution. However, the expansion of *minbo* (extortion) operations in the 1980s meant an increase in victims and rising public discontent with this situation. Media coverage of those victimized by *jiage-ya* (eviction specialists) and *sokaiya*, various other frauds and scams, not to mention violent gang wars lowered public tolerance of yakuza operations and ratcheted up pressure for more concerted state action.

In Heisei Japan, the yakuza are facing a two-pronged challenge—economic and legal. The collapse of the bubble economy in the early 1990s and the prolonged recession since then hit the yakuza hard by saddling them with investment losses and reducing lucrative opportunities. The weak economy and a shrinking pie generated greater competition among the yakuza groups that has erupted in violence and intensified turf wars that have inflicted collateral damage on ordinary Japanese citizens. With more civilians caught in the crossfire, corporations complaining of systematic shakedowns in the form of *sokaiya*, and facing international pressures to join in the "war on drugs," the government was forced to abandon its averted eyes approach to organized crime. As a result, in 1992 the government passed legislation, revised and expanded several times since (1993, 1997, 2004), targeting the yakuza and their ways of making money.

Botaiho, the organized crime legal countermeasures, target the grey zone of yakuza activities by criminalizing them and subjecting blacklisted crime syndicates to various sanctions. *Minbo*, including the various scams, squeezes, extortion, loan sharking, bankruptcy management, evictions, dispute resolution, and shakedowns by the yakuza, rely on implicit threats of violence. For most citizens an encounter with a yakuza is fraught with peril and anxiety precisely because they know what might happen if they don't comply with the demands. The yakuza, through his demeanor, way of speaking, casual presentation of a card indicating his gang affiliation, or display of a tattoo or severed pinky, is threatening without actually voicing a threat. This meant that yakuza in the pre-*botaiho* era could get what they wanted without explicitly threatening people, thus avoiding a criminal offense.

Under the *botaiho*, a Public Safety Commission can blacklist certain groups who meet various criteria. To blacklist a syndicate the PSC must determine that: (1) it has considerable influence and power as an organization; (2) it has many members with a criminal record; and (3) it has a tightly knit structure of command and control. The PSC can issue injunctions prohibiting certain activities by members of blacklisted syndicates. Violations of the injunctions are subject to small fines and/or short prison terms. Members of a blacklisted group are prohibited from making demands or gaining some financial advantage by invoking or otherwise using their gang affiliation. By broadening the definition of what constitutes a threat, focusing on institutional affiliation, and essentially declaring yakuza organizations a social evil, the government changed the rules of the game, cutting off yakuza from some lucrative scams and giving the police more power and citizens more protection.

In addition, the government established Centers for the Elimination of Boryokudan, staffed by retired police officers, designed to raise public awareness about the threats of yakuza to society and advise people and communities on how to respond. The yakuza have relied on their glamorized image and quiescent, fearful communities. Now, communities affected by yakuza activities are learning how to organize, mobilize media coverage, and fight back in the courts.

By international standards, these countermeasures are relatively tame in terms of both scope and penalties. Designating certain activities as illegal does not necessarily discourage yakuza persisting in such activities, especially if they know that the odds of detection are low and the penalties relatively light. The countermeasures' value is in reducing, at least to some extent, "yakuza intervention in the private and business affairs of law-abiding members of society." Now the state has more power and citizens can seek legal redress in response to predatory activities.

The shortcomings of laws targeting the yakuza hamper effective enforcement. The countermeasures, by proscribing certain yakuza activities, drive yakuza into other scams in a criminal version of whack-a-mole, a game center staple where hammering a mole in one hole is followed by its popping out another. In addition, out of respect for constitutional guarantees, the government has not outlawed gang membership. More importantly there is no conspiracy law like the RICO Act used in the US to put mafia dons in prison, and Japanese prosecutors cannot offer immunity and witness protection/relocation as inducements to testify against fellow mobsters.

In 1999, however, the government upped the ante by passing new laws that target the yakuza where it hurts. Now in cases of "serious crimes" (chiefly involving drugs and guns), the police have wider scope to engage in wiretapping and sting operations. These new laws are crucial for gathering evidence to prosecute yakuza. The government has also increased penalties for serious crimes and allows seizure of gangsters' assets. Again every initiative elicits a response, but this expansion of police powers gives them new weapons to make life harder for organized crime.

The first wiretap under this law, which took effect in 2000, was not conducted until 2002. Wiretapping remains limited, but in 2008 the police conducted 11 authorized wiretaps that led to the arrest of 34 suspects. The government says that none of the wiretaps lasted more than 30 days and all focused on mobile phone conversations, mainly in connection with illegal drug sales and gun possession. Thus far, the impact appears limited, but as police, prosecutors, the media, and the public become more accustomed to such surveillance, the probability of expanded use, and more successful prosecutions, is high.

The crackdown may be a mixed blessing. If the expanded police powers become more effective in weakening the major crime syndicates, who will oversee and encourage a degree of stability in the criminal world and prevent competition from overheating into intensified turf wars? By targeting the Big Three oligopoly that now manages organized crime, the police may unwittingly spark a free-for-all among new contenders for domination in battles that will put a premium on demonstrating ruthlessness and the skills of violence specialists, meaning higher risks for non-combatants.

Red Queen Syndrome

In Lewis Carroll's *Through the Looking Glass*, Alice encounters the Red Queen who runs ever faster just to stay in the same place. Biologists use this as a metaphor to describe evolution evident in the contest between a host and a virus, with the host's defenses constantly adapting to new mutations in the virus. Like the Red Queen running faster just to stand still, the government countermeasures against the yakuza elicit a response that requires a new round of actions and adaptations, a flurry of activity that sustains an evolutionary arms race with the parasite. In Japan, this seems a race that the police are destined to lose.

The yakuza have responded to legal reforms by modifying their institutional structure, insulating bosses from criminal activity, slashing membership by ousting those with criminal records, abandoning gang offices, cutting ties with police, and otherwise lowering their profile. Yakuza groups have adopted varied strategies, and they are evolving all the time, but have worked to avoid intra-gang wars that could create opportunities for a police crackdown, not always with success, and sought to lessen the victimization of ordinary citizens.

The countermeasures have also sparked consolidation of yakuza syndicates. Many smaller groups disbanded and forged ties with or merged with the Big Three—the Yamaguchi-gumi, the Inagawa-kai, and the Sumiyoshi-kai. The Yamaguchi-gumi, with a total of some 40,000 soldiers, is based in the Kansai region with headquarters in Kobe. However, it has steadily expanded operations in the Kanto region during the twenty-first century and through alliances and sheer power has grown to some 3,000 affiliated gangsters in Tokyo. Although it has cultivated cordial ties with Kanto-based Inagawa-kai, this infringement on the turf of the Tokyo-based gangs that began in 1991 has sparked a series of violent gang conflicts and killings that have intensified since 2004 with Sumiyoshi-kai. Yamaguchi-gumi has taken the risk of expanding into Tokyo because there are more attractive opportunities in the capital where economic power is concentrated than in the Kansai region. By sparking gang violence the Yamaguchi-gumi is providing police the pretext they need to crack down and thus there are strong pressures to pursue diplomacy with its rivals. However, the impulse to grow is irresistible.

The legal changes restricting *minbo* activities have also generated increased inequalities among yakuza, mirroring one of the controversies animating public discourse in the early twenty-first century. The widening income gap among ordinary Japanese is also evident among yakuza, as those with good networks and financial savvy are doing well while those with more limited skills and contacts are facing tougher times. These "lumpen yakuza" have responded by moving into less sophisticated operations involving drug peddling, especially amphetamines, organized robbery, illegal dumping, Internet pornography, credit card fraud, and various phone scams. These are all good earners, but the barriers to entry are not high and competition from non-yakuza operators is stiff because yakuza have no insuperable comparative advantage as they do in other fields.

Miyazaki, the gangster writer, reminds us, however, that the yakuza are the ultimate entrepreneurs, constantly reinventing themselves, flexibly adapting their core strengths in intimidation and violence to new niches and angles. Despite the new laws, hostile public attitudes, and more aggressive law enforcement, he remains hopeful about the future of the yakuza. Ultimately, if one believes that human nature involves "traits of violence, pleasure-seeking, and dissipation," smart money is on the yakuza.

International

The yakuza have not been content to rest on their laurels at home and have expanded aggressively throughout Asia and also made inroads in Europe and the US. They are involved in gambling, prostitution, human trafficking, drug and gun smuggling, and money laundering as well as corporate extortion. They also invest in real estate, buy art and antiquities, and establish legitimate businesses. The Yamaguchi-gumi is the major international player among the Japanese crime syndicates, drawing on its experiences in organizing sex tours and drug deals in Southeast Asia in the 1960s and 1970s. With slimmer pickings in Heisei era Japan, diversifying into international markets has made sense, at least to the mob.

At home too the yakuza have been involved with foreign crime syndicates, especially from China and Korea, but also from Russia. There has been a degree of media sensationalizing the foreign peril, focusing on cases where foreign criminals have preyed on Japanese ranging from Korean pickpockets to trafficking, robberies, and murder involving Chinese criminals. In reality, the yakuza is partnering with foreign crime syndicates operating in Japan and outsources some jobs to them. For example, some of the heists attributed to foreign gangs could not happen without the inside information supplied by the yakuza. By co-opting foreign gangs and involving them in operations that don't pose a threat to core operations, the yakuza tap new sources of income, insulate themselves from prosecution, and also thwart police unable to deal with non-Japanese criminals speaking a variety of foreign languages and dialects. Thus, rather than the Japanese streets being taken over by foreign gangsters, the yakuza are shrewdly bringing in hired help who are boosting profits.

In the world of international crime, money speaks louder than history, as gangsters from countries with long-standing enmities like Japan, Korea, China, and Russia have put aside the past and focus on raking it in. Russian and Japanese government relations are chilly due to disputes over Russian control of northern islands that Japan claims, but that hasn't stopped a brisk trade in poached seafood netted from northern waters for sale in Japanese markets by arrangement between the yakuza and their Russian counterparts. Russia has also been a lucrative source of prostitutes and hostesses as statuesque blond-haired, blue-eyed beauties command a premium in Japan, while the trade in second-hand cars exported from Japan to the Russian Far East has thrived, at least until 2009 when the Russian government imposed prohibitive import taxes. It is clear, however, that international cooperation among criminal syndicates has been mutually rewarding and will continue as long as this is the case.

Citizens Fight Back

Japanese, widely known as deferential to authority, inclined to harmony, politically apathetic, and averse to lawsuits, are undermining these stereotypes by taking the mob to court. Japanese courts, often depicted as protectors of the wealthy and powerful, have now become a weapon of the weak; gang bosses are now being hit with civil suits by victimized citizens demanding compensation. In 2008, fed up with a two-year-long succession battle between rivals featuring bombs, sub-machine-guns and seven deaths, 1,500 residents of Kurume, a small city on the island of Kyushu, decided to fight the yakuza in the courts. They are suing to shut down the head office of a blacklisted organized crime organization located in their neighborhood. Whether or not they succeed in driving the mobsters out of town, this case is a watershed in yakuza history as they have now become the target of NIMBY (not-in-my-back-yard) activism. It has inspired Japanese elsewhere as residents of the posh Akasaka district in Tokyo filed a similar case in 2009 to bar a gang from moving in.

Glamorized in film and manga, the yakuza are now on the defensive, forced to fight back with lawyers rather than their weapons of choice. The people are trying to take back the streets and oust the violence specialists through non-violent means. Much of the ire directed against the mob is due to their killing of non-combatants. In the Kurume war, in an incident that shocked the nation, a gangster walked into a hospital ward and fatally shot a man he mistook for a rival, putting the yakuza in an unwanted and unflattering media spotlight.

The gang in Kurume, however, is wealthy and well entrenched in the town, so even if the residents push them out of their area, they can just move to another neighborhood and continue conducting business as usual. The problem in fighting organized crime is that society and the police have become resigned to their presence and are not confident they can be eliminated, for the very good reason that the yakuza are constantly adapting.

The 2004 anti-yakuza legislation makes gang bosses responsible for injuries or losses caused by gangland wars, allowing victims to sue them for compensation. The law states that when any member of a blacklisted syndicate has killed or injured a citizen or damaged their property as a result of gangland conflict or internal strife, the leader of that syndicate is liable for damages. There are some two dozen blacklisted syndicates, including the Yamaguchi-gumi, so designated by the Public Safety Commission because they routinely encourage acts of violence. Each of these groups runs a pyramid-like network of subsidiaries and affiliates that pay it large amounts of tribute and protection money.

Previously gang bosses were immune from responsibility for the actions of their rank-and-file members, but now they are liable. And, as ordinary gangsters usually cannot afford to pay much compensation, the new legislation benefits victims and puts a financial squeeze on the bosses. The new law also lowers the bar for plaintiffs who previously had difficulty in gathering evidence and proving a command–supervision, boss–subordinate relationship.

It is a sign of the times that, in 2009, two top members of a crime syndicate agreed to pay nearly JPY100 million in compensation to the relatives of a man fatally shot by yakuza in Maebashi, Gunma Prefecture, acknowledging their liability as employers in a court settlement. In the settlement, the bosses also agreed to apologize to the relatives. The victim was a customer at a bar who died in the 2003 shooting when three yakuza entered and tried to kill the ex-boss of a rival group. The attackers also killed a former gangster and seriously injured the ex-boss along with another ordinary citizen.

The three gangsters are all appealing death sentences while their bosses, unexpectedly, are paying off plaintiffs. The first case under the 2008 law holding gang bosses liable for their underlings' actions was actually filed by a Thai restaurant owner in Tokyo in 2009, claiming that when she refused to continue paying protection money, the mob came in and busted up her joint. She is suing Kenichi Shinoda, kingpin of the Yamaguchi-gumi, for JPY15 million in damages stemming from the alleged assault and robbery carried out by gang members who beat her with wooden swords. With even foreigners suing them, the yakuza must be wondering what's next.

These disparate cases stretching from Kurume to Tokyo and Maebashi are the tip of the iceberg, demonstrating that the yakuza have alienated the public, and now citizens are willing to risk taking them to court to hold them accountable and curtail their operations. Yakuza believe that the police are orchestrating these lawsuits, but even if this is true it is clear that ordinary citizens, foreigners, and the lawyers representing them have crossed a line that nobody in his right mind would have considered 20 years ago. Anybody taking gangsters to court then would have been deemed suicidal, but now this is a rational response given tremendous changes in laws, attitudes, and context.

In pushing greater accountability, the government is also trying to help insulate citizens from the yakuza by including a provision in the lay judge system enacted in 2009 that allows prosecutors to petition for permission not to try certain serious cases involving yakuza under this quasi-jury system. This opt-out clause addresses concerns that yakuza might attend trials involving associates and identify, otherwise intimidate, or exact revenge on the citizen judges. Given that polls in 2009 show lukewarm support for the new lay judge system, making sure that those who do participate are safe from mob retribution is good public relations.

Clearly, the yakuza remain scary violence specialists, and their adversaries remain wary, but they have worn out their welcome and are finding powerful and persistent adversaries among citizens, courts, police, and media.

In Transition

The yakuza's high-profile ties within the corridors of political power during much of the latter half of the twentieth century until now are remarkable. Politicians have relied on the yakuza to help battle left-wing radical groups while also using them in election campaigns for fundraising, voter organizing, and digging up dirt on rivals.

In general, however, the Japanese establishment is now repudiating the yakuza and trying, with episodic commitment, to put them out of business. Gone are the days that the yakuza could operate openly and ostentatiously, comfortable in the knowledge that the police tolerated them and the public bought into the myth of their chivalrous *samurai* spirit. Gone too are the days when they were treated as valued customers by major securities companies such as Nomura and Nikko who lent them billions of yen and helped ramp share prices to their benefit.

As with many other aspects of contemporary Japanese society, what were once considered ineradicable verities are now yesterday's news. Now the government has passed a series of laws that make the yakuza more vulnerable while the prolonged Heisei recession has slashed revenues from gambling, loan sharking, and prostitution, traditional core businesses. To offset these setbacks the mob has been developing new rackets involving cybercrime, financial scams, and stock manipulation. Grossing an estimated $21 billion annually, and probably far more, organized crime remains a major industry, one that is increasingly efficient with a much smaller workforce. Thus, it's a bit early to be lamenting their plight and betting on their demise. After all, they are prominent stockholders in listed companies and have a web of front companies that provide lucrative opportunities in legitimate business to go along with some of their more traditional recession-proof "entertainment" operations. But there are some powerful demographic trends working against them.

The aging crisis is a significant threat to the yakuza, many of who develop lifestyle-related health problems at relatively early ages. After all, older violence specialists can't take care of business like they used to. Aside from engaging in risky businesses and enduring stressful situations, most yakuza are hedonists who love heavy drinking, smoking, and carousing. This takes a physical toll, especially on livers, and there is a big need for transplants in a country that banned such operations until 1997. Since then, organ transplants remain rare and are strictly regulated.

A doctor at UCLA hospital helped out by performing four liver transplants for gangsters between 2000 and 2004, including a prominent gang boss named Tadamasa Goto in 2001. Since known gangsters are routinely denied visas to the US, clearly someone had put in the fix—the FBI as it turns out. In exchange for revealing inside information to FBI agents about yakuza operations in the US, especially money laundering, the FBI helped arrange the visas and liver transplants. The FBI had long suspected that the yakuza were actively using US gambling casinos to launder their illicit earnings, and maintains that such deals are an effective way of getting necessary information for effective law enforcement. Critics maintain the FBI got little valuable information in exchange for aiding and abetting some dangerous crooks who now have a new lease on life. The transplants also sparked controversy because the yakuza jumped the queue and got preferential treatment despite long waiting lists. While the good doctor was stitching up the mob, in each of the years from 2000 to 2004 more than 100 patients died awaiting liver transplants in greater Los Angeles.

Now, even as yakuza lifestyles remain dissolute, all the negative publicity has closed mob access to US healthcare options.

Even if the yakuza can sort out their ailments, the real demographic challenge is recruiting and retaining productive members amidst a looming labor shortage. The marginal and dispossessed will remain a key pool of recruits, but their lack of education and twenty-first-century skills make them ill suited for some of the mob's important new lines of business in finance and cybercrime. And, Japan has become a more affluent society, raising everyone's expectations and hopes, meaning that getting in on the ground floor of the yakuza hierarchy, never all that appealing, is even less so, especially given that the money, perks, and prospects aren't what they used to be.

The yakuza have addressed this problem to some degree by outsourcing, but foreign crime syndicates have been relegated to non-core operations. There is always some danger that partners today might turn into tomorrow's ruthless competitors, but foreign crime syndicates remain dependent on inside contacts, networks, and information that only the yakuza can provide. So the yakuza does not look in danger of being pushed off Japan's streets by the international competitors; but by the same token they can only solve the yakuza's manpower problems at the margins. The yakuza have also taken to hiring a handful of foreigners to work as members, but again this is not a panacea for the aging problem. In the end, aging violence specialists have a limited shelf life and the yakuza will need to restructure and streamline operations in the best traditions of corporate downsizing.

In some respects, however, the aging problem may be exaggerated. It is worth recalling that the mafia membership in the US peaked at 5,000 in a much bigger and more populous country and did okay for themselves until aggressive law enforcement, legal reforms, and political will turned the tide. A more compact yakuza focusing its core strengths on maximizing returns will mean reducing some of the labor-intensive retail protection rackets, but that is where quasi-members can fill the void.

For all the gloomy news about economic recession and an establishment backlash, the yakuza continue to work profitably in the mainstream because in certain lines of business they are peerless. The *jiage* business, for example, still thrives even if it is a pale shadow of the booming bubble days. In 2008 it was revealed that a formerly listed company, Suruga Corporation employed gangsters between 2003 and 2007 to evict tenants from properties that Suruga had acquired and wanted to develop. The company explained that gangsters are good at what they do, producing speedy and cost-effective results that were key to its business strategy, results that could not be achieved by legitimate means. In the five buildings targeted, tenants were ousted within 12 to 18 months, a process that could drag on for several years through legitimate means without the desired outcome, given strong legal protection of tenants' rights in the courts.

Mob involvement with major companies in Japan is also highlighted in the 2008 police white paper on organized crime. The police assert that the yakuza are major players in security trading and have invested in hundreds of listed companies. This raises concerns about corporate governance and stock manipulation, factors that will give foreign fund managers pause as they consider their options. The yakuza have also bilked many corporations, even blue-chip firms, of large sums of cash in artful cons launched from front companies that conceal their involvement. Thus, Japan does have a treacherous business operating environment if one falls in with the wrong crowd. The problem is that identifying them is not as easy as it used to be and has generated a brisk business in due diligence.

Prospects

The long-term future for the yakuza appears grim due to incremental legal reforms, tougher enforcement by the police, and judicial support for these initiatives. Moreover, Japanese society is rapidly changing in various ways that are shrinking the social and economic space that has allowed the yakuza to thrive for so long. Citizens are aroused against them and working collectively to bring pressure on law enforcement to act. Judicial and quasi-judicial remedies are increasingly taking over dispute resolution and arbitration, areas where yakuza have been profitably active. Greater transparency is also shining a light on the darker recesses where yakuza thrive and making operations involving establishment players more difficult.

Successful law enforcement targeting the major criminal syndicates carries its own risks. Rather than eliminating organized crime, weakening the stabilizing influence of the current yakuza oligopoly could spark greater violence as new contenders emerge and make it more difficult to restore law and order. A less centralized yakuza could well become more dangerous and more difficult to police. But a weaker and divided yakuza with fewer resources could also be a boon precisely because they would have less potential to conduct criminal activities. This is the gamble the police are taking.

But betting against the yakuza seems like a losing gamble. The yakuza were on the ropes in the 1930s under military-dominated governments when state actors took over the operations of violence specialists. As we know, they recovered quickly following WWII and became major players in cahoots with the Iron Triangle (business, bureaucracy, and politicians), expanding their influence most dramatically during the bubble era in the late 1980s. The subsequent recession has been tough on business, but crisis has created new opportunities and the yakuza are reinventing themselves, staying a step ahead of law enforcement, maintaining their underworld rackets, and straying further into mainstream pursuits. It is worth bearing in mind that the new yakuza are ruthless investment bankers, intimidating guys in Armani suits and Gucci shoes with a penchant for violence and a gift for lucrative frauds, manipulating stocks, and hiding their illicit activities behind legitimate front companies. Rumors circulate that a yakuza front company even conned Lehman Brothers out of nearly $350 million only months before the once-venerable investment bank went bankrupt, and similar sophisticated scams have involved other blue-chip firms. Ultimately, the continuing demand for yakuza services by the mainstream world, and the primordial impulses of violence, greed, thrill-seeking, and sex, mean that the yakuza are likely to survive even the most concerted actions by authorities to wipe them out. Make no mistake, the yakuza will not go gently into the night.

CHINA AND JAPAN'S SIMMERING RIVALRY

Kent E. Calder

The Great Illusion

China and Japan, the giants of Asia, account for nearly three-quarters of the region's economic activity and more than half of the region's military spending. Despite their deep economic ties and a doubling of their bilateral trade in the past five years, their relationship is increasingly strained, with dangerous implications for the United States and the world at large.

Historically, relations between Japan and China were clearly structured. One country was always more prosperous or powerful than the other. Before the nineteenth century, China was usually dominant; since the Meiji Restoration, in 1868, Japan has generally been preeminent. The prospect that China and Japan could both be powerful and affluent at the same time has only recently emerged, largely because while China's economy and influence have grown rapidly, Japan's have remained stagnant. China has nuclear weapons and intercontinental ballistic missiles, and its military budget has grown by double-digit rates for 17 consecutive years. Although Japan has a relatively low military profile, with its "no-war" constitution and strong alliance with the United States, its defense-relevant technology is sophisticated and it has recently become more proactive. The stage is now set for a struggle between a mature power and a rising one.

Some liken current Sino-Japanese relations to the Anglo-German rivalry prior to World War I. As with the United Kingdom and Germany a century ago, the contest for regional leadership between China and Japan today is creating new security dilemmas, prompting concerns over Chinese ambitions in Japan and fears of renewed Japanese militarism in China. Both states are adopting confrontational stances, partly because of rising popular involvement in politics and resurgent nationalism exacerbated by revived memories of World War II; mutually beneficial economic dealings alone are not effectively soothing these tensions. Fluid perceptions of power and fear, Thucydides observed, are the classic causes of war. And they are increasingly present in Northeast Asia today.

Many contentious issues confront China and Japan. Among the most pressing is their thirst for energy. Japan depends on imports for 99 percent of its oil and natural gas; coastal China is similarly bereft of resources. Thus, the offshore oil and gas fields under the East China Sea are attractive "domestic" sources of energy for both Beijing and Tokyo—and both have laid claim to them. China argues that the entire East China Sea continental shelf, extending eastward nearly all the way to Okinawa, is a "natural prolongation" of the Chinese mainland. Japan has declared its boundary to be a median line between its undisputed territory and China—a line that runs roughly 100 miles west of the Okinawa Trough, which lies undersea just west of Okinawa and is where the richest petroleum deposits in the area are believed to be concentrated.

The conflict began escalating in May 2004 when China started serious exploratory operations in the Chunxiao gas fields, only four kilometers from the median line. Actions by both parties have since raised tensions. In November 2004, a Chinese nuclear-powered attack submarine intruded into Japanese waters near Okinawa for more than two hours, ostensibly by accident. Since the spring of 2005, the number of flights into disputed airspace by Chinese military surveillance aircraft has risen to record levels. In May 2005, Japan's Ministry of Economy, Trade, and Industry (meti) authorized Japanese companies to explore contested areas for natural gas. On the eve of the Japanese elections in September 2005, Chinese warships patrolled near the now-active Chunxiao fields. In response, both Japan's ruling coalition, led by the Liberal Democratic Party (LDP), and the opposition Democratic Party of Japan (DPJ) have prepared bills proposing to protect the operations of Japanese drillers and fishermen in disputed waters—by force, if necessary.

The Korean Peninsula and the Taiwan Strait also present challenges for the Sino-Japanese relationship and for regional stability. Since the Pyongyang summit in June 2000, trade between South Korea and North Korea has grown by 150 percent, cross-border tourism has boomed, railway lines across the demilitarized zone have been reconnected, and a special economic zone in the peninsula's ancient capital of Kaesong, now in North Korea, has begun to flourish with South Korea's backing. As the likelihood of inter-Korean conflict declines, the long-term rivalry between China and Japan for influence on the peninsula may be rekindled—a rivalry that helped spark the First Sino-Japanese War, of 1894–95. Unification or reconciliation could also deepen the sense Japan has that its position in Northeast Asia is under siege. Were the military forces of North Korea and South Korea to be combined, they would number close to ten times those in Japan's Self-Defense Forces (SDF).

Like the Koreas, Taiwan and China have grown more intertwined economically. According to most estimates, investment across the Taiwan Strait now totals over $100 billion. More than 70 percent of Taiwan's foreign investment went to the mainland in 2004, 10 percent of Taiwan's labor force works in China, and four Taiwanese-owned firms are among the mainland's top ten exporters. (Taiwan now trades substantially more with China than it does with the United States.) There have also been signs of an emerging political détente between Beijing and Taiwan's opposition parties: Lien Chan, chair of the Kuomintang Party (KMT) that Chiang Kai-shek led to Taiwan at the end of 1949, went to the mainland in April 2005, where he visited his ancestors' graves and the former KMT capital of Nanjing and met with China's president, Hu Jintao. Meanwhile, both countries' military capabilities have increased. China has deployed dozens of submarines and frigates, 800 short-range missiles, over 1,200 fighter aircraft, and tens of thousands of troops along the Taiwan Strait. Taiwan has countered by deploying its own missiles and nearly 300 top-of-the-line fighter planes, mainly U.S.-built F-16s.

Beijing's military buildup has implications for Tokyo: the missiles China has aimed at Taiwan could easily reach Japan's main islands as well as Okinawa, where 70 percent of U.S. defense facilities in Japan, including the indispensable Kadena Air Force Base, are located. Both U.S. and Japanese defense specialists thus view neutralizing this potential threat as a vital goal. The United States and Japan will conduct missile tests in Hawaii during the spring of 2006 to establish the efficacy of ballistic missile defenses. If a missile defense system were deployed, the U.S.-Japanese alliance's capabilities would be enhanced—and Beijing would be alarmed by the weakening of its relative position. The issue is therefore emerging as yet another area of controversy in Sino-Japanese relations.

As Sino-Japanese tensions increase, it is becoming more and more likely that Japan will revise its constitution in ways that will allow the SDF greater freedom of action, even as other nonmilitary reforms are achieved as well. (The constitution, written in 1947, limits the SDF to a narrowly defensive role.) Beyond the regional tensions themselves, important long-term structural changes in Japanese politics are at work: the combined socialist and communist representation in the Diet has fallen from 14 to 3 percent over the past decade, leaving the conservative LDP and its coalition partner with the two-thirds majority needed to begin amendment of the constitution and leaving the left with only 16 of 480 seats in the Diet's dominant lower house. The recent ascendancy of defense hawks in the DPJ has also amplified the left's collapse.

The current LDP draft amendment, published in October 2005, would retain the historic Article 9, which states that "the Japanese people forever renounce war as a sovereign right of the nation." But the proposal would also clearly legitimate the SDF (an institution whose role has been constitutionally ambiguous); clarify Japan's prerogative to participate in collective self-defense, the linchpin of the security cooperation between Japan and the United States; and simplify procedures for amending the constitution in the future. This procedural change could further exacerbate Sino-Japanese tensions by increasing uncertainty regarding Japan's future rearmament.

The Nightmare of Politicized History

The prospect, however distant, of Japanese remilitarization has a disturbing historical resonance in the region. Although World War II is more than a half century in the past and Japanese expansionism in Asia dates back another half century still, this history continues to haunt relations between Japan and China. The War of Resistance Against Japan, as the Chinese call their version of World War II, lasted more than twice as long as Japan's conflict with the United States; it had already been raging for more than four years when Japan attacked Pearl Harbor. By the time the war ended, it had caused far more casualties and atrocities than had the bitter struggle between Japan and the United States.

The debate over the war's legacy remains volatile, hindering efforts at cooperation. There have been occasional signs of progress: Japan's emperor, Akihito, whose father reigned during the conflict, visited Beijing in 1992, for example. Sadly, however, the situation has worsened lately, although generational change might have been expected to bring greater prospects for reconciliation. In China, the legitimacy of the Chinese Communist Party (CCP) is bound up with its perceived role as the stalwart defender of national interests during the war with Japan. The deference the party derives from that legacy grows ever more important to sustaining its rule as social inequities resulting from economic growth increase. Government policy, reflecting CCP concerns, promotes nationalist curricula in schools and intensive broadcasting of accounts of the war. The Internet has facilitated the expression of nationalist sentiments. In the spring of 2005, 44 million Chinese signed an electronic petition opposing Japan's quest for a permanent seat on the U.N. Security Council.

Positive sentiments toward China among the Japanese have also declined dramatically. According to polls conducted by the secretariat of Japan's cabinet, in October 2005, only 32 percent of respondents felt warmly toward China, down from 38 percent in 2004 and 48 percent in October 2001 (just after Japanese Prime Minister Junichiro Koizumi's only visit to China so far while in office). During the 1980s, before the massacre in Tiananmen Square, similar polls reported that more than 75 percent of respondents had positive feelings about China. The dramatic hardening of sentiment toward China is clearly a reaction to anti-Japanese demonstrations in China, as well as to China's military actions, including the nuclear submarine intrusion into Japanese waters in November 2004.

Five times in four years, Koizumi has visited the Yasukuni Shrine in Tokyo, a memorial where the names of the fallen of Japan's wars are enshrined—including 14 convicted Class A war criminals from World War II. Only two other sitting prime ministers in the past twenty years visited the shrine at all, and each only went once. In Japan, opinion over Koizumi's visits to Yasukuni is almost evenly split, with six former prime ministers and five of Japan's six largest newspapers opposing them. But the dominant Mori faction of the LDP, to which both Koizumi and the influential chief cabinet secretary, Shinzo Abe, belong, has strong connections to Japan's political leadership of the 1930s and 1940s. (Abe, for instance, is the grandson of Nobusuke Kishi, a member of Prime Minister Hideki Tojo's wartime cabinet; Kishi's legacy remains controversial even though later, as prime minister, Kishi began Japan's policy of providing large-scale reparations to Southeast Asia.) Such ties make the Koizumi government prone to holding conservative conceptions of national interests and render it more suspect than its predecessors in the eyes of many Asians, including the Chinese.

Koizumi has consistently stressed the personal and unofficial nature of his visits to the Yasukuni Shrine. Beijing has nevertheless criticized them sharply. Seasoned U.S. diplomats suggest privately that the Yasukuni issue is more damaging to Japanese regional influence now than it was even two or three years ago, because China is emerging as a skilled diplomatic player that can use the history card more effectively to marginalize Japan than previously due to its growing political and economic clout. Two months after the February 2005 U.S.-Japan Security Consultative Committee meetings, at which Washington and Tokyo decided to make a priority of peacefully resolving Taiwan Strait issues, major demonstrations broke out in Beijing and Shanghai against Koizumi's Yasukuni visits and the standard depiction of the war in Japanese textbooks (which the Chinese see as downplaying Japan's culpability for the conflict). Many observers note that Beijing has particularly strong incentives to prevent any strengthening of the U.S.-Japanese alliance on Taiwan-related matters. And China, claiming that Japan has not sincerely atoned for its wartime aggression, has also used the issue to hinder Japan's bid for the permanent U.N. Security Council seat that many feel it richly deserves (Tokyo, after all, funds 20 percent of the U.N. budget, compared to China's 3 percent).

Whatever the personal or political rationale for Koizumi's visits, Yasukuni is a flashpoint for widespread, if often ill-informed, international misgivings about Japan's foreign policies, misgivings that erode the regional and global effectiveness of Japanese diplomacy. The visits make it difficult for leaders in both Japan and China to manage bilateral economic and security relations; hurt Japan's ability to take proactive diplomatic steps (for instance, by preventing Tokyo from taking a leadership role, amply justified by its capabilities, in regional energy and environmental cooperation); reduce Japan's leverage with third countries, such as Russia, that may care little about the visits themselves but care about tensions between Japan and China, with which they do business; and divert Japanese public attention from the serious security issues looming over Northeast Asia. There is a danger that, down the road, Japan could find itself increasingly isolated diplomatically from other countries in the region. Coupled with the security challenges that Tokyo faces, such a situation could drive Japan toward counterproductive unilateralism or an overly militarized variant of the U.S.-Japanese alliance. Either outcome would greatly intensify regional tensions.

Confidence Building

The United States has a crucial role to play in easing the tensions between Japan and China. Rather than prescribing specific solutions for every problem, the U.S. approach should continue to be what it has been since the mid-1980s: reaffirming the importance of the U.S.-Japanese alliance while encouraging Japan and China to develop a dialogue of their own.

The United States' long-standing alliance with Japan has been the pillar of U.S. policy in the Pacific for over half a century. Much has been achieved over the past decade on the military side of the relationship, including operational planning since the late 1990s for emergencies in "areas surrounding Japan," as opposed to Japan itself. Since the attacks of September 11, 2001, the SDF has extended its area of operational responsibility to the Arabian Sea, and in January 2004, Japan sent troops to Iraq. In December 2005, Chief Cabinet Secretary Abe announced Japan's decision to begin developing a next-generation missile interceptor with the United States.

Increasingly close bilateral defense relations have not, however, generated equally strong grass-roots support. Many Japanese appear uneasy with U.S. policies on Iraq, military transformation, host-nation support, and the environment, even as they are frustrated by seemingly lukewarm U.S. support for Japan's aspirations to become a permanent member of the Security Council. These undercurrents showed up in a revealing December 2005 Yomiuri-Gallup poll: although 76 percent of U.S. respondents said they trusted Japan, 53 percent of Japanese said they did not trust the United States, 43 percent said they felt that the U.S. military presence in Japan should be reduced, and 27 percent characterized U.S.-Japanese relations as bad.

Clearly, more should be done to deepen the bilateral U.S.-Japanese partnership, with special sensitivity to the complex economic and security issues raised by the rise of China. A bipartisan U.S.-Japanese task force consisting of both countries' best specialists on trilateral relations is needed. The model could be the Japan-United States Economic Relations Group (which brought together prominent businesspeople and academics of both nations to consider long-term economic and security issues) of the late 1970s. Such a step would help consolidate support for the alliance by making it more responsive to broad national sentiments and less tied to parochial interests.

Once the alliance between Tokyo and Washington is consolidated, the best way to defuse the rivalry between China and Japan would be to increase multilateral contacts, both through official mechanisms and through unofficial relations among nongovernmental actors ("Track II"). Enhancing trilateral cooperation among China, Japan, and the United States, especially regarding energy policy, should be a priority. Together, the three countries account for over 40 percent of the world's energy consumption, and they are the three largest oil importers, making their cooperation especially vital. Japan could take a useful step by creating an "energy and environment exception" to its contemplated 2008 termination of development assistance to China, possibly including a provision for U.S.-Japanese-Chinese energy cooperation. The United States, Japan, and China should also form the core of a new North Pacific Regional Energy Consortium, to focus on improving energy efficiency, particularly in China (which currently operates at 40 percent of the United States' efficiency levels and 11 percent of Japan's). Measures such as these could be a balm for the greatest sore in the region, the spiraling rivalry across the East China Sea. Given rising strategic dangers and political uncertainties, a broad Northeast Asia Strategic Dialogue involving China, Japan, the United States, and others is also needed. Such a body could be a spin-off of the existing six-party talks over North Korea's nuclear program (which include China, Japan, North Korea, Russia, South Korea, and the United States), omitting North Korea if necessary. The group's creation should be supplemented by confidence-building measures such as a Sino-Japanese military-to-military dialogue and multilateral contingency planning for disaster-relief activities. Multilateralism keeps nationalism in check, as has been demonstrated by Europe's experience with the Organization for Security and Cooperation in Europe, which provides the continent with a regional security framework.

To improve Sino-Japanese relations, the two countries will also have to stabilize their bilateral policies and cultural networks. During the period between the normalization of relations between Beijing and Tokyo in 1972 and the advent of the Koizumi government in 2001, Sino-Japanese networks were relatively vigorous, particularly those involving the political heirs of former Japanese Prime Minister Kakuei Tanaka (who presided over the normalization). But they have atrophied over the past five years. There have been no full-scale Sino-Japanese summits since mid-2001, and the crucial networks of midlevel bureaucratic coordination have badly frayed. The quiet yet devastating process of generational change has also been a corrosive factor. Veteran statesmen from both China and Japan who really knew the other country and its importance, such as Zhou Enlai, Deng Xiaoping, former Japanese Prime Minister Noboru Takeshita, and former Chief Cabinet Secretary Hiromu Nonaka, are now gone. From a Japanese perspective, it would be sensible to resume ministerial-level dialogues on finance, trade, and energy as well as to reinvigorate networks with China by appointing as ambassador to Beijing a heavyweight political or business figure with strong personal ties to both the United States and China. China has already made a gesture of this sort by naming the well-regarded (and Japanese-speaking) former vice minister of foreign affairs, Wang Yi, ambassador to Tokyo.

Track II conferences about history (especially World War II), involving academics from neutral countries such as Canada as well as Asian specialists from within the region, could improve relations by fostering less-politicized discussions of the war. Germany and Poland, as well as Japan and South Korea, already have joint textbook commissions that could serve as models for China and Japan. An initiative such as this could be particularly effective at de-escalating tensions in the wake of progress in the strategic dialogues outlined above. To help those dialogues along, moreover, U.S. officials should refrain from making casual pronouncements on the delicate matter of wartime commemoration in Japan. As Koizumi has noted, many personal issues are involved in such events. The Japanese people themselves, however, deserve the broadest possible range of options about how to remember the war. For several years, there has been spirited discussion about building a national secular war memorial to supplement Yasukuni, and this deserves serious consideration. Such a model has worked well in both Hiroshima and Okinawa. Apart from providing a way to commemorate the sacrifice of civilians and other heroes of past conflicts not enshrined at Yasukuni, a secular memorial would clearly help improve Japan's relations with other countries in the region and provide foreign leaders with a way to gracefully honor the past sacrifices of the Japanese people.

The United States should encourage regional cultural communication as well. In many areas, such an approach will be far more effective than official action, given the importance of personal networks in Asia. Using mechanisms such as the State Department's International Visitors

Program to bring to the United States Japanese and Chinese experts who specialize in the other country's affairs could help create new intellectual networks and generate specific ideas for improving trilateral relations. Informal groups and more formal deliberative forums, such as congressional hearings, should address the deteriorating Sino-Japanese relationship, which is the storm center of the political and military crisis in Northeast Asia. Such discussions could also usefully consider the diplomatic implications of the Yasukuni issue in addition to pressing security concerns such as China's military buildup.

Change in Japan's policy toward China ultimately must come from within. It is unlikely that any significant shift in foreign policy can be made while Koizumi remains in office. He is locked into his positions, such as his promise to go to Yasukuni annually, and it would be difficult for him to escape such pledges, particularly in the context of continuing geopolitical challenges in Northeast Asia. A window of opportunity could well open this September, when Koizumi is scheduled to leave office. Japan's new leader will have opportunities to innovate pragmatically in relations with Beijing without being seen to knuckle under to Chinese influence—by resuming summit meetings between Japan and China, reinvigorating energy and environmental dialogues, exploring the concept of a secular war memorial, and tacitly refraining from visits to Yasukuni, even as he or she comprehensively strengthens relations with India, Australia, and the Association of Southeast Asian Nations (ASEAN), and takes a hardheaded approach to deepening security concerns. Such actions would enable Japan to take the diplomatic high ground, and allow both Japan and China to focus on the very real challenges of stabilizing their relationship, less distracted by the peripheral yet politically contentious issues of history.

Stabilizing the Sino-Japanese relationship is crucial for both the region and the world. Doing so is a matter primarily for China and Japan, but there is an important role for the United States as well. The United States must honor its vital alliance with Japan. Yet it will also have to transcend its "hub and spoke" diplomacy and recognize that many issues need multilateral treatment. If it can do so, the United States will indeed be the "essential power" in Asia, as its diplomatic rhetoric has so often claimed.